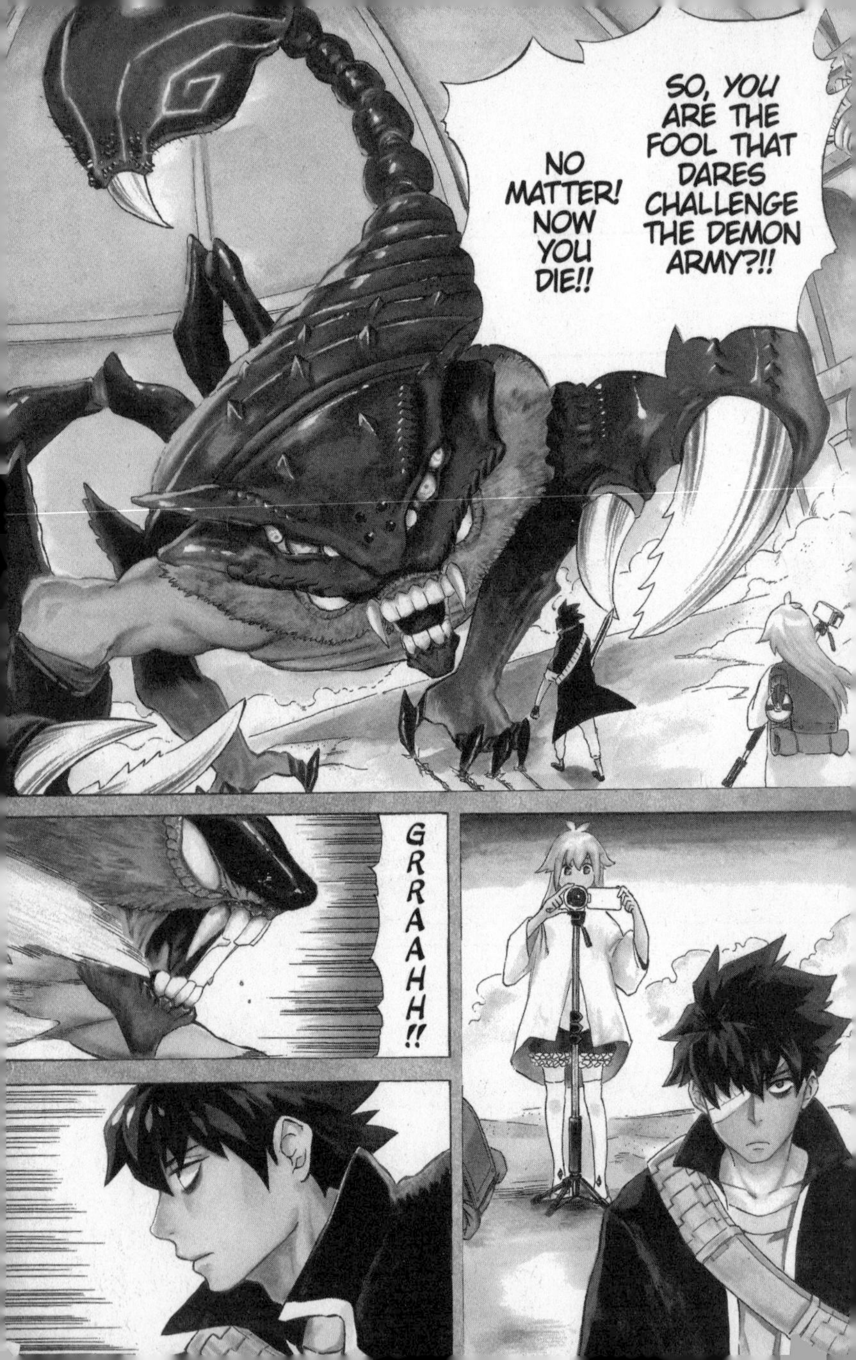
SO, YOU ARE THE FOOL THAT DARES CHALLENGE THE DEMON ARMY?!!
NO MATTER! NOW YOU DIE!!
GRRAAHH!!

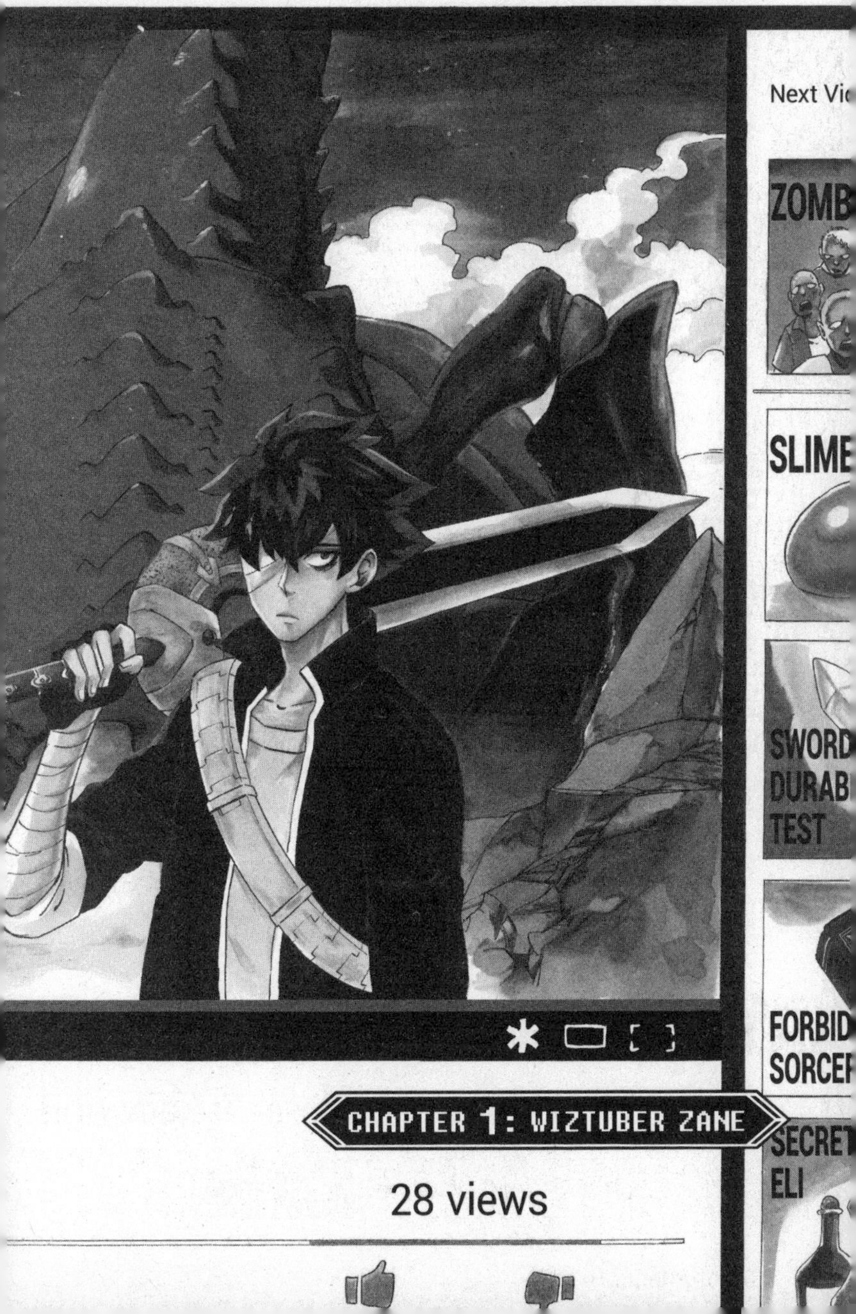
Next Vi
ZOMB
SLIME
SWORD
DURAB
TEST
FORBID
SORCER
CHAPTER 1: WIZTUBER ZANE
SECRET
ELI
28 views

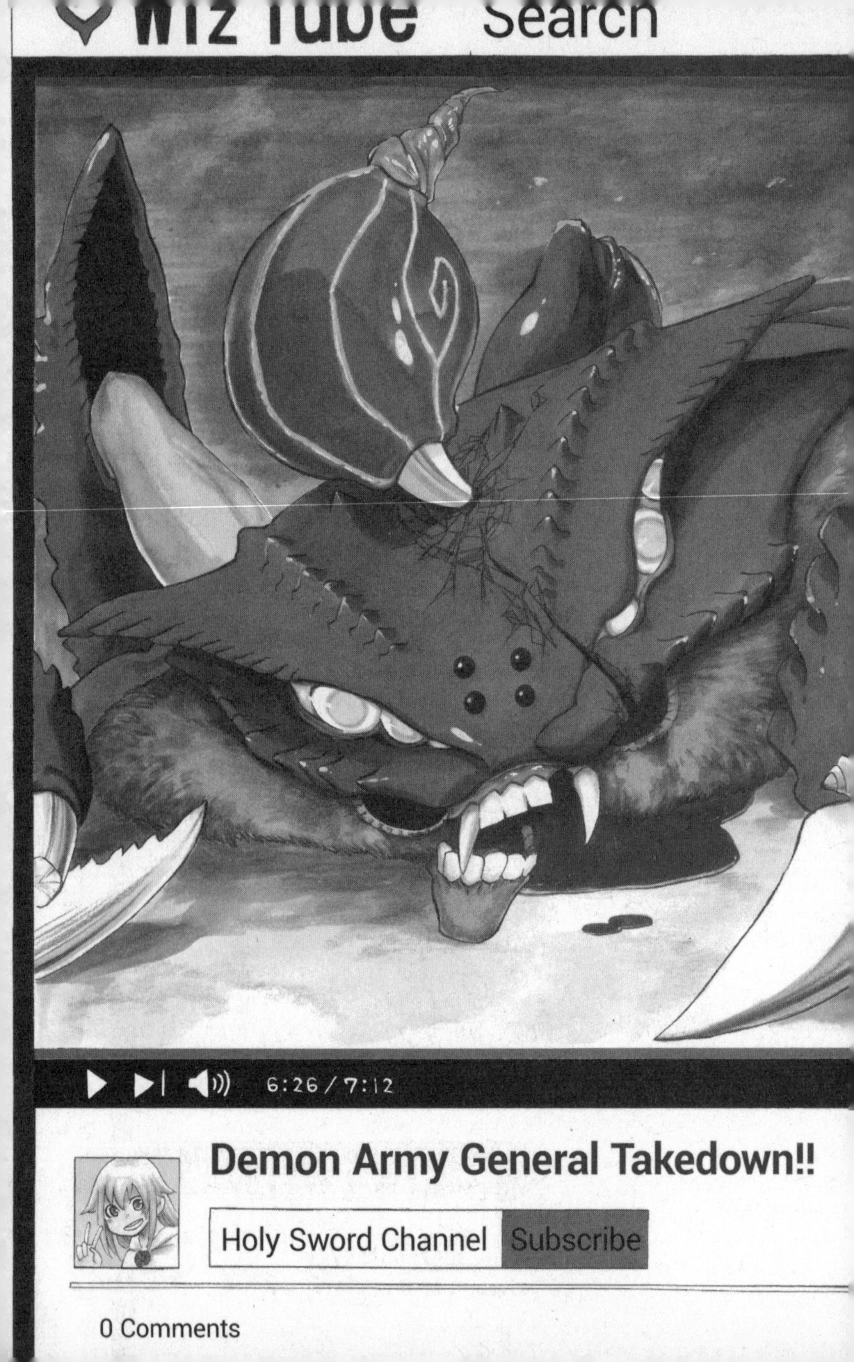
WizTube Search
6:26 / 7:12
Demon Army General Takedown!!
Holy Sword Channel
Subscribe
0 Comments

THE BRAVE TUBER

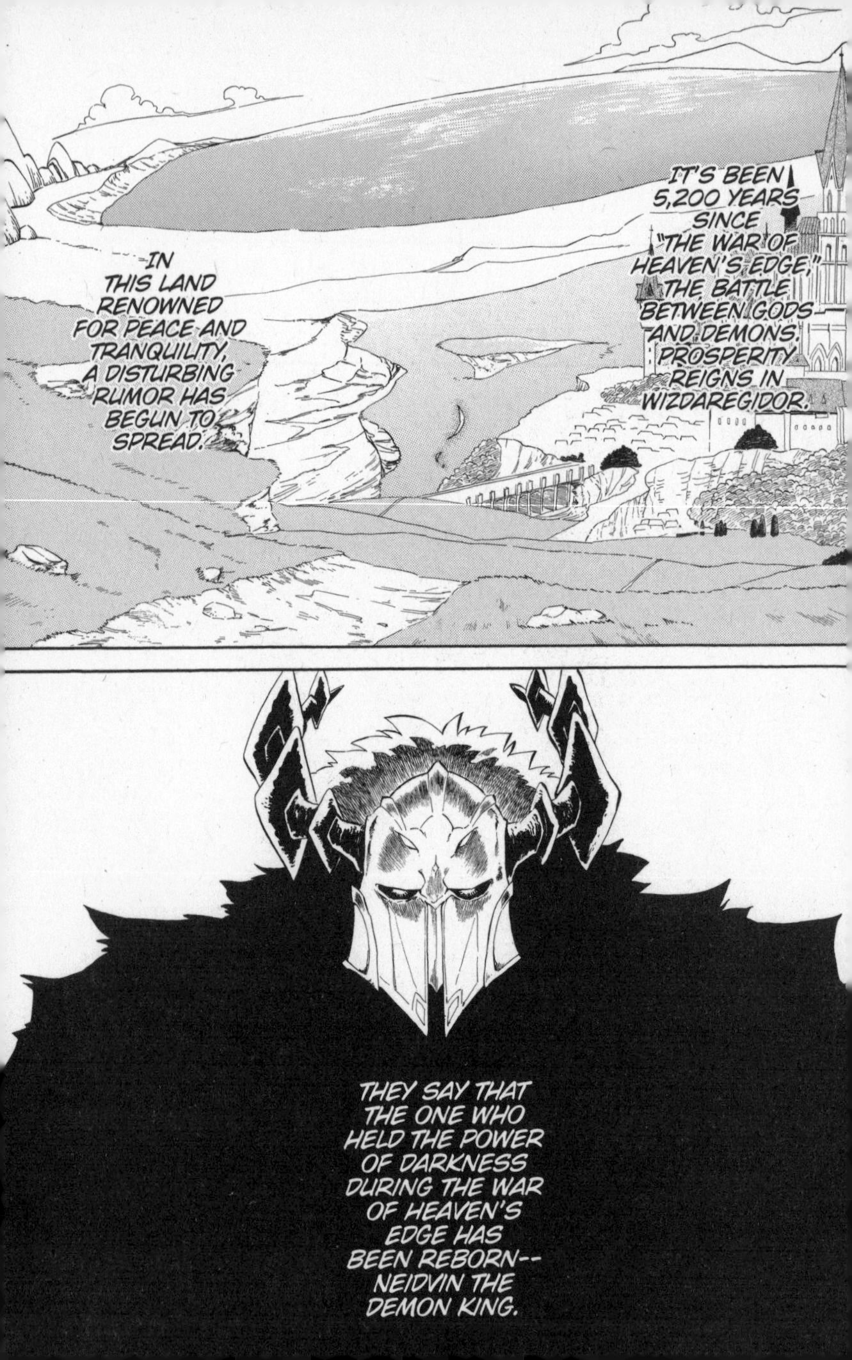
IT'S BEEN 5,200 YEARS SINCE "THE WAR OF HEAVEN'S EDGE," THE BATTLE BETWEEN GODS AND DEMONS. PROSPERITY REIGNS IN WIZDAREGIDOR.
IN THIS LAND RENOWNED FOR PEACE AND TRANQUILITY, A DISTURBING RUMOR HAS BEGUN TO SPREAD.
THEY SAY THAT THE ONE WHO HELD THE POWER OF DARKNESS DURING THE WAR OF HEAVEN'S EDGE HAS BEEN REBORN-- NEIDVIN THE DEMON KING.

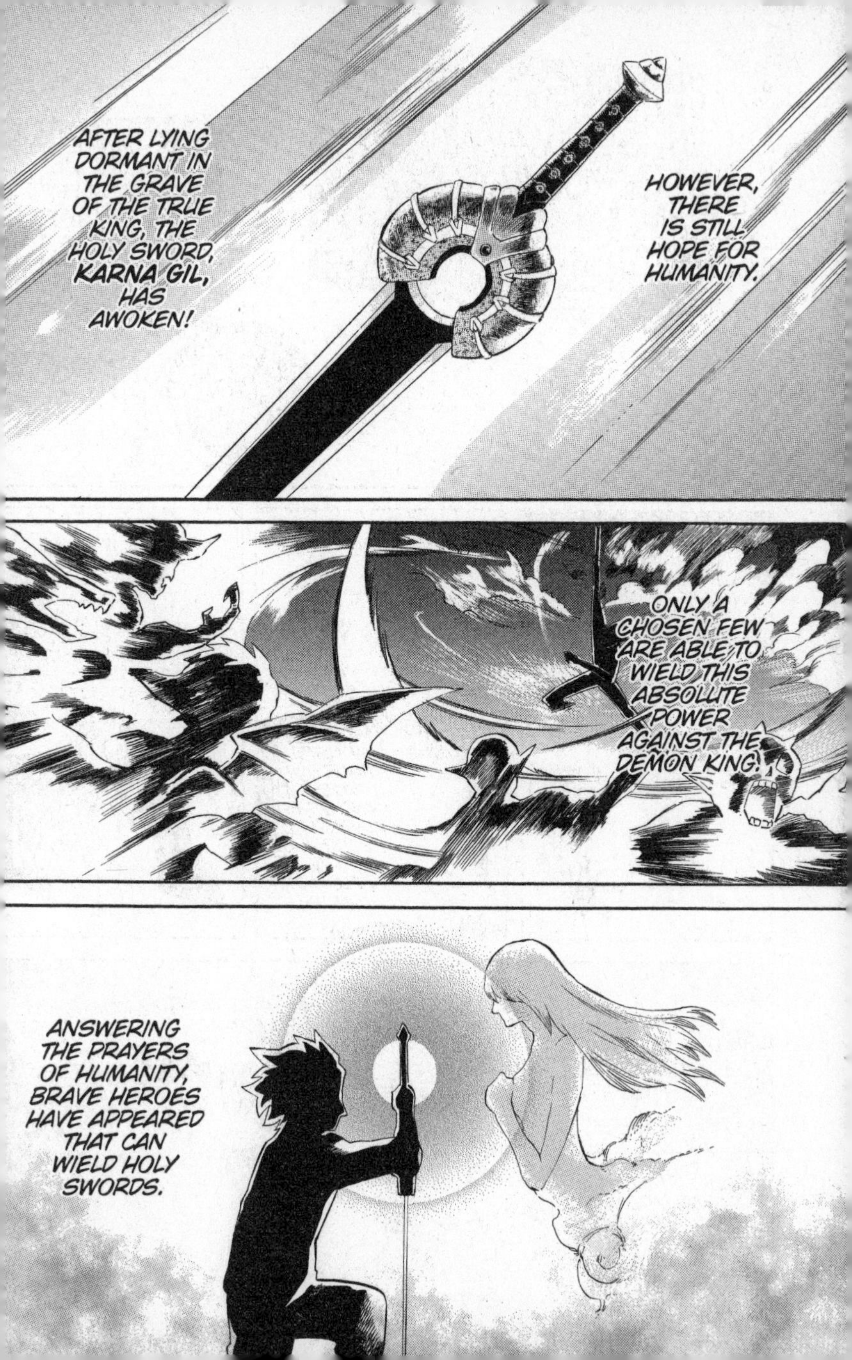
HOWEVER, THERE IS STILL HOPE FOR HUMANITY.
AFTER LYING DORMANT IN THE GRAVE OF THE TRUE KING, THE HOLY SWORD, KARNA GIL, HAS AWOKEN!
ONLY A CHOSEN FEW ARE ABLE TO WIELD THIS ABSOLUTE POWER AGAINST THE DEMON KING.
ANSWERING THE PRAYERS OF HUMANITY, BRAVE HEROES HAVE APPEARED THAT CAN WIELD HOLY SWORDS.

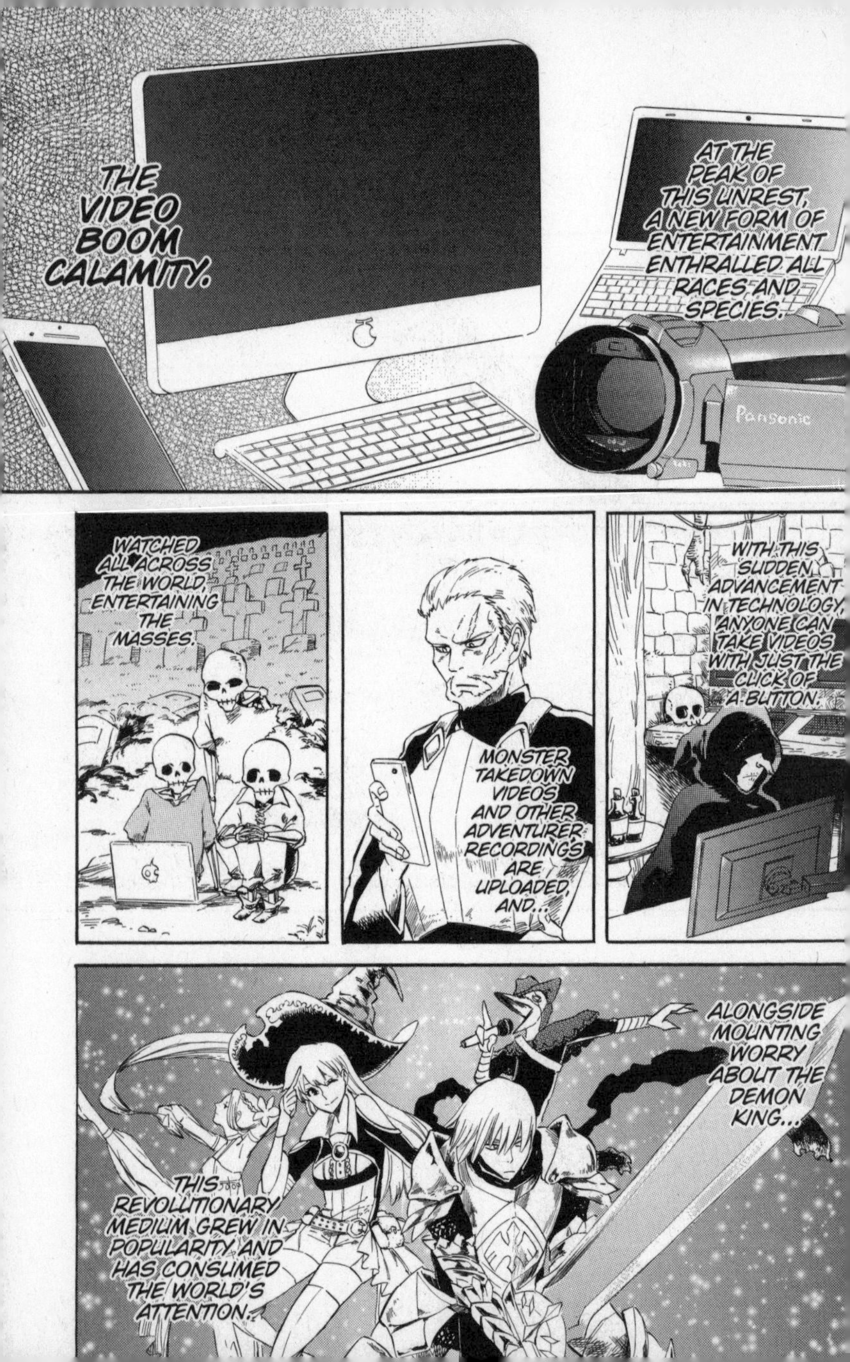
AT THE PEAK OF THIS UNREST, A NEW FORM OF ENTERTAINMENT ENTHRALLED ALL RACES AND SPECIES.
Pansonic
THE VIDEO BOOM CALAMITY.
WITH THIS SUDDEN ADVANCEMENT IN TECHNOLOGY, ANYONE CAN TAKE VIDEOS WITH JUST THE CLICK OF A BUTTON.
MONSTER TAKEDOWN VIDEOS AND OTHER ADVENTURER RECORDINGS ARE UPLOADED, AND...
WATCHED ALL ACROSS THE WORLD, ENTERTAINING THE MASSES.
ALONGSIDE MOUNTING WORRY ABOUT THE DEMON KING...
THIS REVOLUTIONARY MEDIUM GREW IN POPULARITY AND HAS CONSUMED THE WORLD'S ATTENTION.

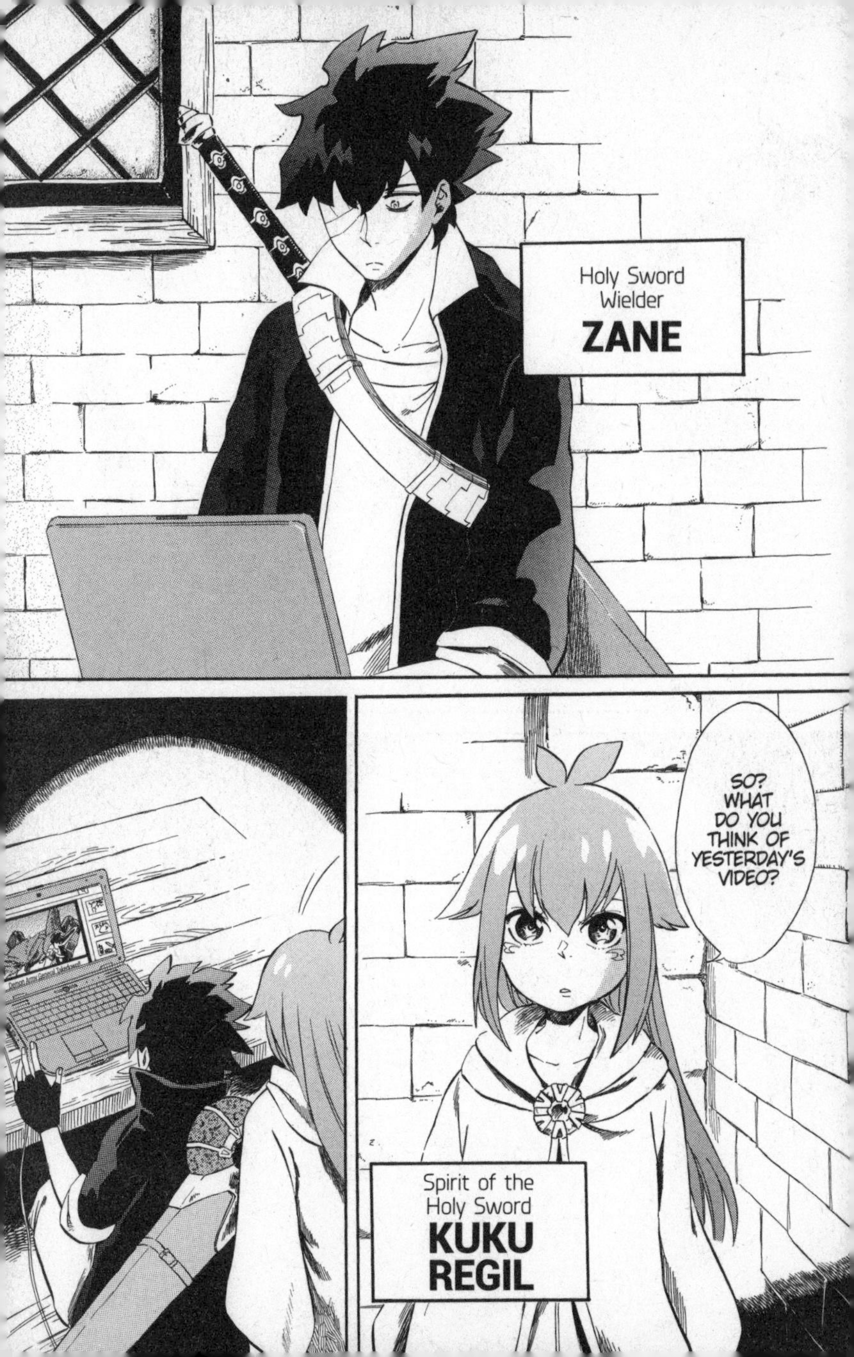
Holy Sword Wielder ZANE
SO? WHAT DO YOU THINK OF YESTERDAY'S VIDEO?
Spirit of the Holy Sword KUKU REGIL

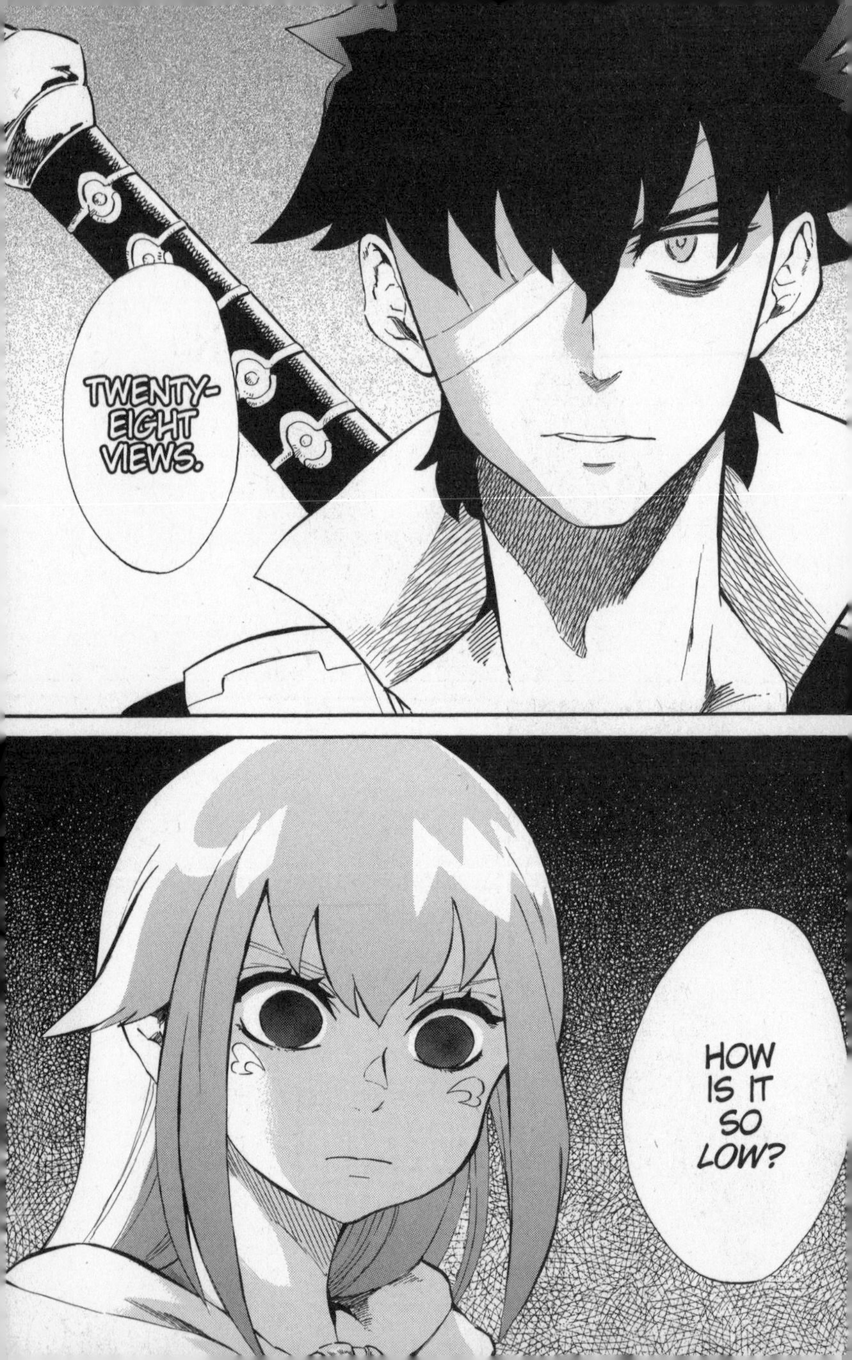
TWENTY-EIGHT VIEWS.
HOW IS IT SO LOW?

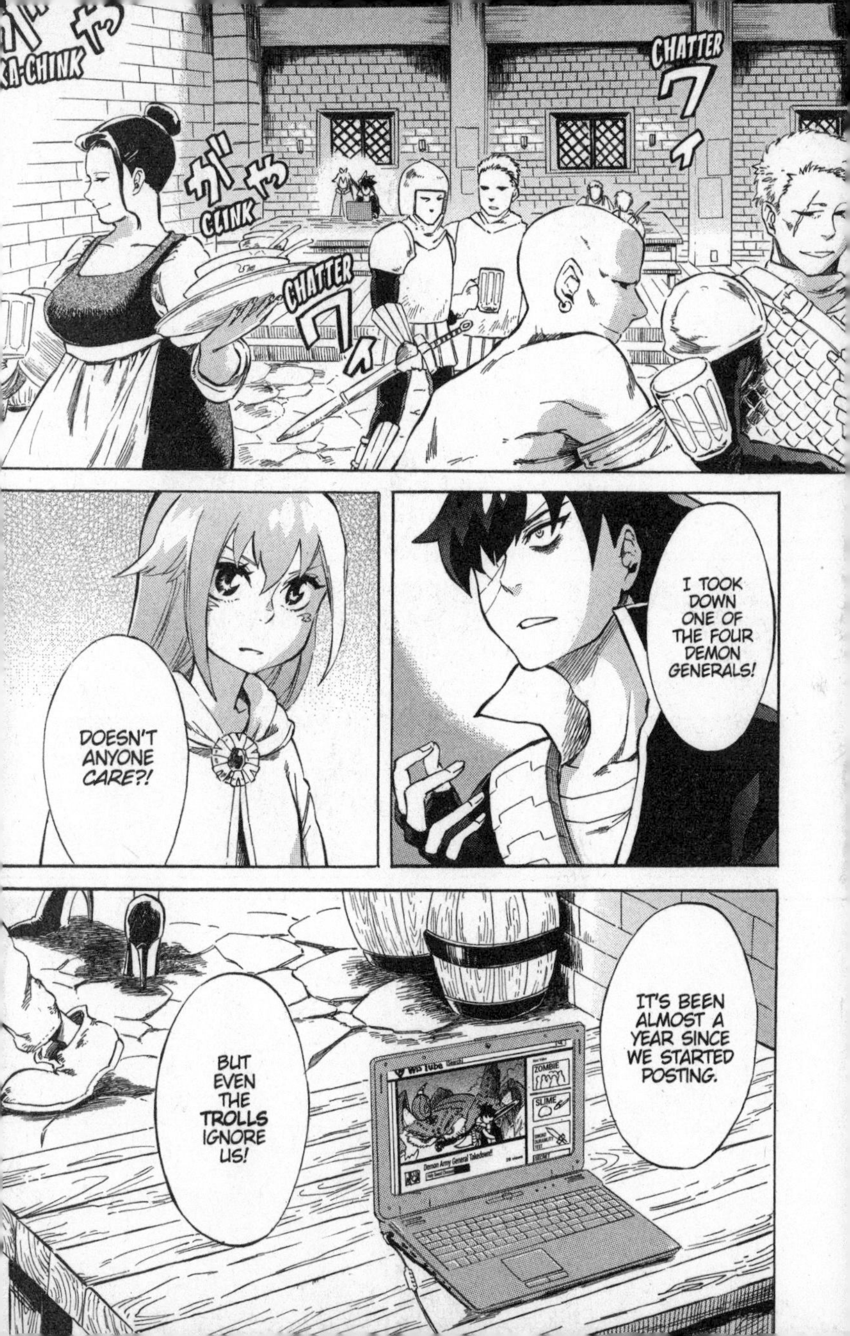
CHATTER
A-CHINK
CLINK
CHATTER
I TOOK DOWN ONE OF THE FOUR DEMON GENERALS!
DOESN'T ANYONE CARE?!
IT'S BEEN ALMOST A YEAR SINCE WE STARTED POSTING.
BUT EVEN THE TROLLS IGNORE US!
ZOMBIE
SLIME
Demon Army General Takedown!

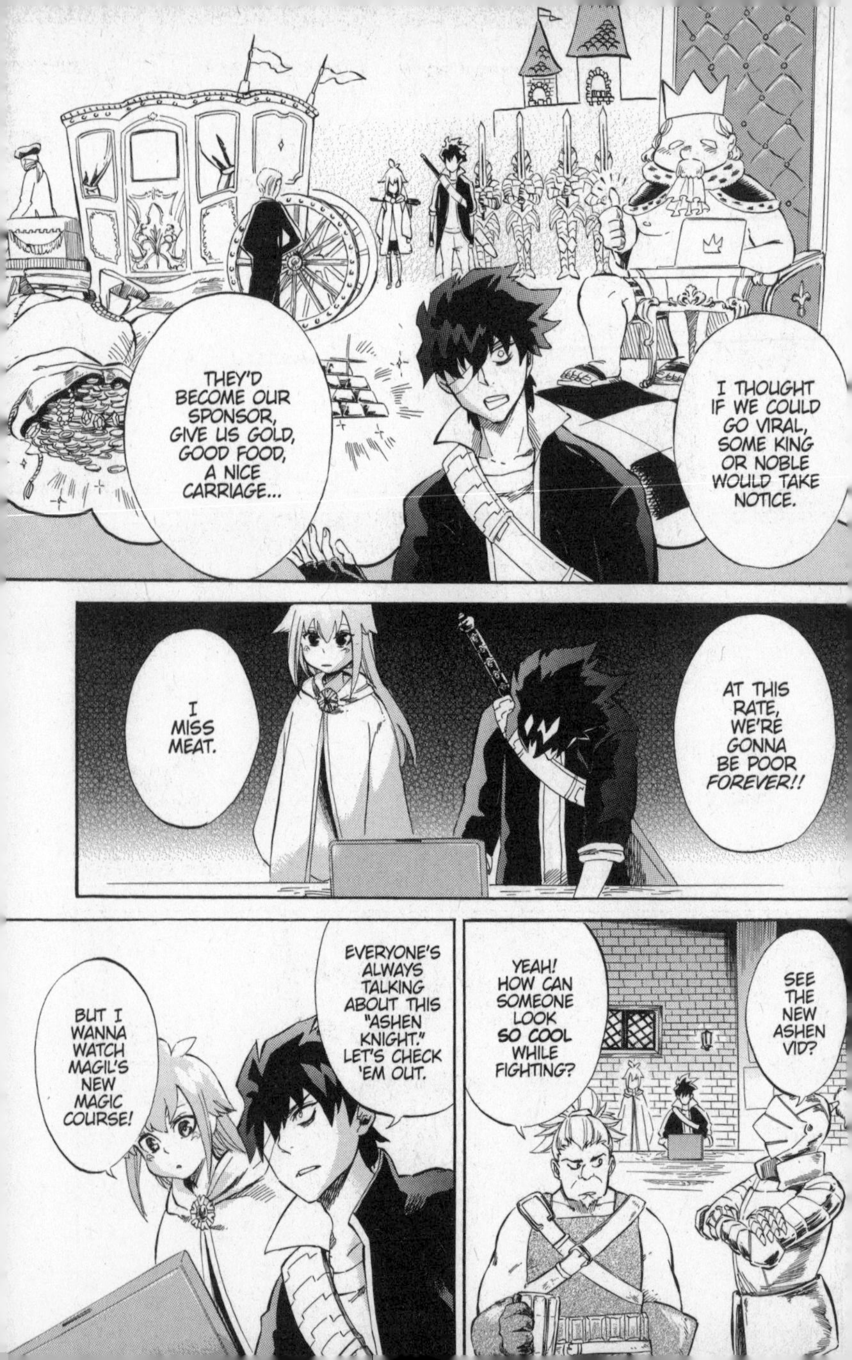
I THOUGHT IF WE COULD GO VIRAL, SOME KING OR NOBLE WOULD TAKE NOTICE.
THEY'D BECOME OUR SPONSOR, GIVE US GOLD, GOOD FOOD, A NICE CARRIAGE...
AT THIS RATE, WE'RE GONNA BE POOR FOREVER!!
I MISS MEAT.
SEE THE NEW ASHEN VID?
YEAH! HOW CAN SOMEONE LOOK SO COOL WHILE FIGHTING?
EVERYONE'S ALWAYS TALKING ABOUT THIS "ASHEN KNIGHT." LET'S CHECK 'EM OUT.
BUT I WANNA WATCH MAGIL'S NEW MAGIC COURSE!

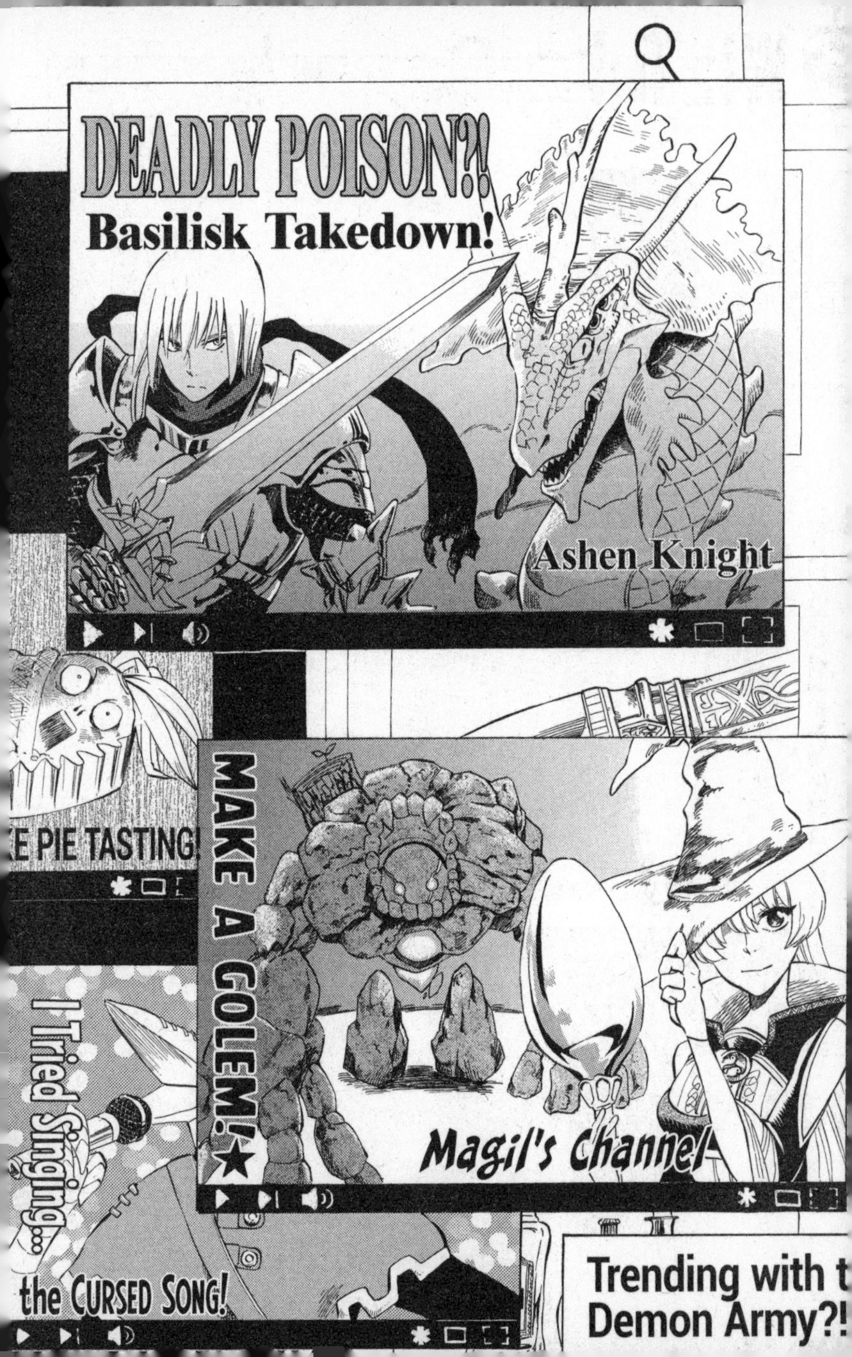
DEADLY POISON?!
Basilisk Takedown!
Ashen Knight
MAKE A GOLEM!★
Magil's Channel
E PIE TASTING!
Trending with t
Demon Army?!
I Tried Singing...
the CURSED SONG!

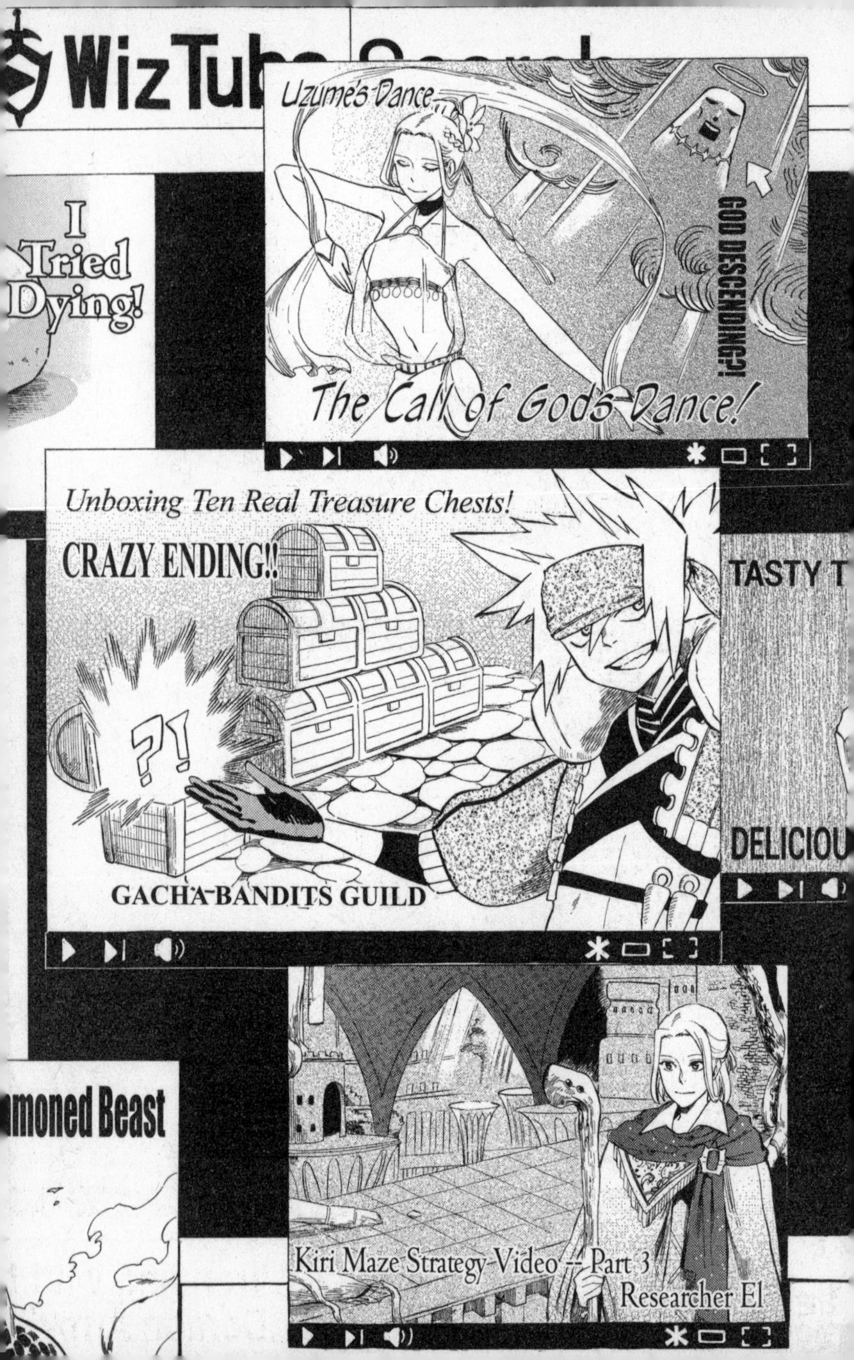
Wiz Tub
Uzume's Dance
GOD DESCENDING?!
The Call of Gods Dance!
I Tried Dying!
Unboxing Ten Real Treasure Chests!
CRAZY ENDING!!
?!
GACHA BANDITS GUILD
TASTY T
DELICIOU
nmoned Beast
Kiri Maze Strategy Video -- Part 3
Researcher El

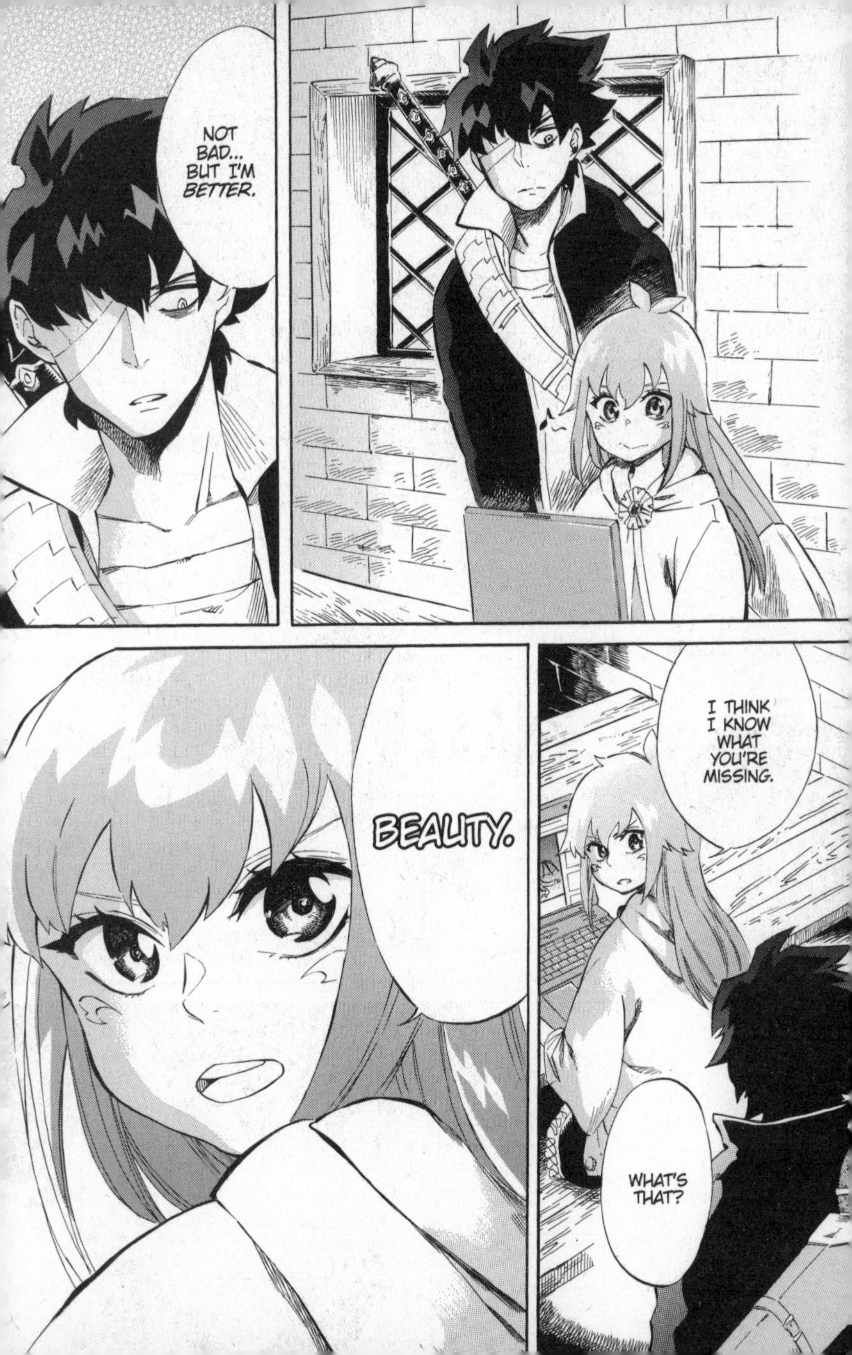
NOT BAD... BUT I'M *BETTER.*
I THINK I KNOW WHAT YOU'RE MISSING.
WHAT'S THAT?
BEAUTY.

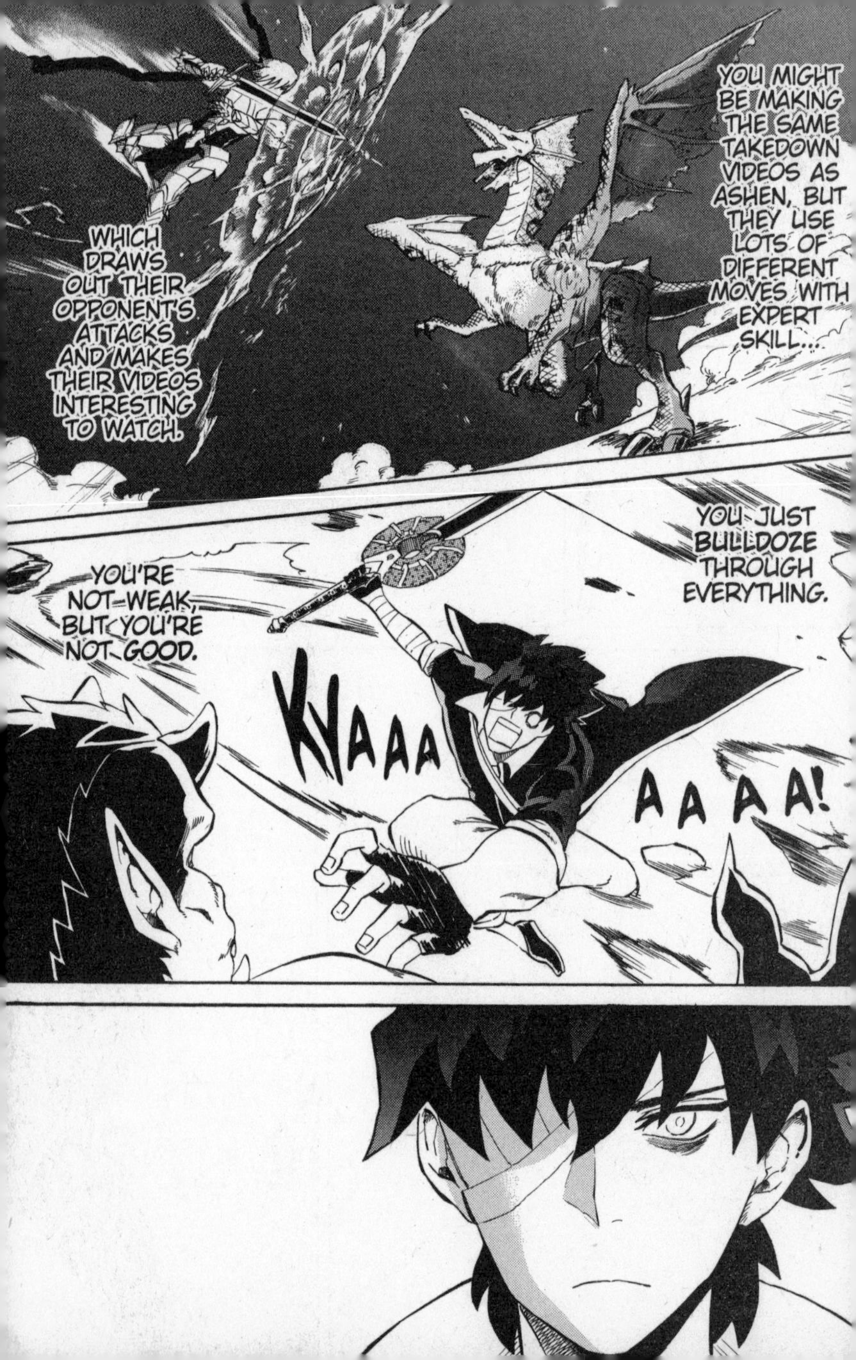
YOU MIGHT BE MAKING THE SAME TAKEDOWN VIDEOS AS ASHEN, BUT THEY USE LOTS OF DIFFERENT MOVES WITH EXPERT SKILL...
WHICH DRAWS OUT THEIR OPPONENT'S ATTACKS AND MAKES THEIR VIDEOS INTERESTING TO WATCH.
YOU JUST BULLDOZE THROUGH EVERYTHING.
YOU'RE NOT WEAK, BUT YOU'RE NOT GOOD.
KYAAAAAAAA!

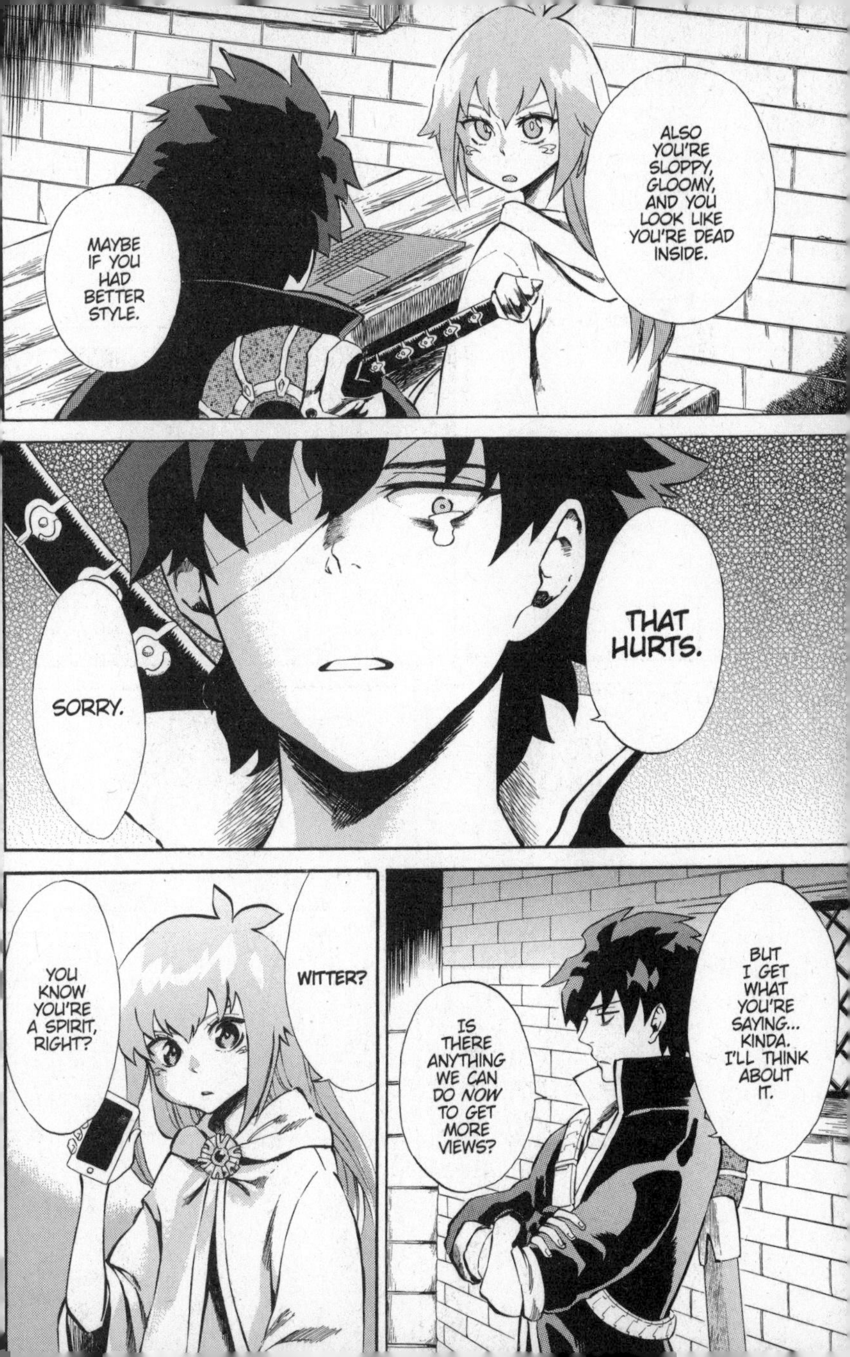
ALSO YOU'RE SLOPPY, GLOOMY, AND YOU LOOK LIKE YOU'RE DEAD INSIDE.
MAYBE IF YOU HAD BETTER STYLE.
THAT HURTS.
SORRY.
BUT I GET WHAT YOU'RE SAYING... KINDA. I'LL THINK ABOUT IT.
IS THERE ANYTHING WE CAN DO *NOW* TO GET MORE VIEWS?
WITTER?
YOU KNOW YOU'RE A SPIRIT, RIGHT?

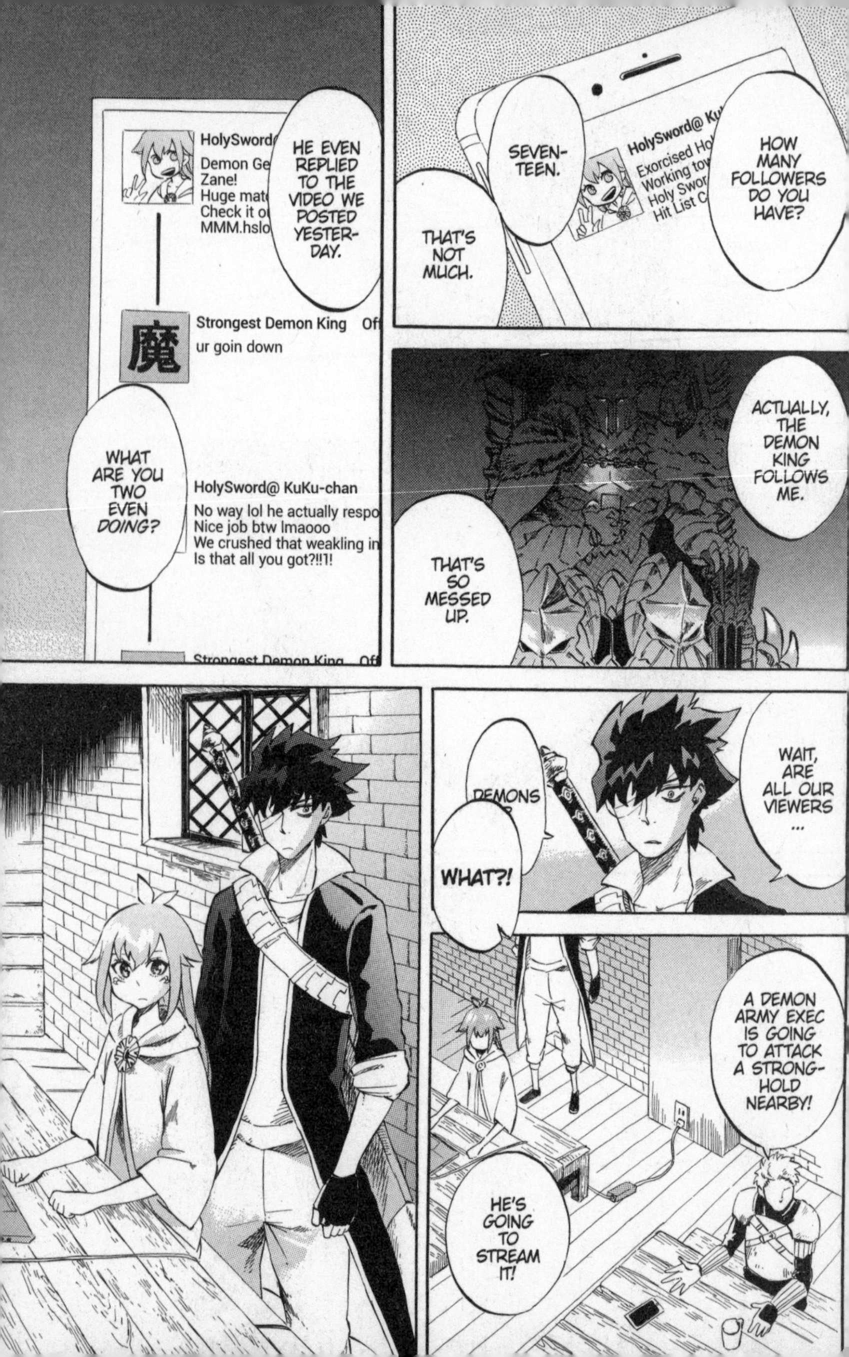
HOW MANY FOLLOWERS DO YOU HAVE?
HolySword@ Ku
Exorcised Ho
Working tow
Holy Swor
Hit List C
SEVEN-TEEN.
THAT'S NOT MUCH.
ACTUALLY, THE DEMON KING FOLLOWS ME.
THAT'S SO MESSED UP.
HE EVEN REPLIED TO THE VIDEO WE POSTED YESTER-DAY.
HolySword@
Demon Ge
Zane!
Huge mat
Check it o
MMM.hslo
魔
Strongest Demon King Off
ur goin down
WHAT ARE YOU TWO EVEN *DOING?*
HolySword@ KuKu-chan
No way lol he actually respo
Nice job btw lmaooo
We crushed that weakling in
Is that all you got?!!1!
Strongest Demon King Off
WAIT, ARE ALL OUR VIEWERS ...
DEMONS
WHAT?!
A DEMON ARMY EXEC IS GOING TO ATTACK A STRONG-HOLD NEARBY!
HE'S GOING TO STREAM IT!

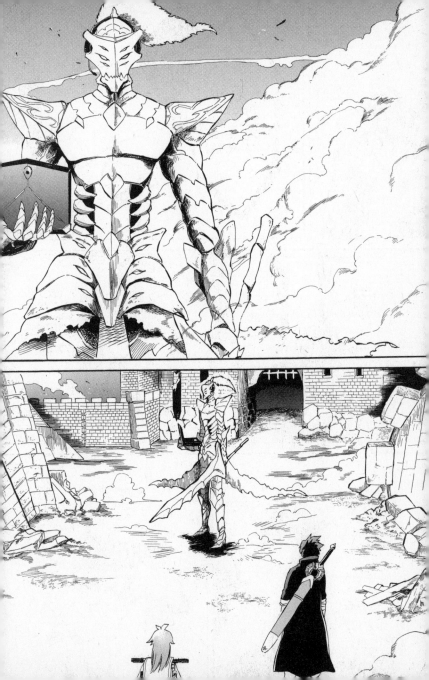

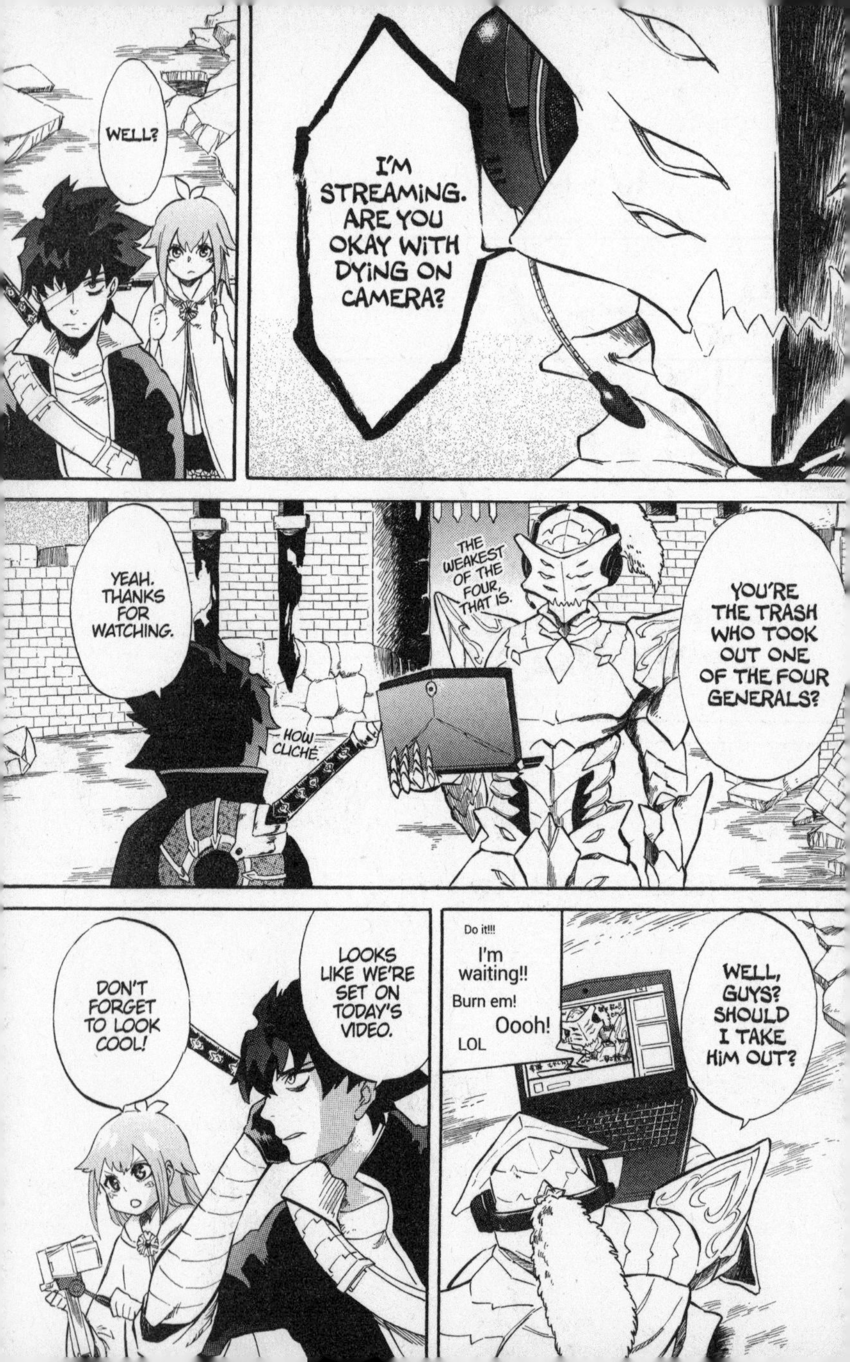
I'M STREAMING. ARE YOU OKAY WITH DYING ON CAMERA?
WELL?
YOU'RE THE TRASH WHO TOOK OUT ONE OF THE FOUR GENERALS?
THE WEAKEST OF THE FOUR, THAT IS.
HOW CLICHÉ.
YEAH. THANKS FOR WATCHING.
WELL, GUYS? SHOULD I TAKE HIM OUT?
Do it!!!
I'm waiting!!
Burn em!
Oooh!
LOL
LOOKS LIKE WE'RE SET ON TODAY'S VIDEO.
DON'T FORGET TO LOOK COOL!

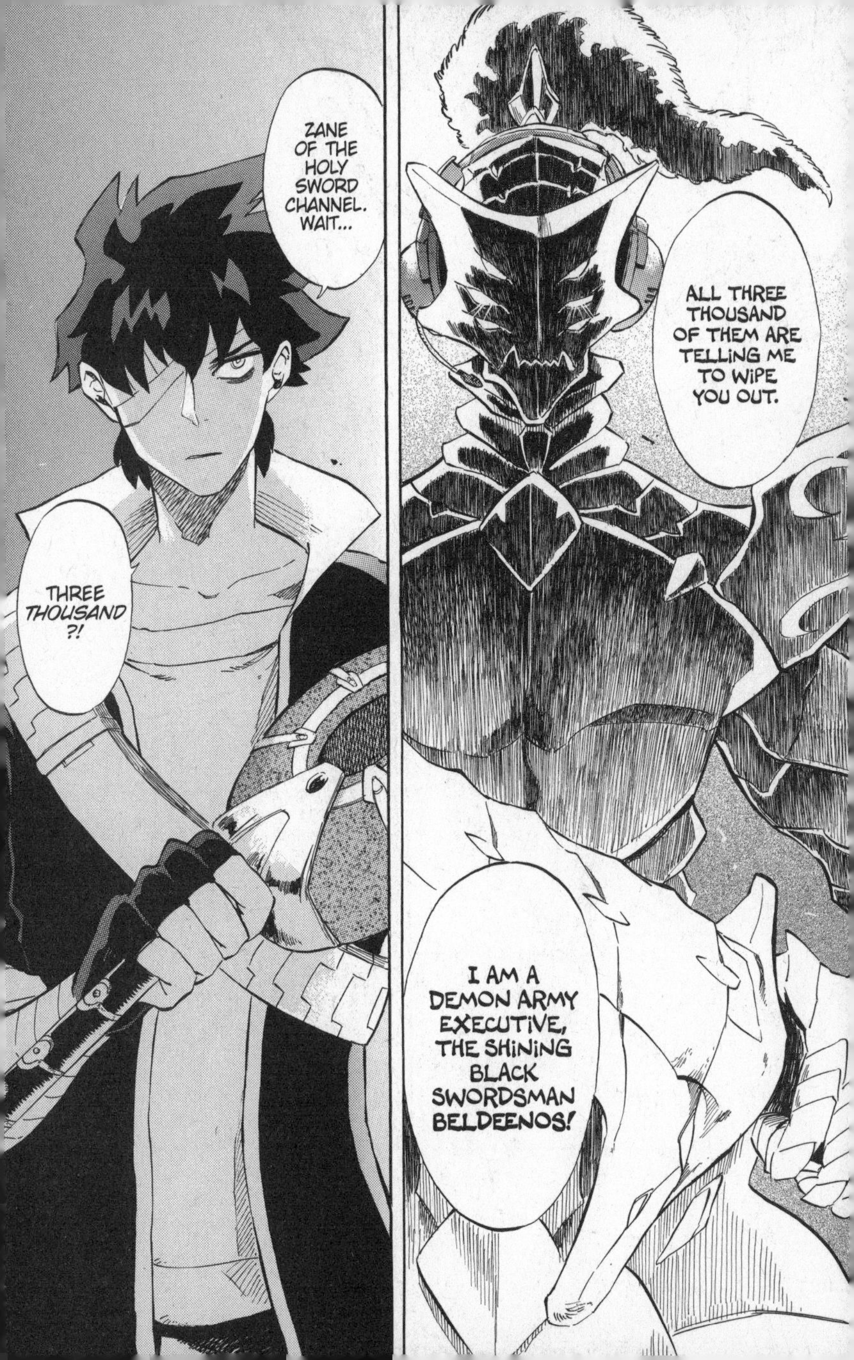
ALL THREE THOUSAND OF THEM ARE TELLING ME TO WIPE YOU OUT.
I AM A DEMON ARMY EXECUTIVE, THE SHINING BLACK SWORDSMAN BELDEENOS!
ZANE OF THE HOLY SWORD CHANNEL. WAIT...
THREE *THOUSAND* ?!

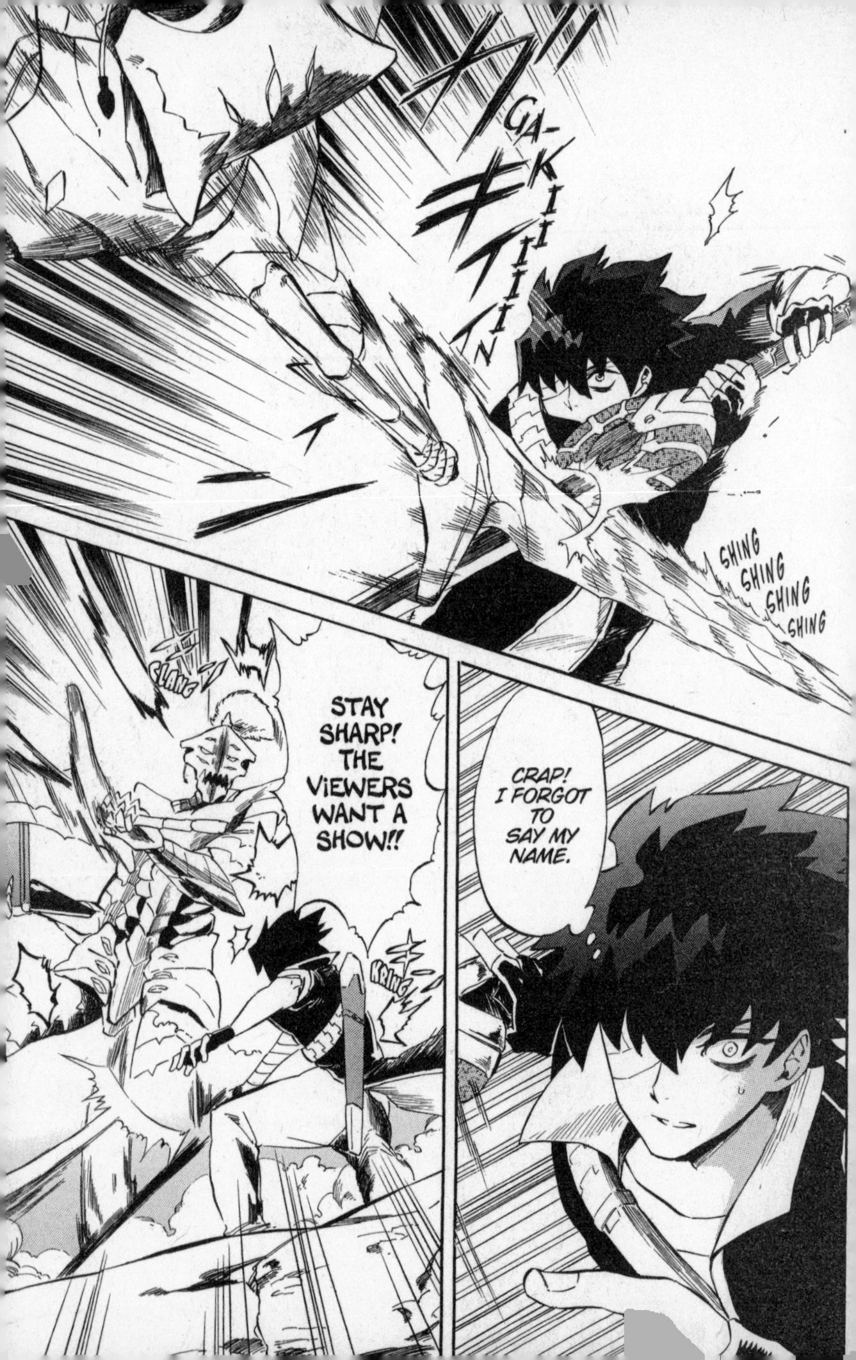
GA-KIIIIIN
SHING
SHING
SHING
SHING
CRAP! I FORGOT TO SAY MY NAME.
CLANG
STAY SHARP! THE VIEWERS WANT A SHOW!!
KRING

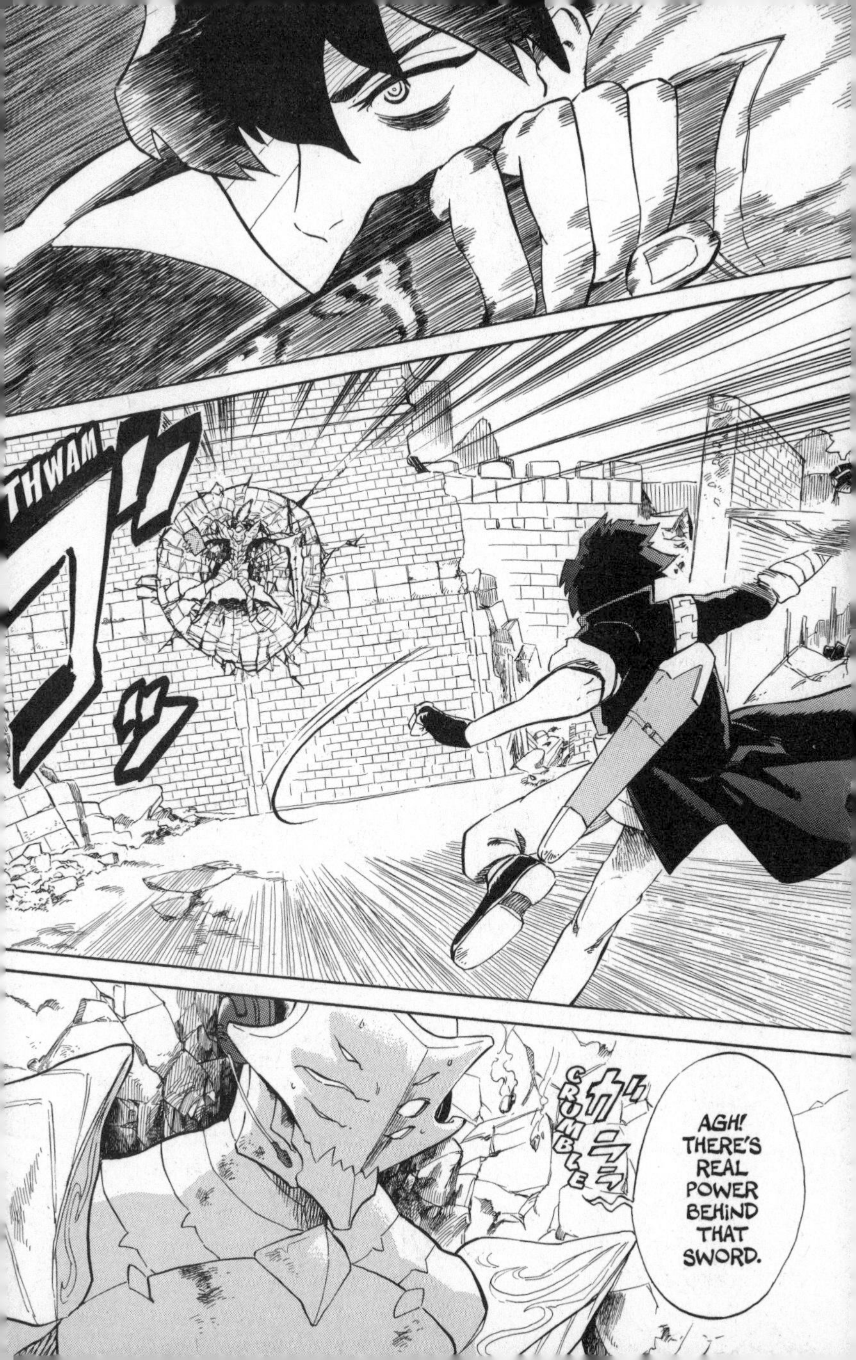
THWAM
CRUMBLE
AGH! THERE'S REAL POWER BEHIND THAT SWORD.

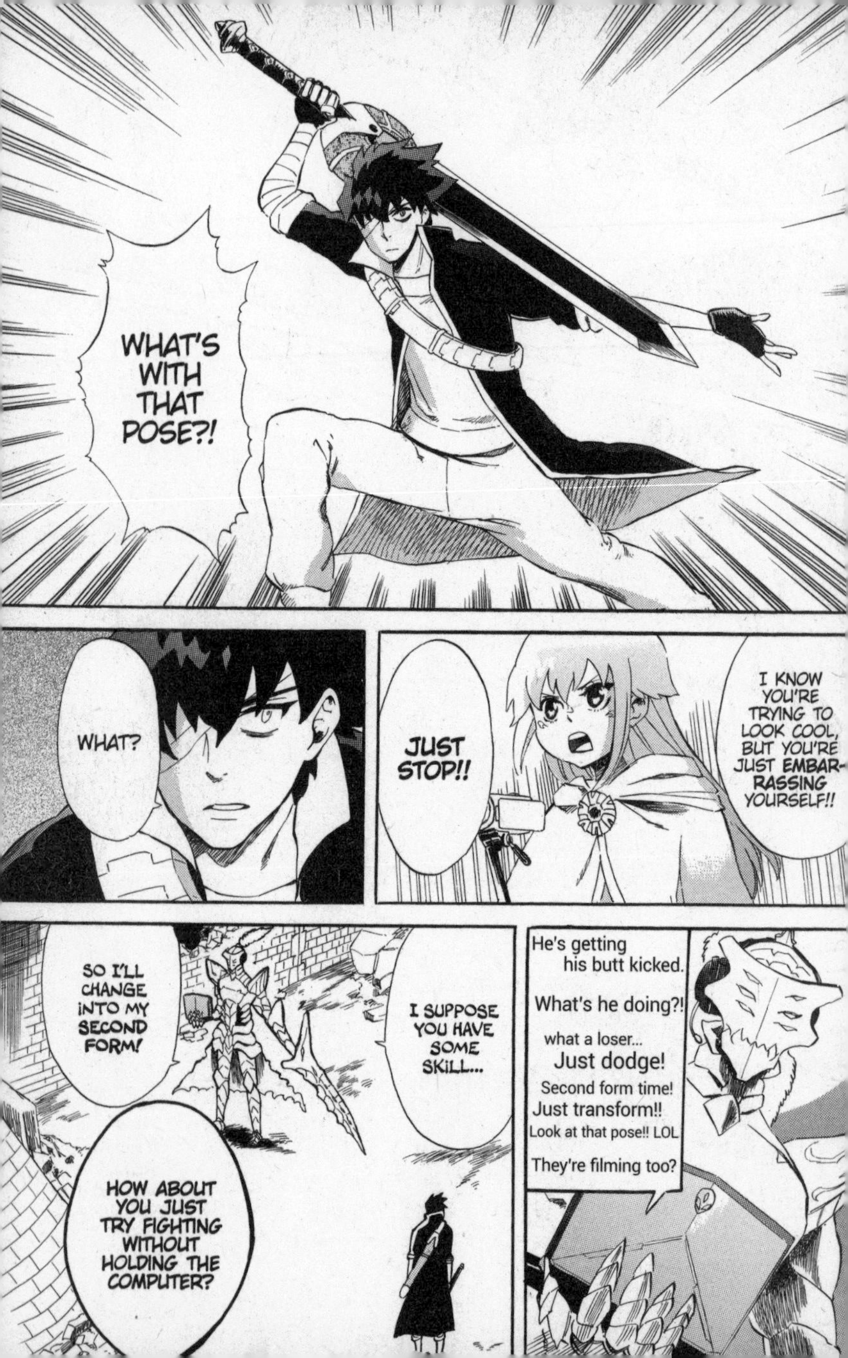
WHAT'S WITH THAT POSE?!
I KNOW YOU'RE TRYING TO LOOK COOL, BUT YOU'RE JUST EMBARRASSING YOURSELF!!
JUST STOP!!
WHAT?
He's getting his butt kicked.
What's he doing?!
what a loser...
Just dodge!
Second form time!
Just transform!!
Look at that pose!! LOL
They're filming too?
I SUPPOSE YOU HAVE SOME SKILL...
SO I'LL CHANGE INTO MY SECOND FORM!
HOW ABOUT YOU JUST TRY FIGHTING WITHOUT HOLDING THE COMPUTER?

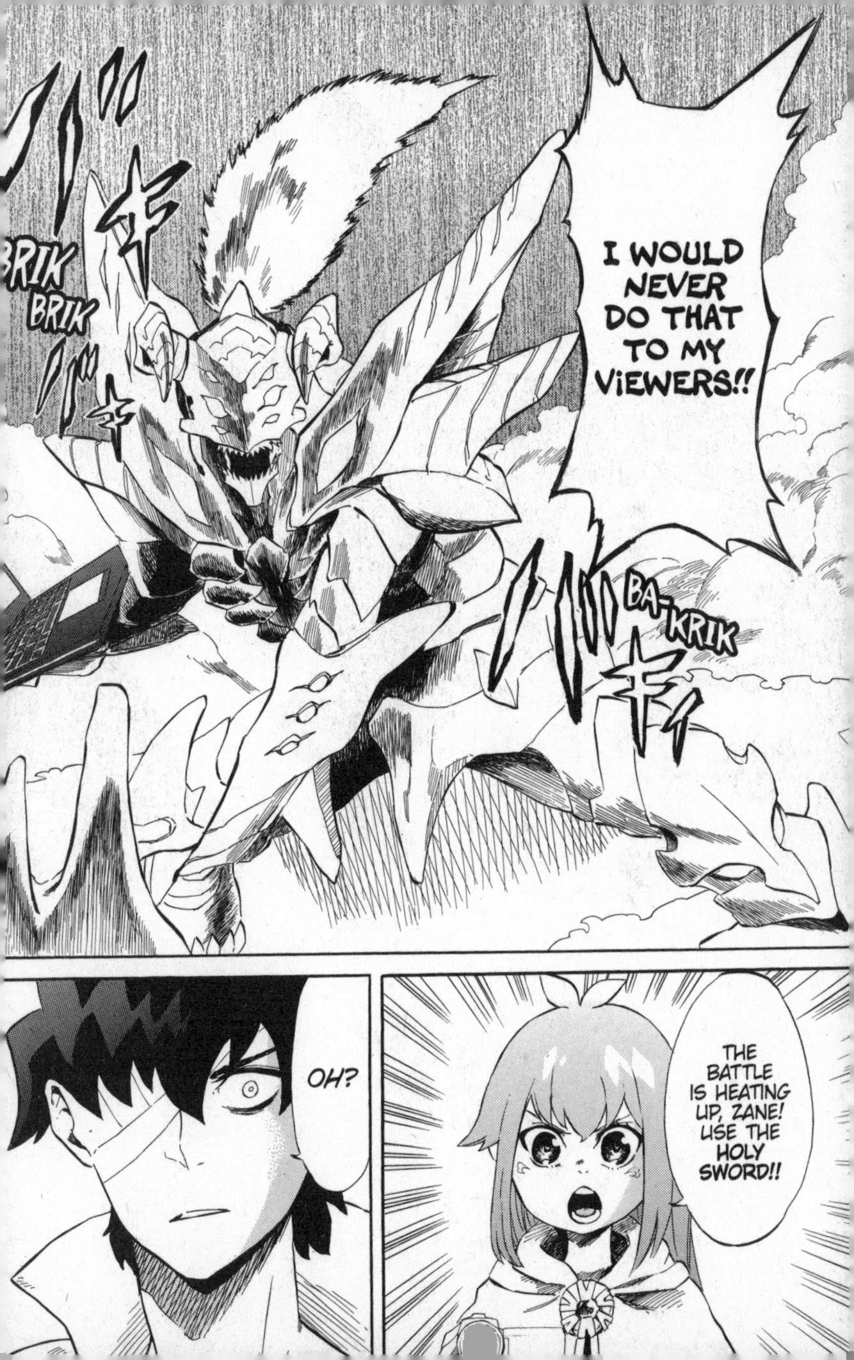
I WOULD NEVER DO THAT TO MY ViEWERS!!
BRIK BRIK
BA-KRIK
THE BATTLE IS HEATING UP, ZANE! USE THE HOLY SWORD!!
OH?

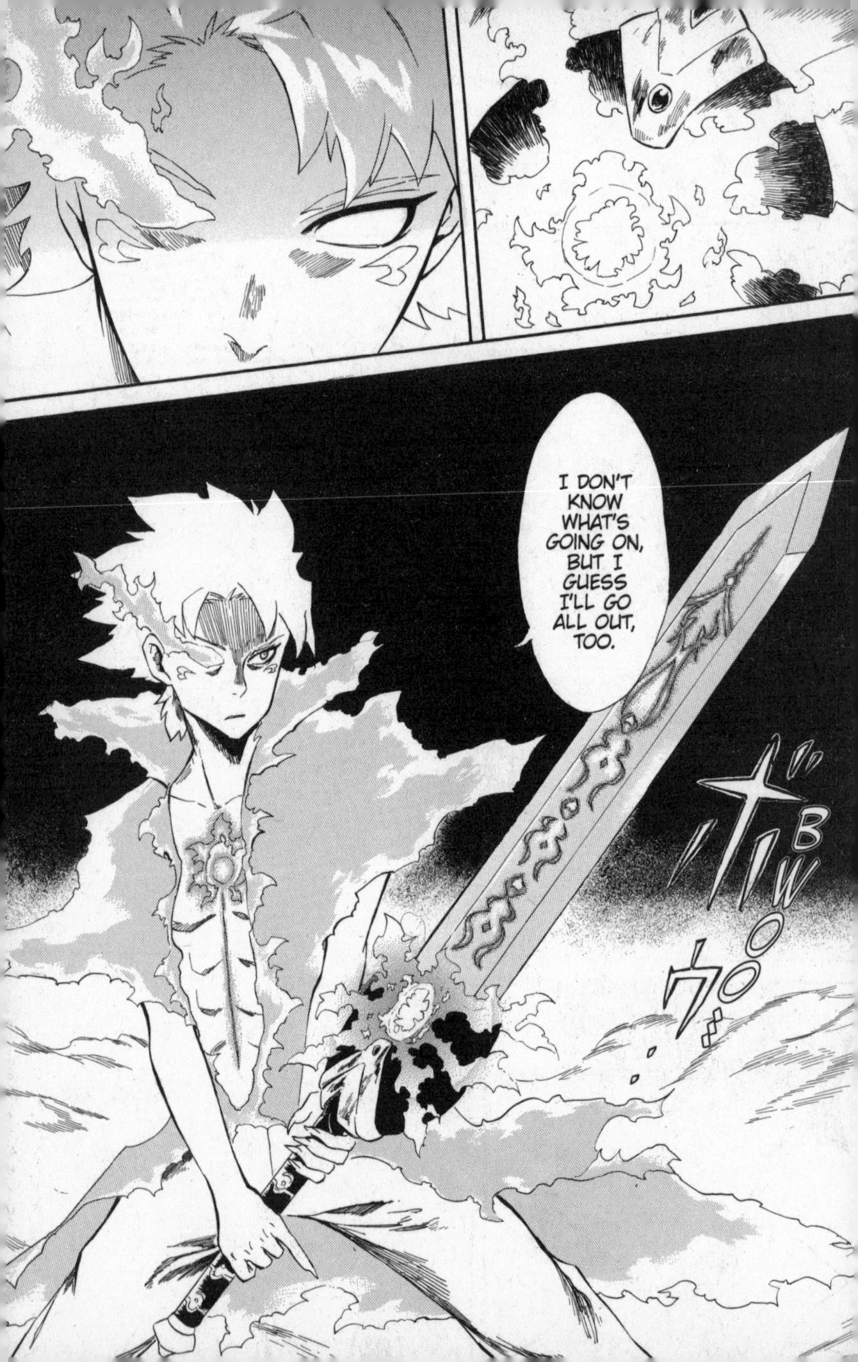
I DON'T KNOW WHAT'S GOING ON, BUT I GUESS I'LL GO ALL OUT, TOO.
BWOOO

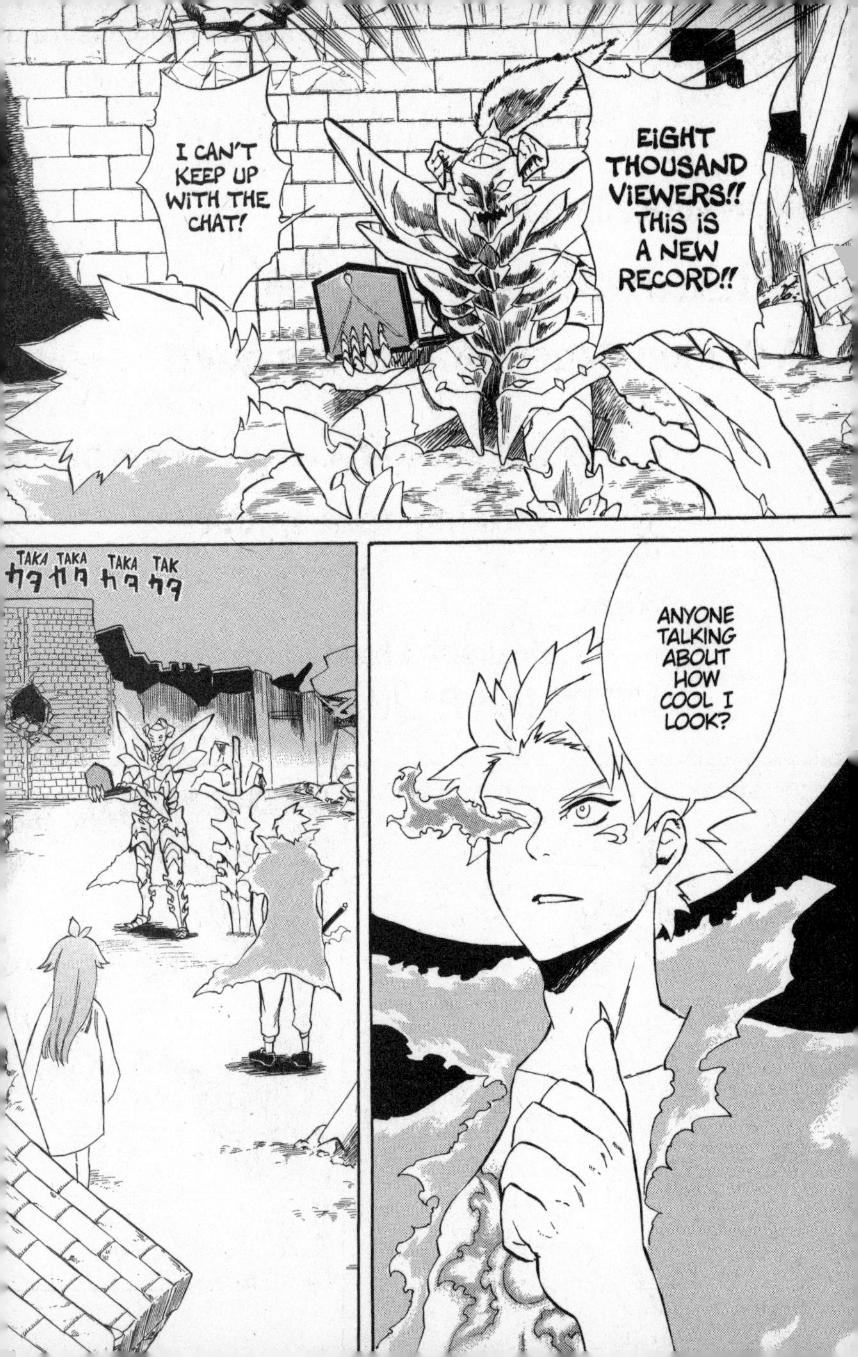
EIGHT THOUSAND VIEWERS!! THIS IS A NEW RECORD!!
I CAN'T KEEP UP WITH THE CHAT!
ANYONE TALKING ABOUT HOW COOL I LOOK?
TAKA TAKA TAKA TAK
カタカタカタカタ

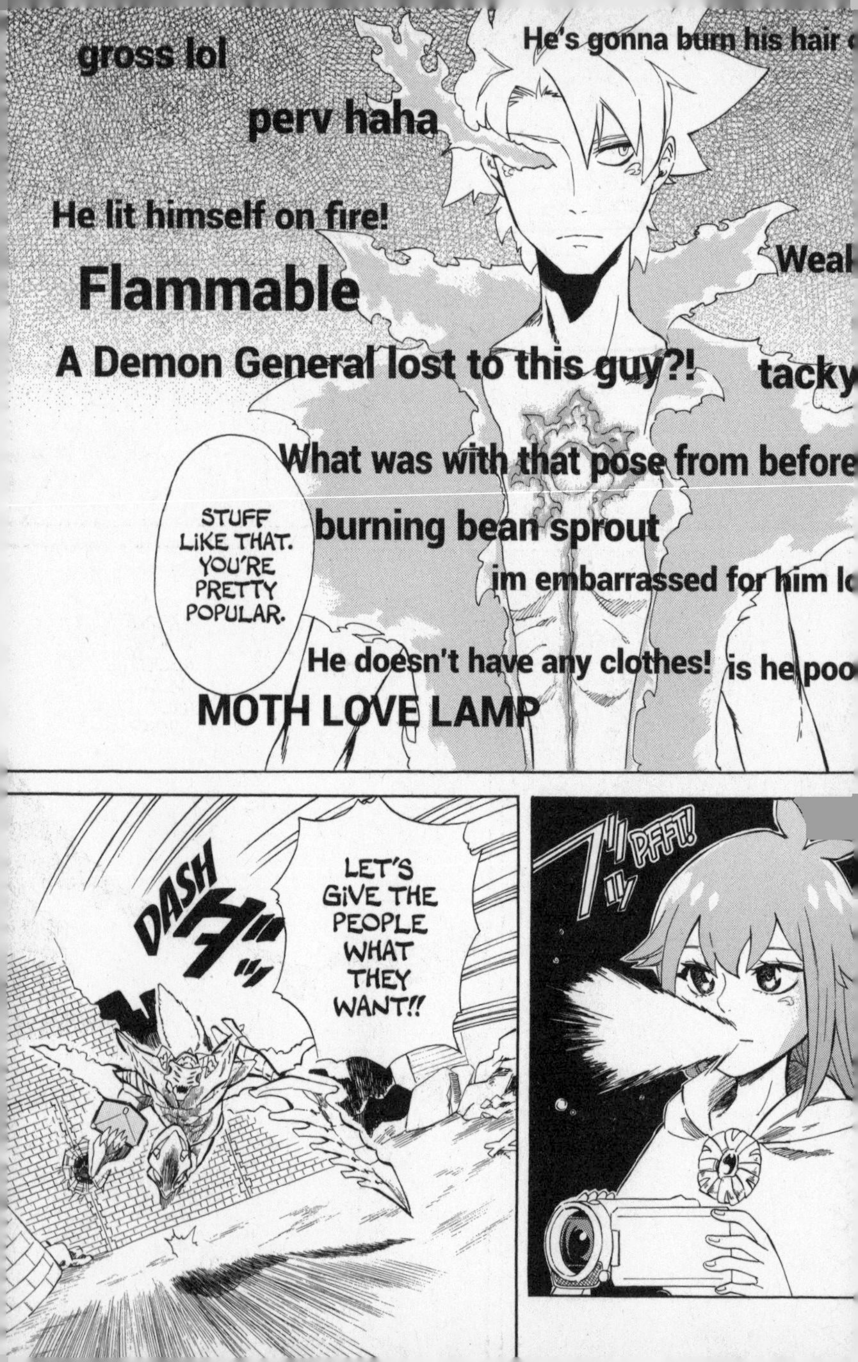
He's gonna burn his hair
gross lol
perv haha
He lit himself on fire!
Wea
Flammable
tacky
A Demon General lost to this guy?!
What was with that pose from before
STUFF LIKE THAT. YOU'RE PRETTY POPULAR.
burning bean sprout
im embarrassed for him l
is he poo
He doesn't have any clothes!
MOTH LOVE LAMP
PFFT!
DASH
LET'S GIVE THE PEOPLE WHAT THEY WANT!!

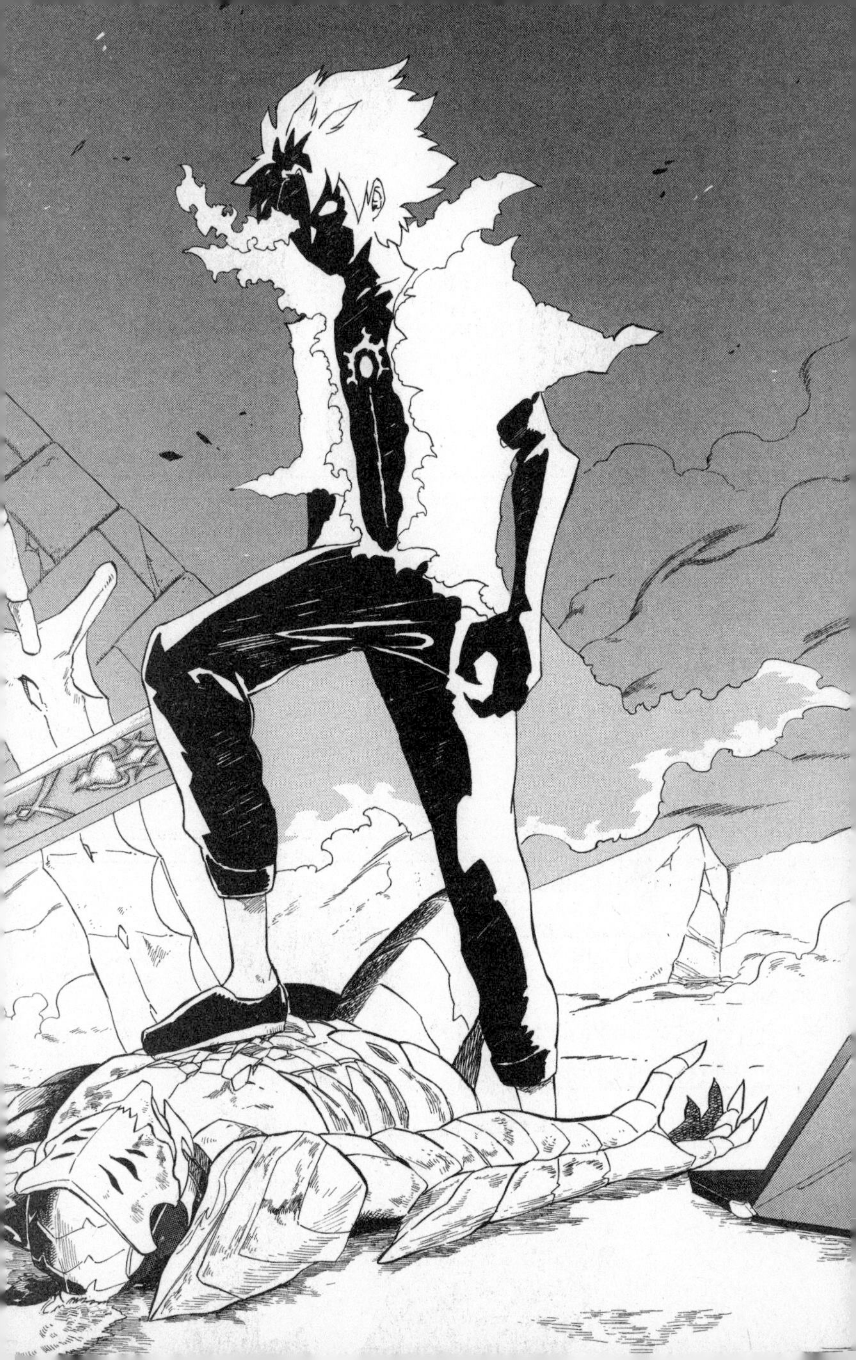

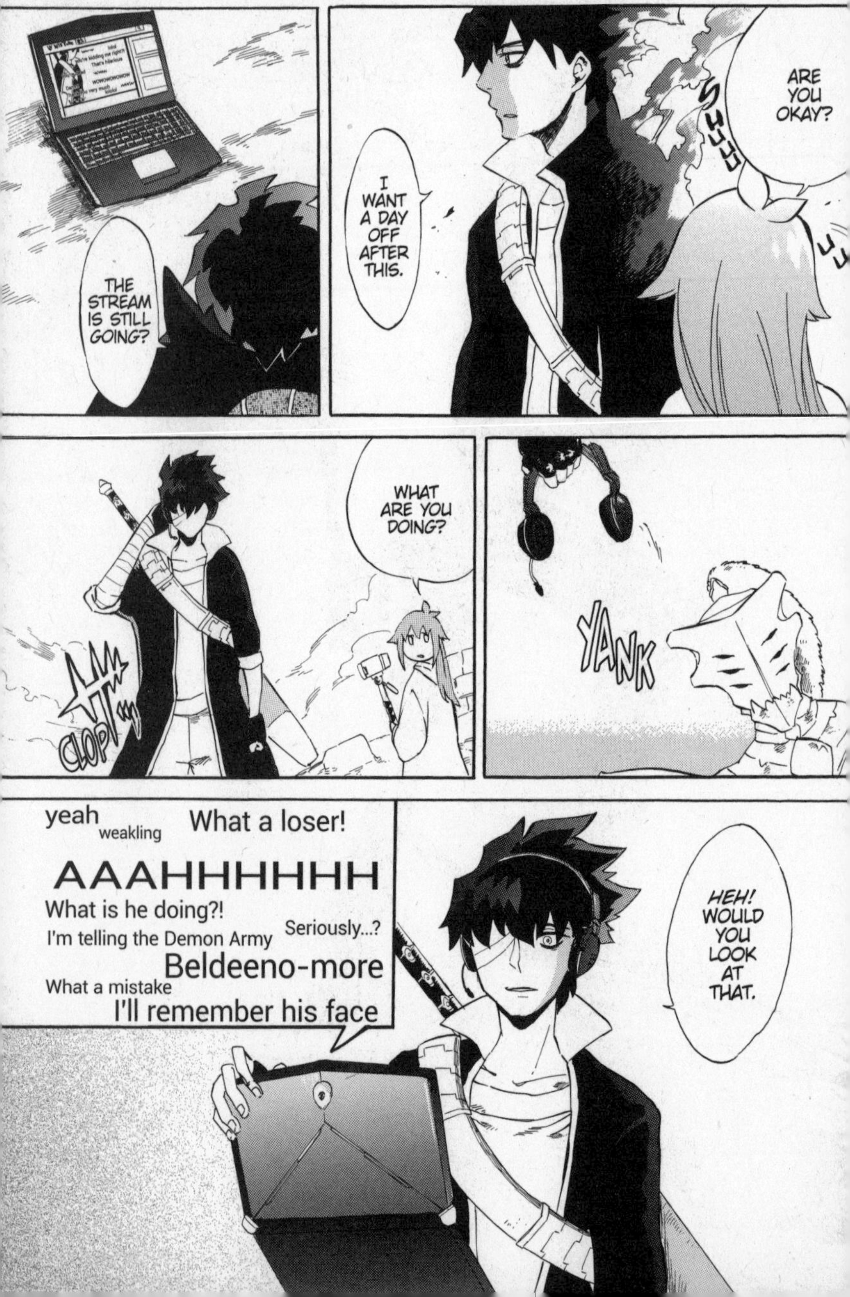
ARE YOU OKAY?
I WANT A DAY OFF AFTER THIS.
THE STREAM IS STILL GOING?
YANK
WHAT ARE YOU DOING?
CLOP!
HEH! WOULD YOU LOOK AT THAT.
yeah
weakling
What a loser!
AAAHHHHHH
What is he doing?!
I'm telling the Demon Army
Seriously...?
Beldeeno-more
What a mistake
I'll remember his face

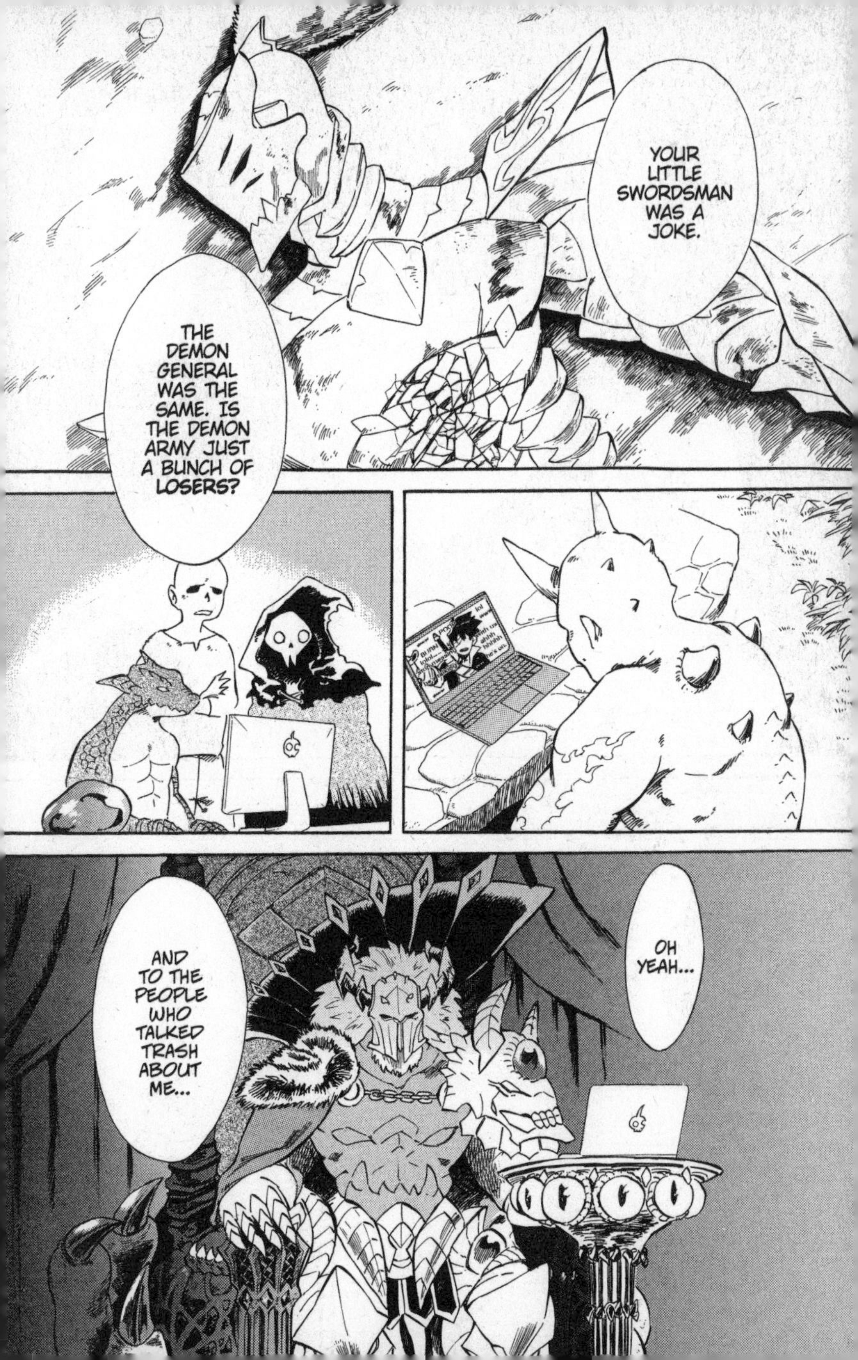
YOUR LITTLE SWORDSMAN WAS A JOKE.
THE DEMON GENERAL WAS THE SAME. IS THE DEMON ARMY JUST A BUNCH OF LOSERS?
OH YEAH...
AND TO THE PEOPLE WHO TALKED TRASH ABOUT ME...

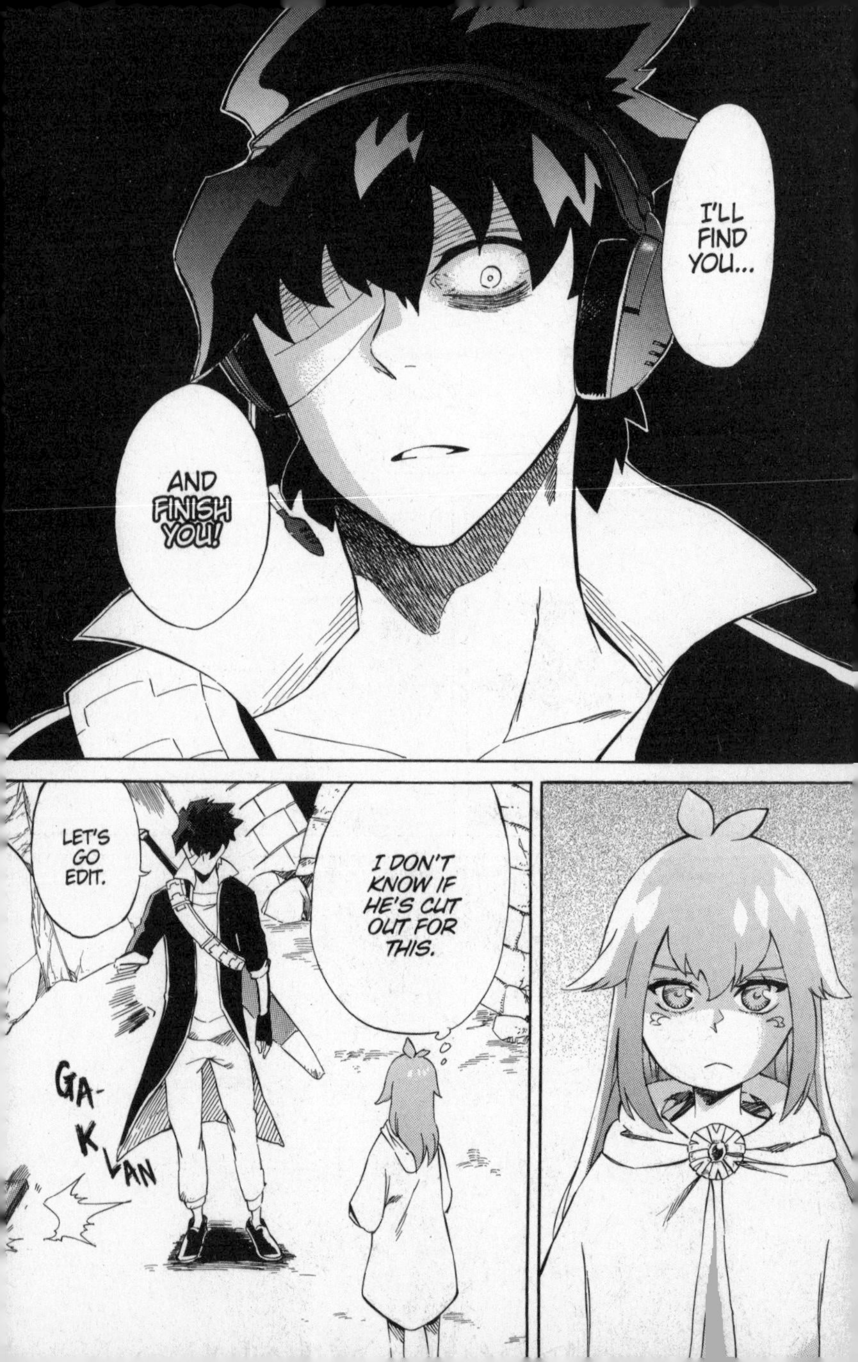
I'LL FIND YOU...
AND FINISH YOU!
I DON'T KNOW IF HE'S CUT OUT FOR THIS.
LET'S GO EDIT.
GA-KLAN

Destroying an Underling Streamer of the Demon Army!

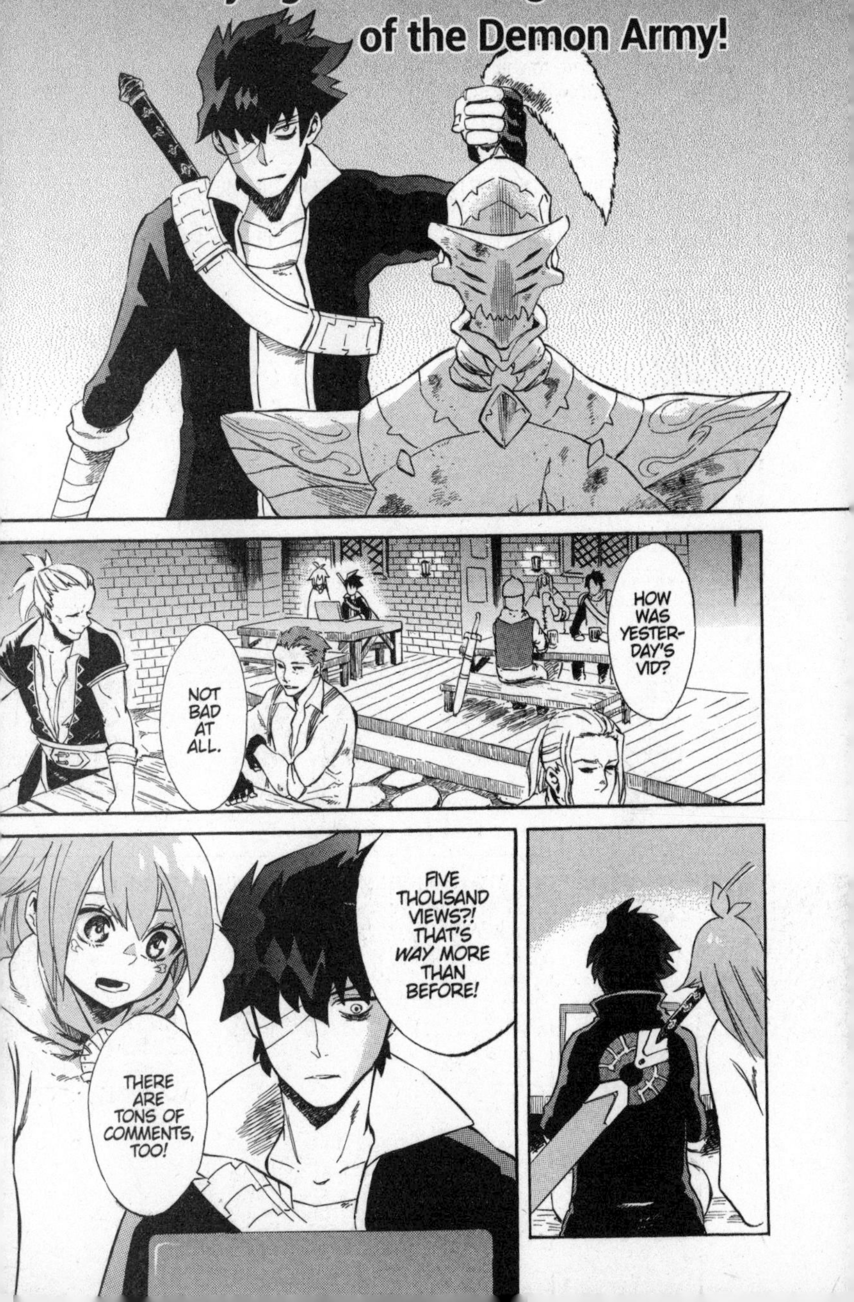
HOW WAS YESTER-DAY'S VID?
NOT BAD AT ALL.
FIVE THOUSAND VIEWS?! THAT'S WAY MORE THAN BEFORE!
THERE ARE TONS OF COMMENTS, TOO!

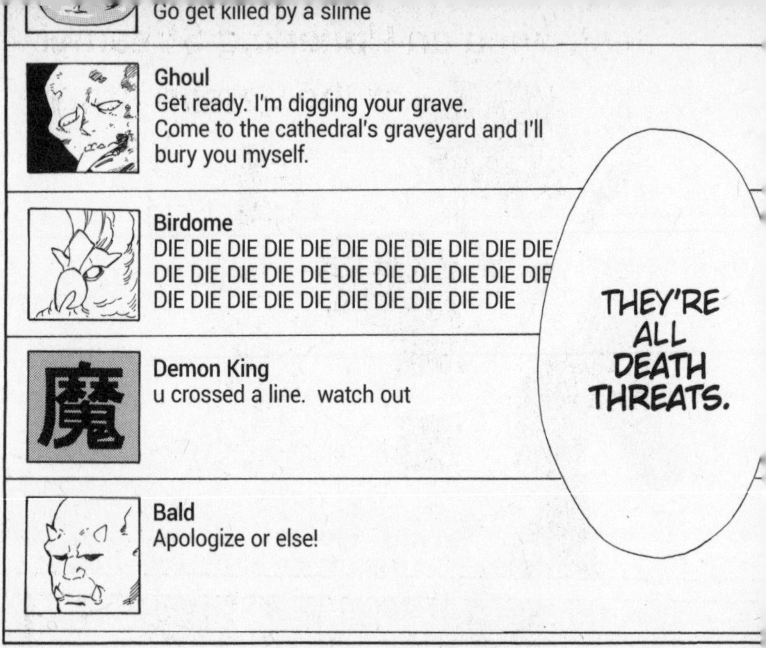
Go get killed by a slime
Ghoul
Get ready. I'm digging your grave. Come to the cathedral's graveyard and I'll bury you myself.
Birdome
DIE DIE DIE DIE DIE DIE DIE DIE DIE DIE DIE DIE DIE DIE DIE DIE DIE DIE DIE DIE DIE DIE DIE DIE DIE DIE DIE DIE DIE DIE DIE DIE
Demon King
u crossed a line. watch out
Bald
Apologize or else!
THEY'RE ALL DEATH THREATS.
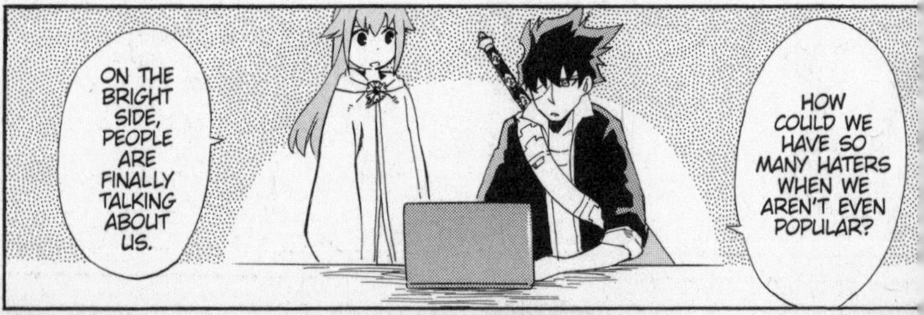
HOW COULD WE HAVE SO MANY HATERS WHEN WE AREN'T EVEN POPULAR?
ON THE BRIGHT SIDE, PEOPLE ARE FINALLY TALKING ABOUT US.
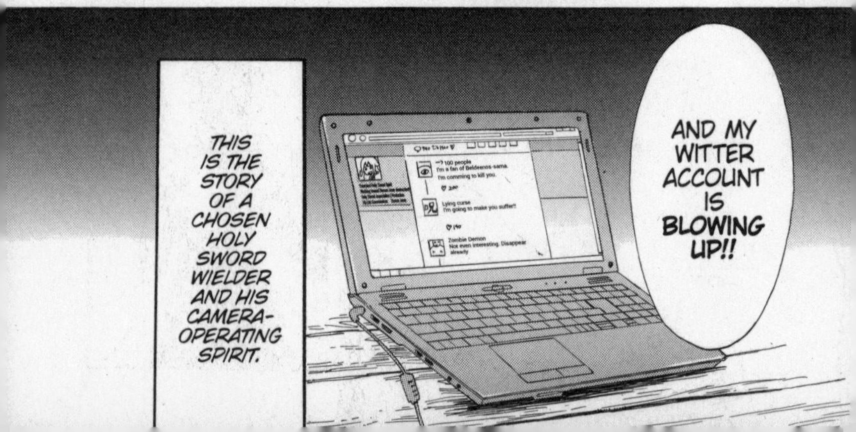
AND MY WITTER ACCOUNT IS BLOWING UP!!
I'm a fan of Beldeenos-sama. I'm comming to kill you.
Lying curse
I'm going to make you suffer!!
Zombie Demon
Not even interesting. Disappear already
THIS IS THE STORY OF A CHOSEN HOLY SWORD WIELDER AND HIS CAMERA-OPERATING SPIRIT.

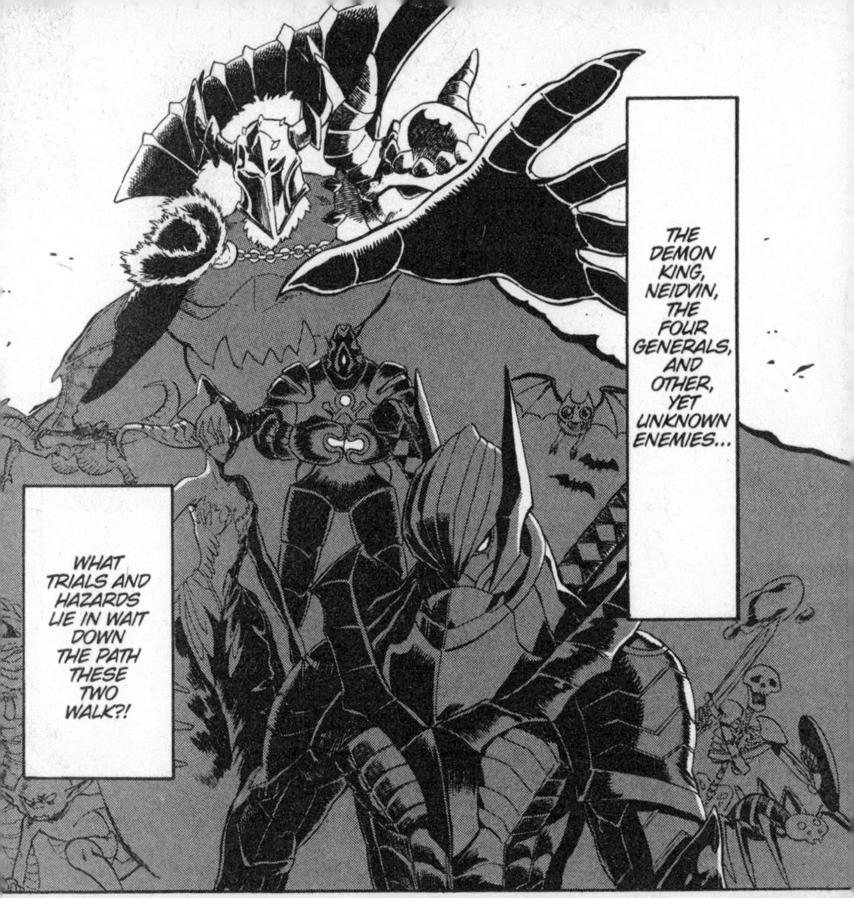
THE DEMON KING, NEIDVIN, THE FOUR GENERALS, AND OTHER, YET UNKNOWN ENEMIES...
WHAT TRIALS AND HAZARDS LIE IN WAIT DOWN THE PATH THESE TWO WALK?!

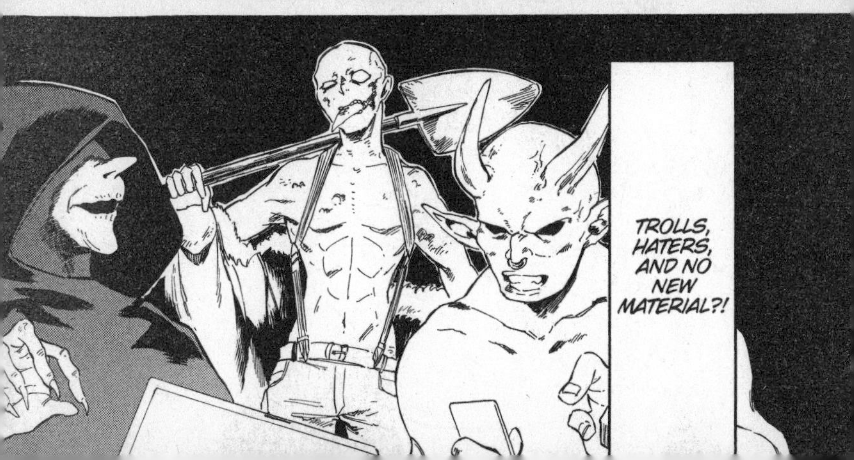
TROLLS, HATERS, AND NO NEW MATERIAL?!

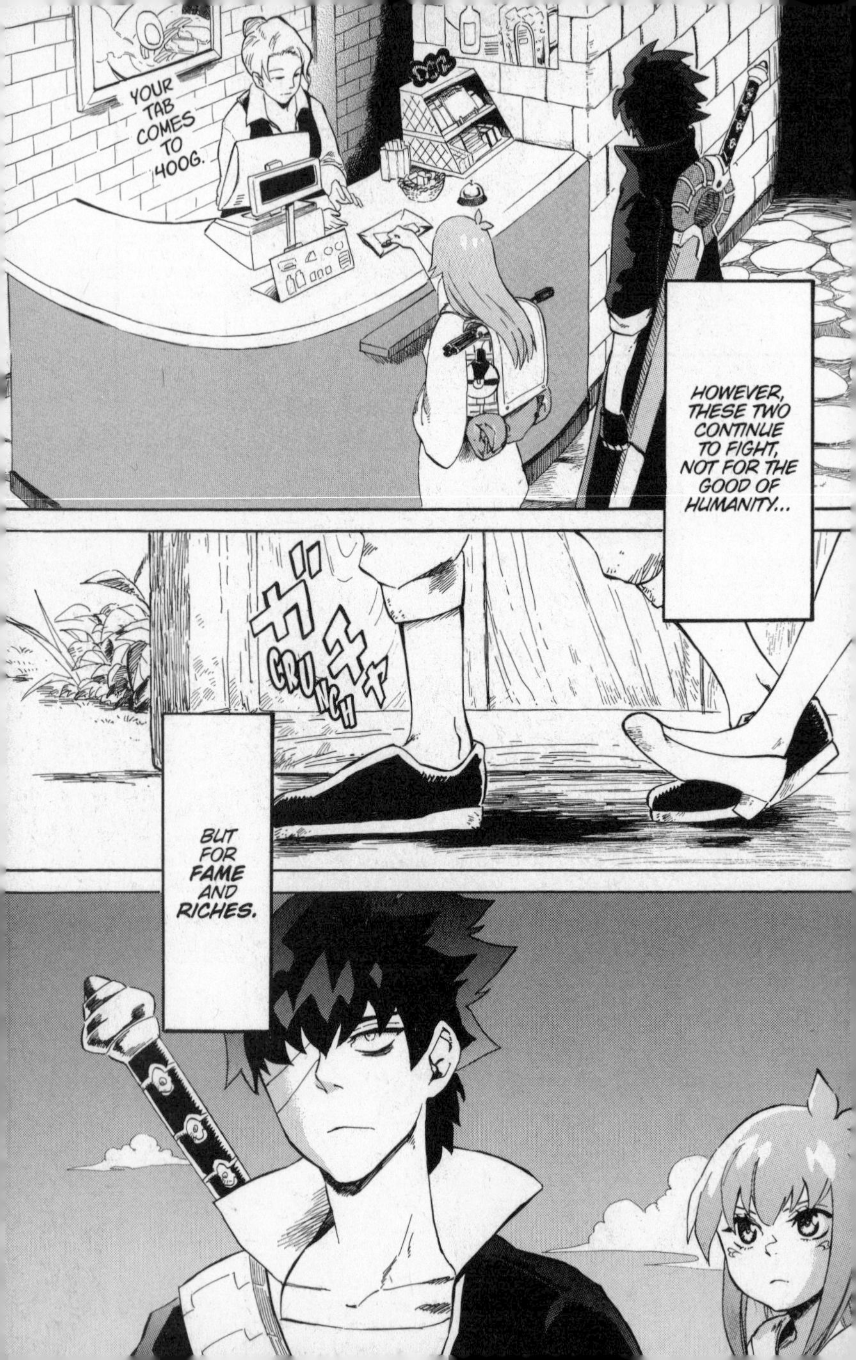
YOUR TAB COMES TO 400G.
HOWEVER, THESE TWO CONTINUE TO FIGHT, NOT FOR THE GOOD OF HUMANITY...
ガチャ
CRUNCH
BUT FOR FAME AND RICHES.

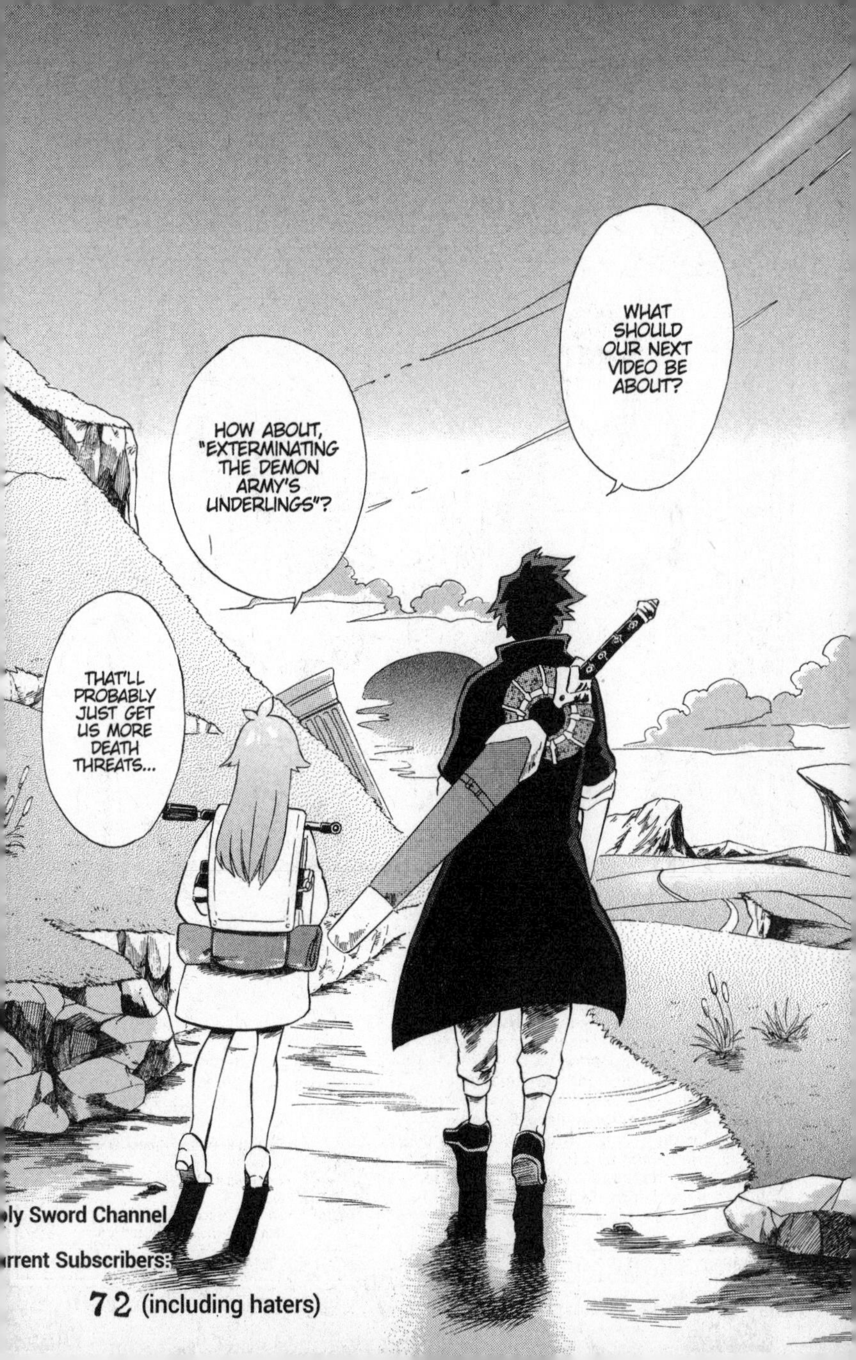
WHAT SHOULD OUR NEXT VIDEO BE ABOUT?
HOW ABOUT, "EXTERMINATING THE DEMON ARMY'S UNDERLINGS"?
THAT'LL PROBABLY JUST GET US MORE DEATH THREATS...
ly Sword Channel
rrent Subscribers:
72 (including haters)

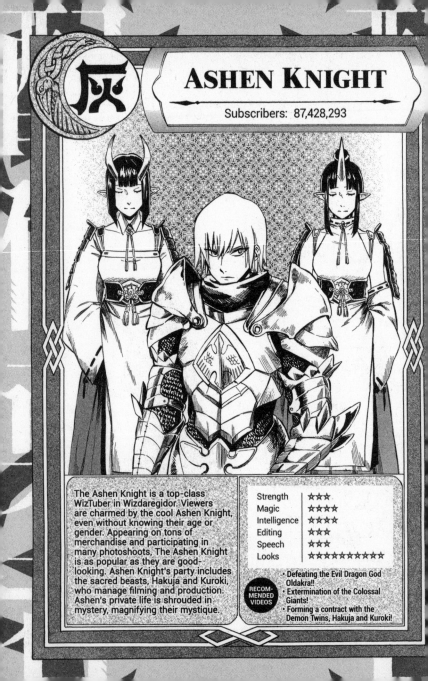

ASHEN KNIGHT

Subscribers: 87,428,293

The Ashen Knight is a top-class WizTuber in Wizdaregidor. Viewers are charmed by the cool Ashen Knight, even without knowing their age or gender. Appearing on tons of merchandise and participating in many photoshoots, The Ashen Knight is as popular as they are good-looking. Ashen Knight's party includes the sacred beasts, Hakuja and Kuroki, who manage filming and production. Ashen's private life is shrouded in mystery, magnifying their mystique.

Strength	★★★
Magic	★★★★
Intelligence	★★★★
Editing	★★★
Speech	★★★
Looks	★★★★★★★★★★

RECOM-MENDED VIDEOS

- Defeating the Evil Dragon God Oldakra!!
- Extermination of the Colossal Giants!
- Forming a contract with the Demon Twins, Hakuja and Kuroki!

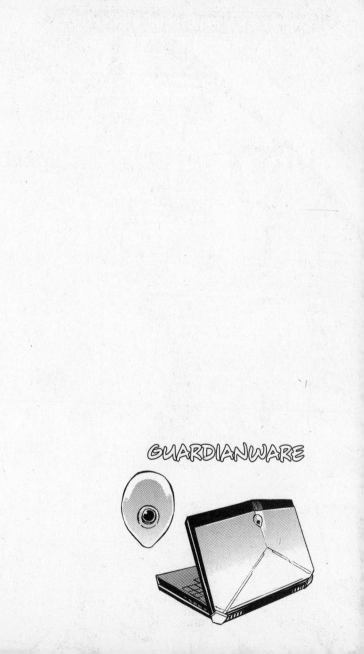

GUARDIANWARE

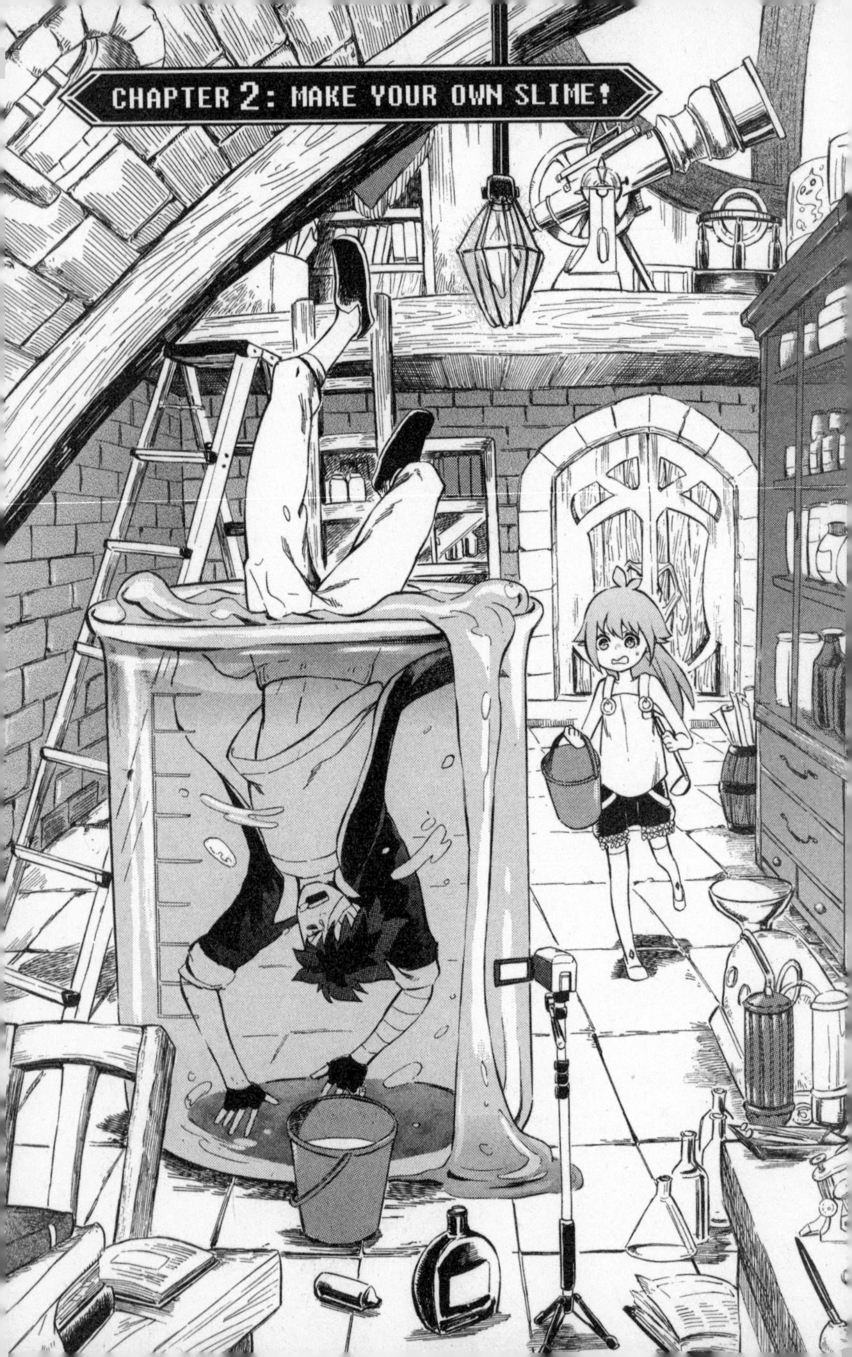
CHAPTER 2: MAKE YOUR OWN SLIME!

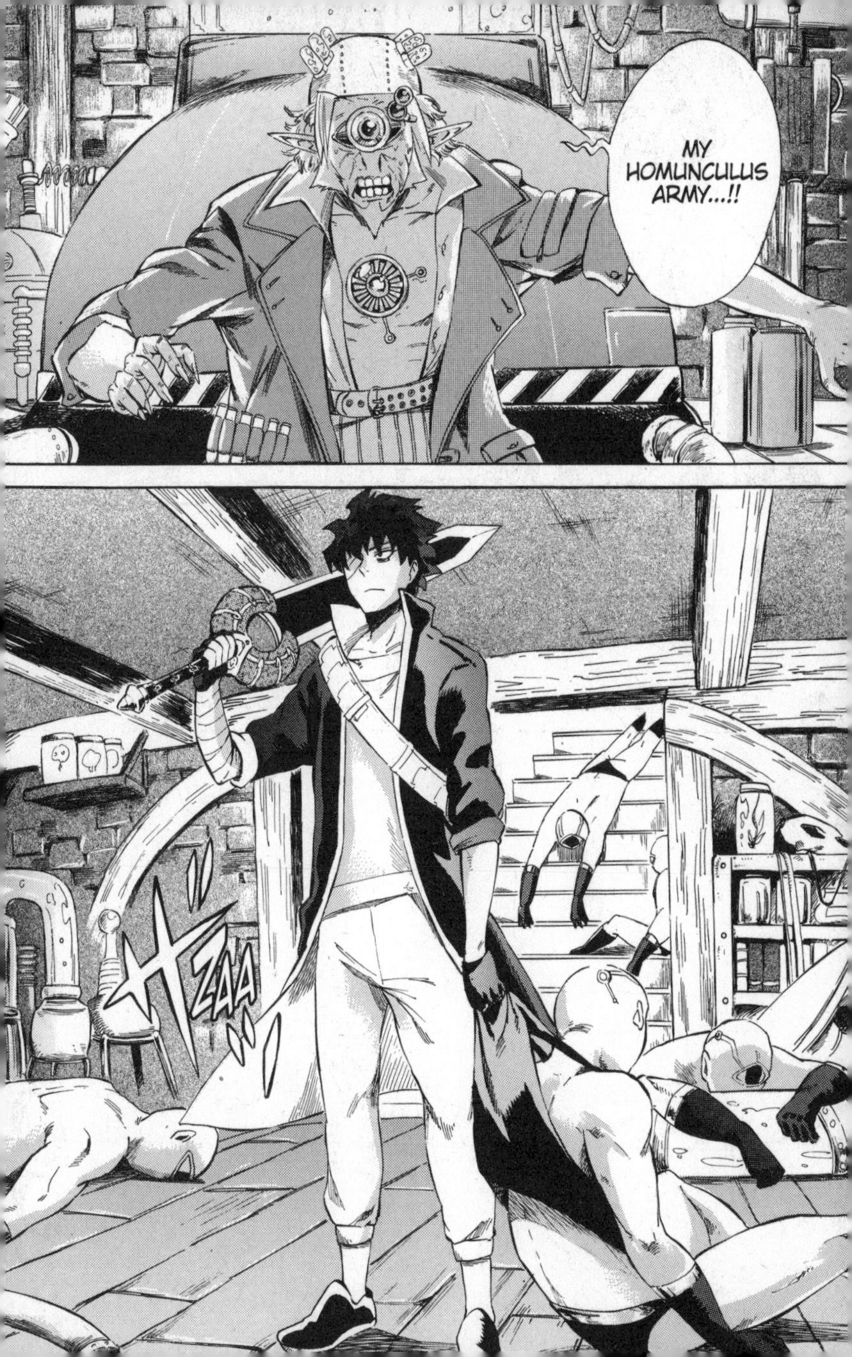
MY HOMUNCULUS ARMY...!!
ZAA

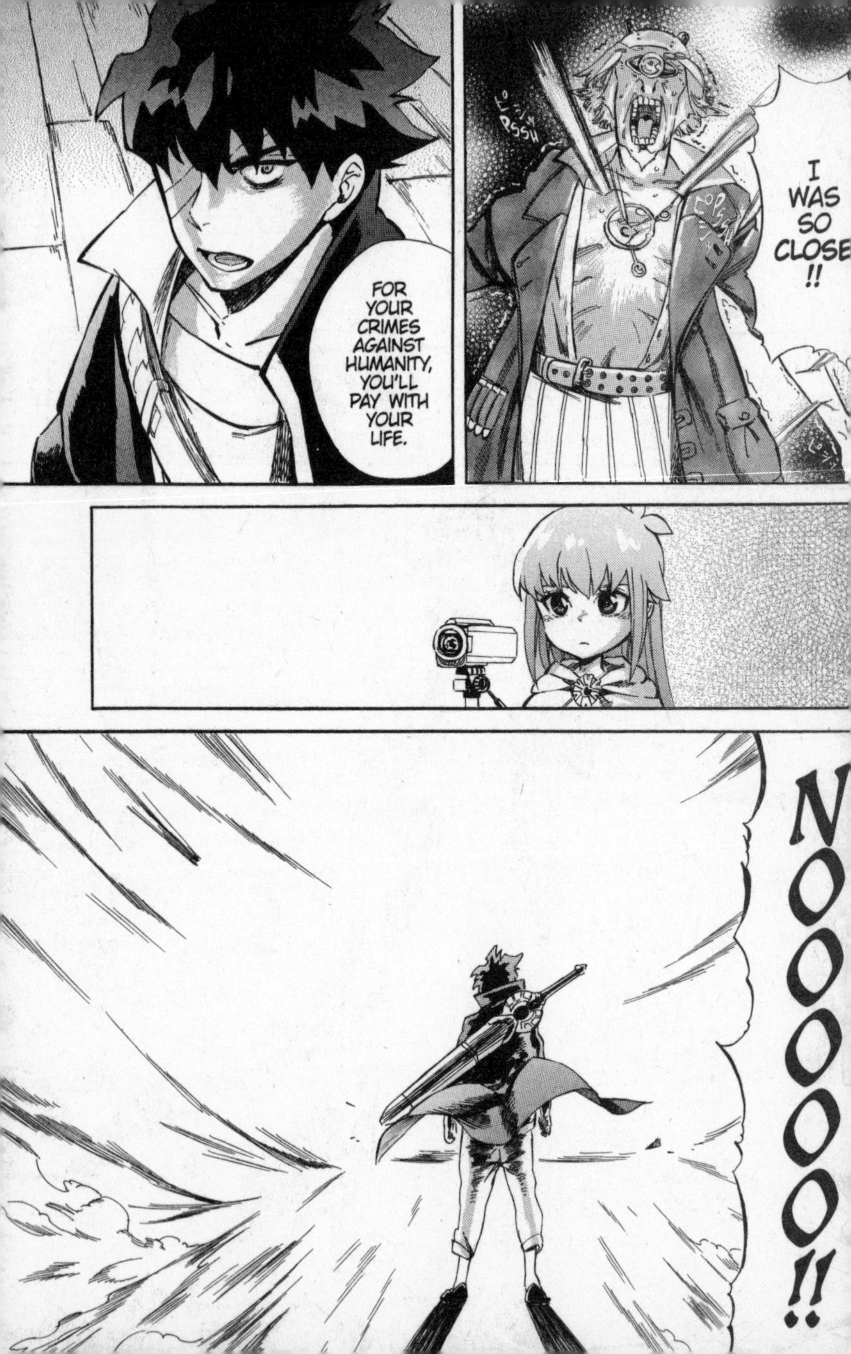
I WAS SO CLOSE!!
PSSH
FOR YOUR CRIMES AGAINST HUMANITY, YOU'LL PAY WITH YOUR LIFE.
NOOOOO!!

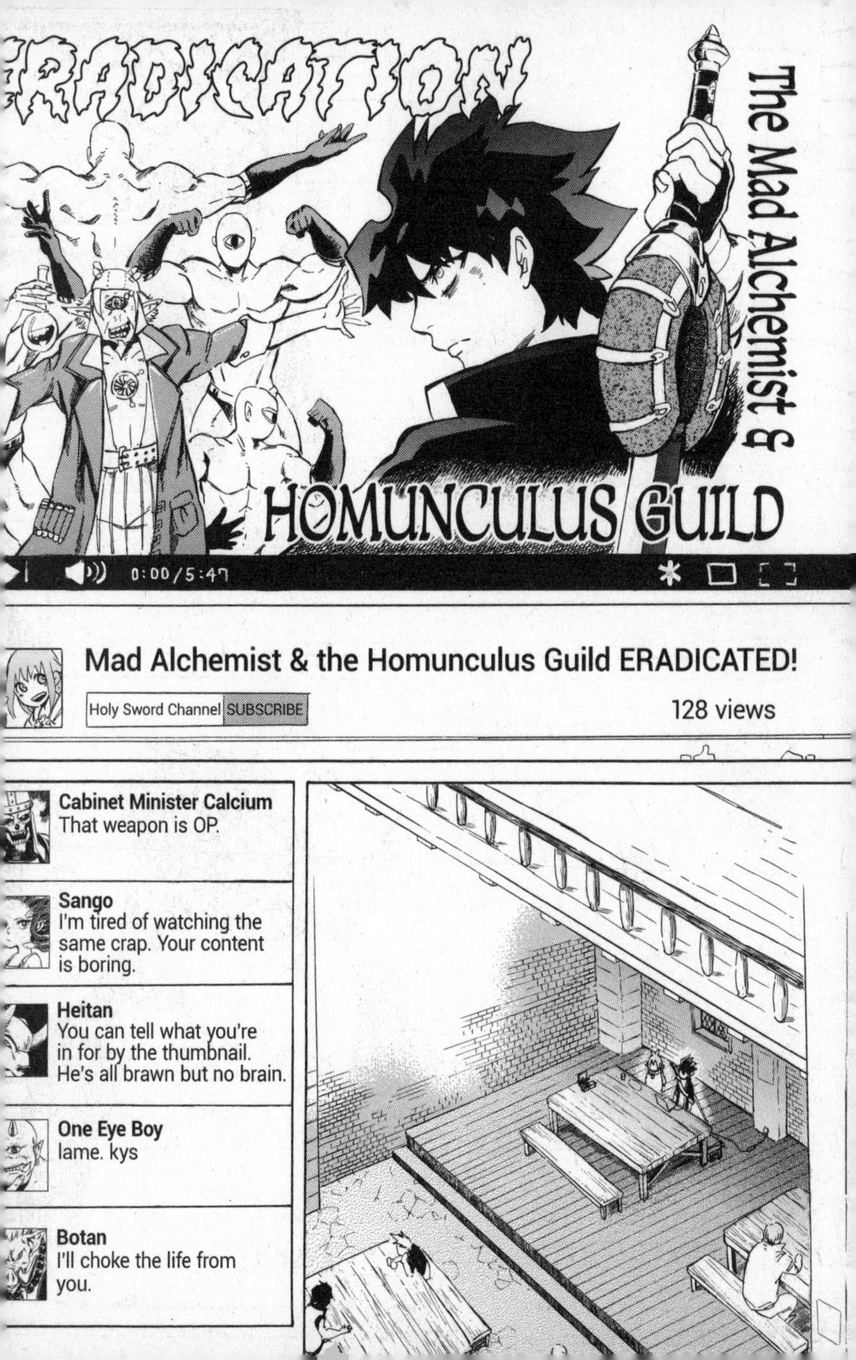
RADICATION
The Mad Alchemist &
HOMUNCULUS GUILD
0:00/5:47
Mad Alchemist & the Homunculus Guild ERADICATED!
Holy Sword Channel
SUBSCRIBE
128 views
Cabinet Minister Calcium
That weapon is OP.
Sango
I'm tired of watching the same crap. Your content is boring.
Heitan
You can tell what you're in for by the thumbnail. He's all brawn but no brain.
One Eye Boy
lame. kys
Botan
I'll choke the life from you.

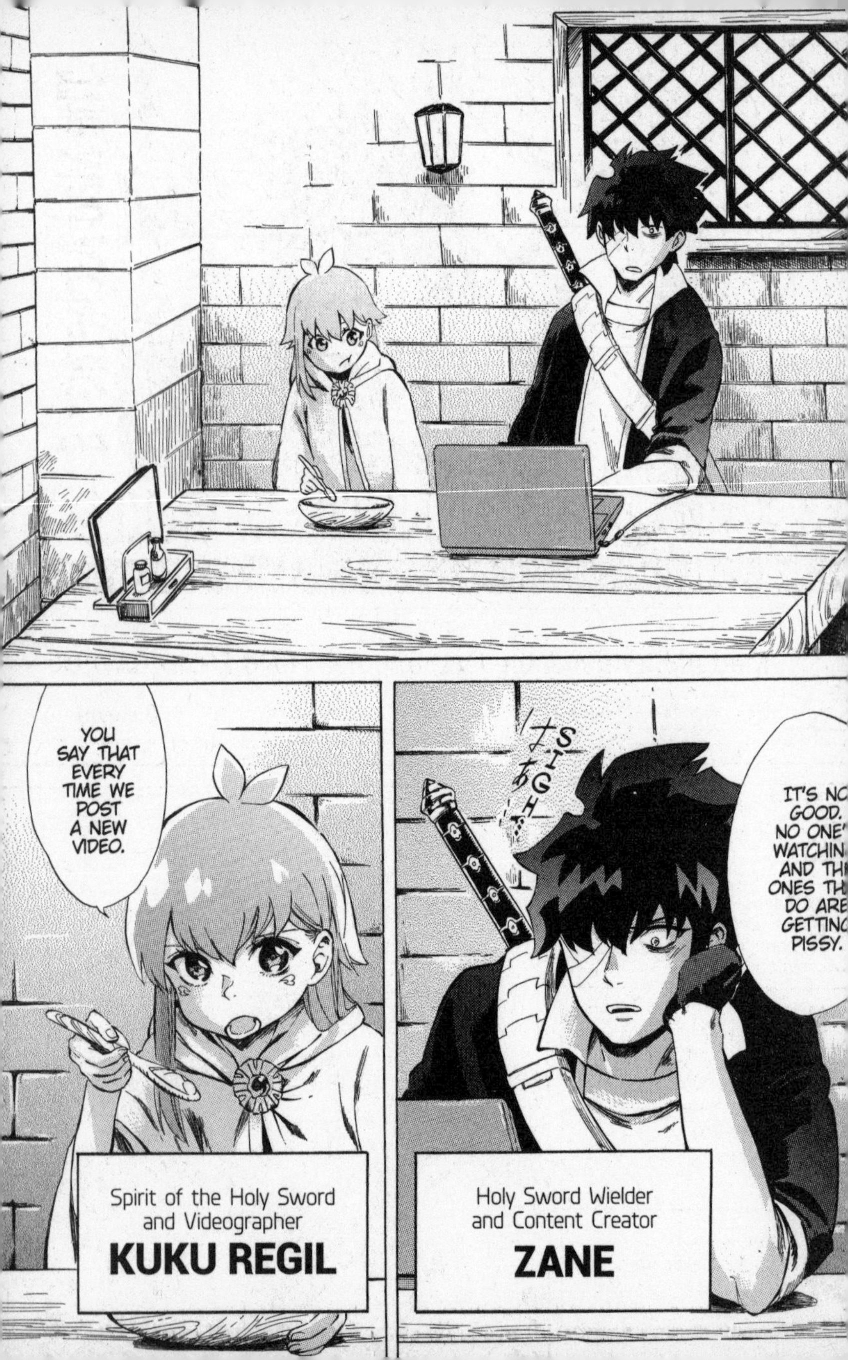

IT'S NO GOOD. NO ONE' WATCHIN AND TH ONES TH DO ARE GETTINC PISSY.
!
はあ
SIGH...
Holy Sword Wielder and Content Creator
ZANE
YOU SAY THAT EVERY TIME WE POST A NEW VIDEO.
Spirit of the Holy Sword and Videographer
KUKU REGIL

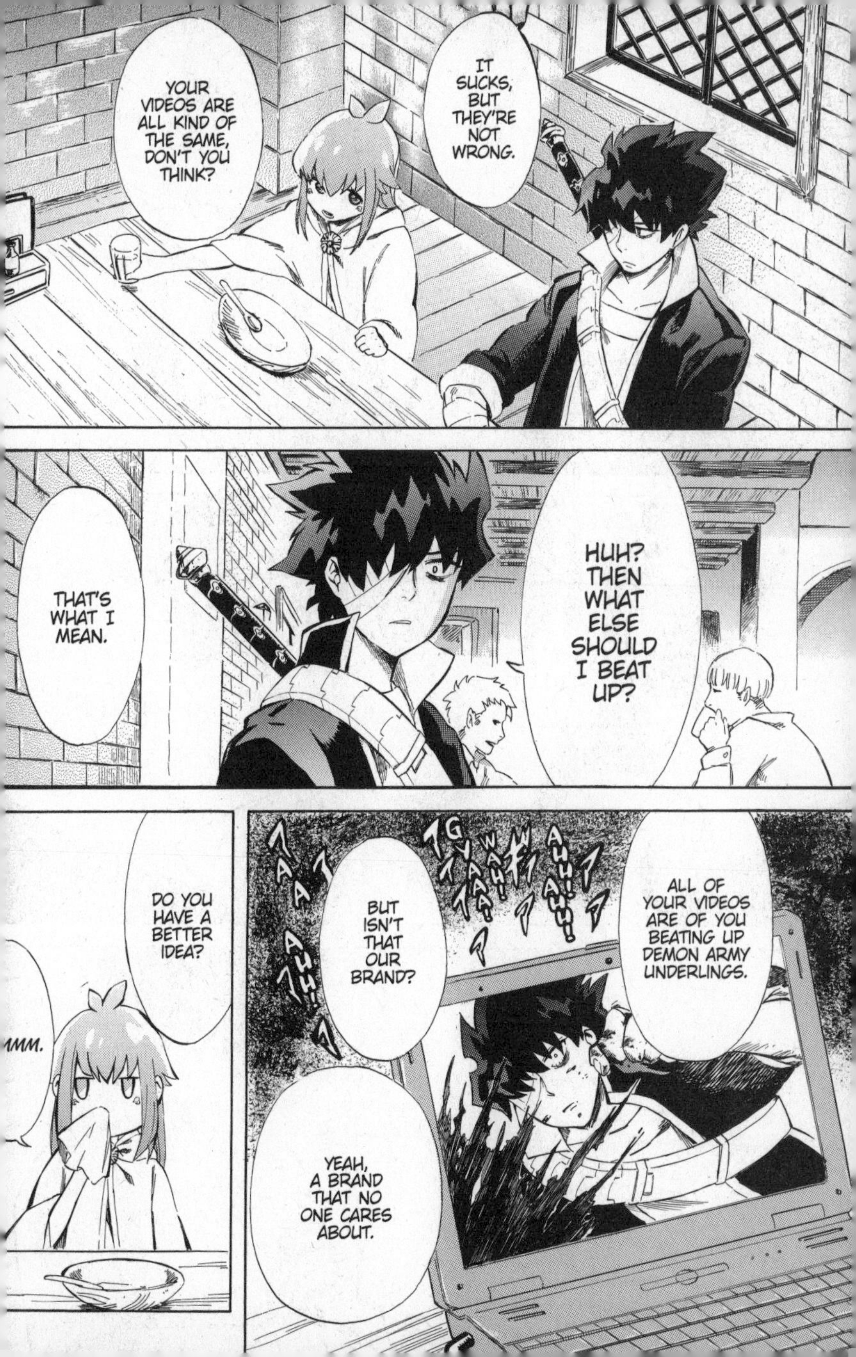
IT SUCKS, BUT THEY'RE NOT WRONG.
YOUR VIDEOS ARE ALL KIND OF THE SAME, DON'T YOU THINK?
HUH? THEN WHAT ELSE SHOULD I BEAT UP?
THAT'S WHAT I MEAN.
ALL OF YOUR VIDEOS ARE OF YOU BEATING UP DEMON ARMY UNDERLINGS.
AHH! AHH!
WAH!
GYAAA
AHH!
BUT ISN'T THAT OUR BRAND?
YEAH, A BRAND THAT NO ONE CARES ABOUT.
DO YOU HAVE A BETTER IDEA?
MMM.

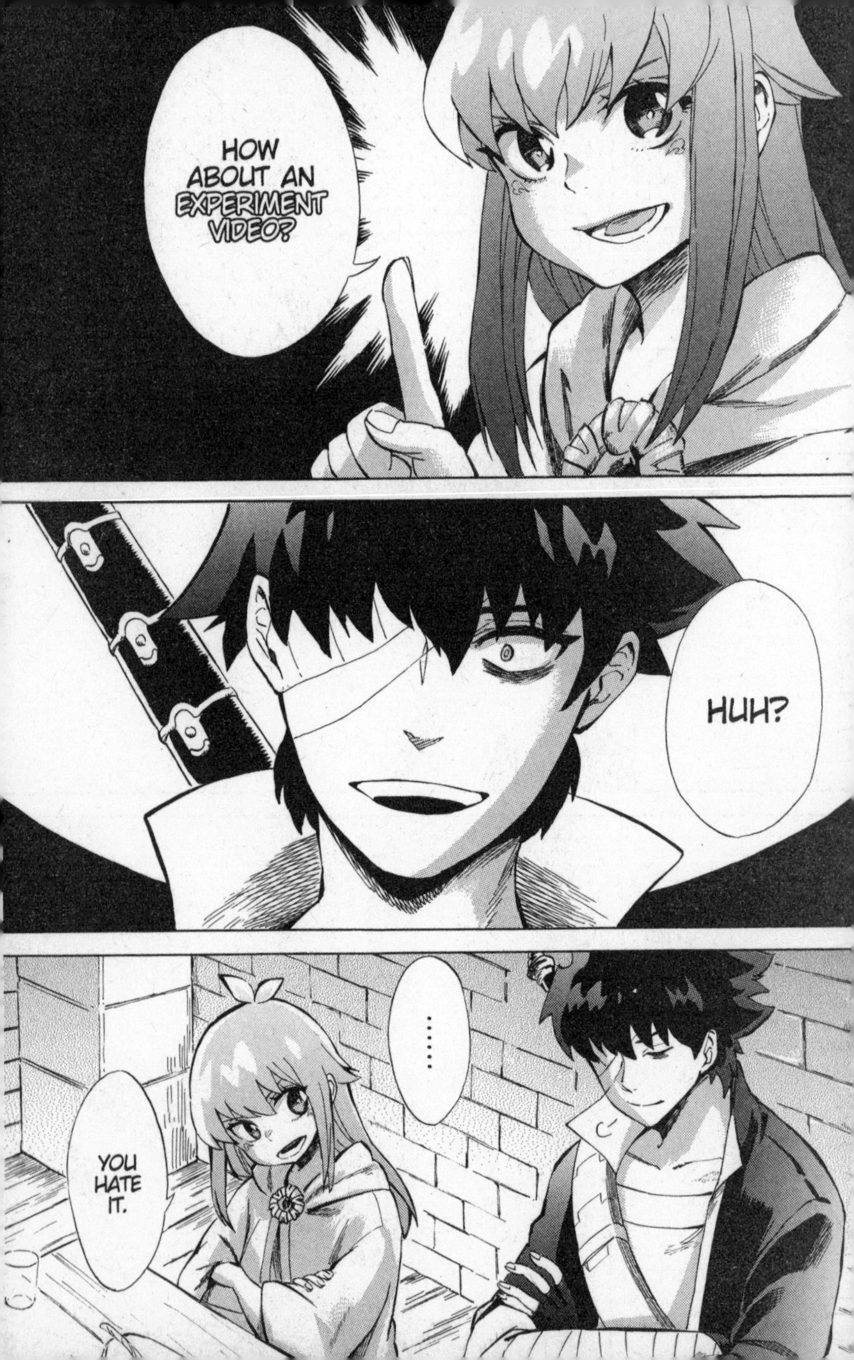
HOW ABOUT AN EXPERIMENT VIDEO?
HUH?
......
YOU HATE IT.

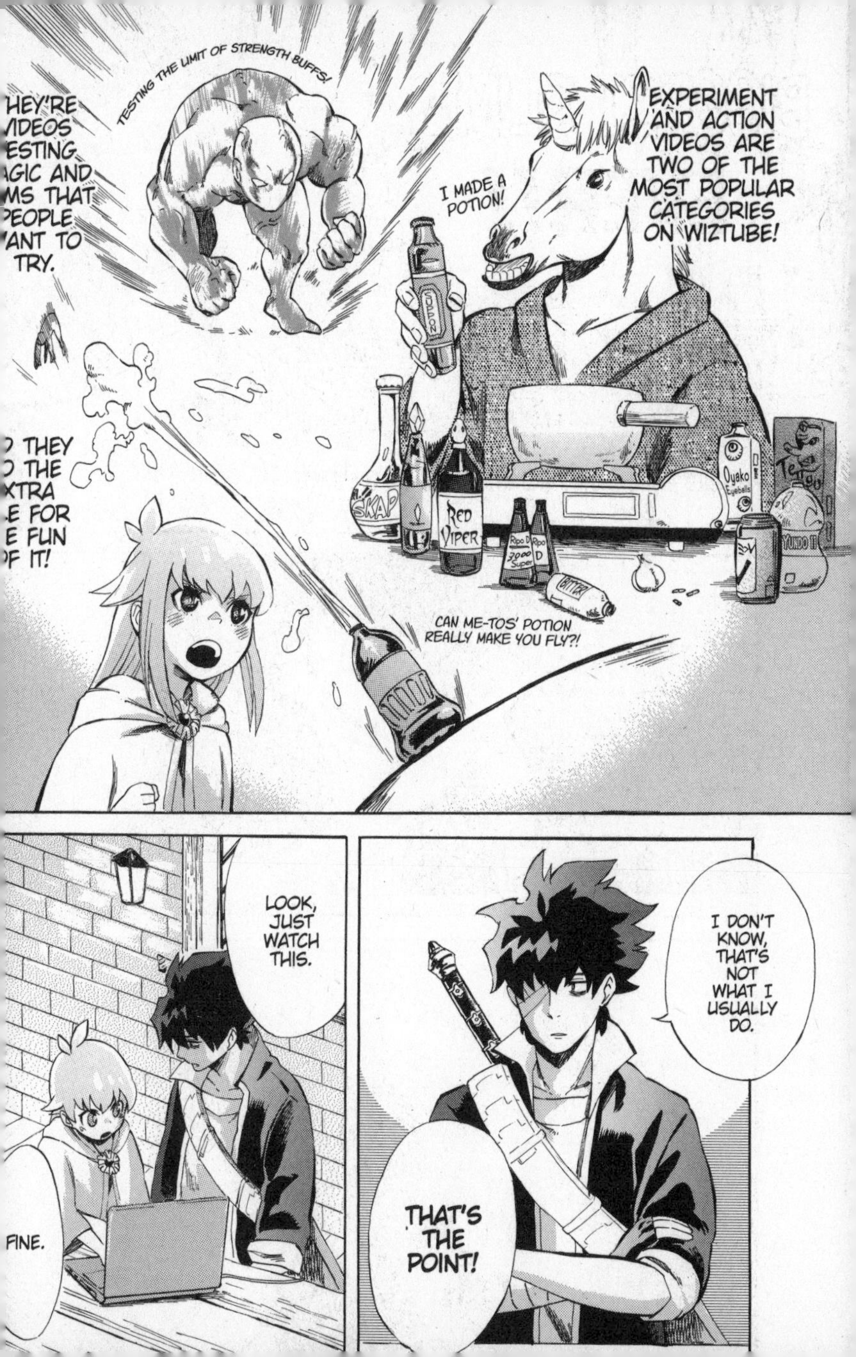
EXPERIMENT AND ACTION VIDEOS ARE TWO OF THE MOST POPULAR CATEGORIES ON WIZTUBE!
I MADE A POTION!
TESTING THE LIMIT OF STRENGTH BUFFS!
HEY'RE VIDEOS ESTING AGIC AND MS THAT PEOPLE ANT TO TRY.
D THEY D THE XTRA E FOR E FUN OF IT!
CAN ME-TOS' POTION REALLY MAKE YOU FLY?!
I DON'T KNOW, THAT'S NOT WHAT I USUALLY DO.
THAT'S THE POINT!
LOOK, JUST WATCH THIS.
FINE.

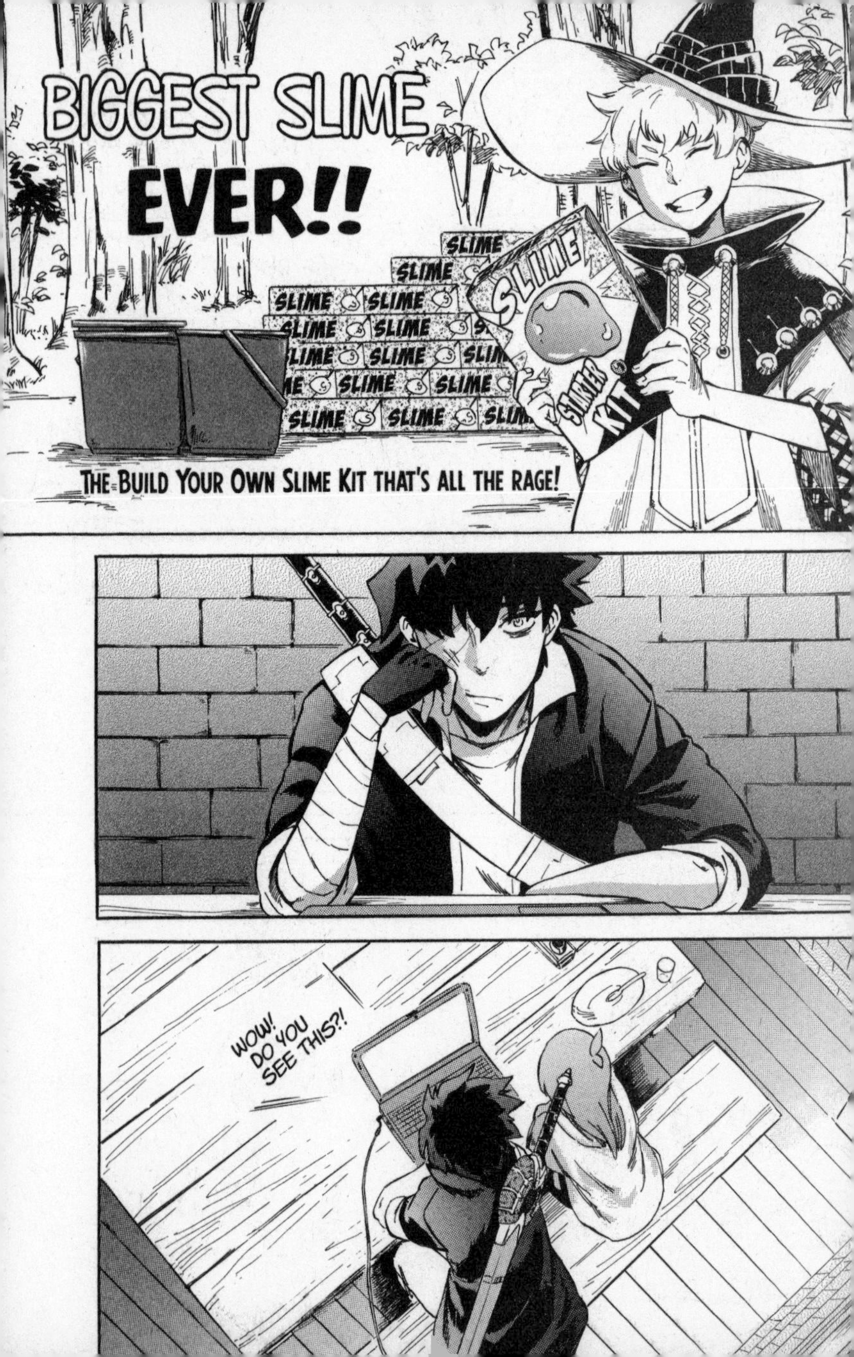
BIGGEST SLIME EVER!!
SLIME STARTER KIT
THE BUILD YOUR OWN SLIME KIT THAT'S ALL THE RAGE!
WOW! DO YOU SEE THIS?!

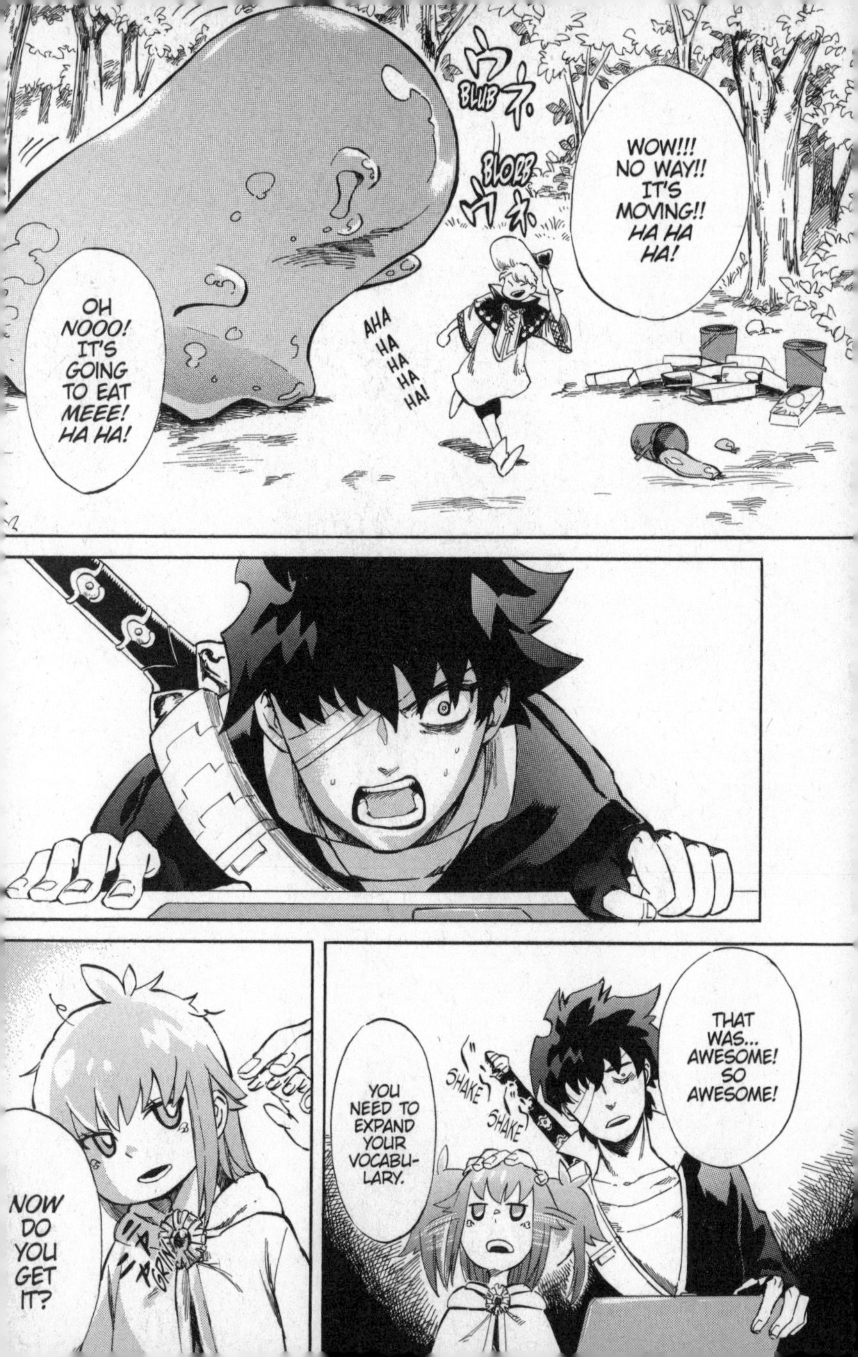
WOW!!! NO WAY!! IT'S MOVING!! HA HA HA!
BLUB
BLORB
AHA HA HA HA HA!
OH NOOO! IT'S GOING TO EAT MEEE! HA HA!
THAT WAS... AWESOME! SO AWESOME!
SHAKE
SHAKE
YOU NEED TO EXPAND YOUR VOCABU-LARY.
NOW DO YOU GET IT?
GRIN

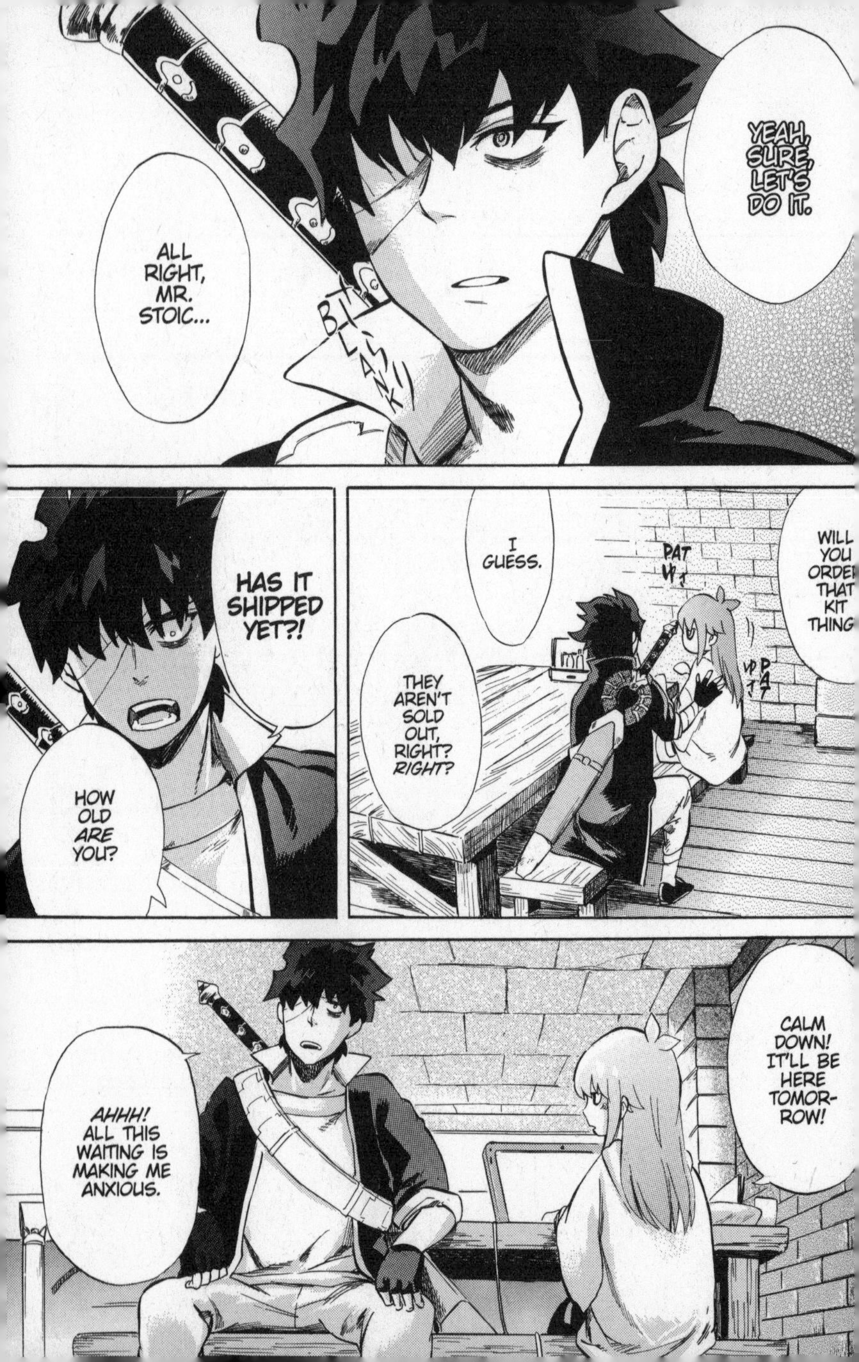
YEAH, SURE, LET'S DO IT.
ALL RIGHT, MR. STOIC...
WILL YOU ORDE THAT KIT THING
PAT PAT
I GUESS.
THEY AREN'T SOLD OUT, RIGHT? *RIGHT?*
HAS IT SHIPPED YET?!
HOW OLD *ARE* YOU?
CALM DOWN! IT'LL BE HERE TOMOR-ROW!
AHHH! ALL THIS WAITING IS MAKING ME ANXIOUS.

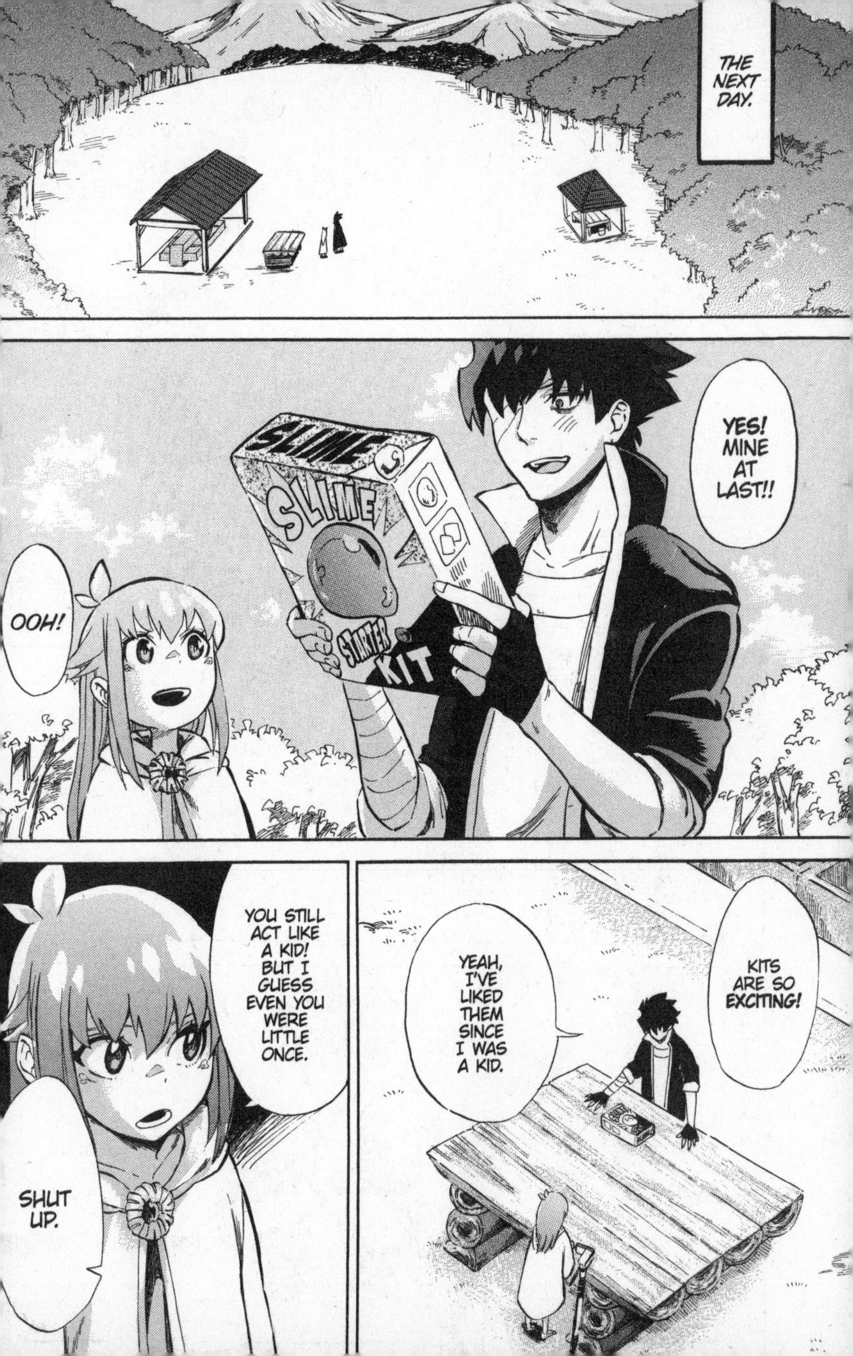
THE NEXT DAY.
YES! MINE AT LAST!!
SLIME
SLIME STARTER KIT
OOH!
KITS ARE SO EXCITING!
YEAH, I'VE LIKED THEM SINCE I WAS A KID.
YOU STILL ACT LIKE A KID! BUT I GUESS EVEN YOU WERE LITTLE ONCE.
SHUT UP.

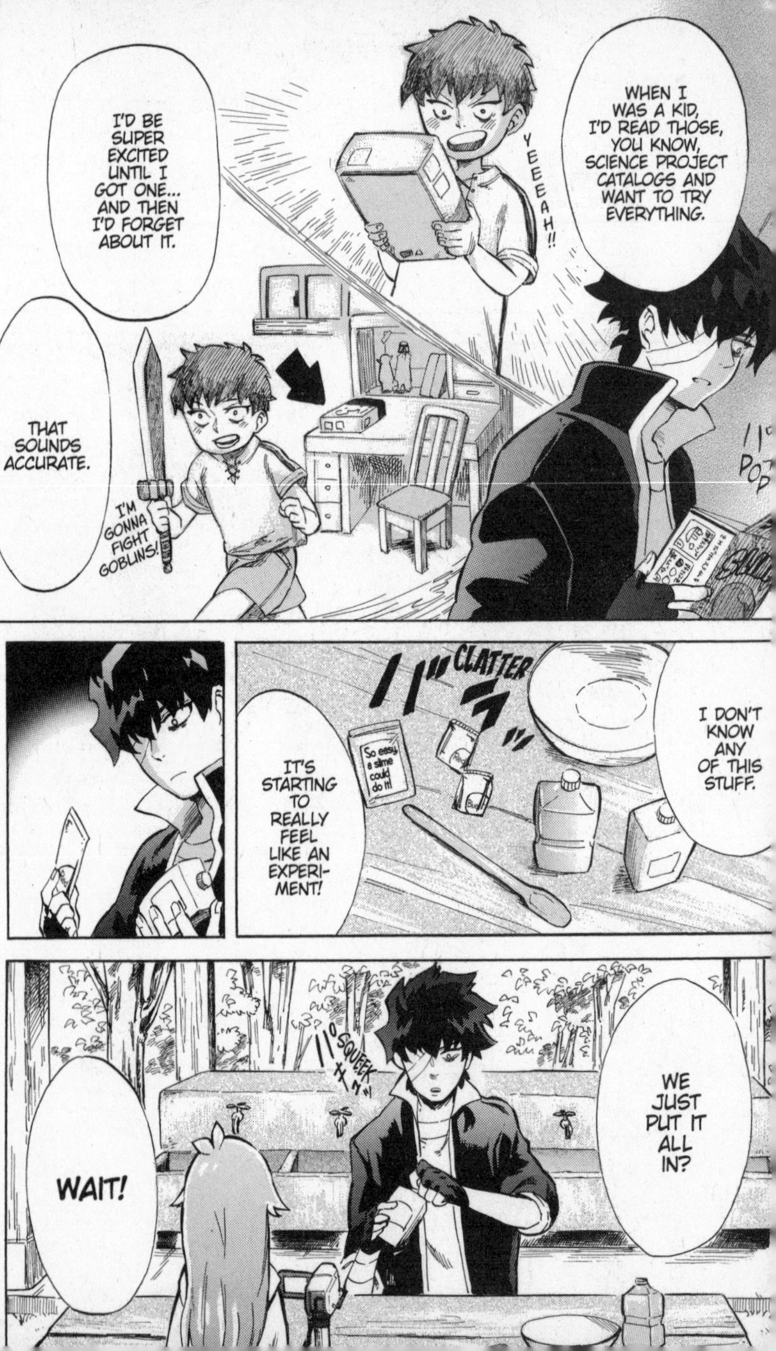
WHEN I WAS A KID, I'D READ THOSE, YOU KNOW, SCIENCE PROJECT CATALOGS AND WANT TO TRY EVERYTHING.
POP
YEEEAH!!
I'D BE SUPER EXCITED UNTIL I GOT ONE... AND THEN I'D FORGET ABOUT IT.
THAT SOUNDS ACCURATE.
I'M GONNA FIGHT GOBLINS!
I DON'T KNOW ANY OF THIS STUFF.
CLATTER
So easy a slime could do it!
IT'S STARTING TO REALLY FEEL LIKE AN EXPERI-MENT!
WE JUST PUT IT ALL IN?
SQUEEK
WAIT!

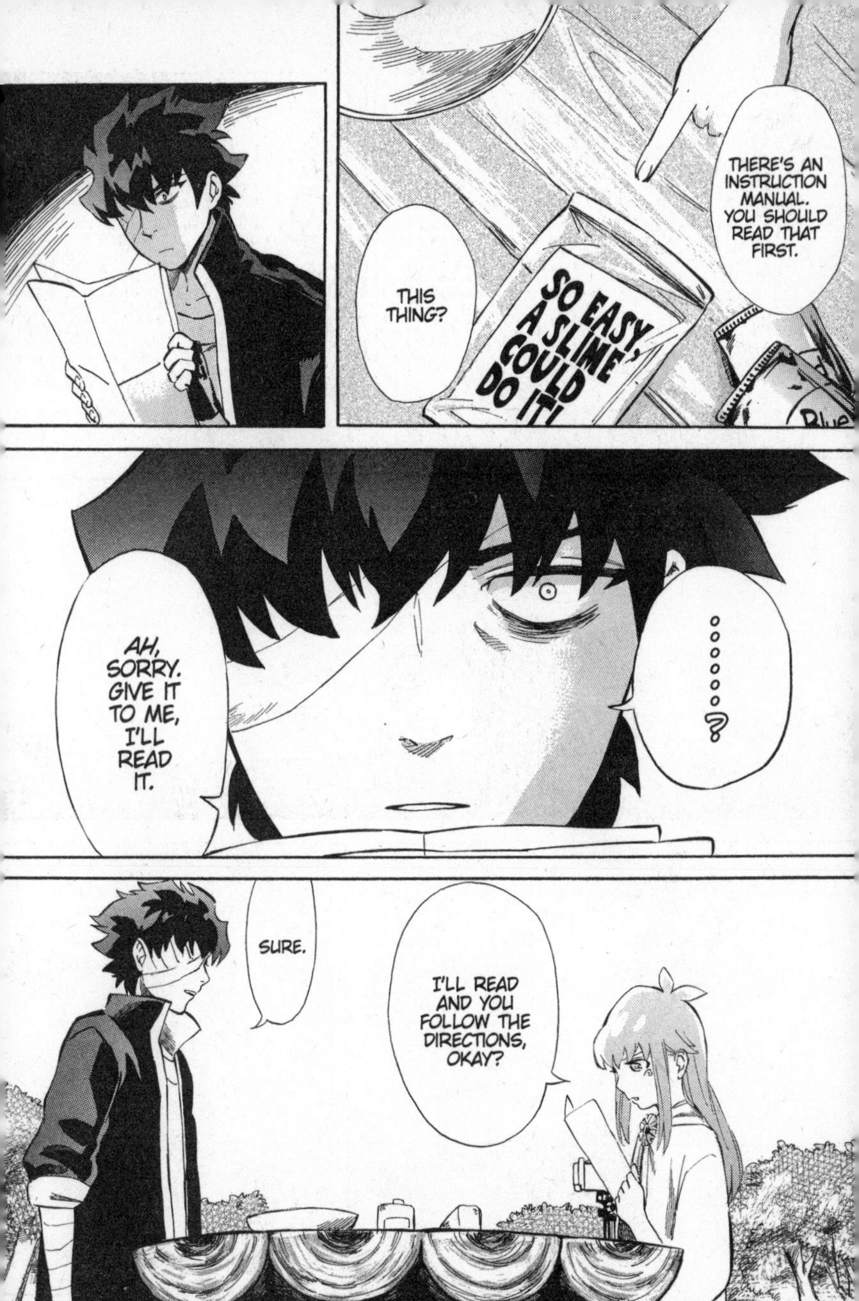
THERE'S AN INSTRUCTION MANUAL. YOU SHOULD READ THAT FIRST.
SO EASY, A SLIME COULD DO IT!
THIS THING?
......?
AH, SORRY. GIVE IT TO ME, I'LL READ IT.
I'LL READ AND YOU FOLLOW THE DIRECTIONS, OKAY?
SURE.

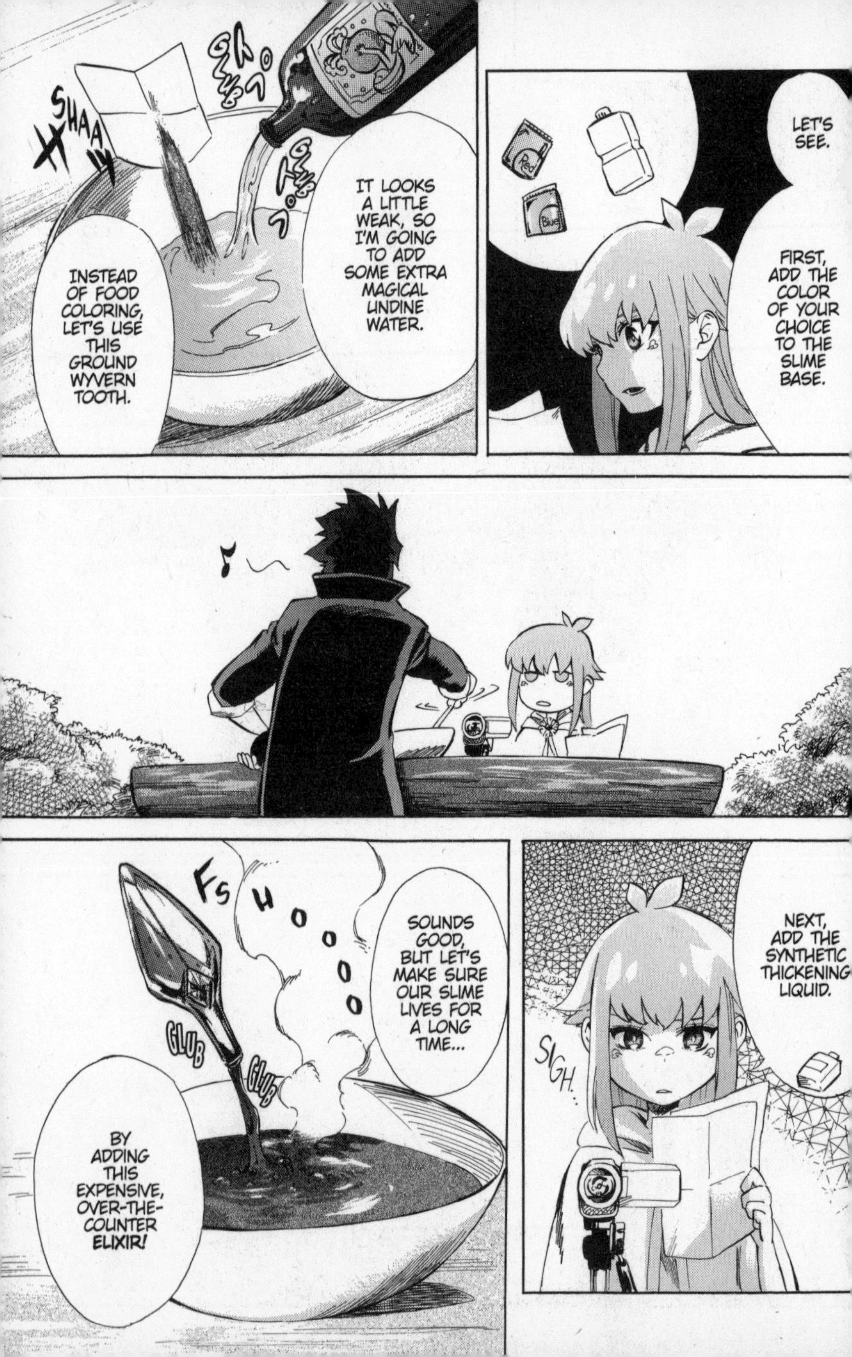
LET'S SEE.
Red
Blue
FIRST, ADD THE COLOR OF YOUR CHOICE TO THE SLIME BASE.
IT LOOKS A LITTLE WEAK, SO I'M GOING TO ADD SOME EXTRA MAGICAL UNDINE WATER.
GLUB
SHAA
INSTEAD OF FOOD COLORING, LET'S USE THIS GROUND WYVERN TOOTH.
NEXT, ADD THE SYNTHETIC THICKENING LIQUID.
SIGH...
SOUNDS GOOD, BUT LET'S MAKE SURE OUR SLIME LIVES FOR A LONG TIME...
FSHOOOO
GLUB GLUB
BY ADDING THIS EXPENSIVE, OVER-THE-COUNTER ELIXIR!

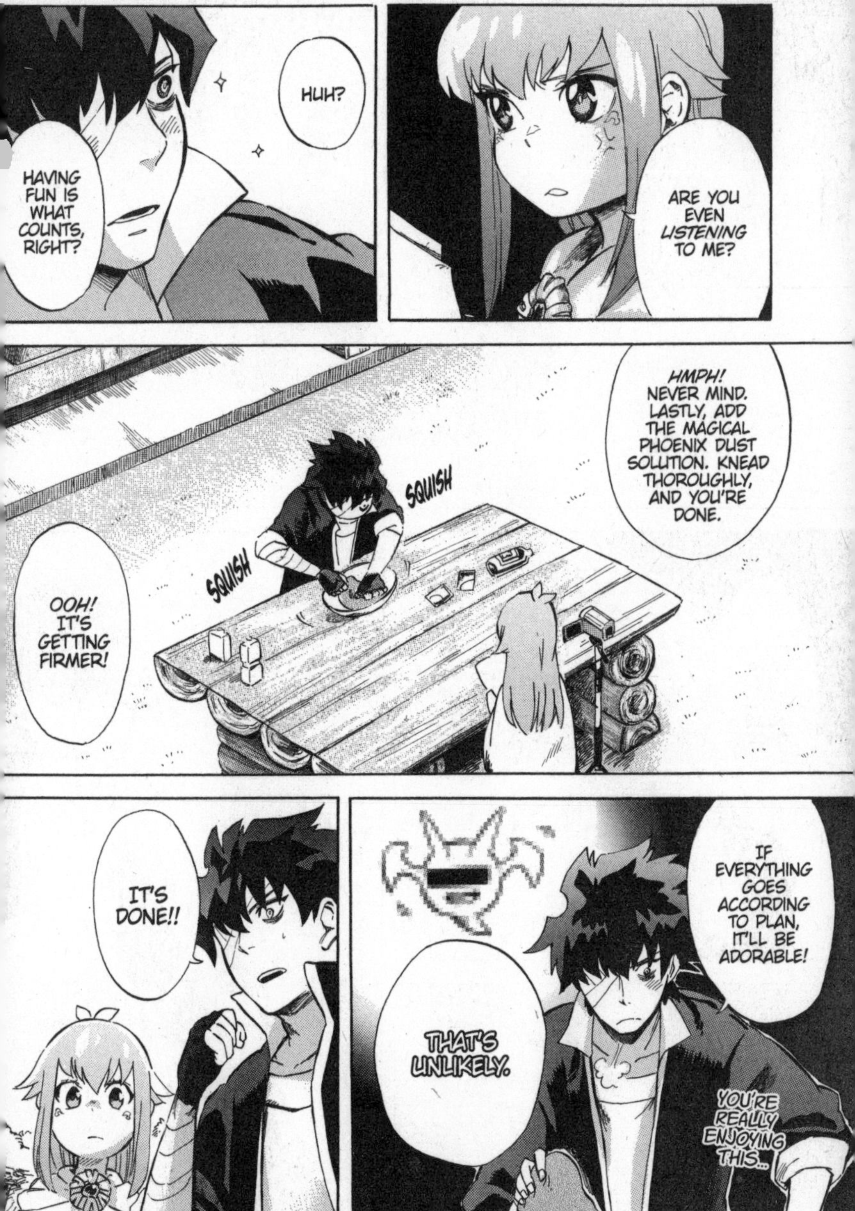
ARE YOU EVEN *LISTENING* TO ME?
HUH?
HAVING FUN IS WHAT COUNTS, RIGHT?
HMPH! NEVER MIND. LASTLY, ADD THE MAGICAL PHOENIX DUST SOLUTION. KNEAD THOROUGHLY, AND YOU'RE DONE.
SQUISH
SQUISH
OOH! IT'S GETTING FIRMER!
IF EVERYTHING GOES ACCORDING TO PLAN, IT'LL BE ADORABLE!
THAT'S UNLIKELY.
YOU'RE REALLY ENJOYING THIS...
IT'S DONE!!

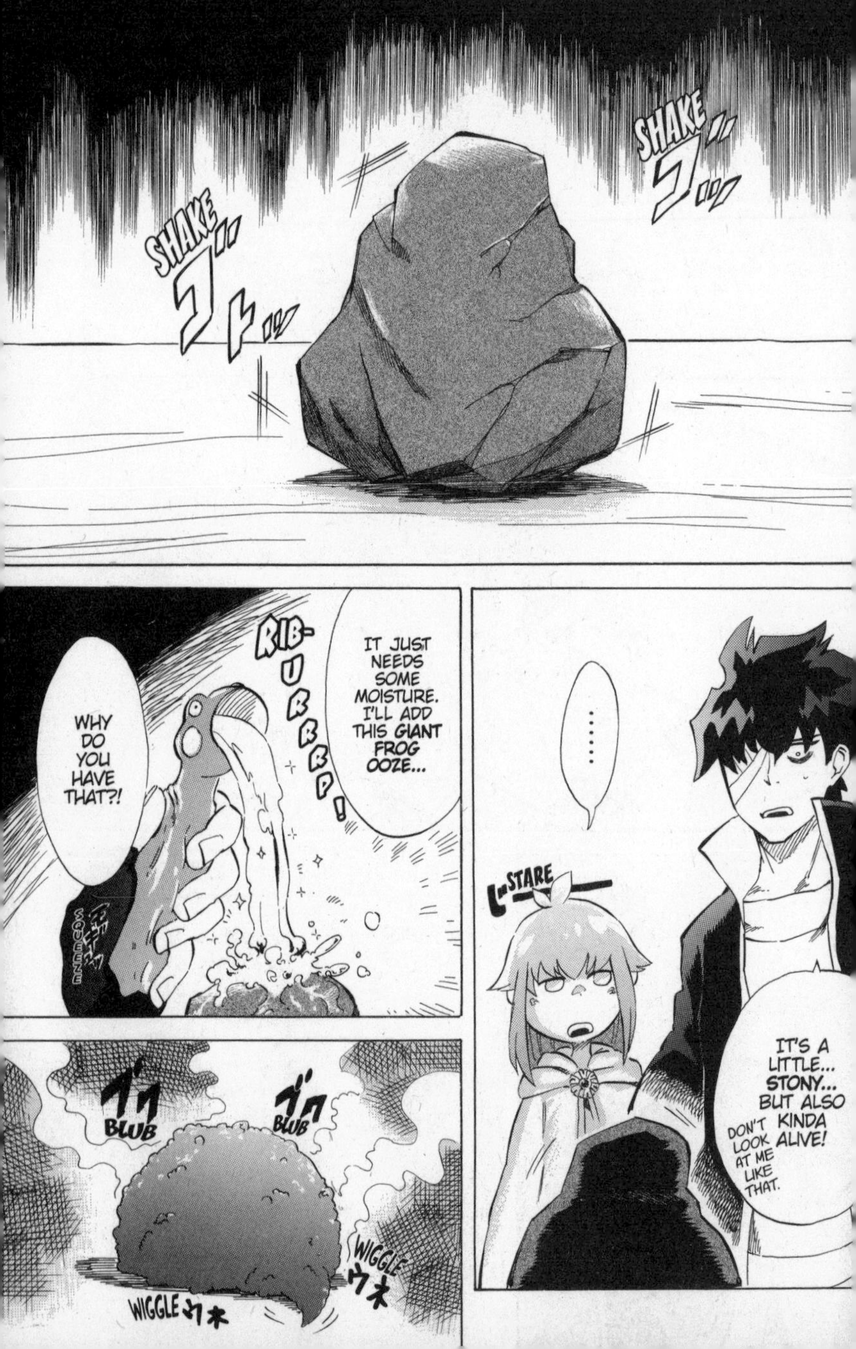
SHAKE
SHAKE
......
STARE
IT'S A LITTLE... STONY... BUT ALSO KINDA ALIVE!
DON'T LOOK AT ME LIKE THAT.
IT JUST NEEDS SOME MOISTURE. I'LL ADD THIS GIANT FROG OOZE...
RIB-URRRP!
WHY DO YOU HAVE THAT?!
SQUEEZE
BLUB
BLUB
WIGGLE
WIGGLE

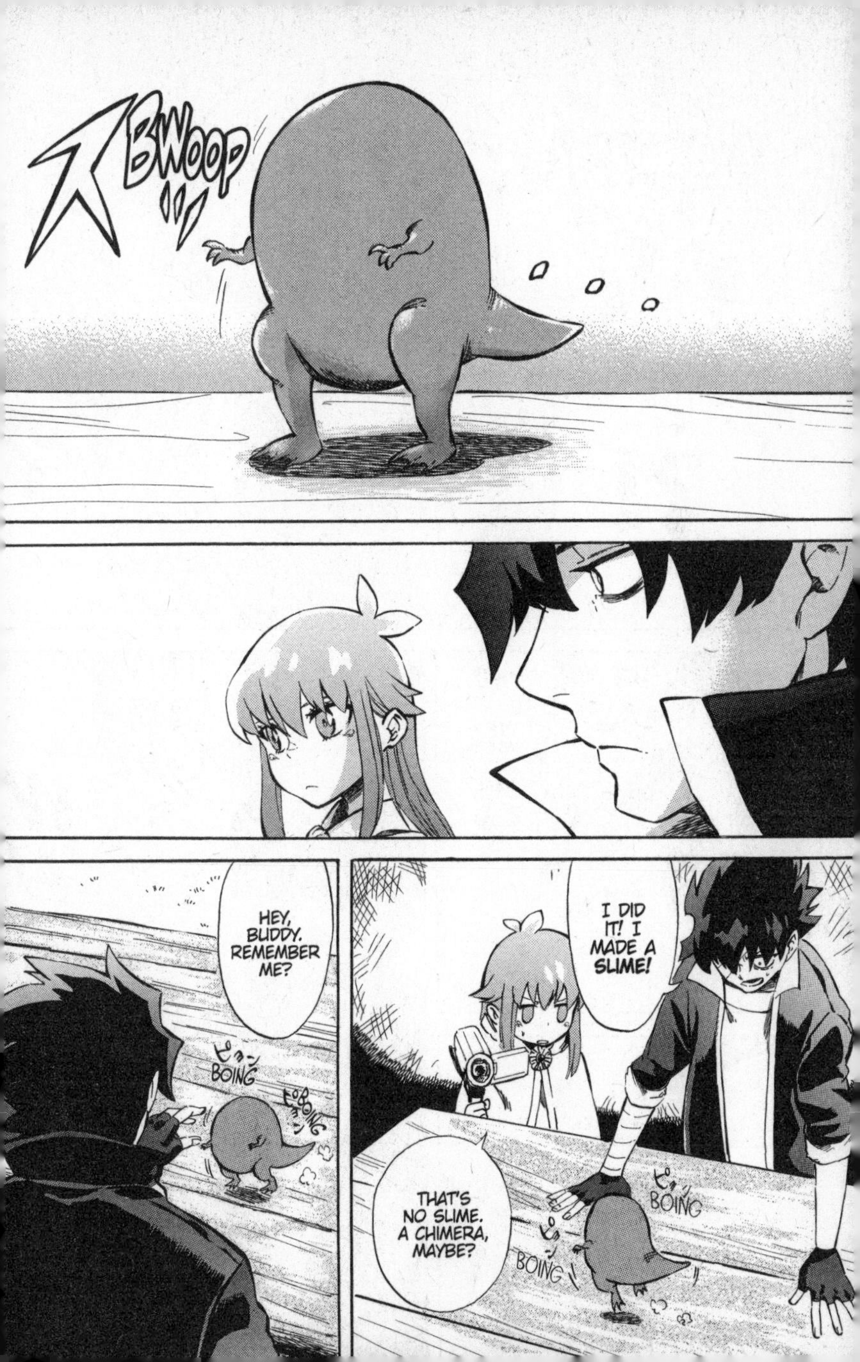
BWOOP
I DID IT! I MADE A SLIME!
THAT'S NO SLIME. A CHIMERA, MAYBE?
ピョン BOING
ピョン BOING
HEY, BUDDY. REMEMBER ME?
ピョン BOING
ピョン BOING

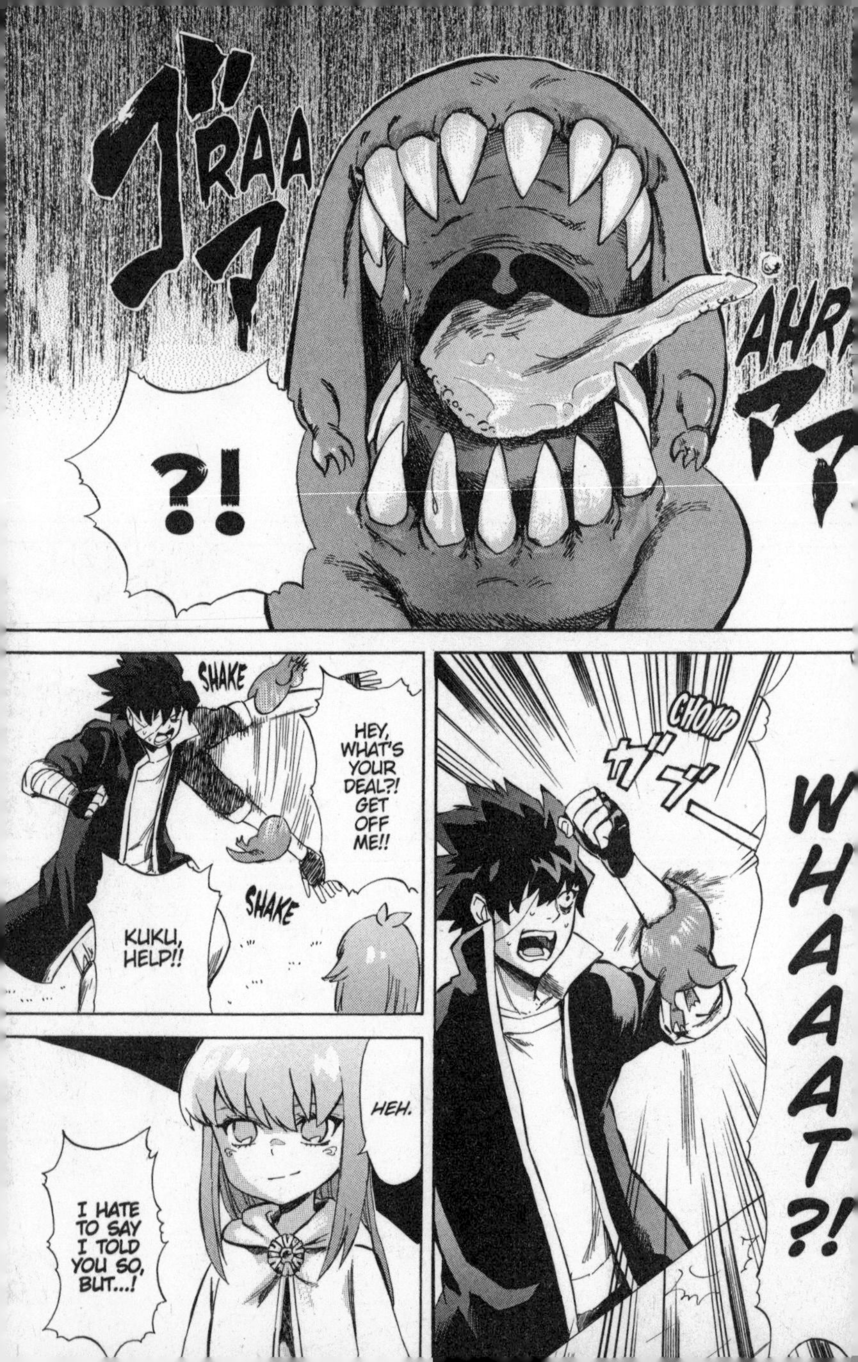
AHR
ゴRAAア
?!
CHOMP
ガブー
WHAAAAT?!
SHAKE
HEY, WHAT'S YOUR DEAL?! GET OFF ME!!
SHAKE
KUKU, HELP!!
HEH.
I HATE TO SAY I TOLD YOU SO, BUT...!

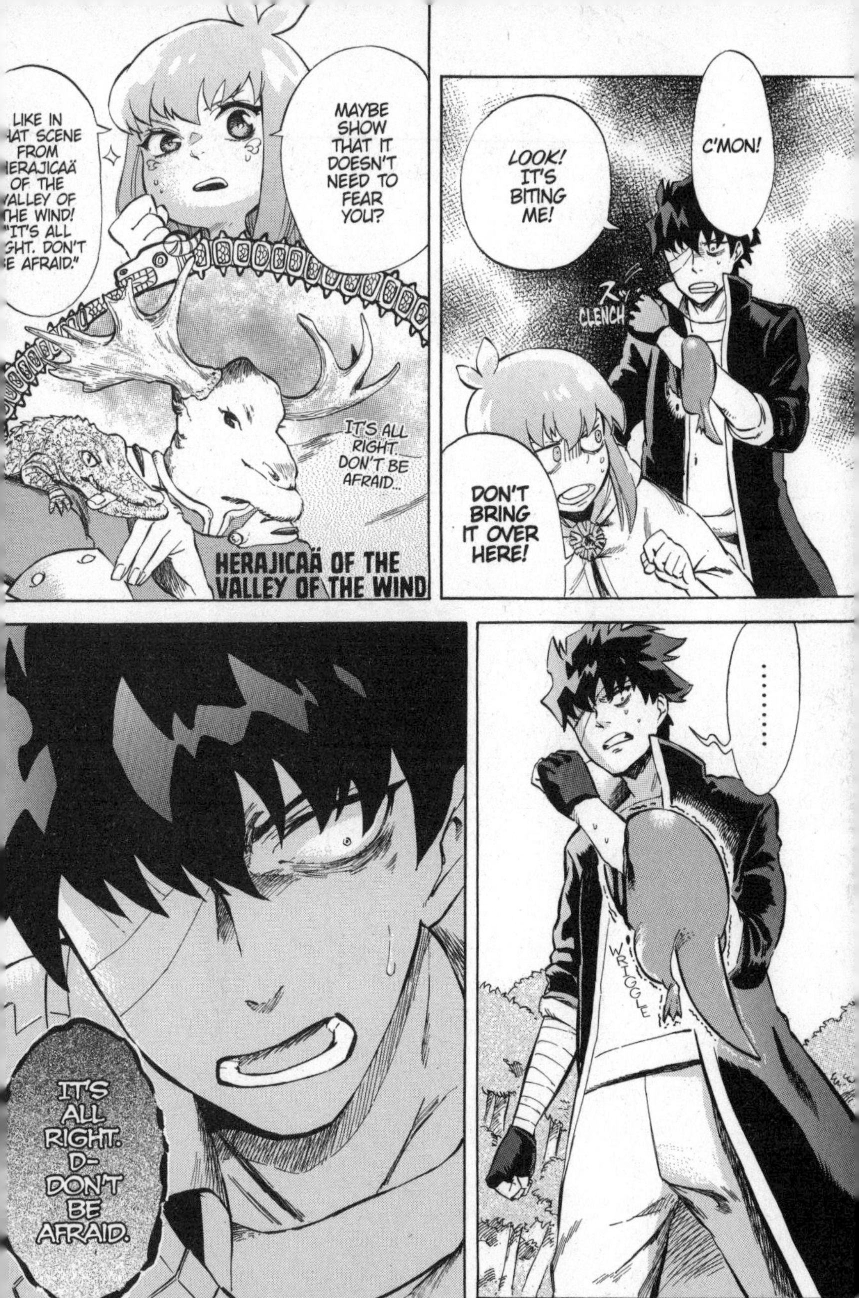
C'MON!
LOOK! IT'S BITING ME!
ス
CLENCH
DON'T BRING IT OVER HERE!
MAYBE SHOW THAT IT DOESN'T NEED TO FEAR YOU?
LIKE IN HAT SCENE FROM HERAJICAÄ OF THE VALLEY OF THE WIND! "IT'S ALL GHT. DON'T E AFRAID."
IT'S ALL RIGHT. DON'T BE AFRAID...
HERAJICAÄ OF THE VALLEY OF THE WIND
......
WRIGGLE
IT'S ALL RIGHT. D-DON'T BE AFRAID.

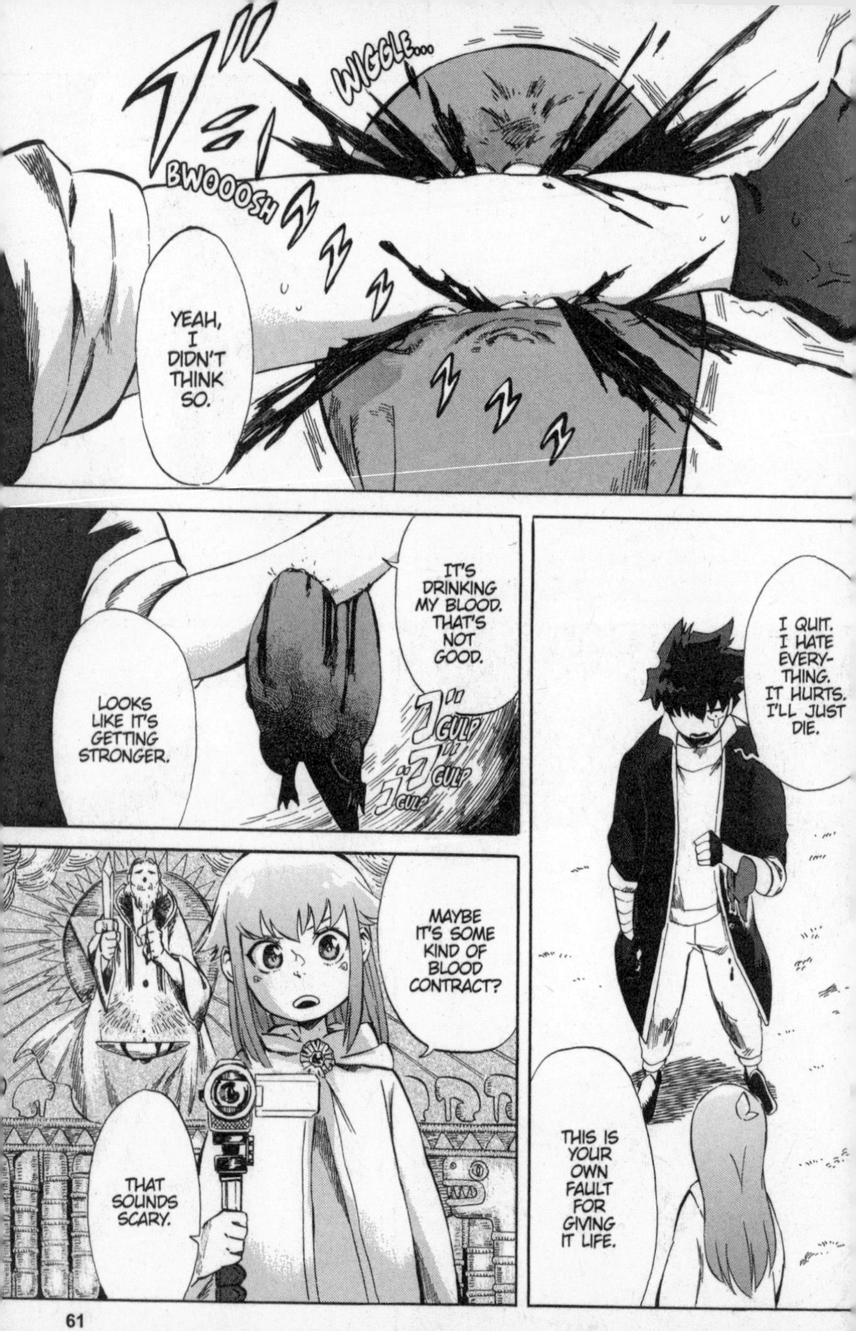
WIGGLE...
BWOOOSH
YEAH, I DIDN'T THINK SO.
I QUIT. I HATE EVERYTHING. IT HURTS. I'LL JUST DIE.
THIS IS YOUR OWN FAULT FOR GIVING IT LIFE.
IT'S DRINKING MY BLOOD. THAT'S NOT GOOD.
GULP
GULP
GULP
LOOKS LIKE IT'S GETTING STRONGER.
MAYBE IT'S SOME KIND OF BLOOD CONTRACT?
THAT SOUNDS SCARY.

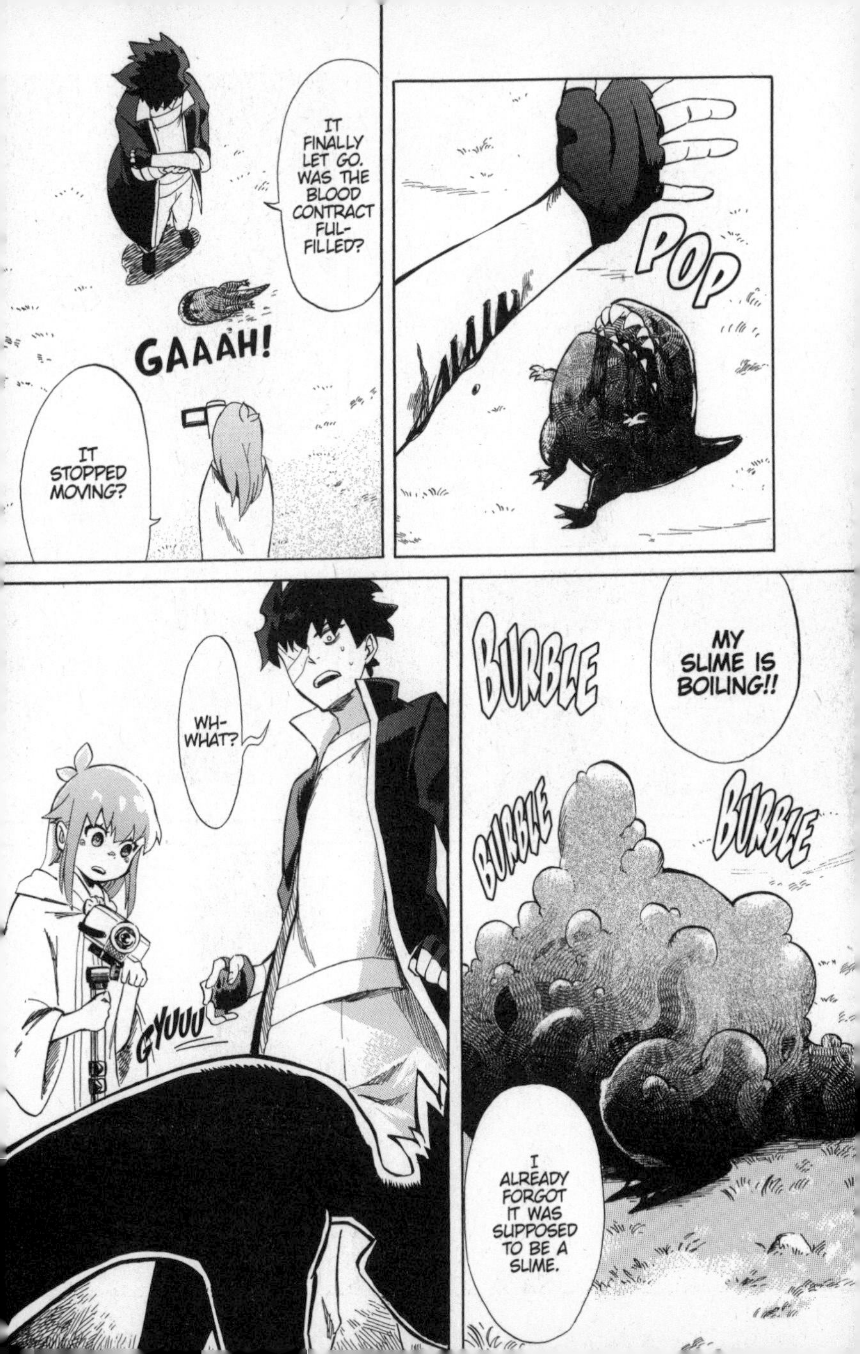
POP
IT FINALLY LET GO. WAS THE BLOOD CONTRACT FUL-FILLED?
GAAAH!
IT STOPPED MOVING?
BURBLE
MY SLIME IS BOILING!!
BURBLE
BURBLE
I ALREADY FORGOT IT WAS SUPPOSED TO BE A SLIME.
WH-WHAT?
GYUUU

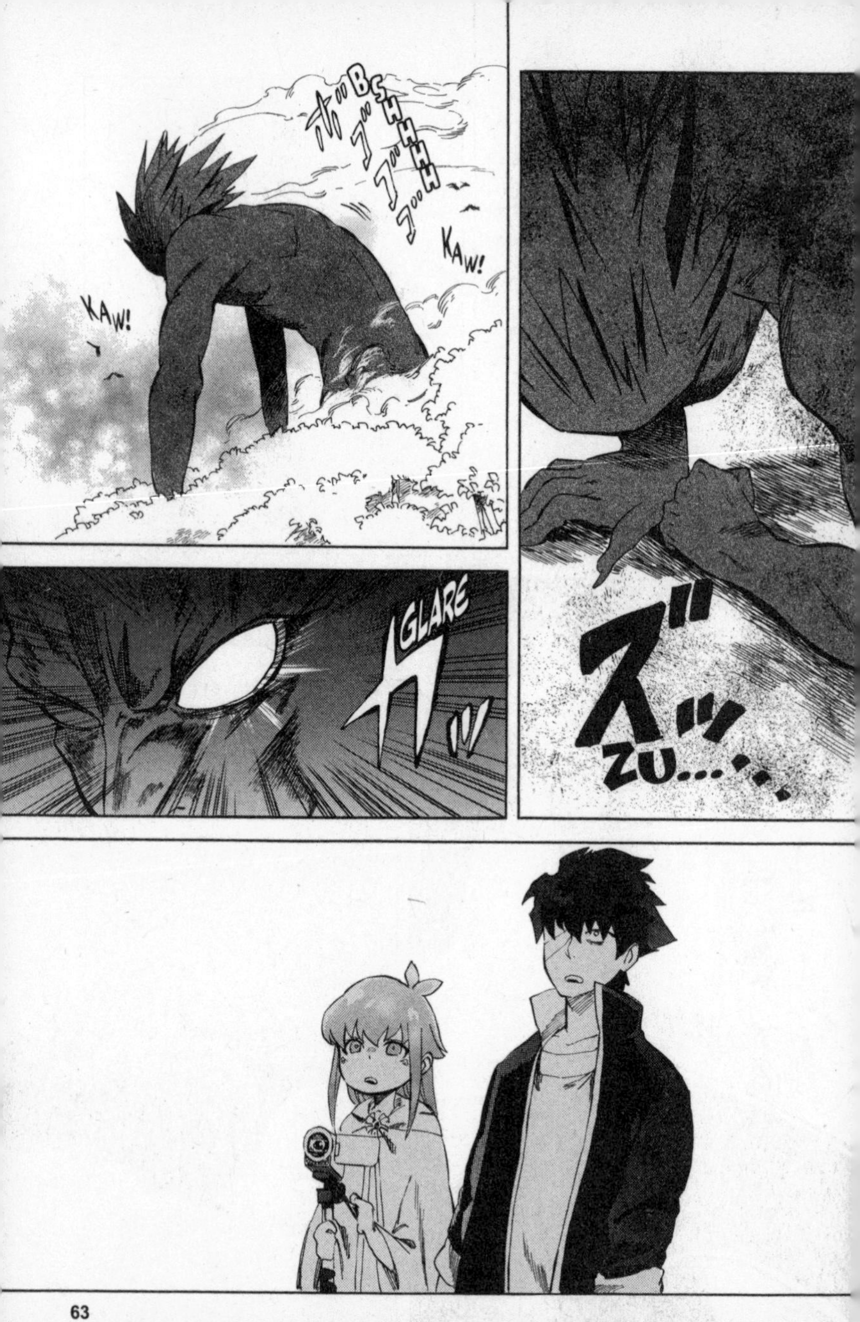
ズッ
ZU......
BSHHHHH
KAW!
KAW!
GLARE

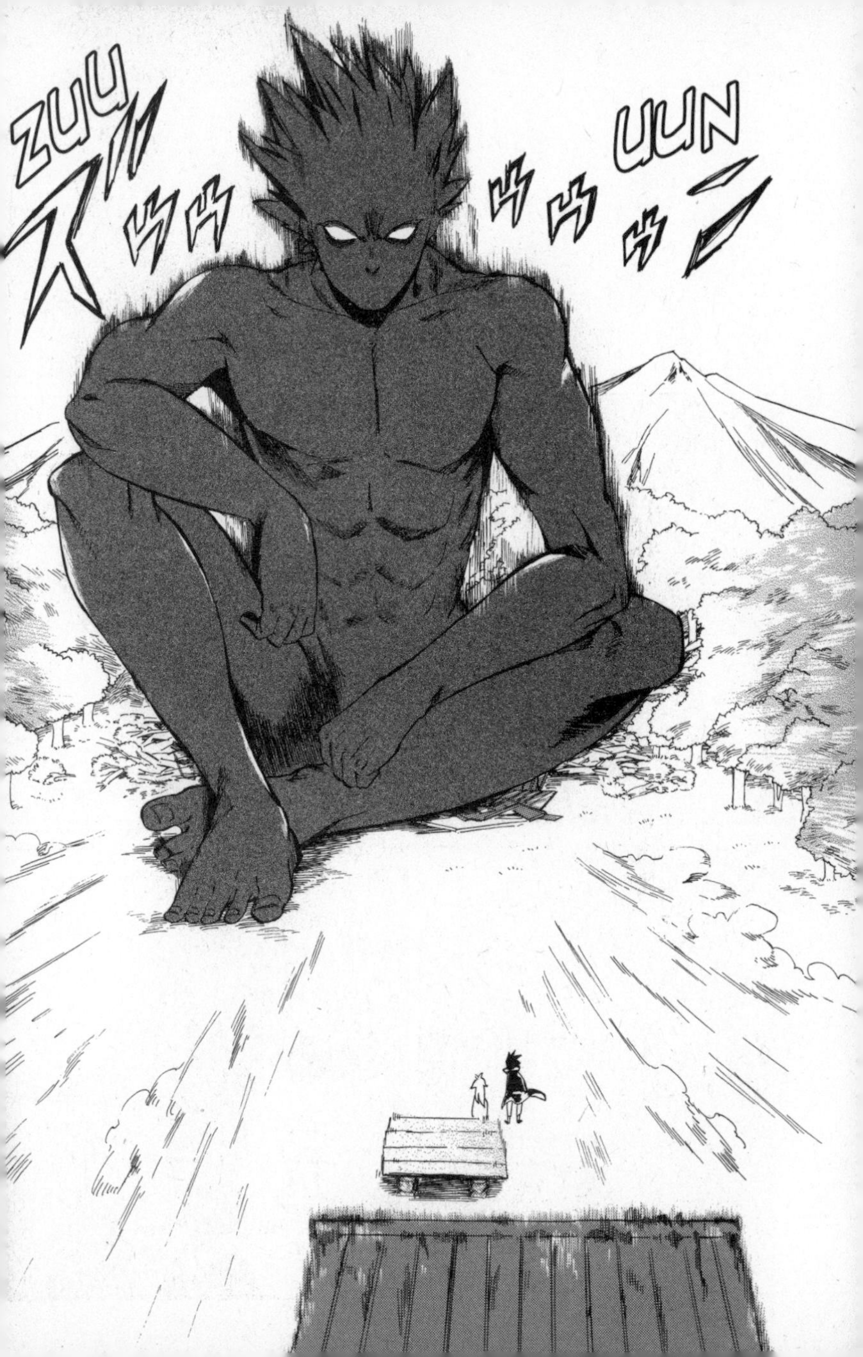
ZUU
UUN
ズゥゥゥゥゥン

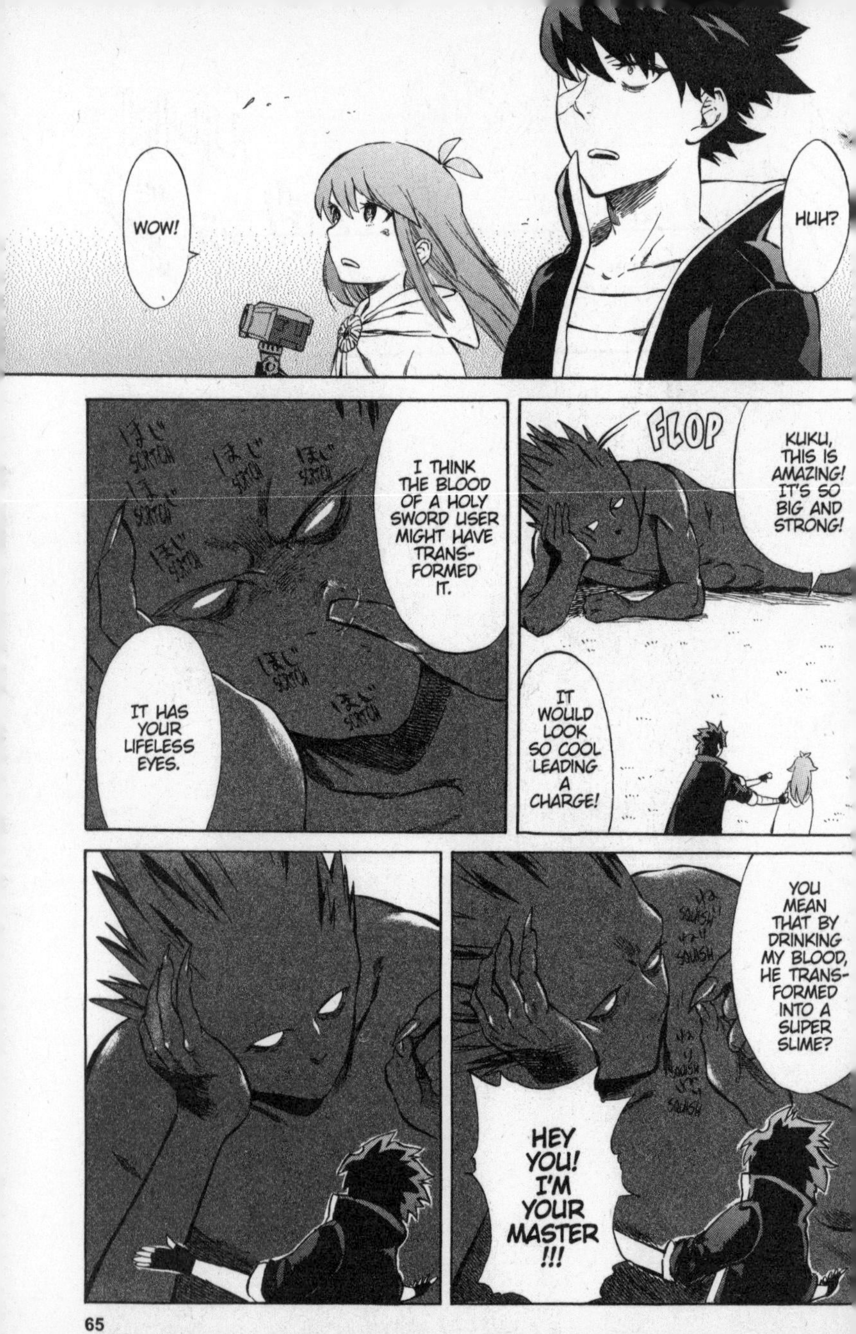
HUH?
WOW!
FLOP
KUKU, THIS IS AMAZING! IT'S SO BIG AND STRONG!
IT WOULD LOOK SO COOL LEADING A CHARGE!
I THINK THE BLOOD OF A HOLY SWORD USER MIGHT HAVE TRANSFORMED IT.
IT HAS YOUR LIFELESS EYES.
YOU MEAN THAT BY DRINKING MY BLOOD, HE TRANSFORMED INTO A SUPER SLIME?
HEY YOU! I'M YOUR MASTER!!!

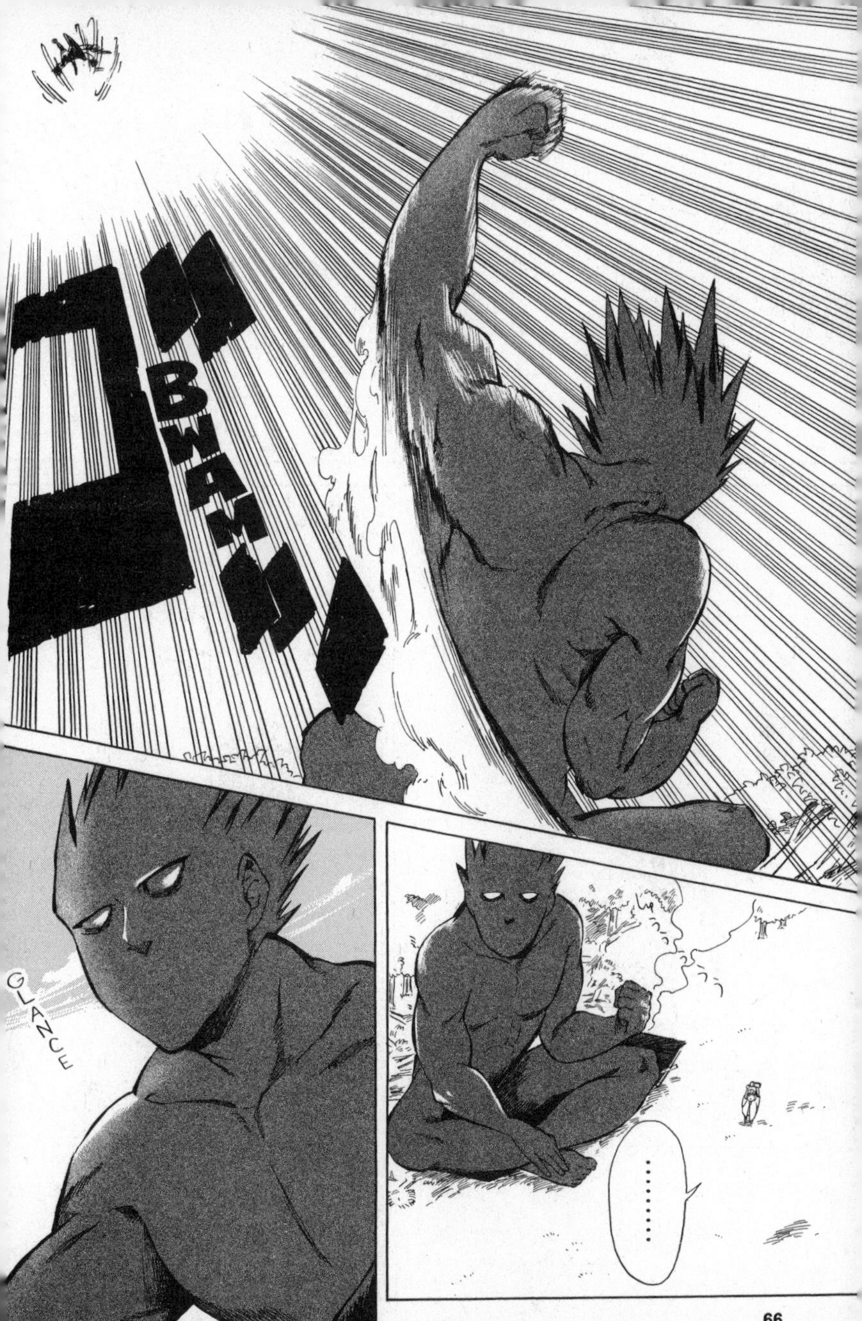
BWAM
....
GLANCE

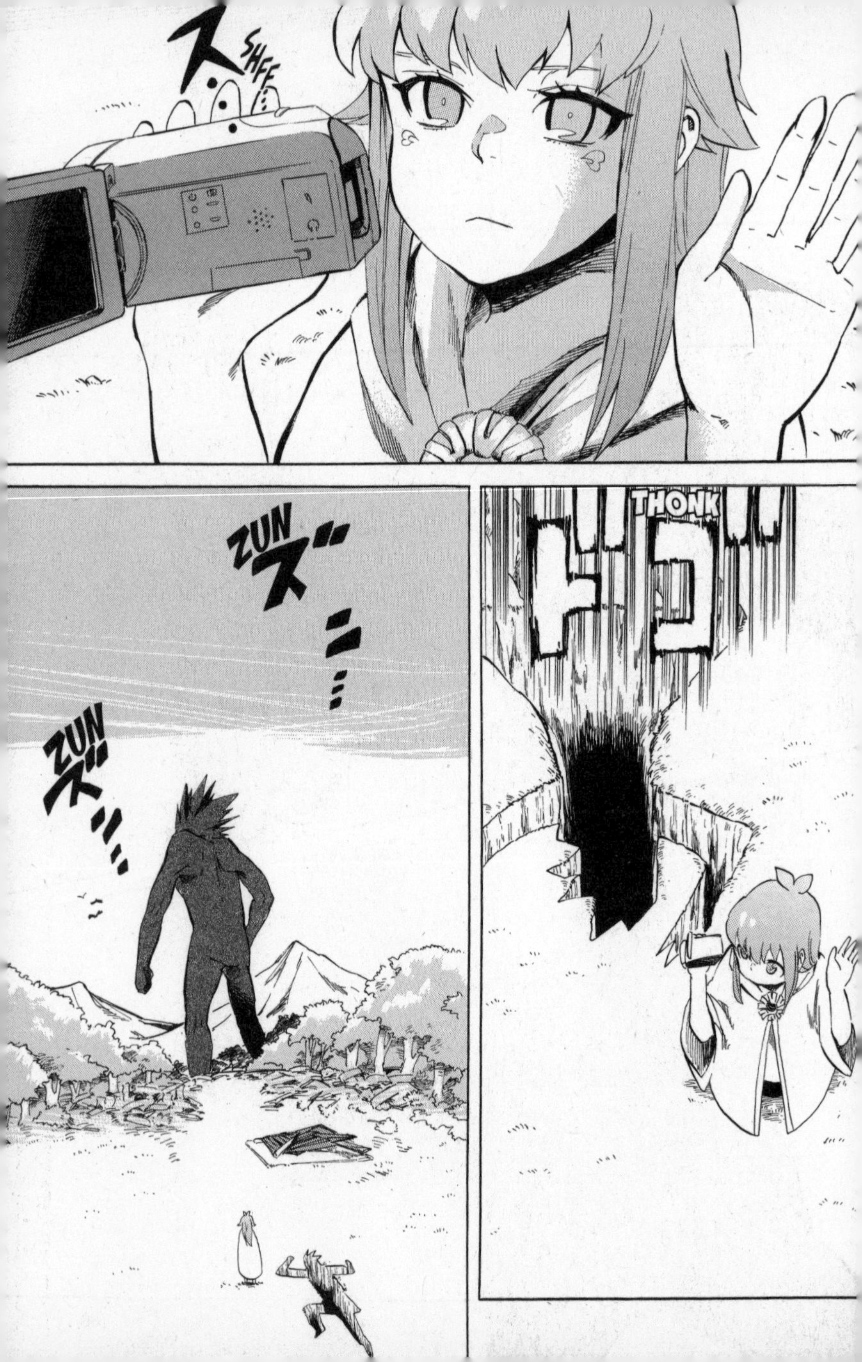
ス
SHFF
THONK
ドン
ZUN
ズ
ZUN
ズ

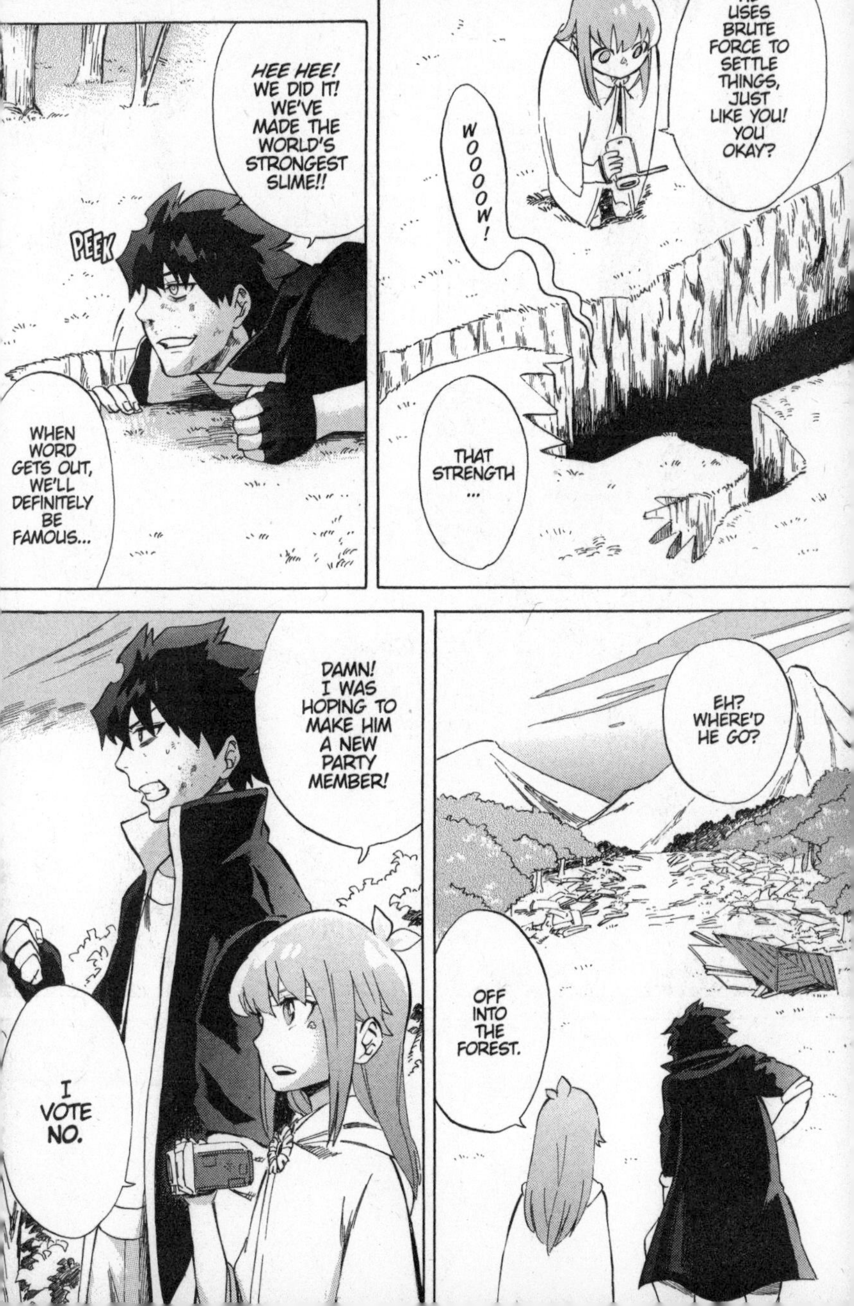
HE USES BRUTE FORCE TO SETTLE THINGS, JUST LIKE YOU! YOU OKAY?
WOOOOOW!
THAT STRENGTH...
HEE HEE! WE DID IT! WE'VE MADE THE WORLD'S STRONGEST SLIME!!
PEEK
WHEN WORD GETS OUT, WE'LL DEFINITELY BE FAMOUS...
EH? WHERE'D HE GO?
OFF INTO THE FOREST.
DAMN! I WAS HOPING TO MAKE HIM A NEW PARTY MEMBER!
I VOTE NO.

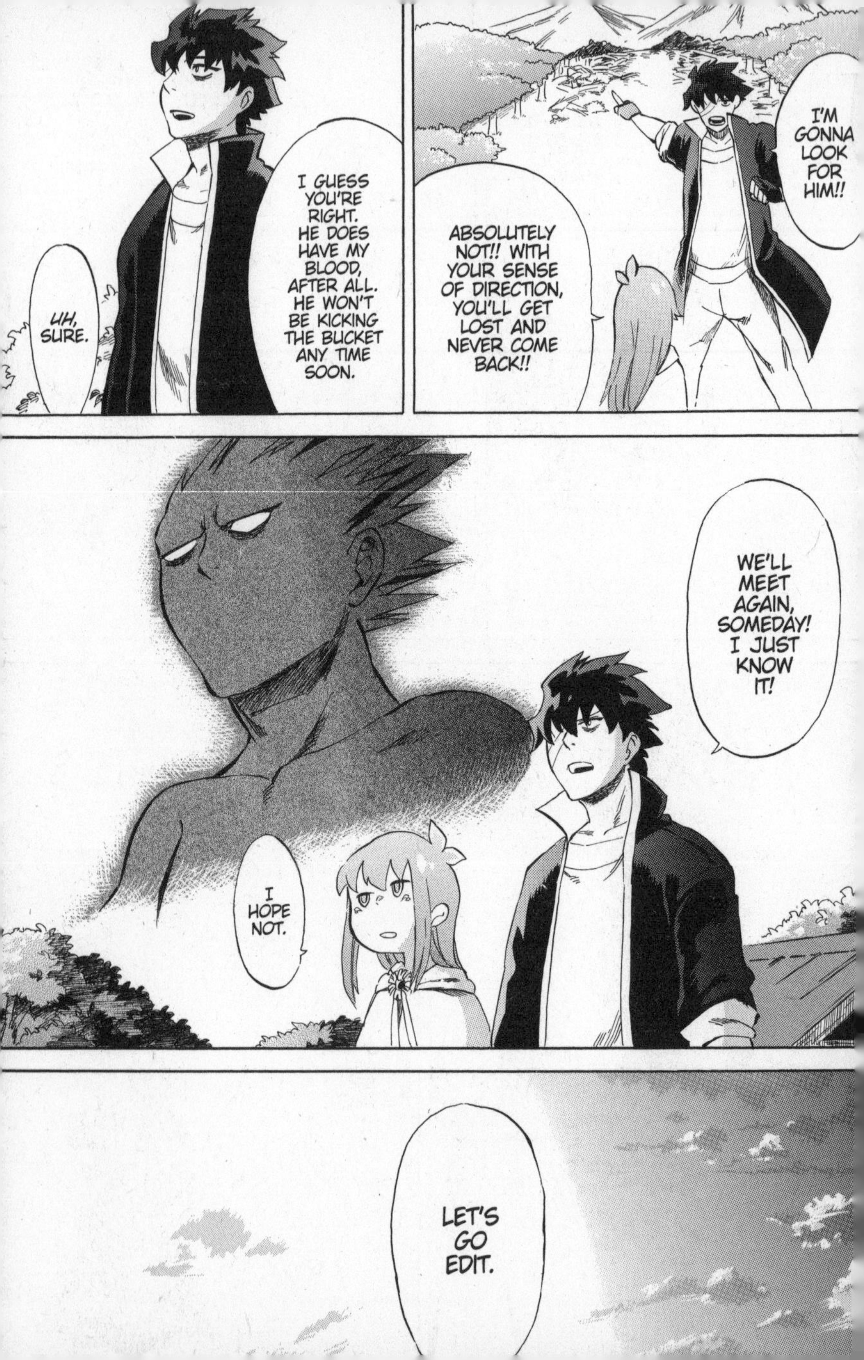
I'M GONNA LOOK FOR HIM!!
ABSOLUTELY NOT!! WITH YOUR SENSE OF DIRECTION, YOU'LL GET LOST AND NEVER COME BACK!!
I GUESS YOU'RE RIGHT. HE DOES HAVE MY BLOOD, AFTER ALL. HE WON'T BE KICKING THE BUCKET ANY TIME SOON.
UH, SURE.
WE'LL MEET AGAIN, SOMEDAY! I JUST KNOW IT!
I HOPE NOT.
LET'S GO EDIT.

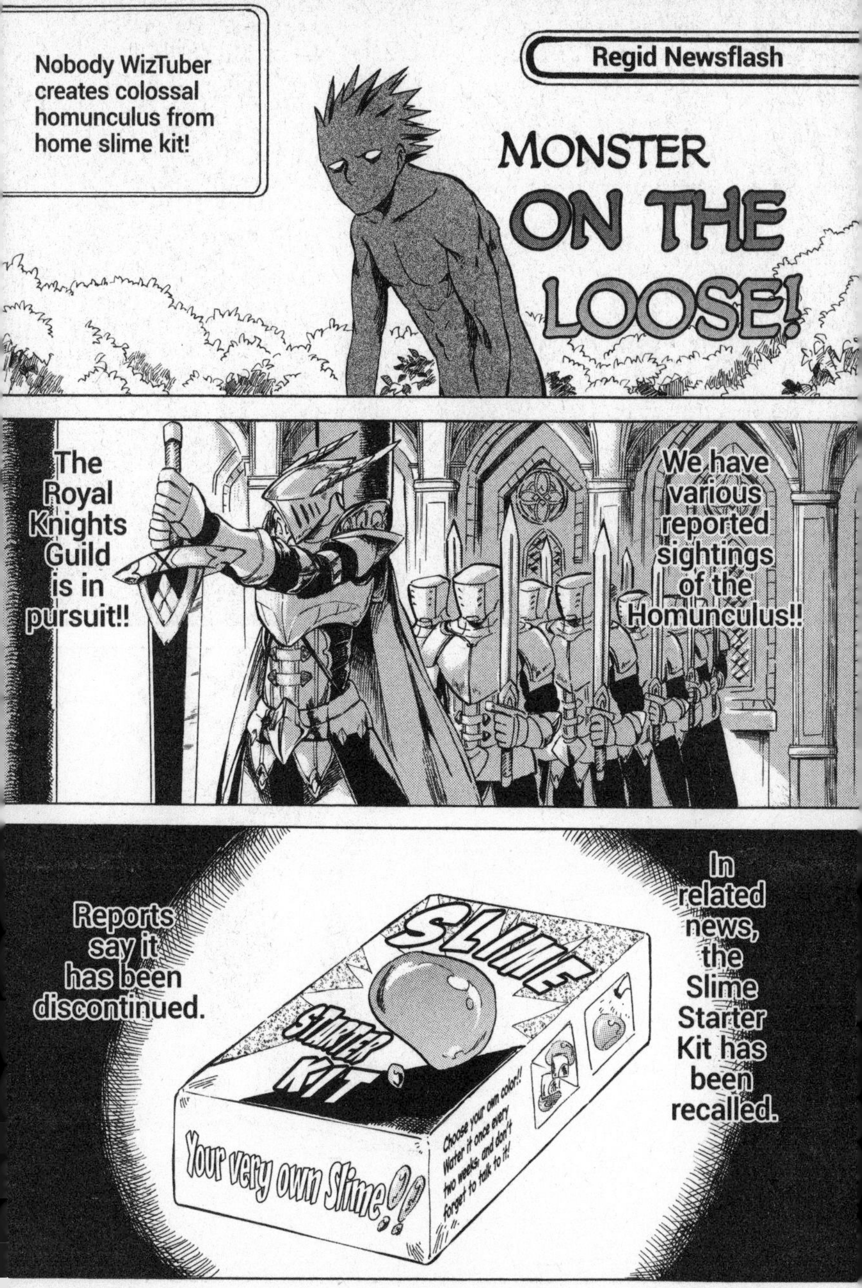
Regid Newsflash
MONSTER ON THE LOOSE!
Nobody WizTuber creates colossal homunculus from home slime kit!
We have various reported sightings of the Homunculus!!
The Royal Knights Guild is in pursuit!!
In related news, the Slime Starter Kit has been recalled.
SLIME STARTER KIT
Your very own Slime?!
Choose your own color!! Water it once every two weeks, and don't forget to talk to it!!
Reports say it has been discontinued.

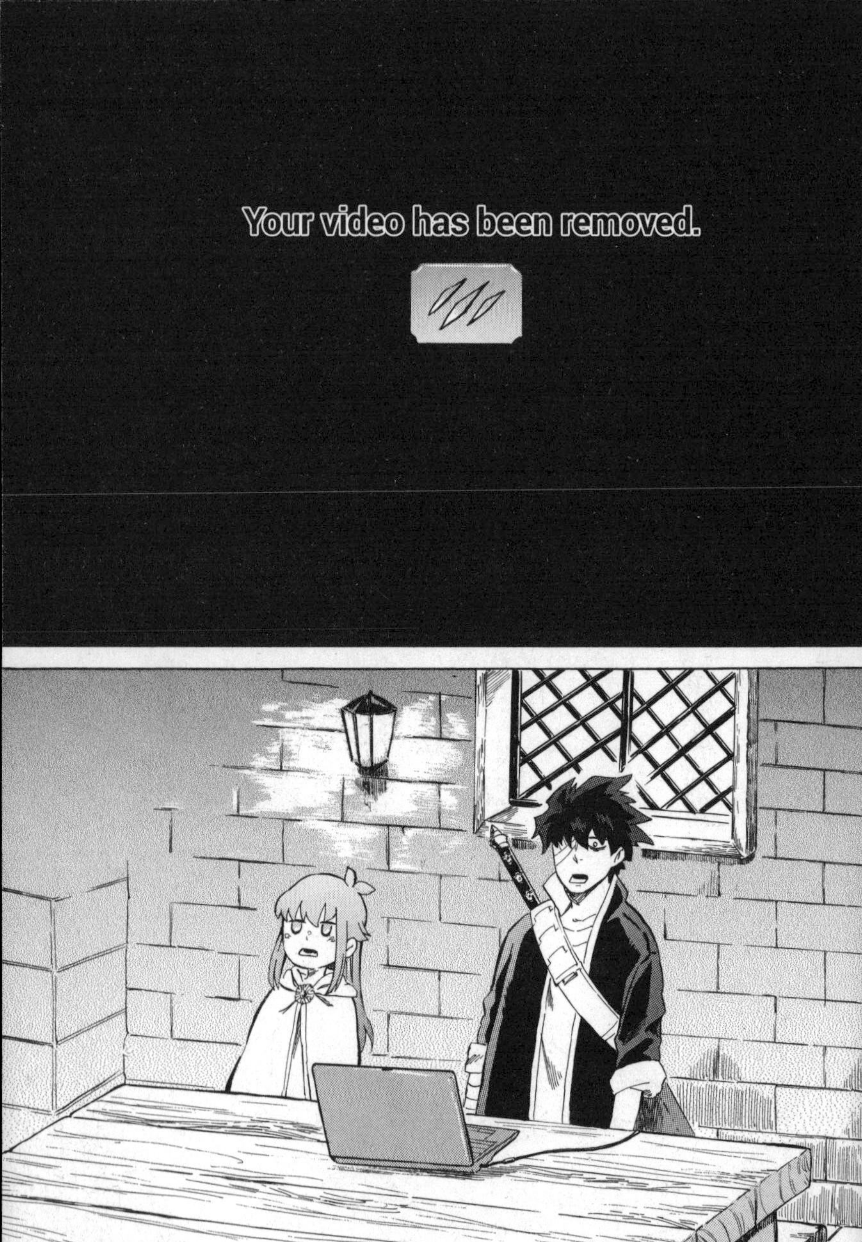
Your video has been removed.

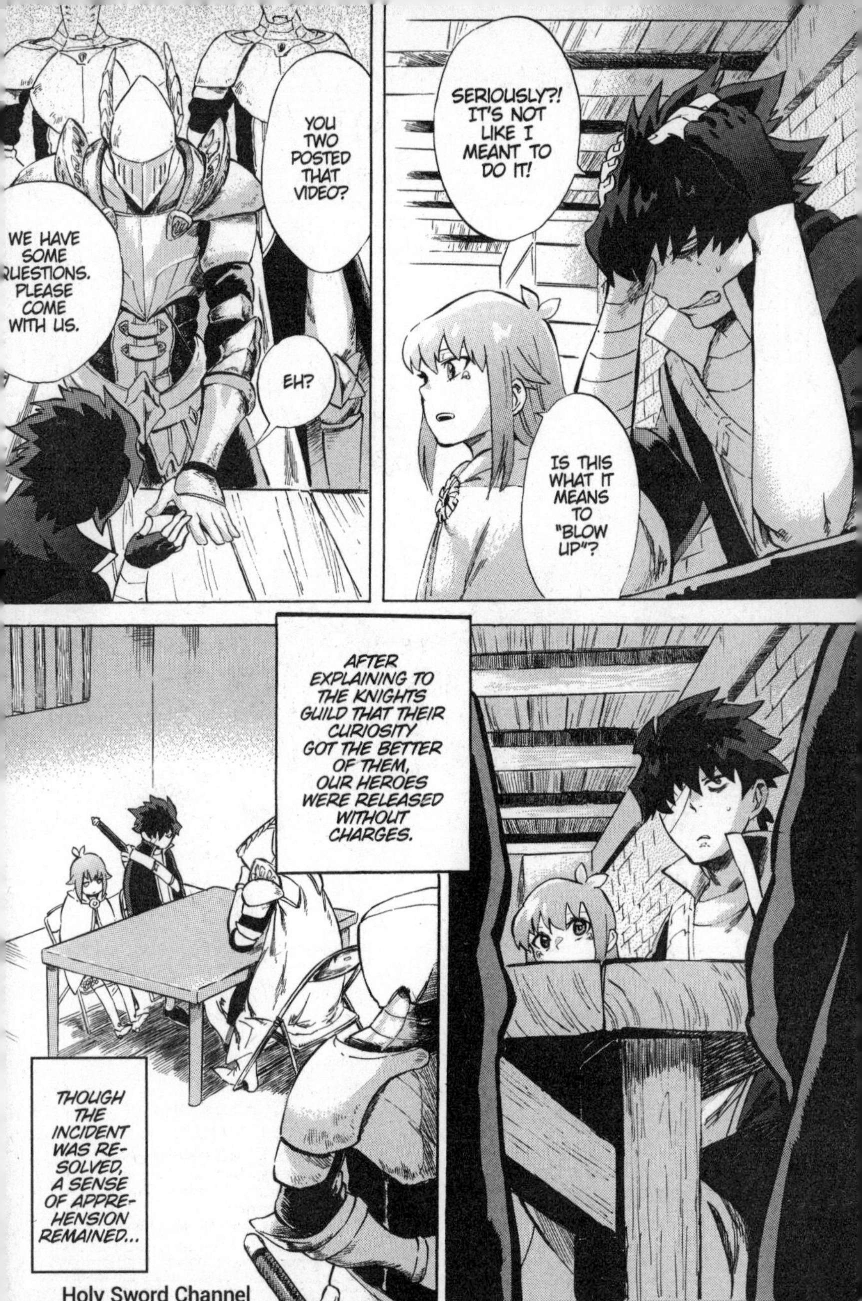
SERIOUSLY?! IT'S NOT LIKE I MEANT TO DO IT!
IS THIS WHAT IT MEANS TO "BLOW UP"?
YOU TWO POSTED THAT VIDEO?
WE HAVE SOME QUESTIONS. PLEASE COME WITH US.
EH?
AFTER EXPLAINING TO THE KNIGHTS GUILD THAT THEIR CURIOSITY GOT THE BETTER OF THEM, OUR HEROES WERE RELEASED WITHOUT CHARGES.
THOUGH THE INCIDENT WAS RE-SOLVED, A SENSE OF APPRE-HENSION REMAINED...

Holy Sword Channel
Subscribers: 68

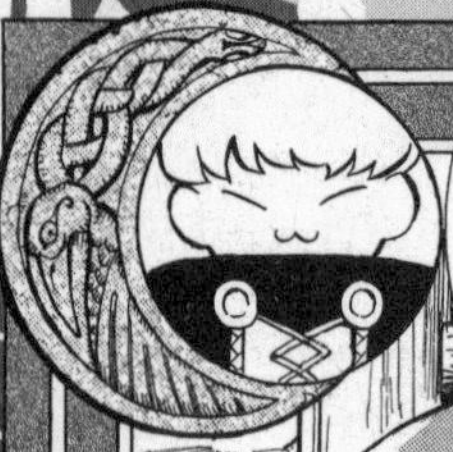

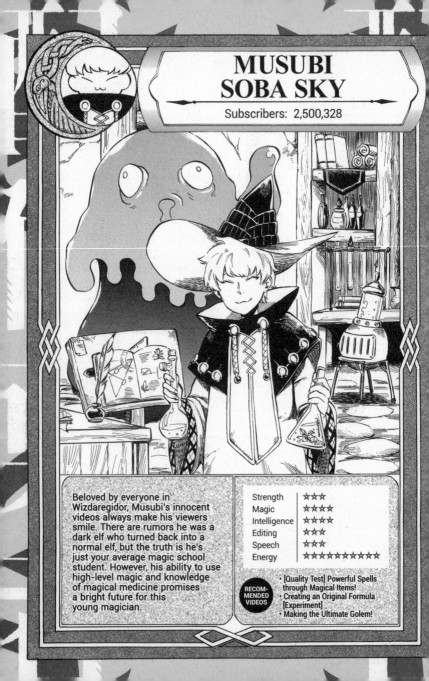

MUSUBI SOBA SKY

Subscribers: 2,500,328

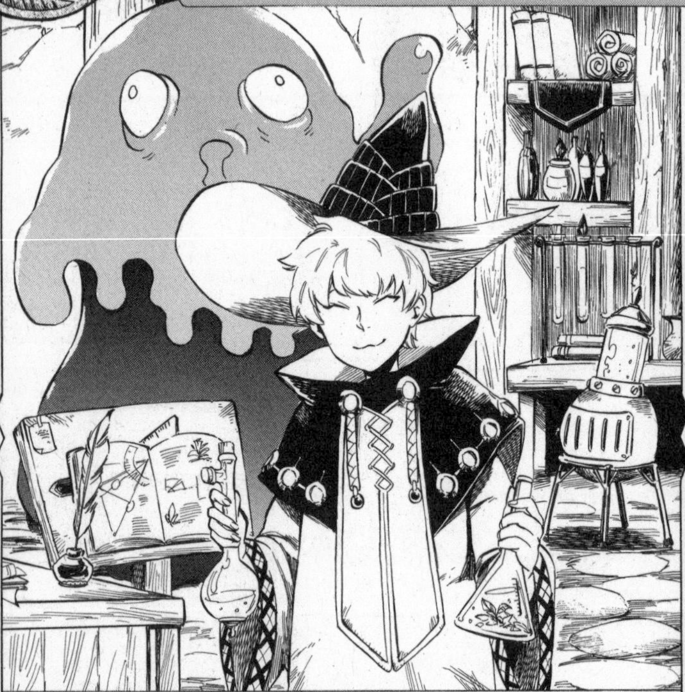

Beloved by everyone in Wizdaregidor, Musubi's innocent videos always make his viewers smile. There are rumors he was a dark elf who turned back into a normal elf, but the truth is he's just your average magic school student. However, his ability to use high-level magic and knowledge of magical medicine promises a bright future for this young magician.

Strength	☆☆☆
Magic	☆☆☆☆
Intelligence	☆☆☆☆
Editing	☆☆☆
Speech	☆☆☆
Energy	☆☆☆☆☆☆☆☆☆☆

RECOMMENDED VIDEOS

- [Quality Test] Powerful Spells through Magical Items!
- Creating an Original Formula [Experiment]
- Making the Ultimate Golem!

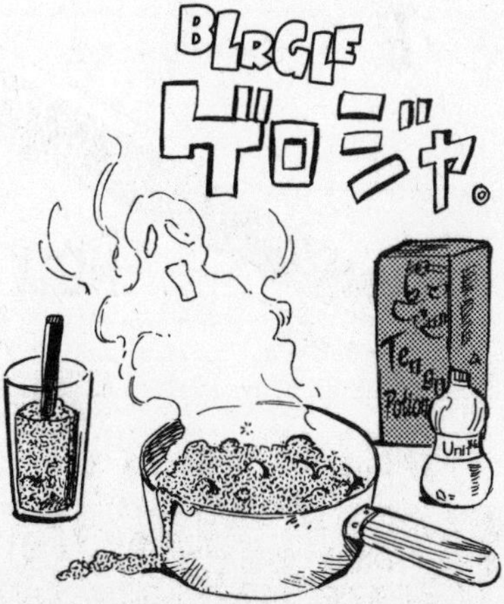
BLRGLE
ゲロジャ。
Tengu
Unit

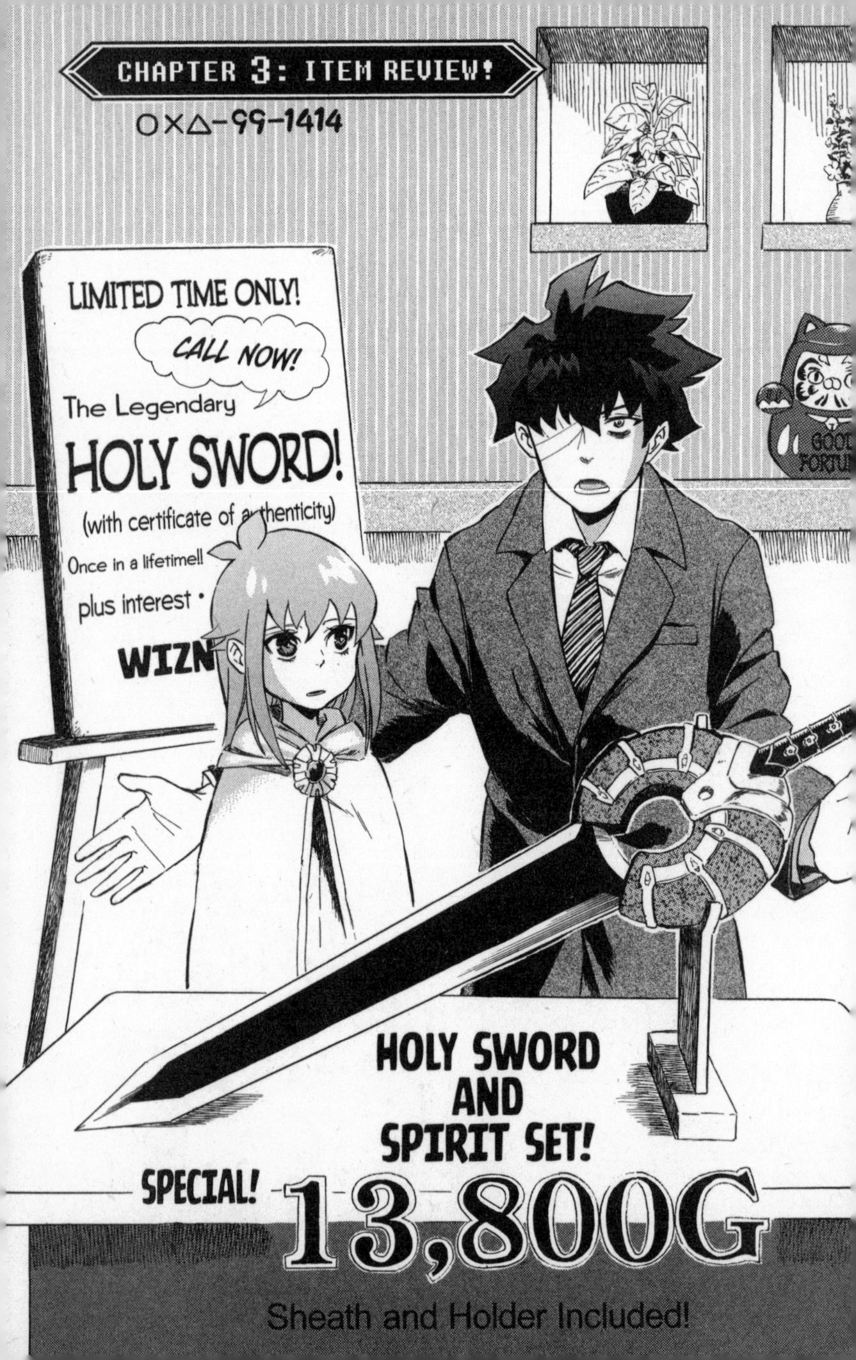

CHAPTER 3: ITEM REVIEW!
○×△-99-1414
LIMITED TIME ONLY!
CALL NOW!
The Legendary
HOLY SWORD!
(with certificate of authenticity)
Once in a lifetime!!
plus interest ·
WIZN
GOOD FORTU
HOLY SWORD AND SPIRIT SET!
SPECIAL! 13,800G
Sheath and Holder Included!

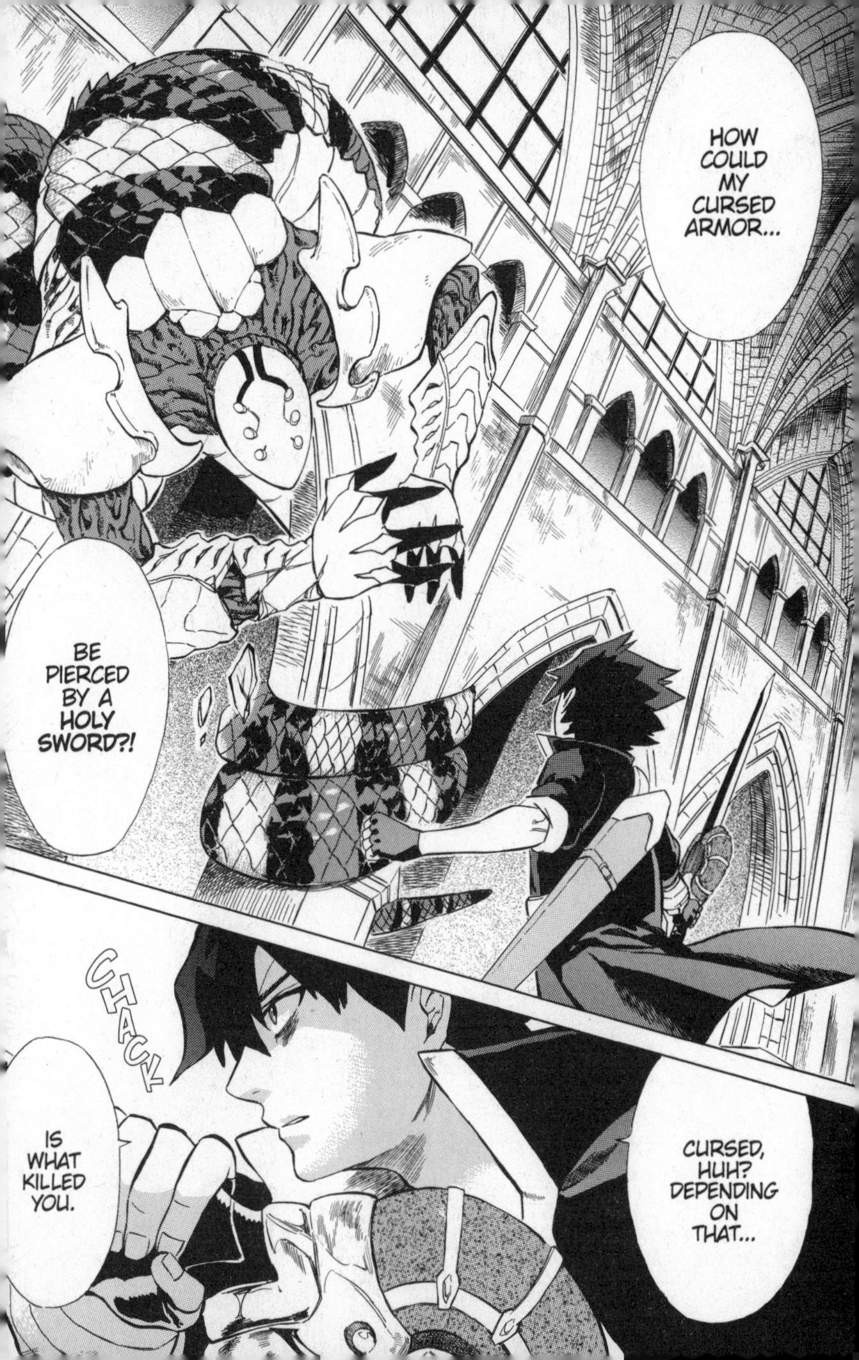
HOW COULD MY CURSED ARMOR...
BE PIERCED BY A HOLY SWORD?!
CURSED, HUH? DEPENDING ON THAT...
CHACK
IS WHAT KILLED YOU.

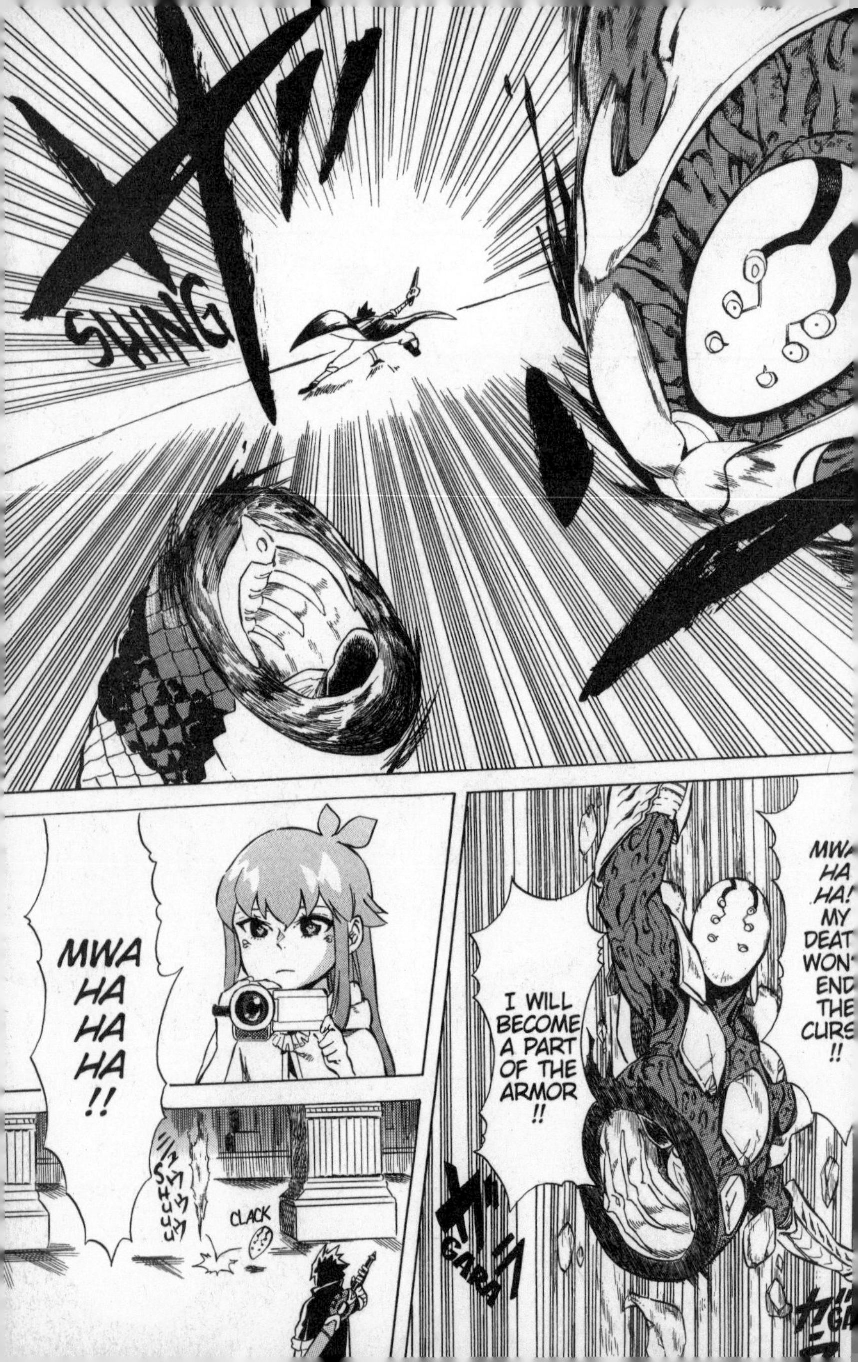
SHING
MWA HA HA! MY DEAT WON' END THE CURS !!
I WILL BECOME A PART OF THE ARMOR !!
GARA
MWA HA HA HA !!
SHUUU
CLACK

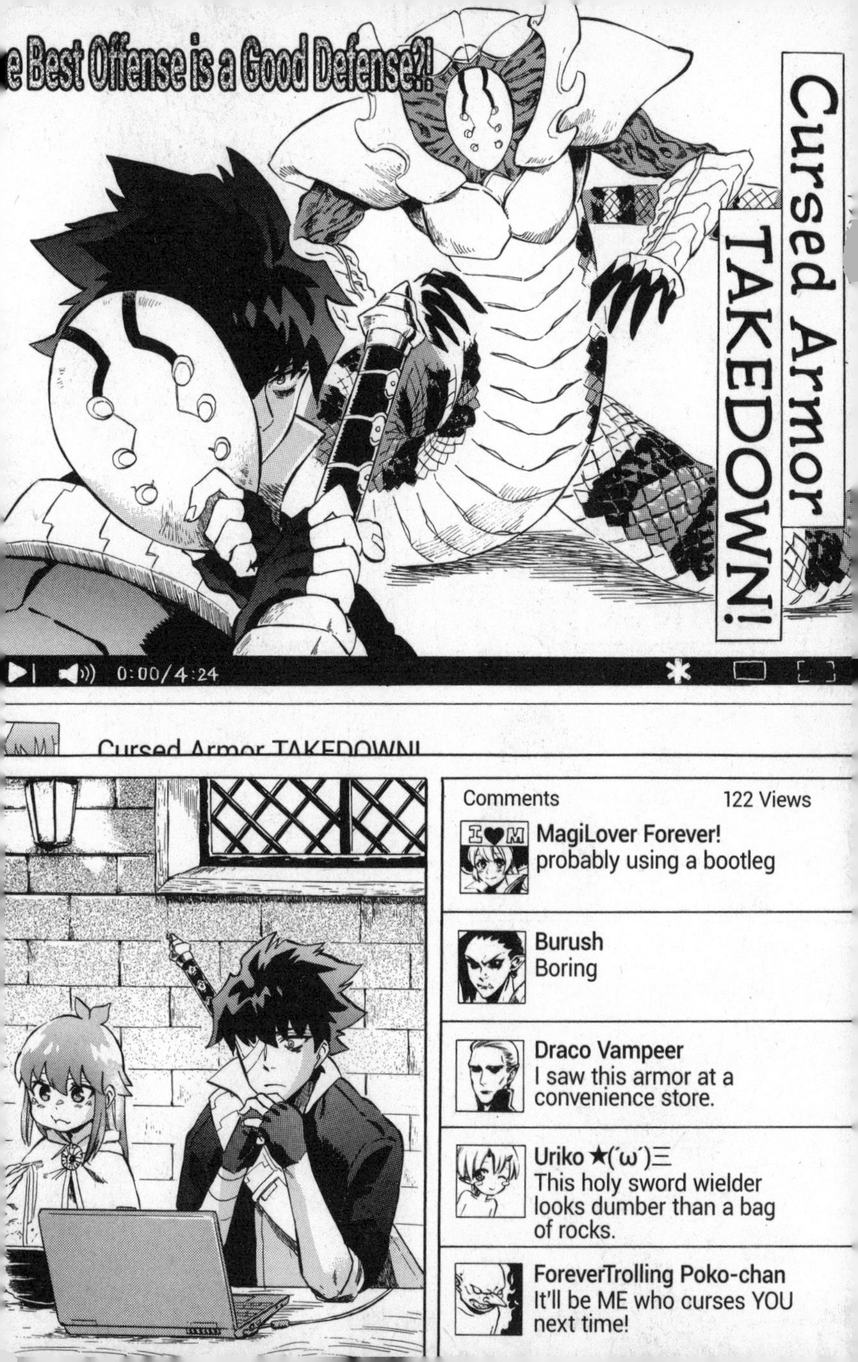

e Best Offense is a Good Defense?!
Cursed Armor TAKEDOWN!
0:00/4:24
Cursed Armor TAKEDOWN!
Comments
122 Views
MagiLover Forever!
probably using a bootleg
Burush
Boring
Draco Vampeer
I saw this armor at a convenience store.
Uriko ★(´ω`)三
This holy sword wielder looks dumber than a bag of rocks.
ForeverTrolling Poko-chan
It'll be ME who curses YOU next time!

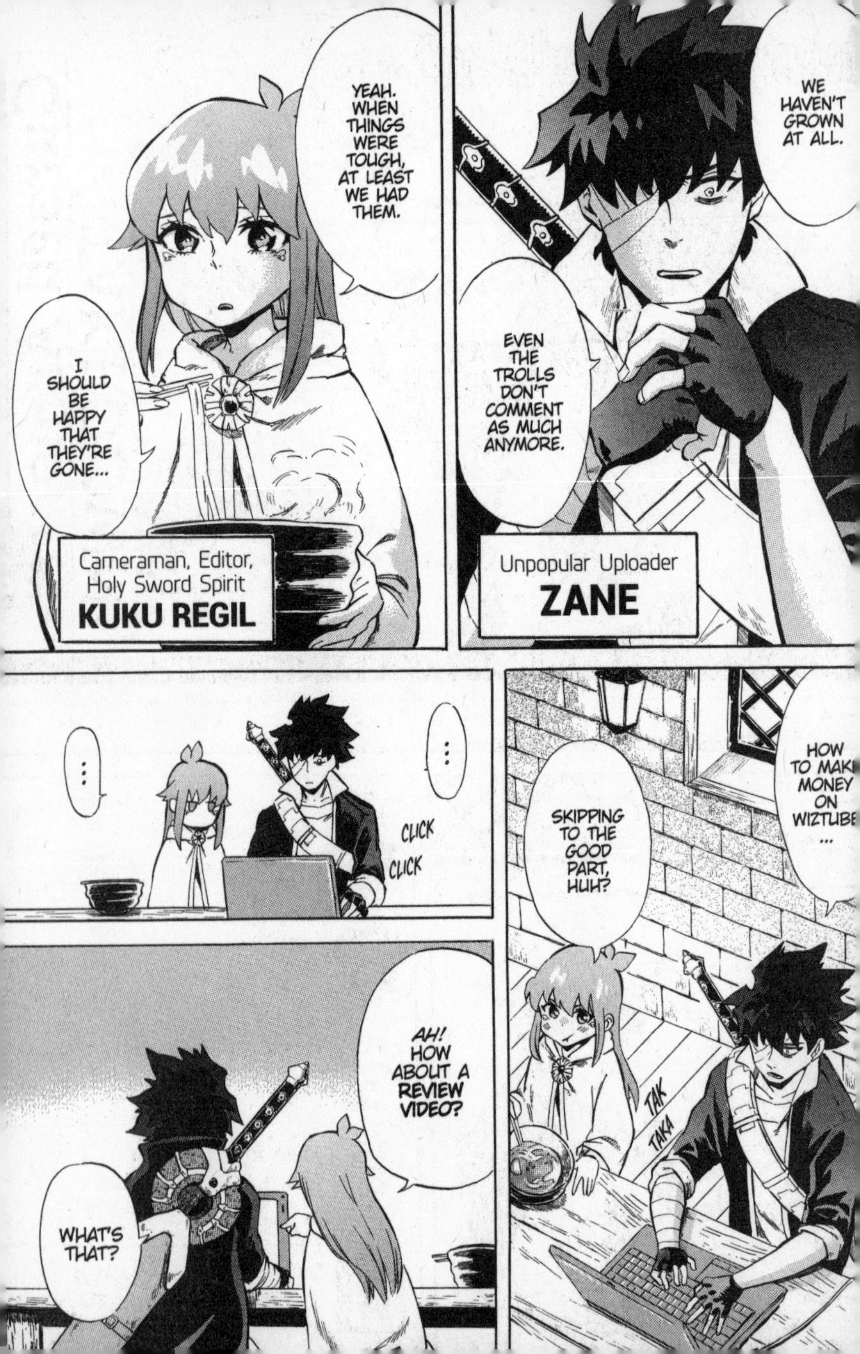
WE HAVEN'T GROWN AT ALL.
EVEN THE TROLLS DON'T COMMENT AS MUCH ANYMORE.
Unpopular Uploader
ZANE
YEAH. WHEN THINGS WERE TOUGH, AT LEAST WE HAD THEM.
I SHOULD BE HAPPY THAT THEY'RE GONE...
Cameraman, Editor, Holy Sword Spirit
KUKU REGIL
HOW TO MAK MONEY ON WIZTUB ...
SKIPPING TO THE GOOD PART, HUH?
TAK
TAKA
...
...
CLICK
CLICK
AH! HOW ABOUT A REVIEW VIDEO?
WHAT'S THAT?

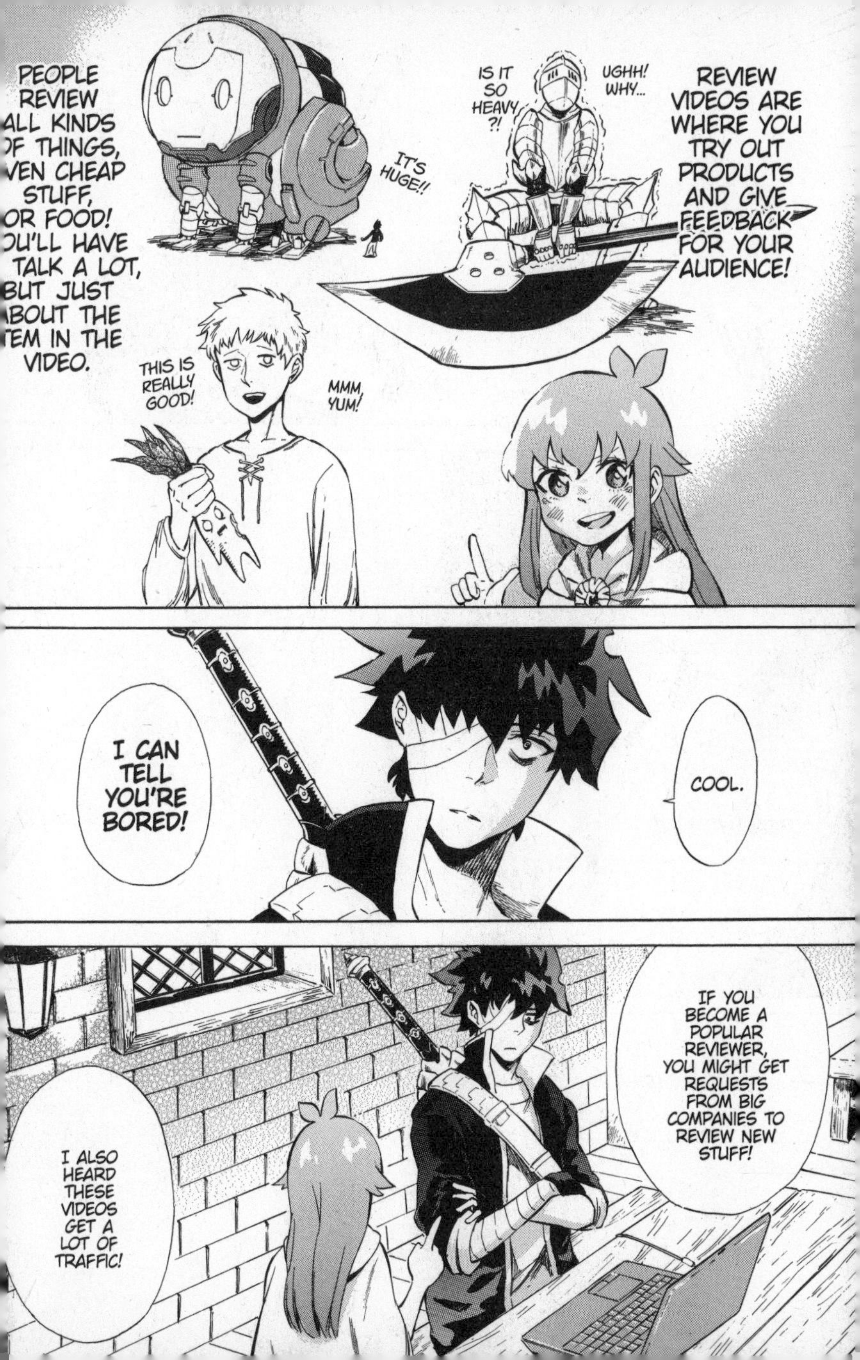
REVIEW VIDEOS ARE WHERE YOU TRY OUT PRODUCTS AND GIVE FEEDBACK FOR YOUR AUDIENCE!
UGHH! WHY...
IS IT SO HEAVY?!
IT'S HUGE!!
PEOPLE REVIEW ALL KINDS OF THINGS, VEN CHEAP STUFF, OR FOOD! OU'LL HAVE TALK A LOT, BUT JUST ABOUT THE TEM IN THE VIDEO.
MMM, YUM!
THIS IS REALLY GOOD!
COOL.
I CAN TELL YOU'RE BORED!
IF YOU BECOME A POPULAR REVIEWER, YOU MIGHT GET REQUESTS FROM BIG COMPANIES TO REVIEW NEW STUFF!
I ALSO HEARD THESE VIDEOS GET A LOT OF TRAFFIC!

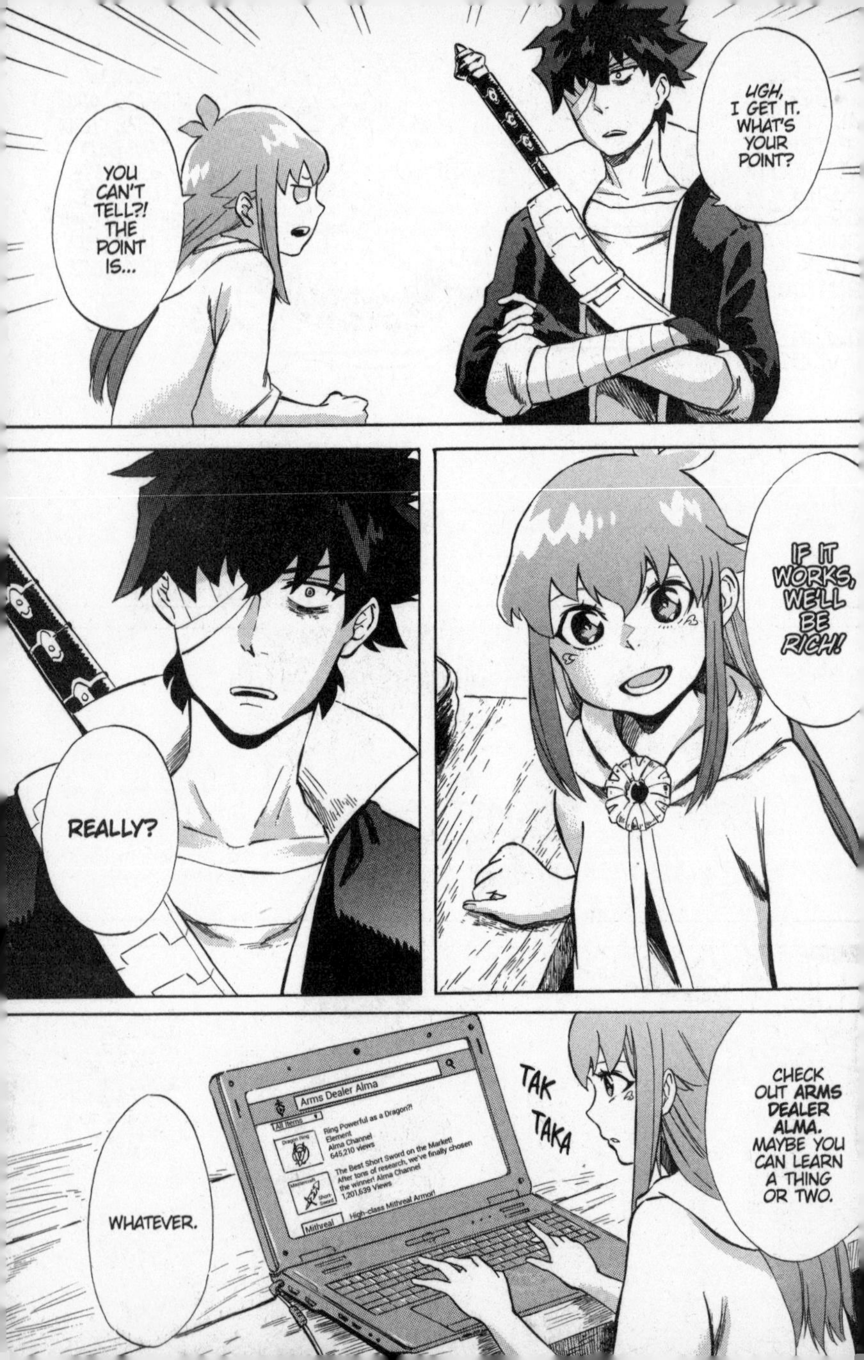
UGH, I GET IT. WHAT'S YOUR POINT?
YOU CAN'T TELL?! THE POINT IS...
IF IT WORKS, WE'LL BE RICH!
REALLY?
CHECK OUT ARMS DEALER ALMA. MAYBE YOU CAN LEARN A THING OR TWO.
TAK TAKA
Arms Dealer Alma
All Items
Dragon Ring
Ring Powerful as a Dragon?! Element Alma Channel 645,210 views
Mastercraft Short-Sword
The Best Short Sword on the Market! After tons of research, we've finally chosen the winner! Alma Channel 1,201,639 Views
Mithreal
High-class Mithreal Armor!
WHATEVER.

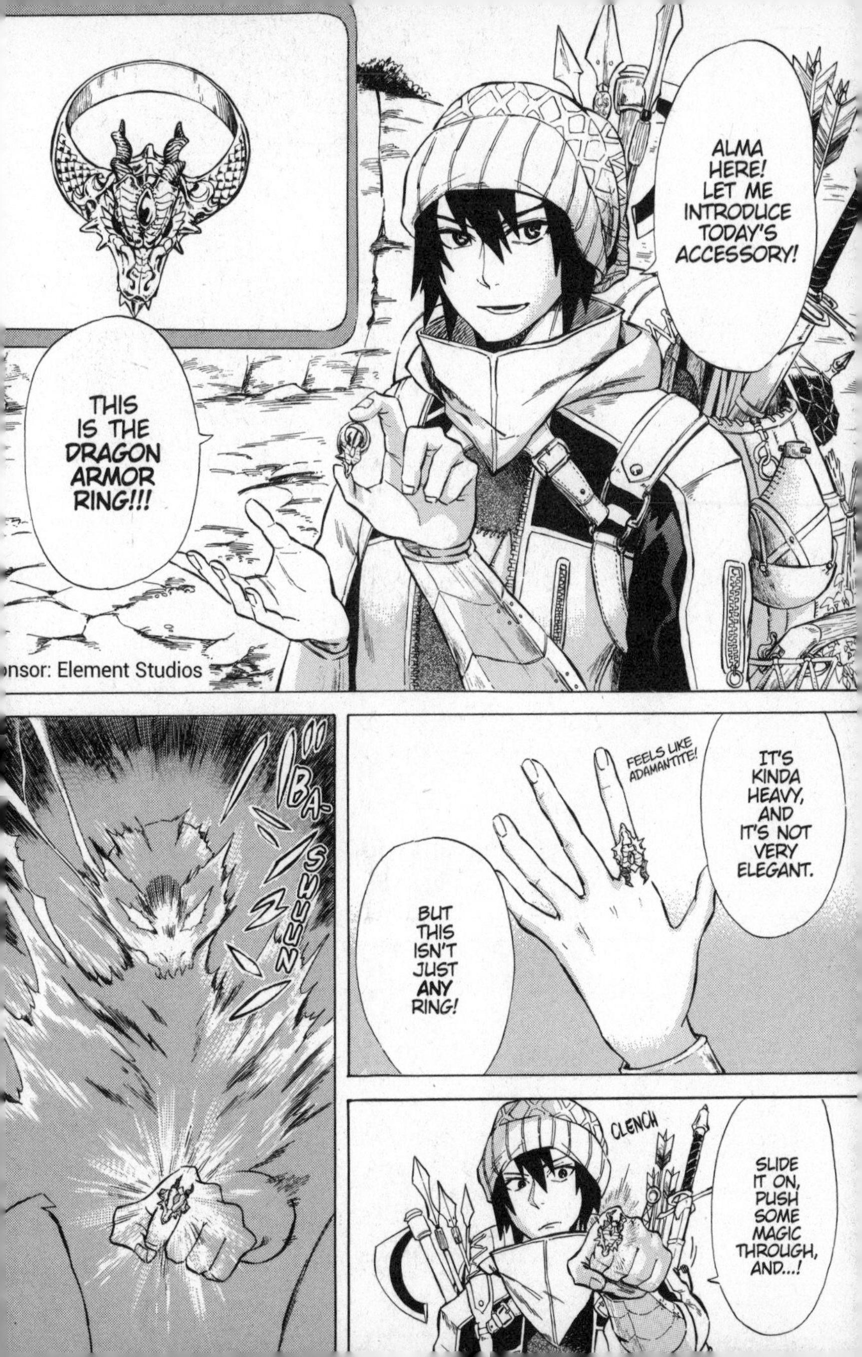
ALMA HERE! LET ME INTRODUCE TODAY'S ACCESSORY!
THIS IS THE DRAGON ARMOR RING!!!
onsor: Element Studios
IT'S KINDA HEAVY, AND IT'S NOT VERY ELEGANT.
FEELS LIKE ADAMANTITE!
BUT THIS ISN'T JUST ANY RING!
CLENCH
SLIDE IT ON, PUSH SOME MAGIC THROUGH, AND...!
BA-SHUUUN

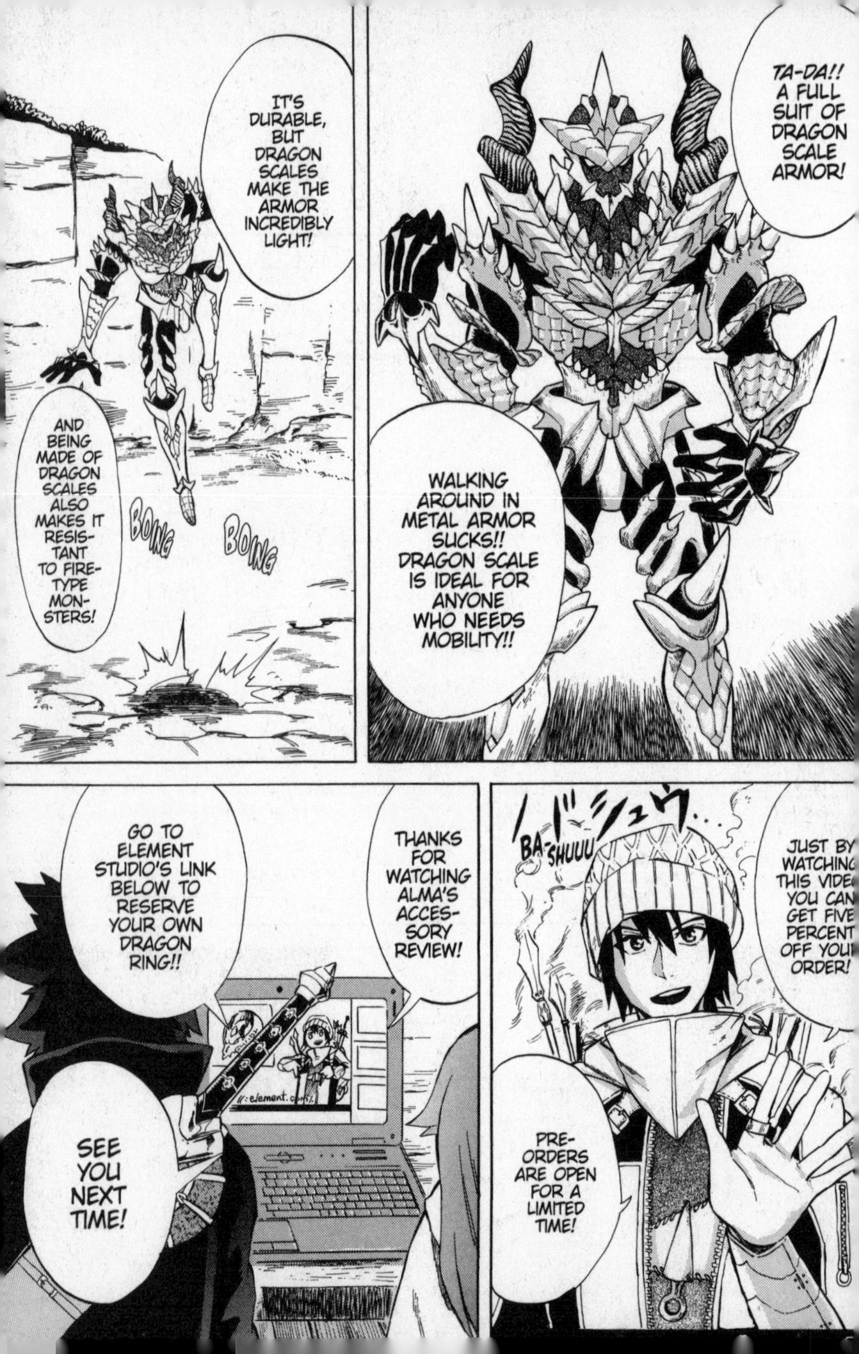

TA-DA!! A FULL SUIT OF DRAGON SCALE ARMOR!
WALKING AROUND IN METAL ARMOR SUCKS!! DRAGON SCALE IS IDEAL FOR ANYONE WHO NEEDS MOBILITY!!
IT'S DURABLE, BUT DRAGON SCALES MAKE THE ARMOR INCREDIBLY LIGHT!
AND BEING MADE OF DRAGON SCALES ALSO MAKES IT RESIS-TANT TO FIRE-TYPE MON-STERS!
BOING
BOING
BA-SHUUU
JUST BY WATCHING THIS VIDE YOU CAN GET FIVE PERCENT OFF YOU ORDER!
PRE-ORDERS ARE OPEN FOR A LIMITED TIME!
THANKS FOR WATCHING ALMA'S ACCES-SORY REVIEW!
GO TO ELEMENT STUDIO'S LINK BELOW TO RESERVE YOUR OWN DRAGON RING!!
SEE YOU NEXT TIME!

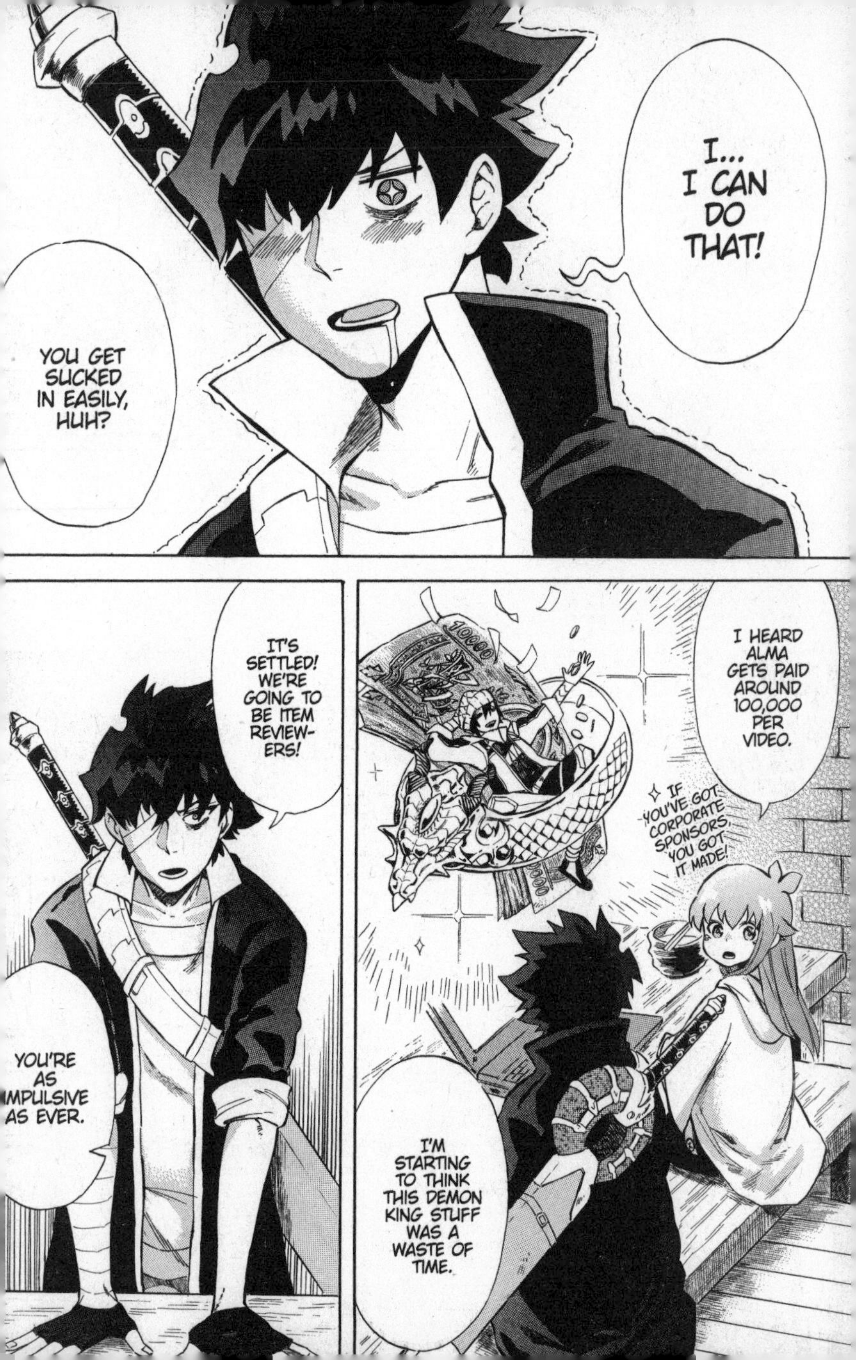
I... I CAN DO THAT!
YOU GET SUCKED IN EASILY, HUH?
I HEARD ALMA GETS PAID AROUND 100,000 PER VIDEO.
IF YOU'VE GOT CORPORATE SPONSORS, YOU GOT IT MADE!
I'M STARTING TO THINK THIS DEMON KING STUFF WAS A WASTE OF TIME.
IT'S SETTLED! WE'RE GOING TO BE ITEM REVIEWERS!
YOU'RE AS MPULSIVE AS EVER.

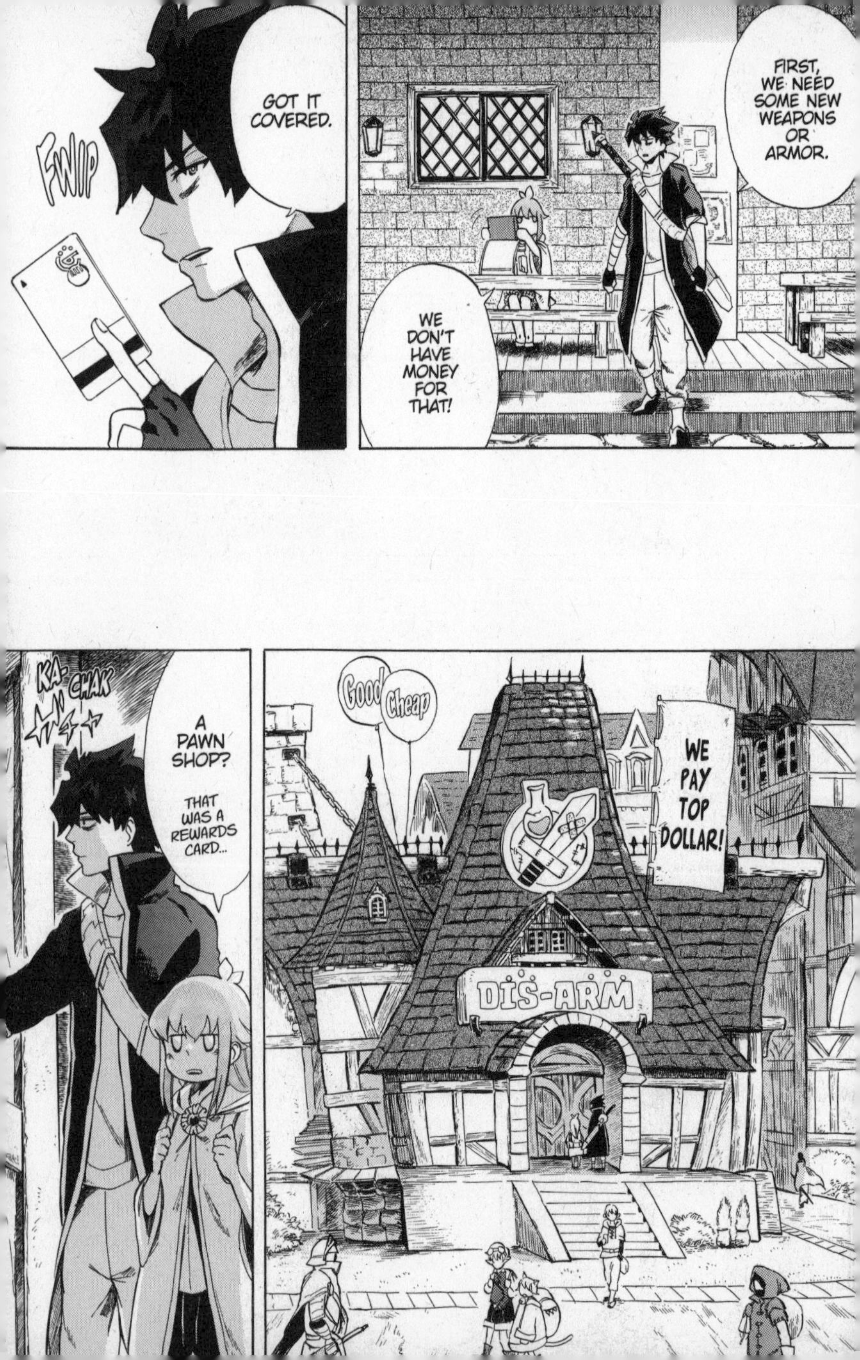
FIRST, WE NEED SOME NEW WEAPONS OR ARMOR.
WE DON'T HAVE MONEY FOR THAT!
FWIP
GOT IT COVERED.
Good
Cheap
WE PAY TOP DOLLAR!
DIS-ARM
KA-CHAK
A PAWN SHOP?
THAT WAS A REWARDS CARD...

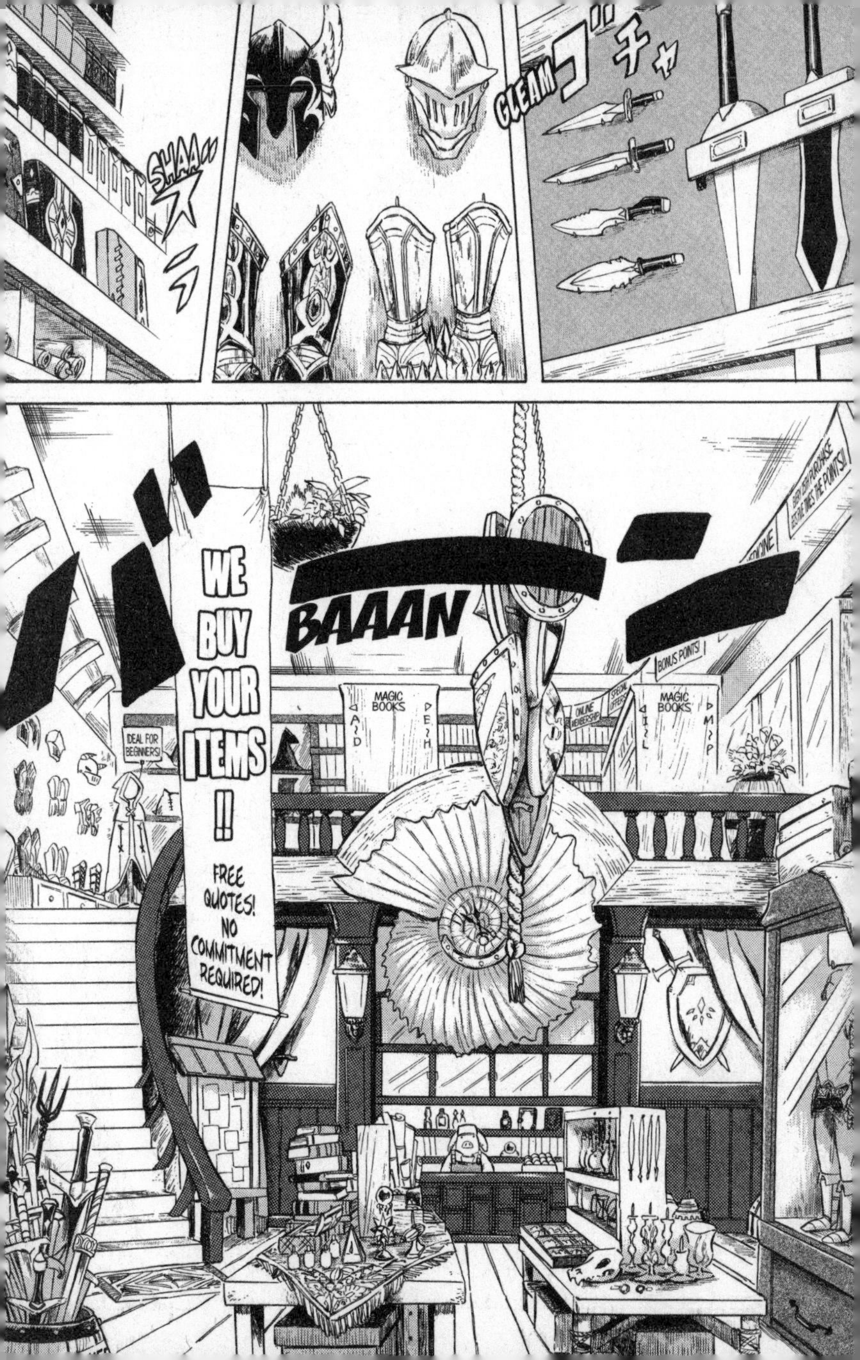
GLEAM
ゴチャ
SHAA
バーン
BAAAN
WE BUY YOUR ITEMS!!
FREE QUOTES! NO COMMITMENT REQUIRED!
EVERY 15TH PURCHASE GETS FIVE TIMES THE POINTS!!
BONUS POINTS!
SPECIAL OFFERS
ONLINE MEMBERSHIP
MAGIC BOOKS
A~D
E~H
MAGIC BOOKS
I~L
M~P
IDEAL FOR BEGINNERS!

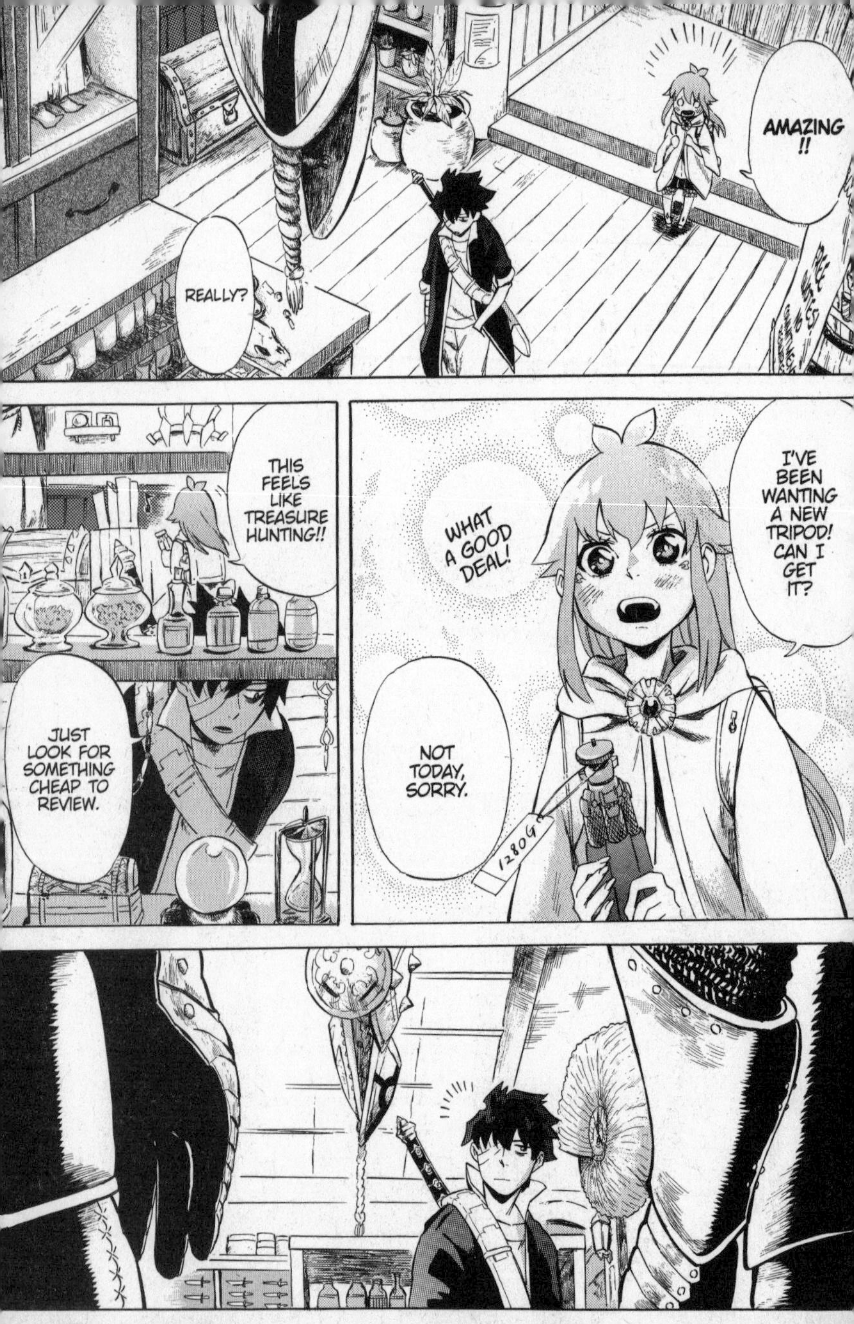
AMAZING !!
REALLY?
I'VE BEEN WANTING A NEW TRIPOD! CAN I GET IT?
WHAT A GOOD DEAL!
1280G
NOT TODAY, SORRY.
THIS FEELS LIKE TREASURE HUNTING!!
JUST LOOK FOR SOMETHING CHEAP TO REVIEW.

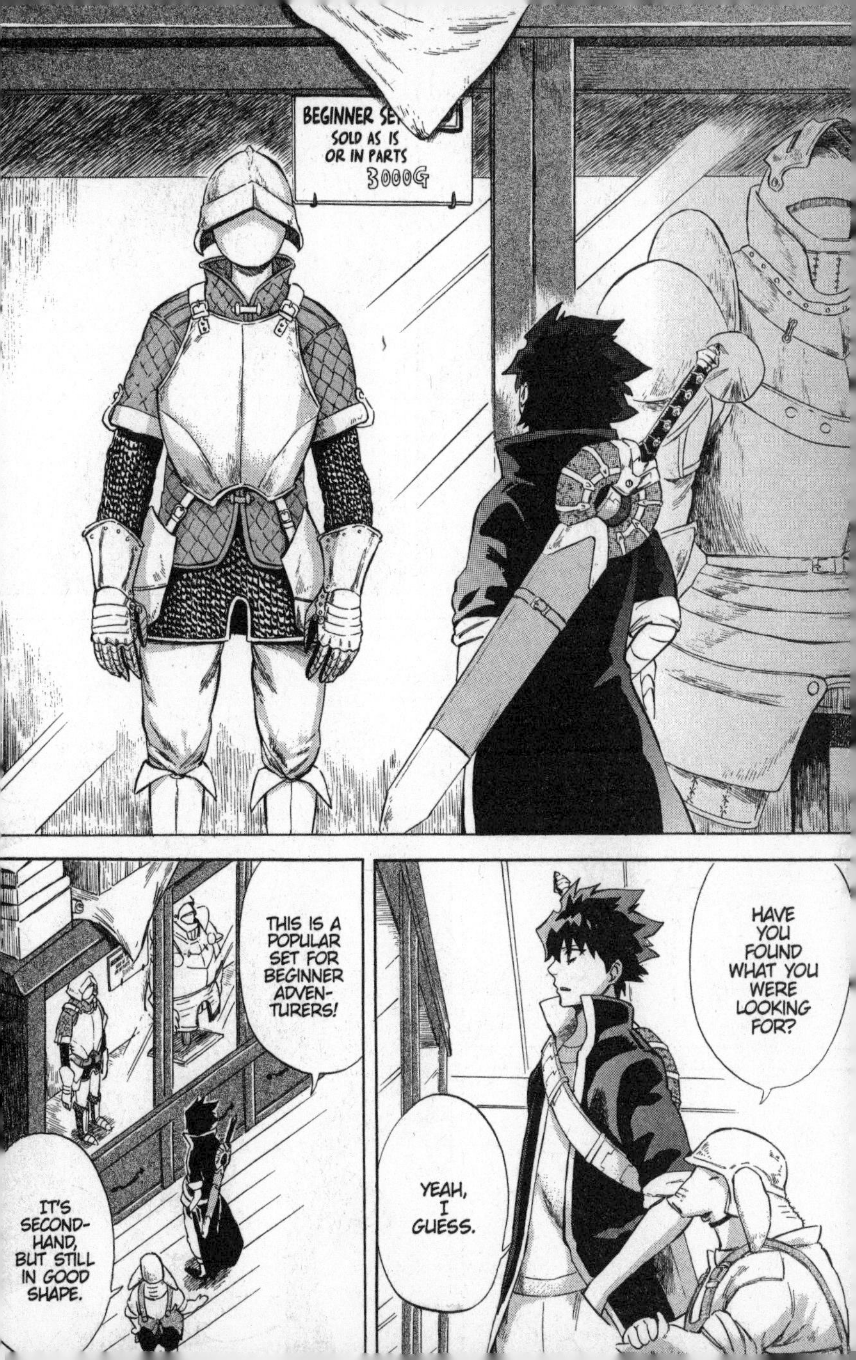
BEGINNER SE
SOLD AS IS OR IN PARTS
3000G
HAVE YOU FOUND WHAT YOU WERE LOOKING FOR?
YEAH, I GUESS.
THIS IS A POPULAR SET FOR BEGINNER ADVEN-TURERS!
IT'S SECOND-HAND, BUT STILL IN GOOD SHAPE.

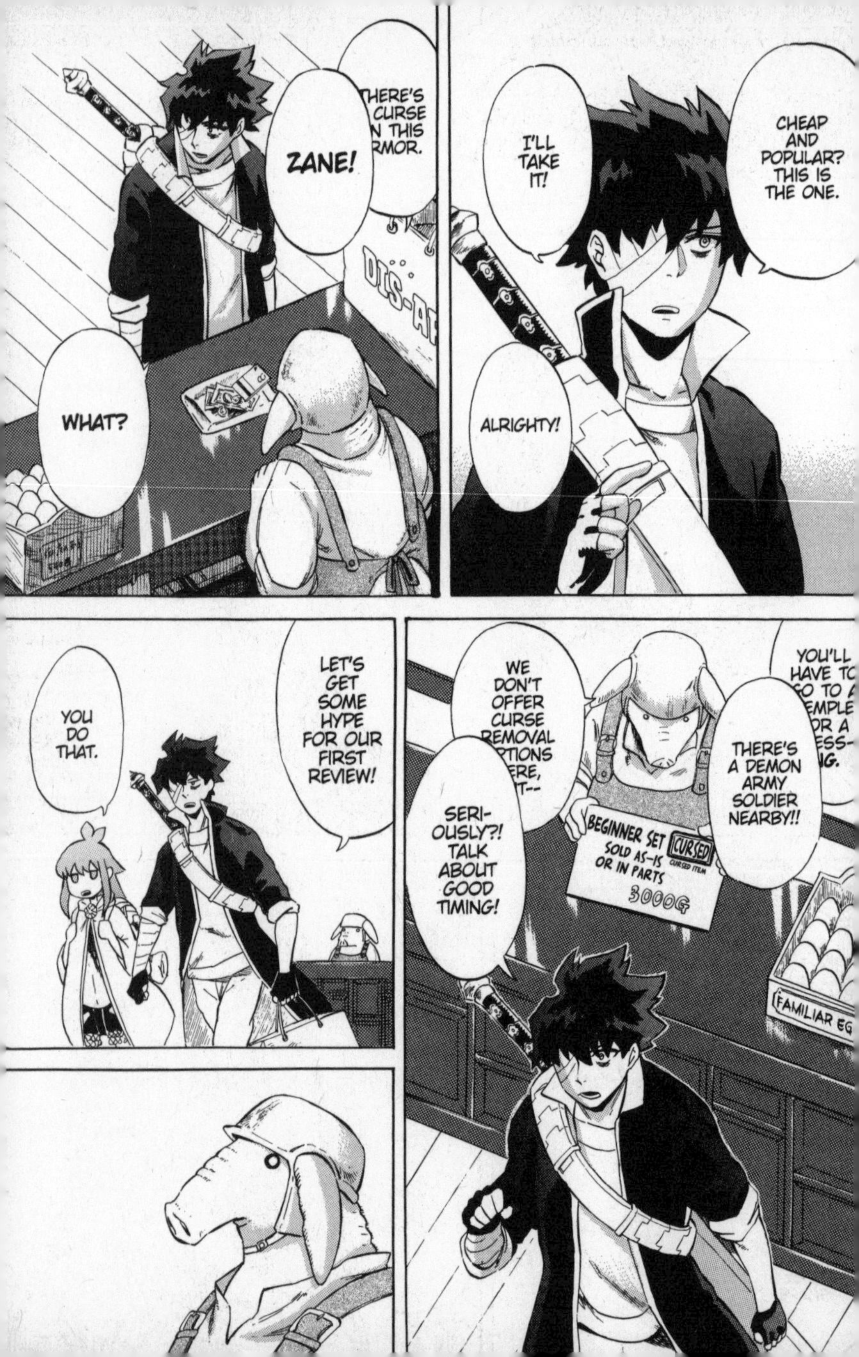
CHEAP AND POPULAR? THIS IS THE ONE.
I'LL TAKE IT!
ALRIGHTY!
THERE'S CURSE N THIS RMOR.
ZANE!
WHAT?
YOU'LL HAVE TO GO TO A EMPLE OR A ESS- NG.
WE DON'T OFFER CURSE REMOVAL PTIONS ERE, T--
THERE'S A DEMON ARMY SOLDIER NEARBY!!
SERI- OUSLY?! TALK ABOUT GOOD TIMING!
BEGINNER SET CURSED CURSED ITEM SOLD AS-IS OR IN PARTS 3000G
FAMILIAR EG
LET'S GET SOME HYPE FOR OUR FIRST REVIEW!
YOU DO THAT.

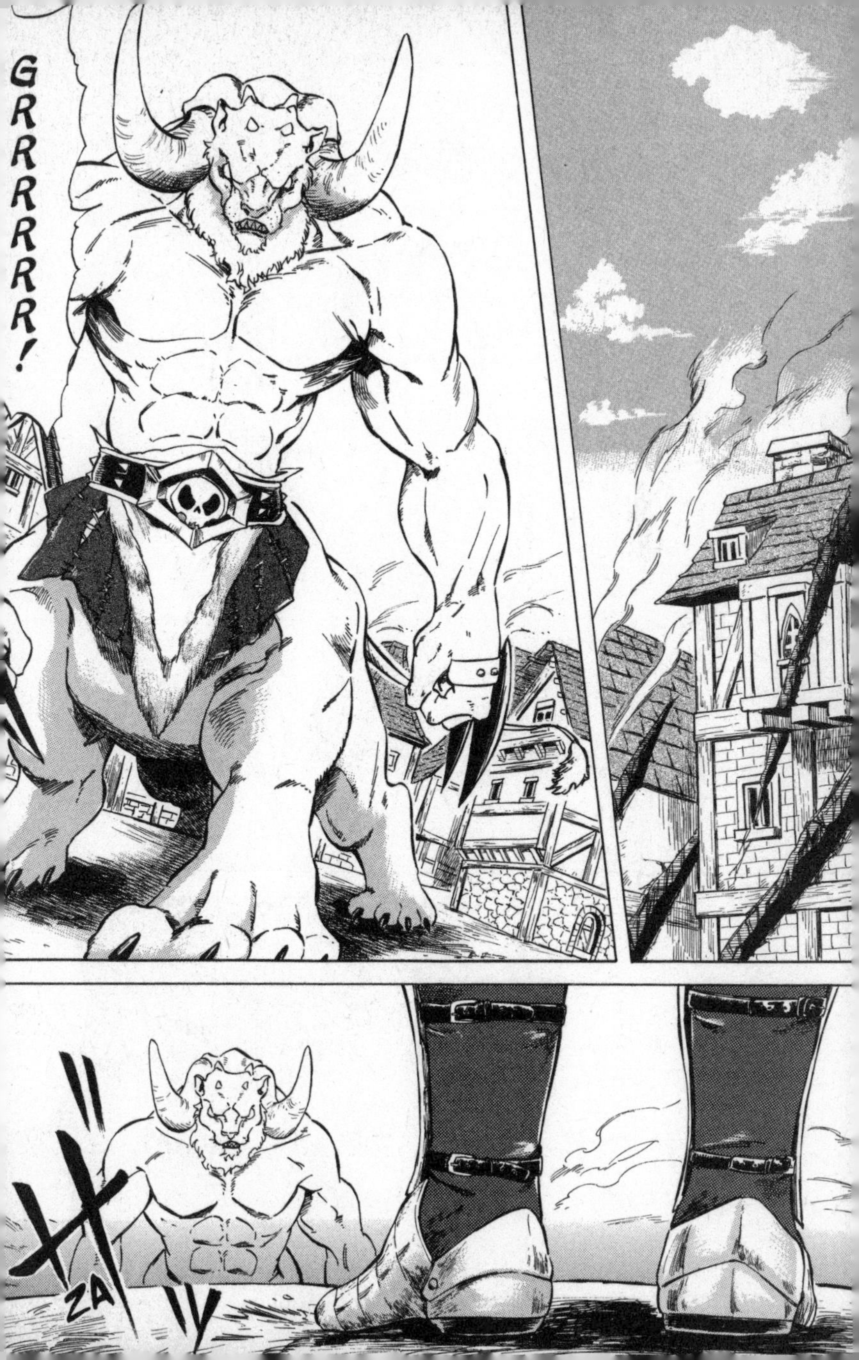
GRRRRRR!
ZA

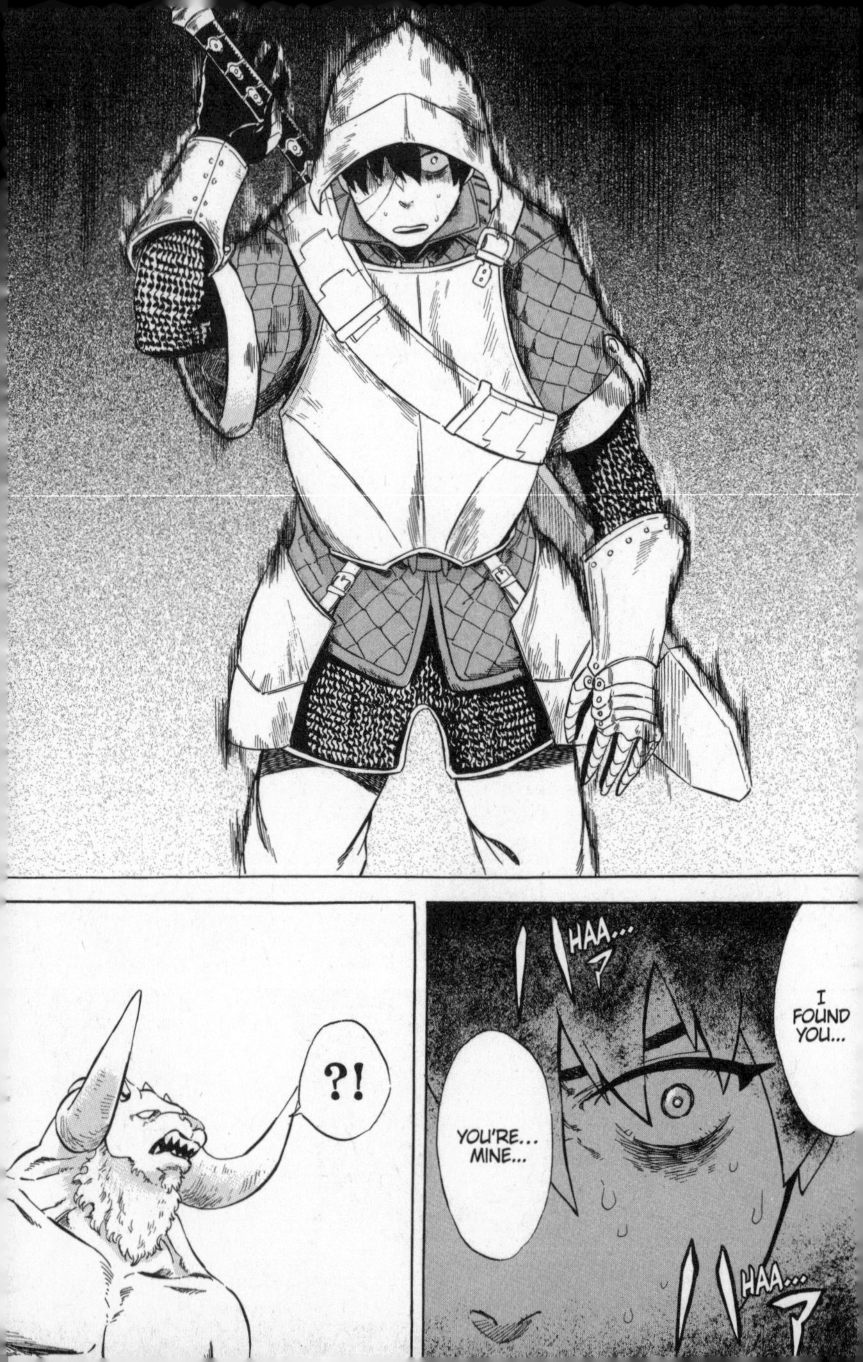

HAA... ア
I FOUND YOU...
YOU'RE... MINE...
HAA... ア
?!

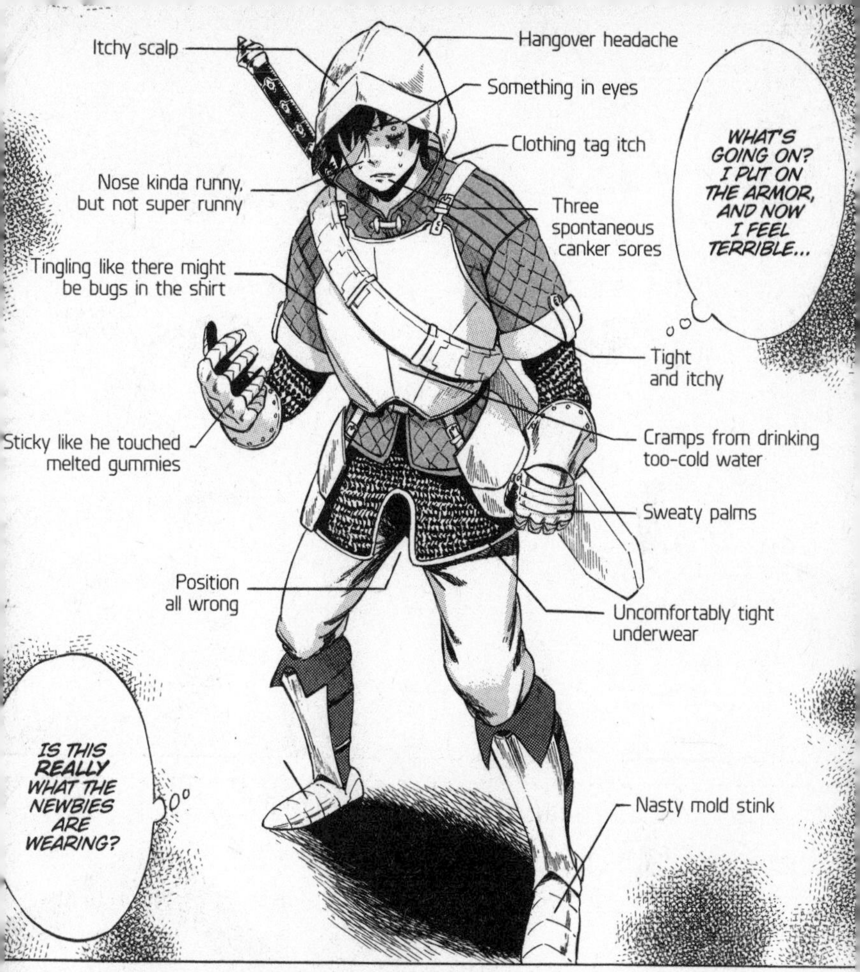
WHAT'S GOING ON? I PUT ON THE ARMOR, AND NOW I FEEL TERRIBLE...
Hangover headache
Itchy scalp
Something in eyes
Clothing tag itch
Nose kinda runny, but not super runny
Three spontaneous canker sores
Tingling like there might be bugs in the shirt
Tight and itchy
Sticky like he touched melted gummies
Cramps from drinking too-cold water
Sweaty palms
Position all wrong
Uncomfortably tight underwear
Nasty mold stink
IS THIS REALLY WHAT THE NEWBIES ARE WEARING?

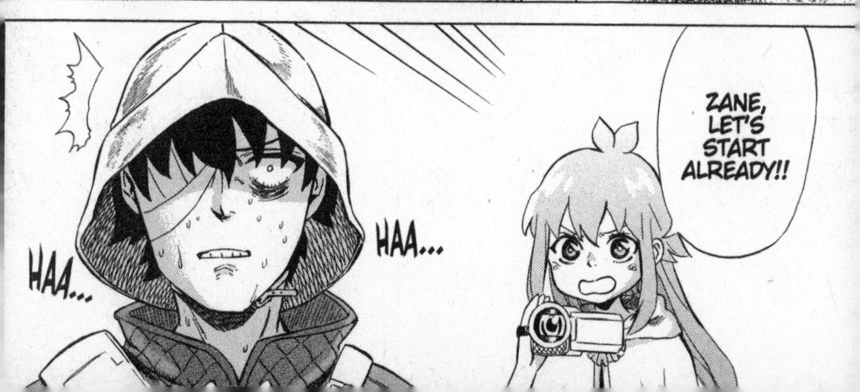
ZANE, LET'S START ALREADY!!
HAA...
HAA...

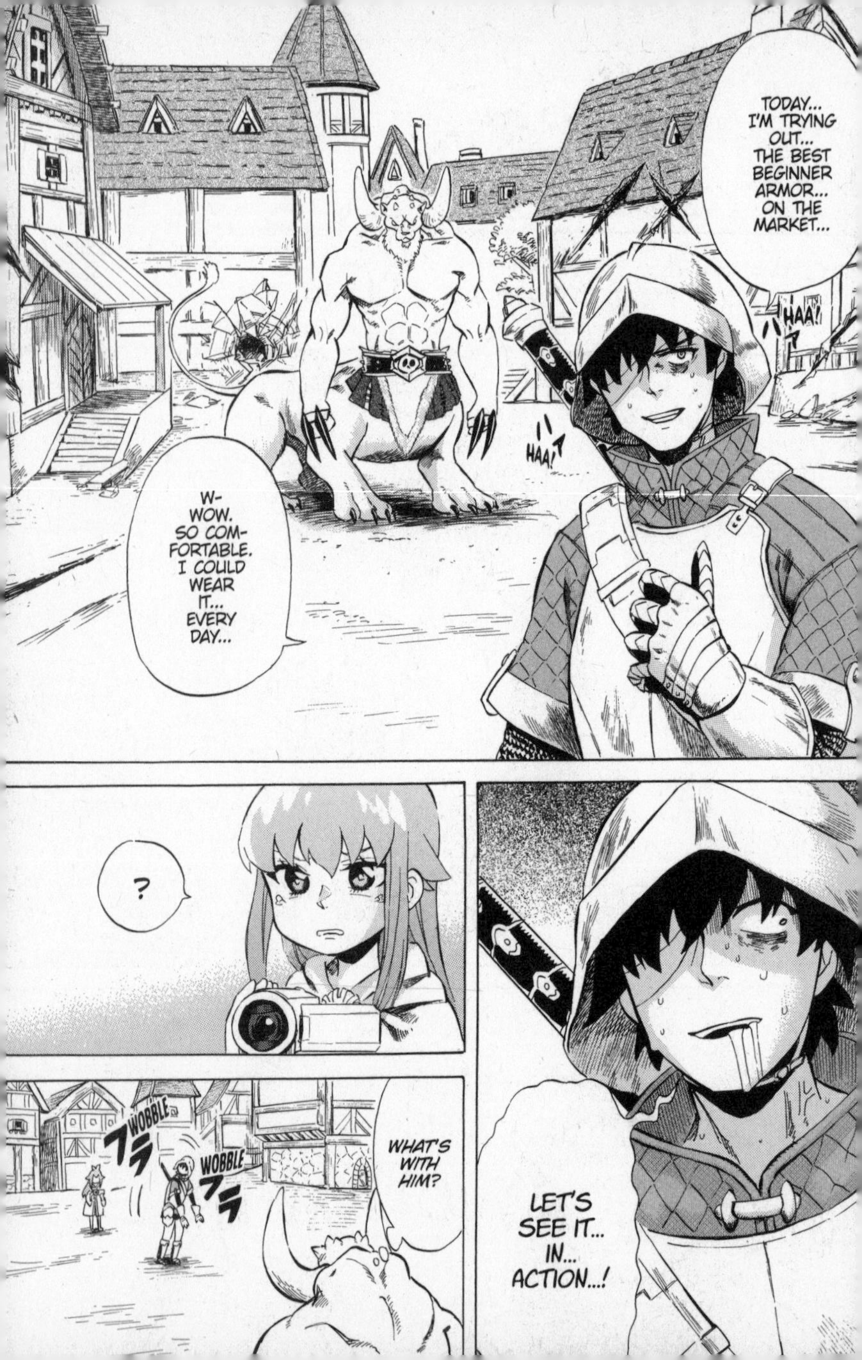
TODAY... I'M TRYING OUT... THE BEST BEGINNER ARMOR... ON THE MARKET...
HAA!
HAA!
W-WOW. SO COM-FORTABLE. I COULD WEAR IT... EVERY DAY...
LET'S SEE IT... IN... ACTION...!
?
WHAT'S WITH HIM?
WOBBLE
WOBBLE

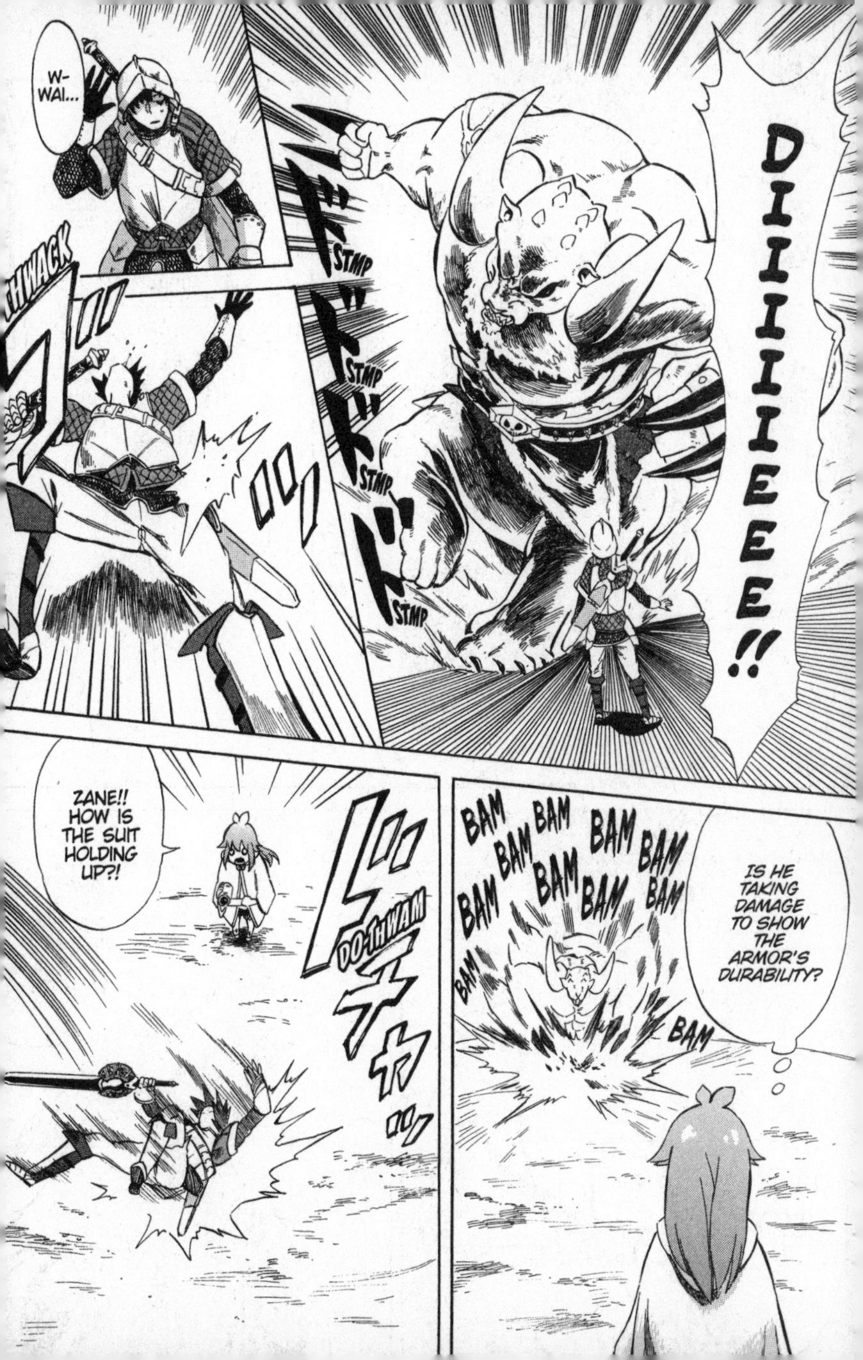

DIIIIEEEE!!
STMP
STMP
STMP
STMP
W-WAI...
THWACK
IS HE TAKING DAMAGE TO SHOW THE ARMOR'S DURABILITY?
BAM BAM BAM BAM BAM BAM BAM BAM BAM BAM BAM BAM
BAM
ZANE!! HOW IS THE SUIT HOLDING UP?!
DO-THWAM

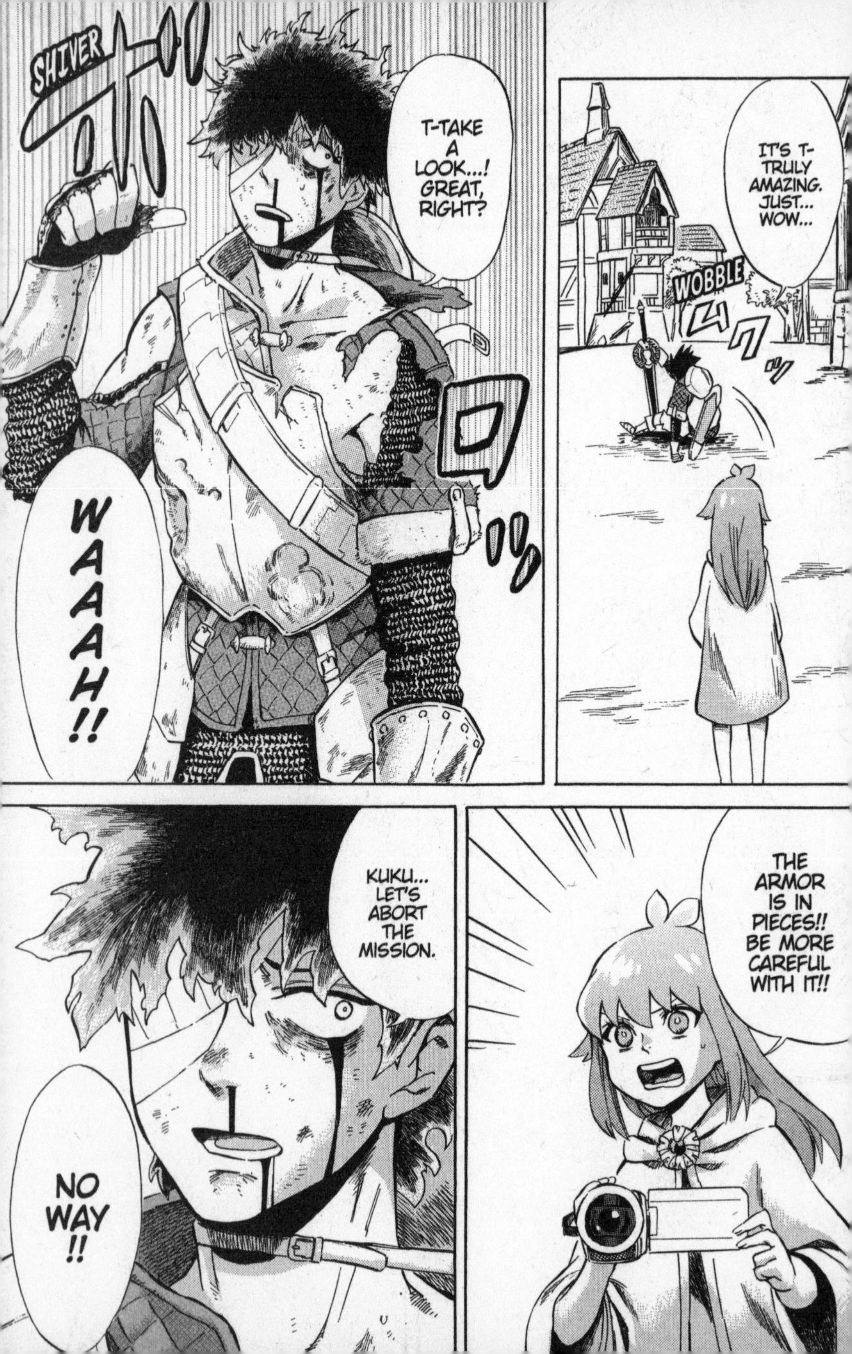
IT'S T-TRULY AMAZING. JUST... WOW...
WOBBLE
T-TAKE A LOOK...! GREAT, RIGHT?
SHIVER
WAAAAH!!
THE ARMOR IS IN PIECES!! BE MORE CAREFUL WITH IT!!
KUKU... LET'S ABORT THE MISSION.
NO WAY!!

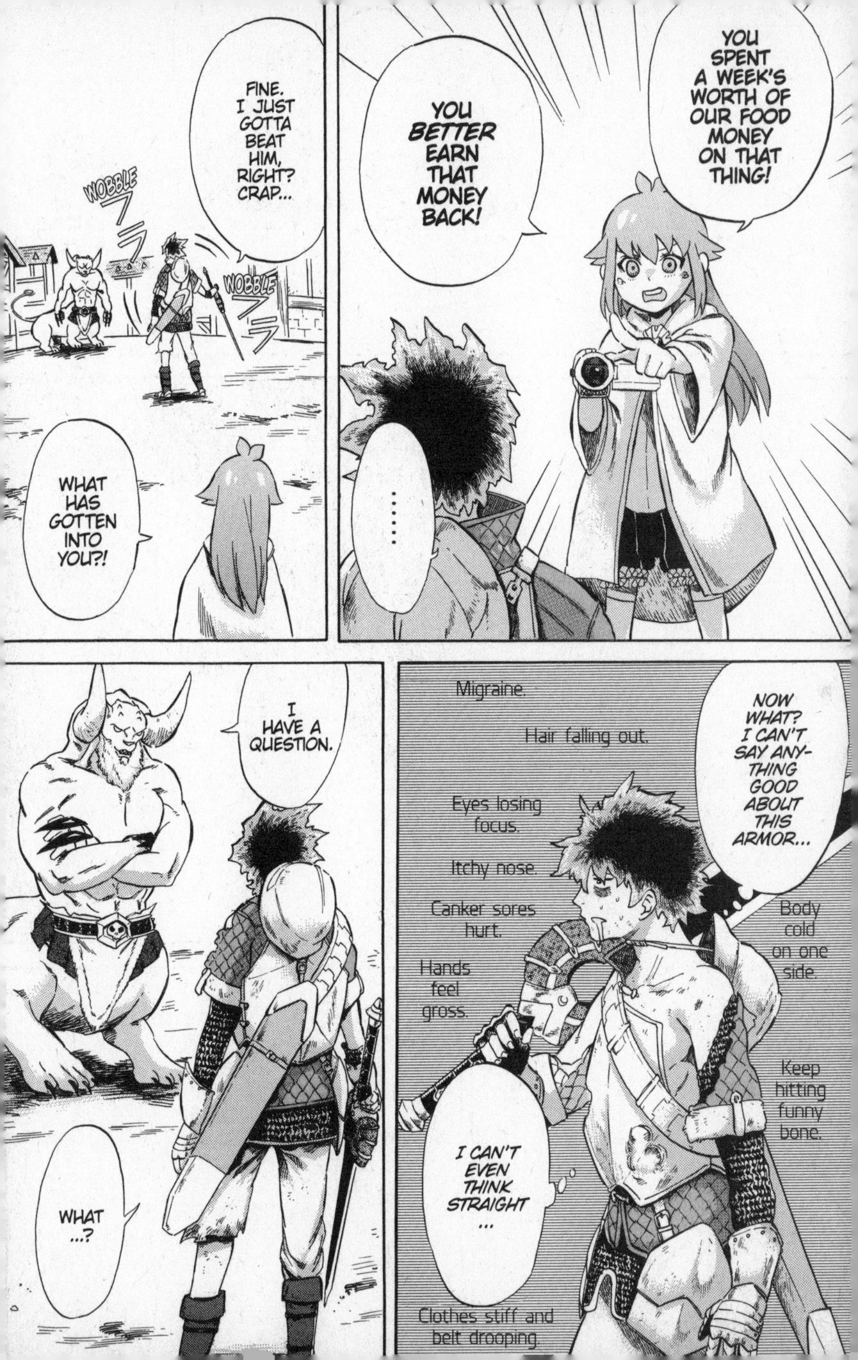
YOU SPENT A WEEK'S WORTH OF OUR FOOD MONEY ON THAT THING!
YOU BETTER EARN THAT MONEY BACK!
......
FINE. I JUST GOTTA BEAT HIM, RIGHT? CRAP...
WOBBLE
WOBBLE
WHAT HAS GOTTEN INTO YOU?!
NOW WHAT? I CAN'T SAY ANYTHING GOOD ABOUT THIS ARMOR...
Migraine.
Hair falling out.
Eyes losing focus.
Itchy nose.
Body cold on one side.
Canker sores hurt.
Hands feel gross.
Keep hitting funny bone.
I CAN'T EVEN THINK STRAIGHT...
Clothes stiff and belt drooping.
I HAVE A QUESTION.
WHAT...?

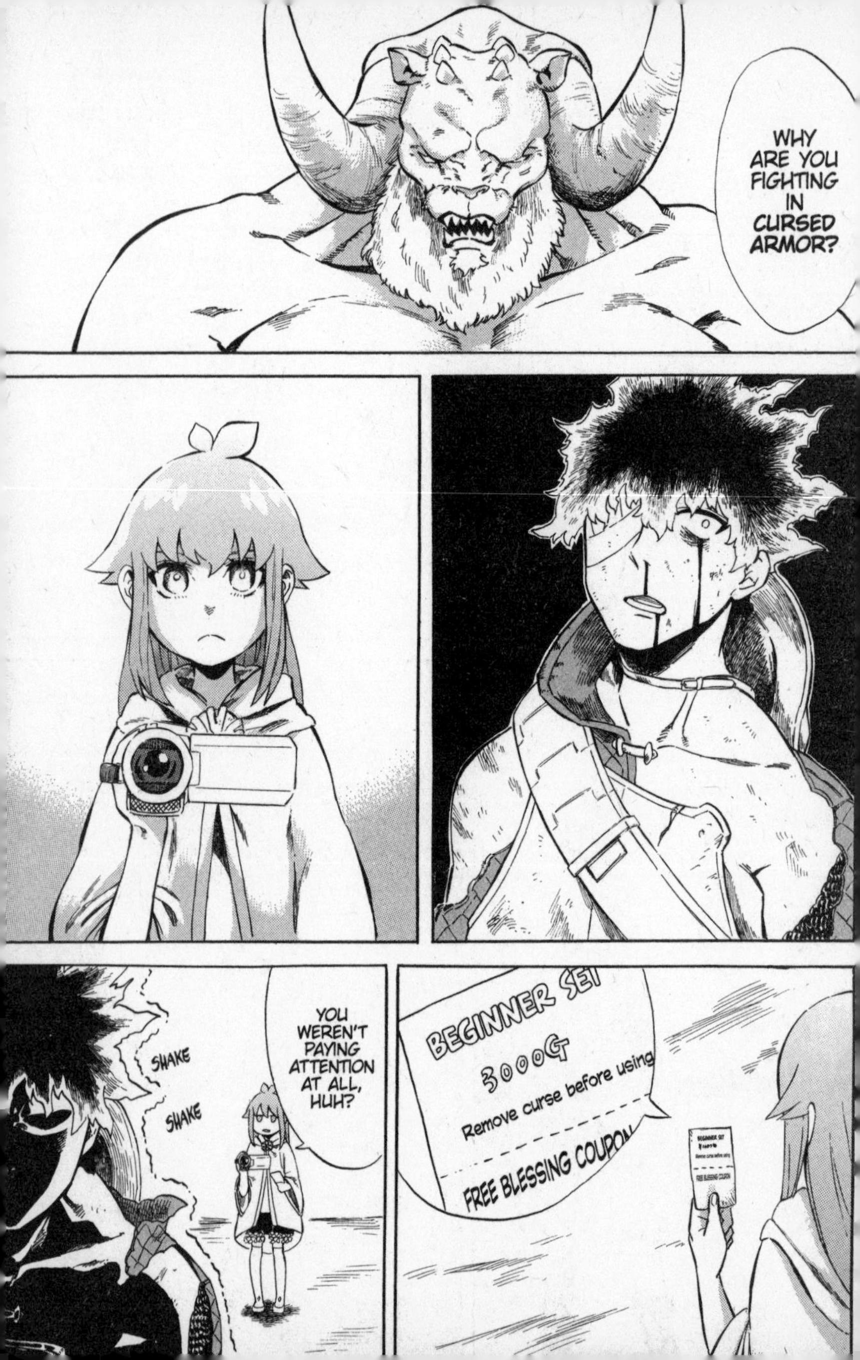
WHY ARE YOU FIGHTING IN CURSED ARMOR?
BEGINNER SET
3000G
Remove curse before using
FREE BLESSING COUPON
YOU WEREN'T PAYING ATTENTION AT ALL, HUH?
SHAKE
SHAKE

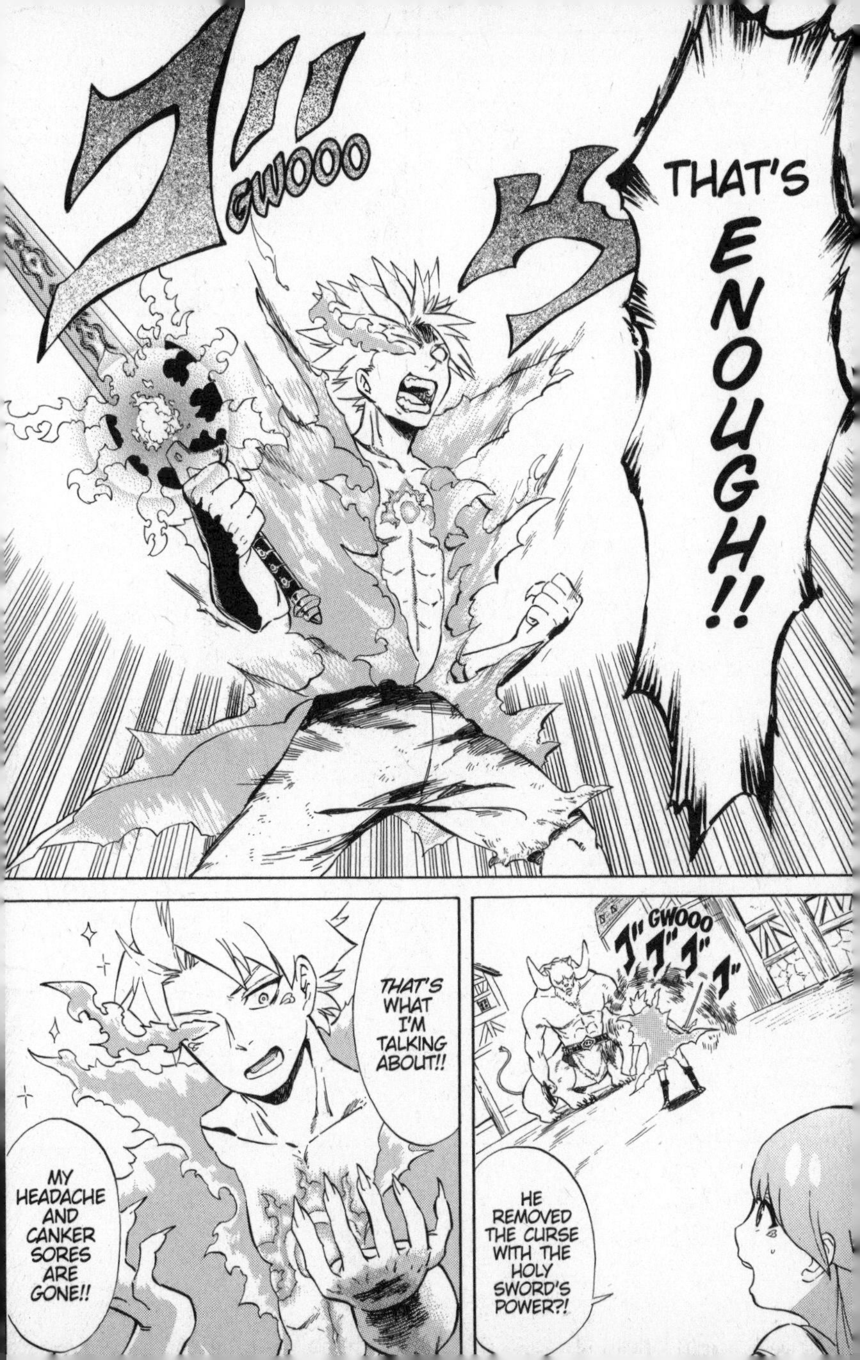
THAT'S ENOUGH!!
GWOOO
GWOOO
HE REMOVED THE CURSE WITH THE HOLY SWORD'S POWER?!
THAT'S WHAT I'M TALKING ABOUT!!
MY HEADACHE AND CANKER SORES ARE GONE!!

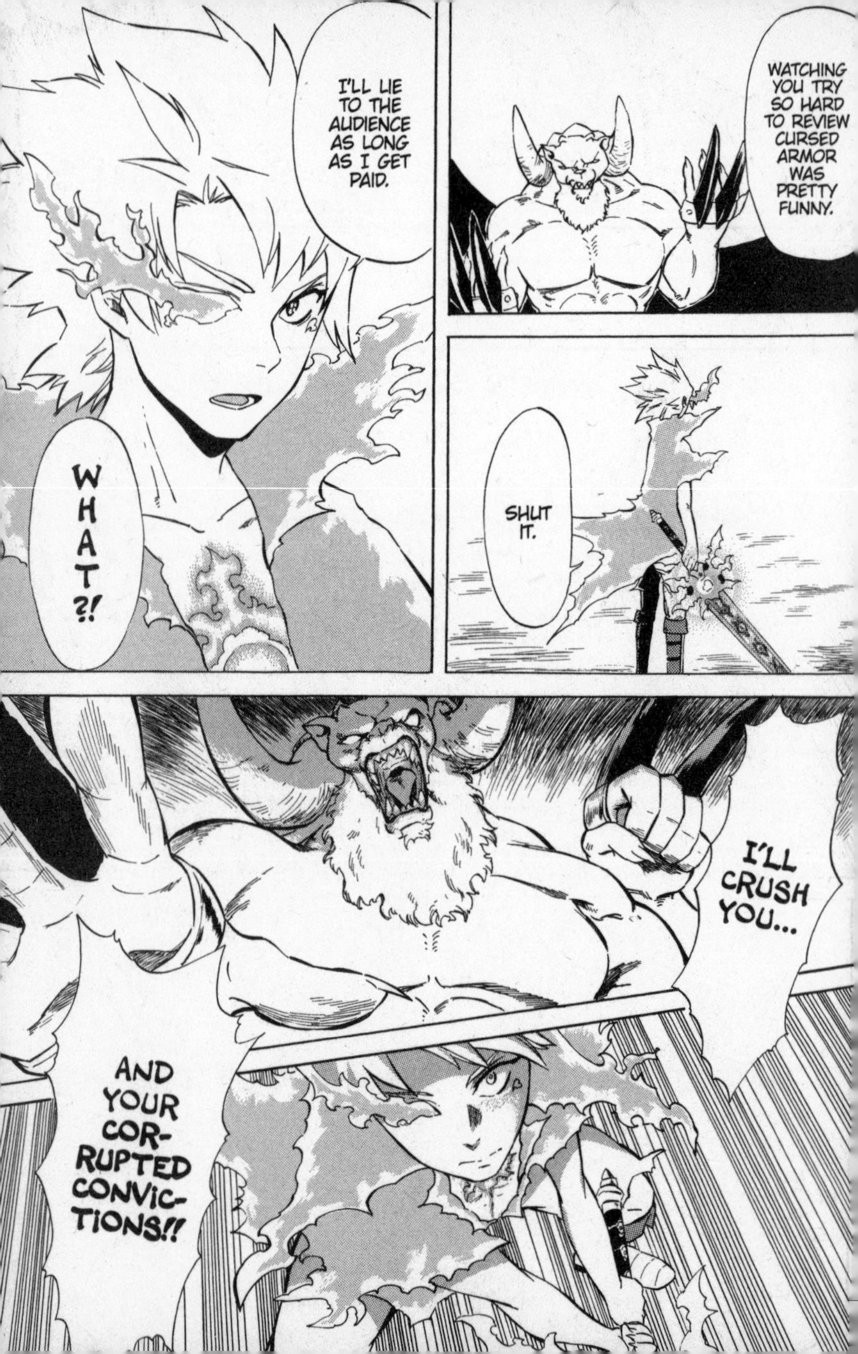
WATCHING YOU TRY SO HARD TO REVIEW CURSED ARMOR WAS PRETTY FUNNY.
SHUT IT.
I'LL LIE TO THE AUDIENCE AS LONG AS I GET PAID.
WHAT?!
I'LL CRUSH YOU...
AND YOUR COR-RUPTED CONVIC-TIONS!!

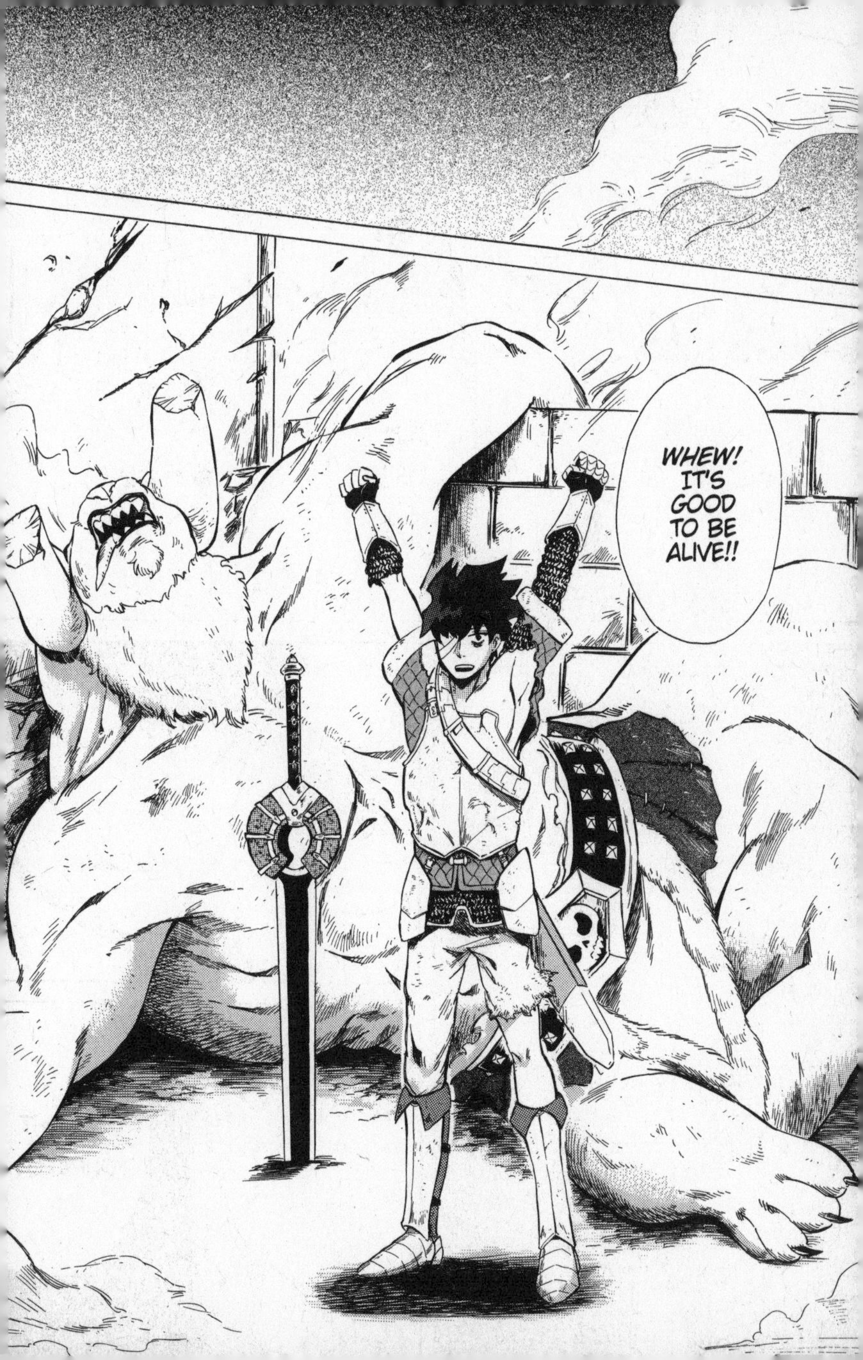
WHEW! IT'S GOOD TO BE ALIVE!!

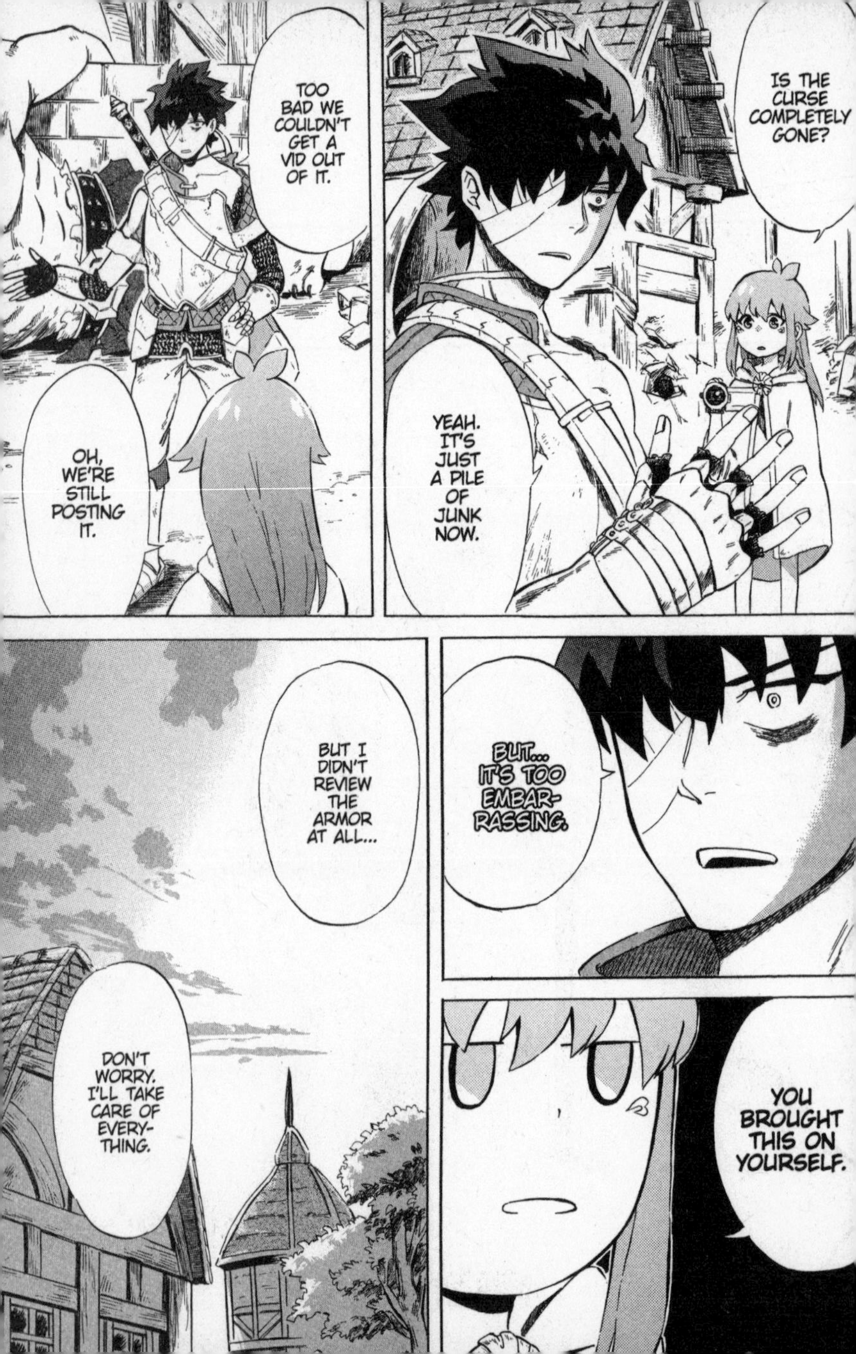
IS THE CURSE COMPLETELY GONE?
YEAH. IT'S JUST A PILE OF JUNK NOW.
TOO BAD WE COULDN'T GET A VID OUT OF IT.
OH, WE'RE STILL POSTING IT.
BUT... IT'S TOO EMBARRASSING.
YOU BROUGHT THIS ON YOURSELF.
BUT I DIDN'T REVIEW THE ARMOR AT ALL...
DON'T WORRY. I'LL TAKE CARE OF EVERYTHING.

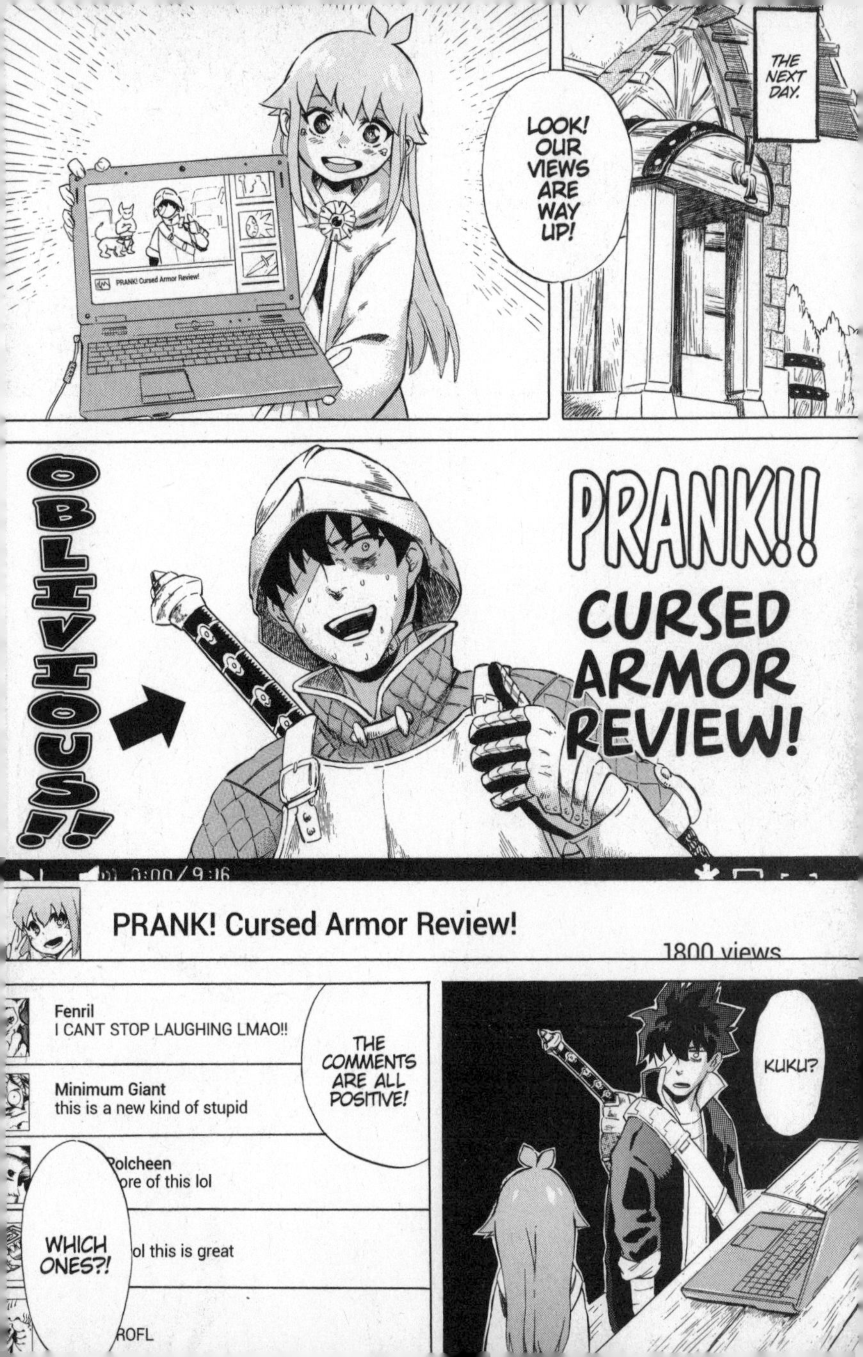
THE NEXT DAY.
LOOK! OUR VIEWS ARE WAY UP!
PRANK! Cursed Armor Review!
PRANK!! CURSED ARMOR REVIEW!
OBLIVIOUS!!
0:00 / 9:16
PRANK! Cursed Armor Review!
1800 views
KUKU?
Fenril
I CANT STOP LAUGHING LMAO!!
Minimum Giant
this is a new kind of stupid
Polcheen
ore of this lol
ol this is great
ROFL
THE COMMENTS ARE ALL POSITIVE!
WHICH ONES?!

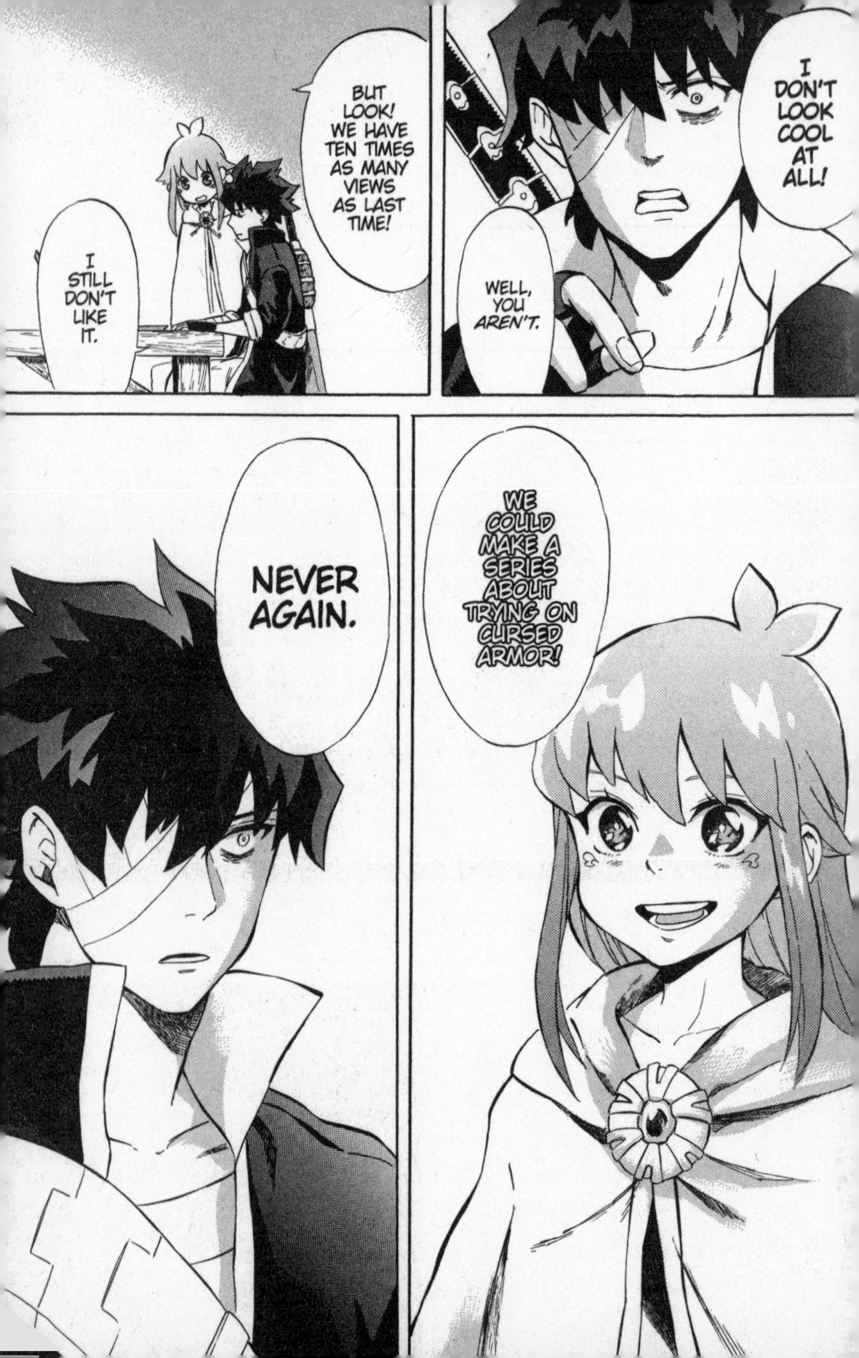
I DON'T LOOK COOL AT ALL!
WELL, YOU AREN'T.
BUT LOOK! WE HAVE TEN TIMES AS MANY VIEWS AS LAST TIME!
I STILL DON'T LIKE IT.
WE COULD MAKE A SERIES ABOUT TRYING ON CURSED ARMOR!
NEVER AGAIN.

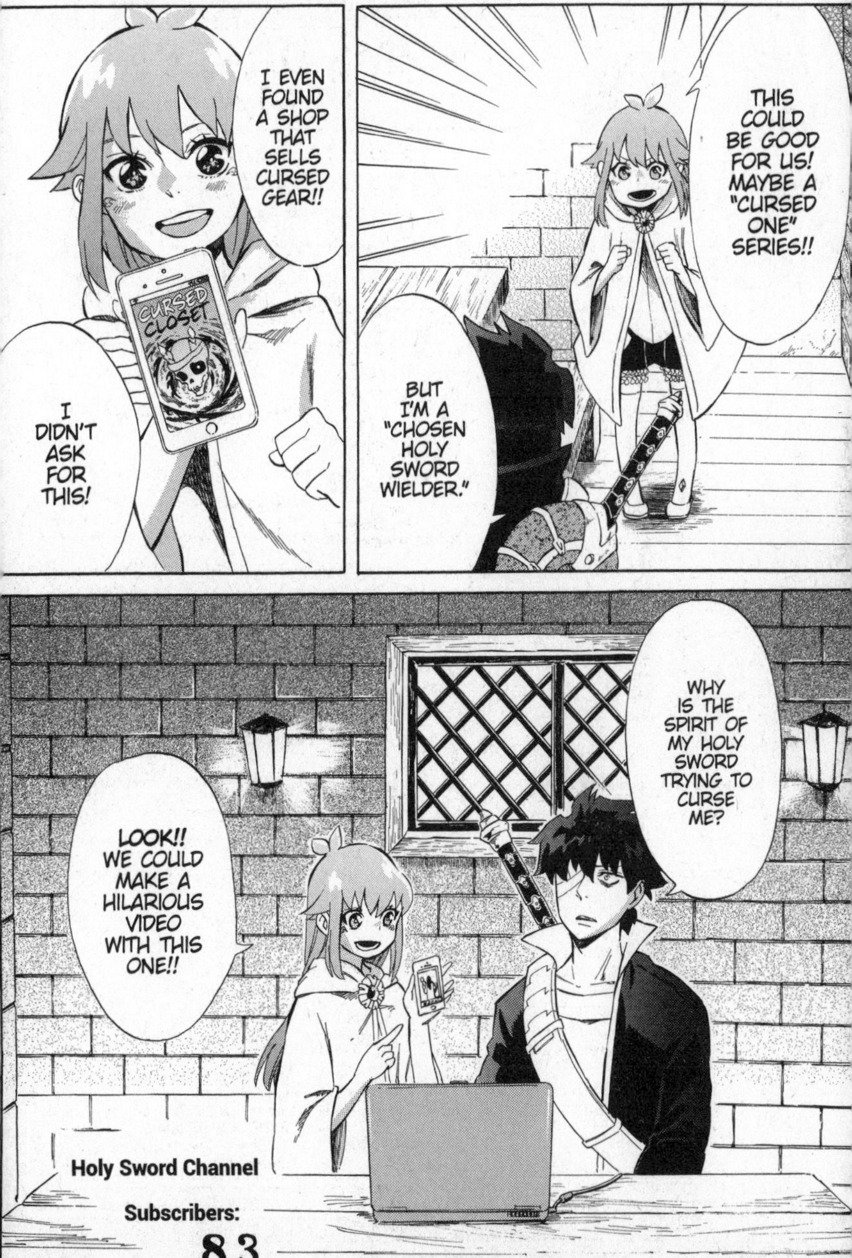
THIS COULD BE GOOD FOR US! MAYBE A "CURSED ONE" SERIES!!
BUT I'M A "CHOSEN HOLY SWORD WIELDER."
I EVEN FOUND A SHOP THAT SELLS CURSED GEAR!!
CURSED CLOSET
I DIDN'T ASK FOR THIS!
WHY IS THE SPIRIT OF MY HOLY SWORD TRYING TO CURSE ME?
LOOK!! WE COULD MAKE A HILARIOUS VIDEO WITH THIS ONE!!
Holy Sword Channel
Subscribers:

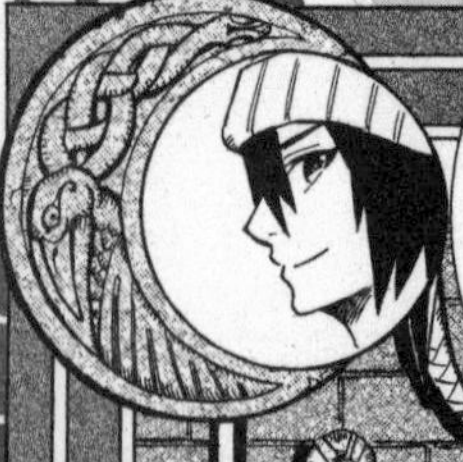

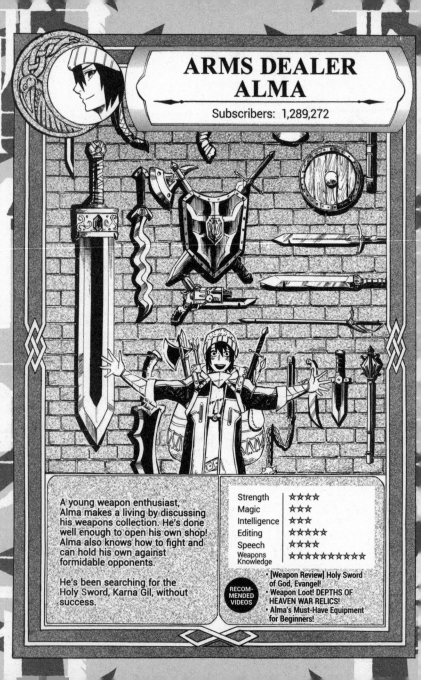

ARMS DEALER ALMA

Subscribers: 1,289,272

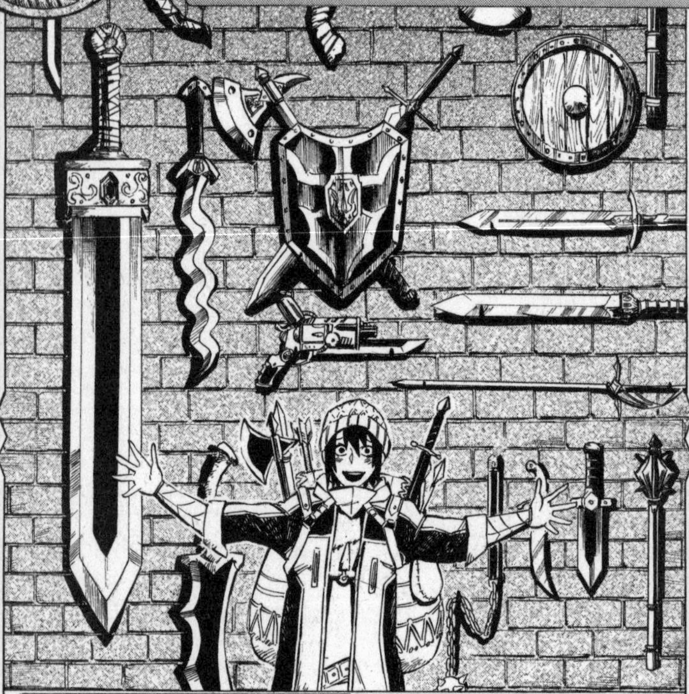

A young weapon enthusiast, Alma makes a living by discussing his weapons collection. He's done well enough to open his own shop! Alma also knows how to fight and can hold his own against formidable opponents.

He's been searching for the Holy Sword, Karna Gil, without success.

Strength	☆☆☆☆
Magic	☆☆☆
Intelligence	☆☆☆
Editing	☆☆☆☆☆
Speech	☆☆☆☆
Weapons Knowledge	☆☆☆☆☆☆☆☆☆☆

RECOMMENDED VIDEOS

- **[Weapon Review] Holy Sword of God, Evangel!**
- **Weapon Loot! DEPTHS OF HEAVEN WAR RELICS!**
- **Alma's Must-Have Equipment for Beginners!**

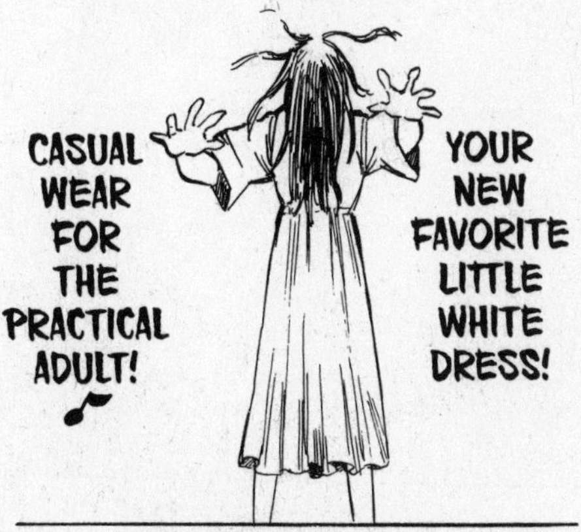
CASUAL WEAR FOR THE PRACTICAL ADULT! ♪
YOUR NEW FAVORITE LITTLE WHITE DRESS!

CURSED ONE-PIECE DRESS IN SOFT COTTON!
M/L/XL AVAILABLE

PRICE 2,990 G (3,229 G WITH TAX)

★★★☆☆ (21 REVIEWS)

※ CURSED ITEMS CANNOT BE RETURNED OR EXCHANGED.

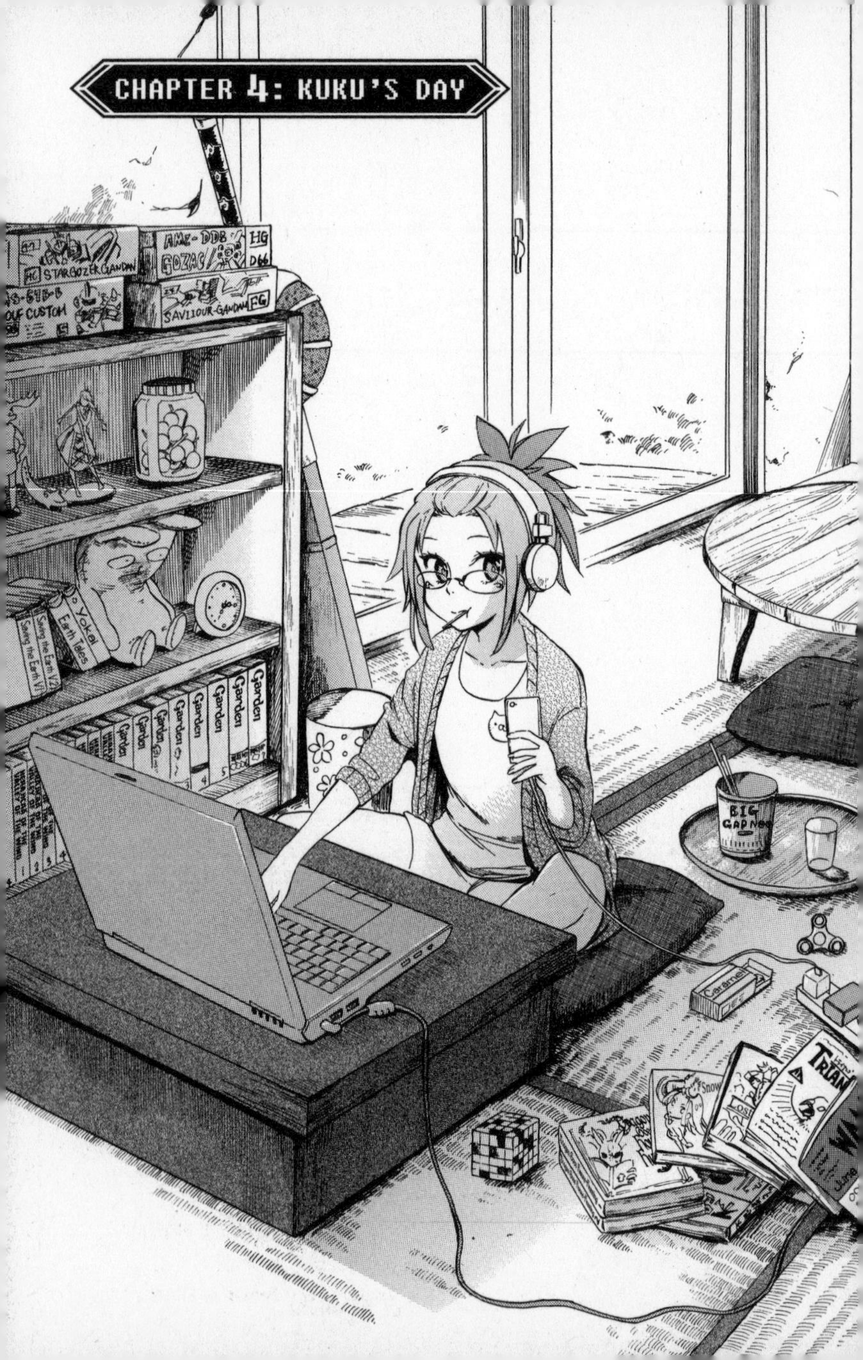
CHAPTER 4: KUKU'S DAY
AMZ-DDB
HG
FG
Yokai Earth Tales
Saving the Earth V2
Saving the Earth V1
Garden
Caramel

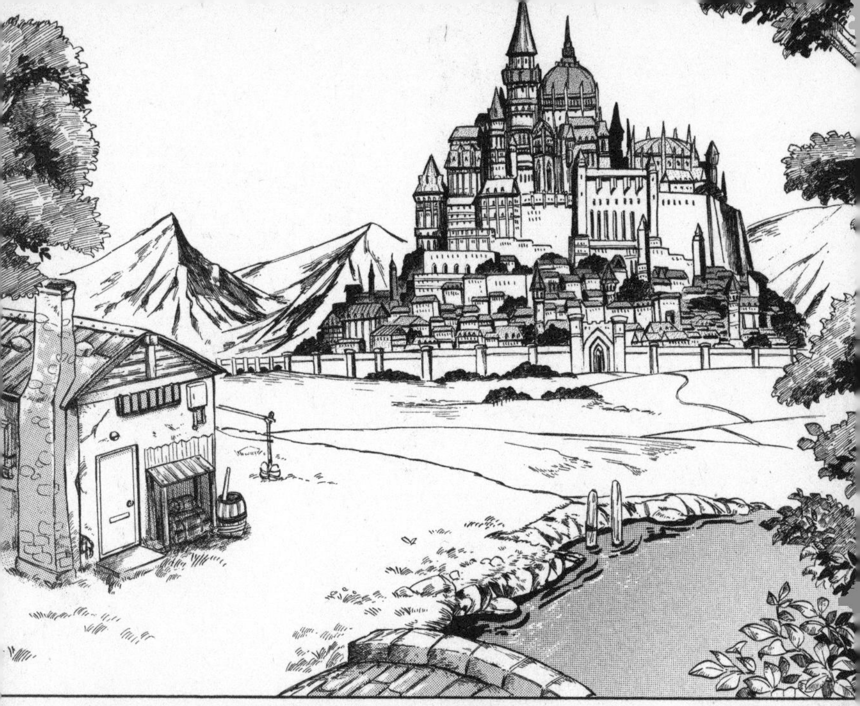
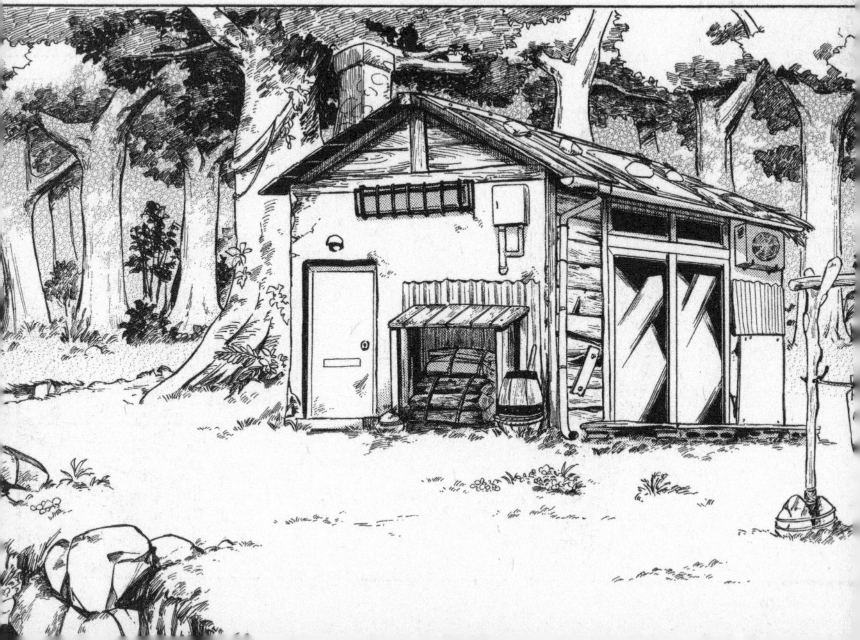

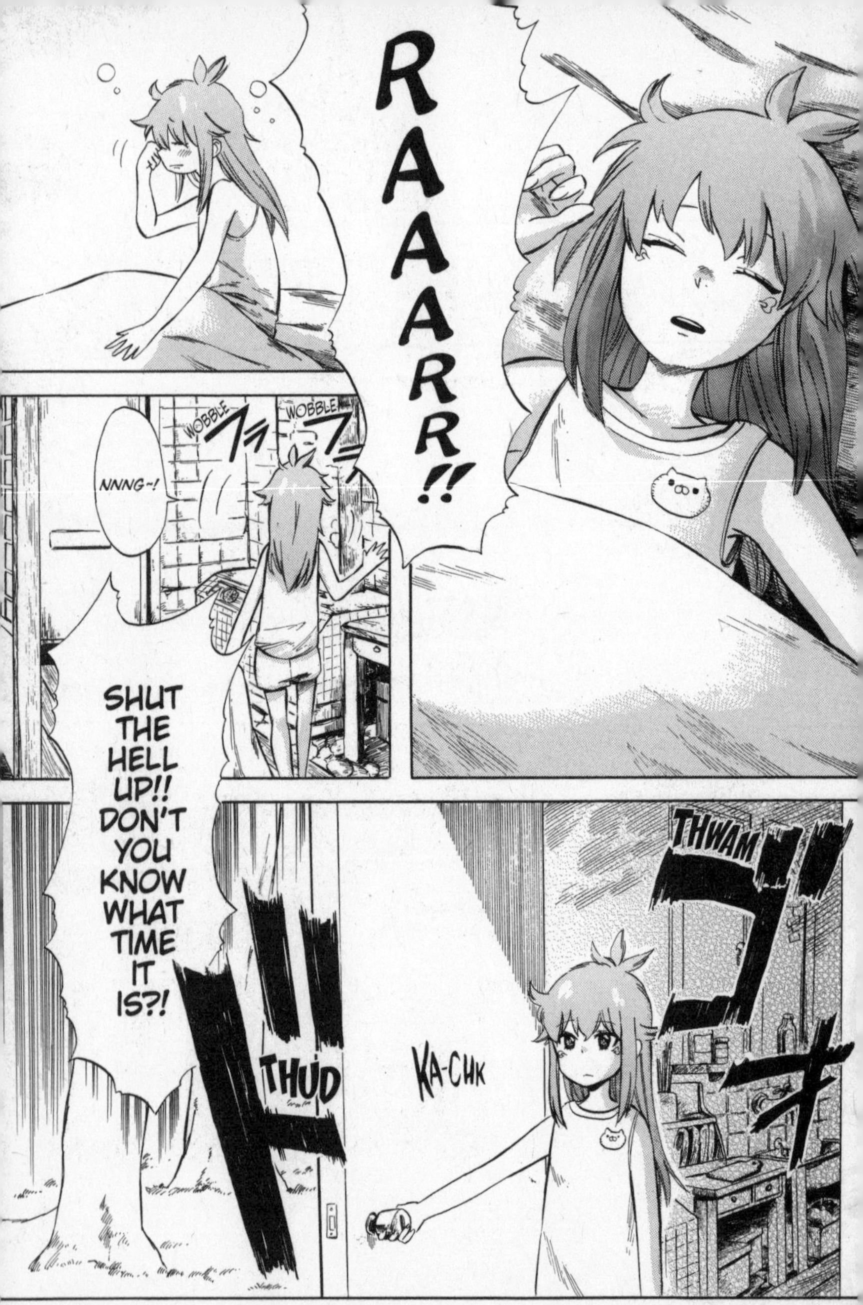
RAAARR!!
WOBBLE
WOBBLE
NNNG~!
SHUT THE HELL UP!! DON'T YOU KNOW WHAT TIME IT IS?!
THWAM
KA-CHK
THUD

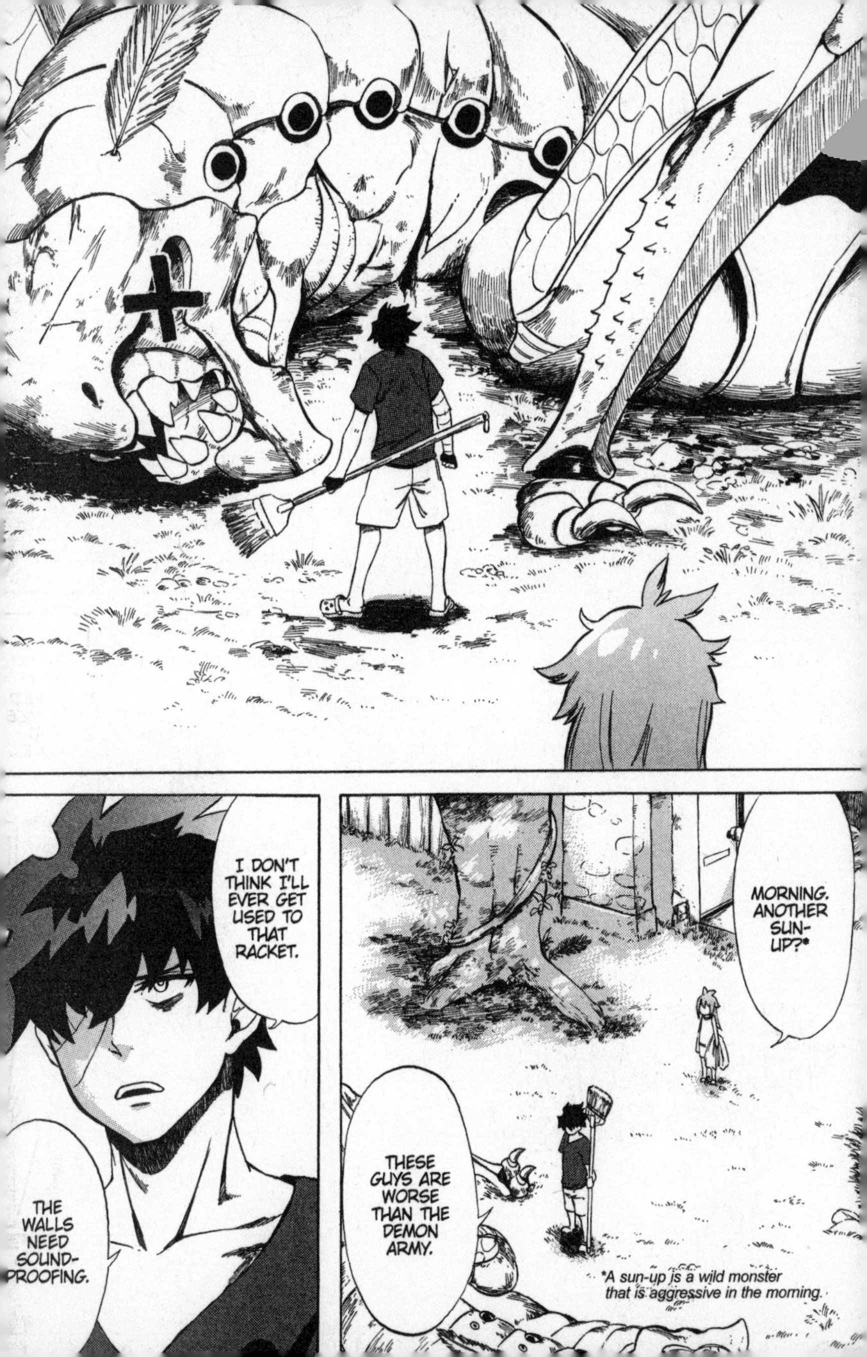
MORNING. ANOTHER SUN-UP?*
THESE GUYS ARE WORSE THAN THE DEMON ARMY.
*A sun-up is a wild monster that is aggressive in the morning.
I DON'T THINK I'LL EVER GET USED TO THAT RACKET.
THE WALLS NEED SOUND-PROOFING.

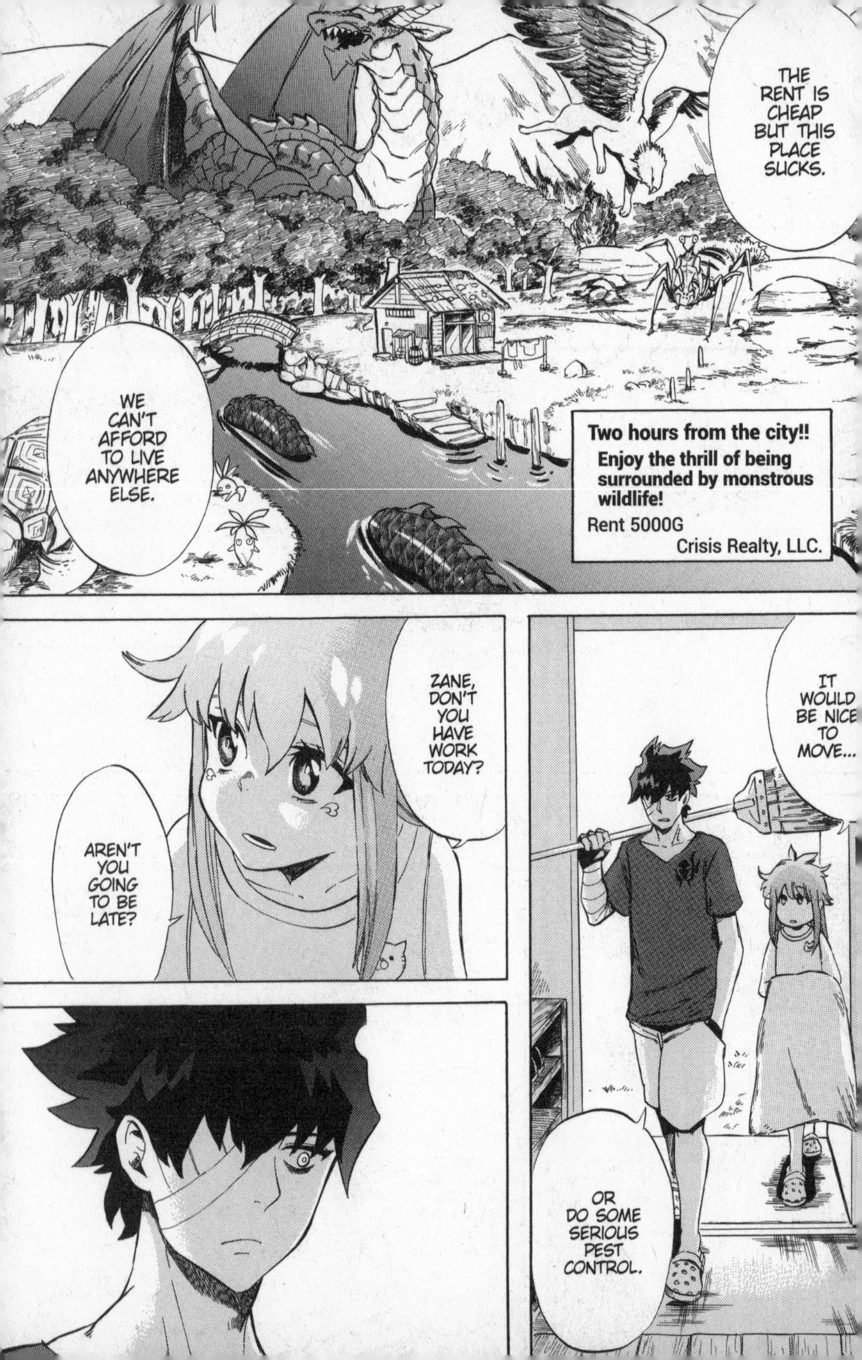
THE RENT IS CHEAP BUT THIS PLACE SUCKS.
WE CAN'T AFFORD TO LIVE ANYWHERE ELSE.
Two hours from the city!!
Enjoy the thrill of being surrounded by monstrous wildlife!
Rent 5000G
Crisis Realty, LLC.
IT WOULD BE NICE TO MOVE...
OR DO SOME SERIOUS PEST CONTROL.
ZANE, DON'T YOU HAVE WORK TODAY?
AREN'T YOU GOING TO BE LATE?

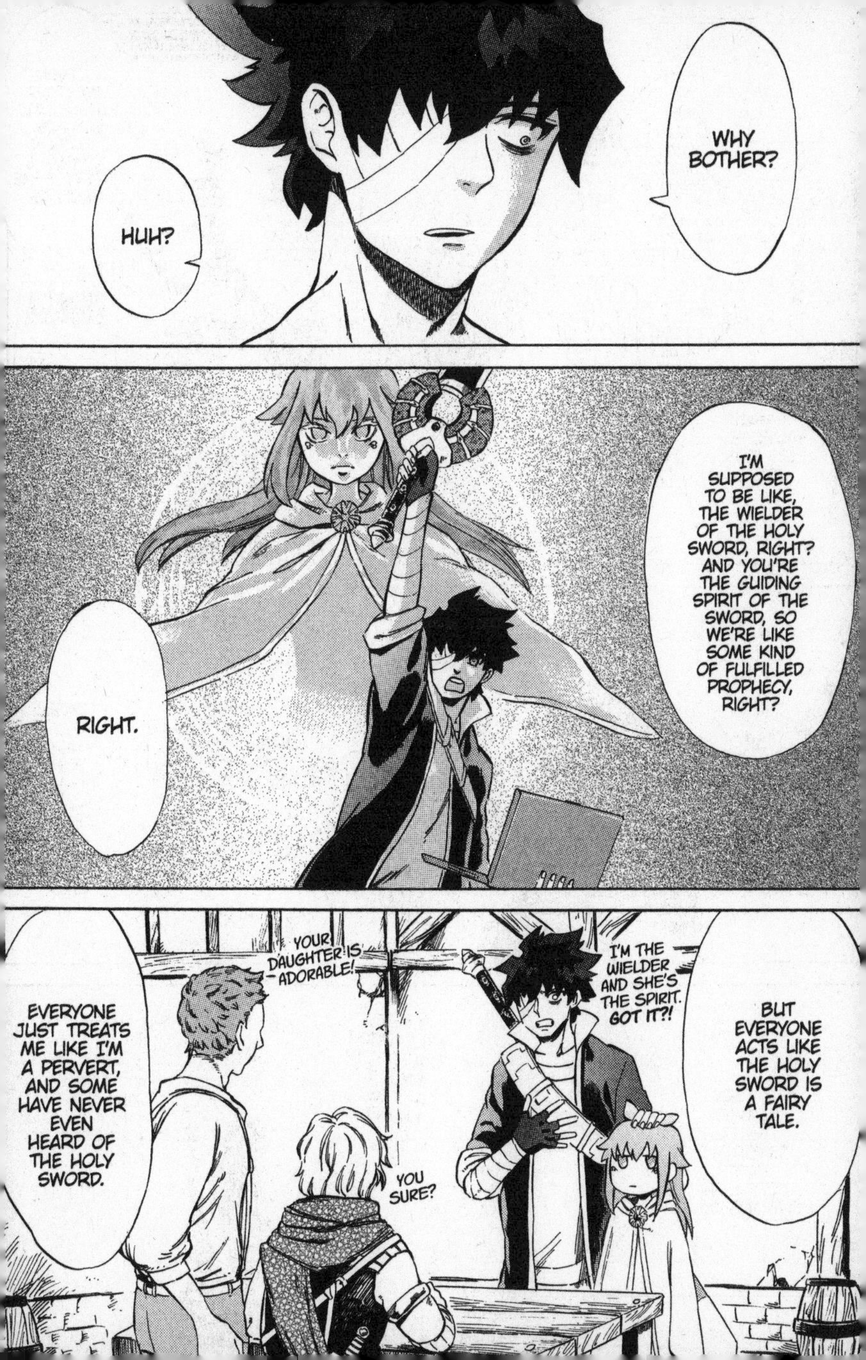
WHY BOTHER?
HUH?
I'M SUPPOSED TO BE LIKE, THE WIELDER OF THE HOLY SWORD, RIGHT? AND YOU'RE THE GUIDING SPIRIT OF THE SWORD, SO WE'RE LIKE SOME KIND OF FULFILLED PROPHECY, RIGHT?
RIGHT.
BUT EVERYONE ACTS LIKE THE HOLY SWORD IS A FAIRY TALE.
I'M THE WIELDER AND SHE'S THE SPIRIT. GOT IT?!
YOUR DAUGHTER IS ADORABLE!
EVERYONE JUST TREATS ME LIKE I'M A PERVERT, AND SOME HAVE NEVER EVEN HEARD OF THE HOLY SWORD.
YOU SURE?

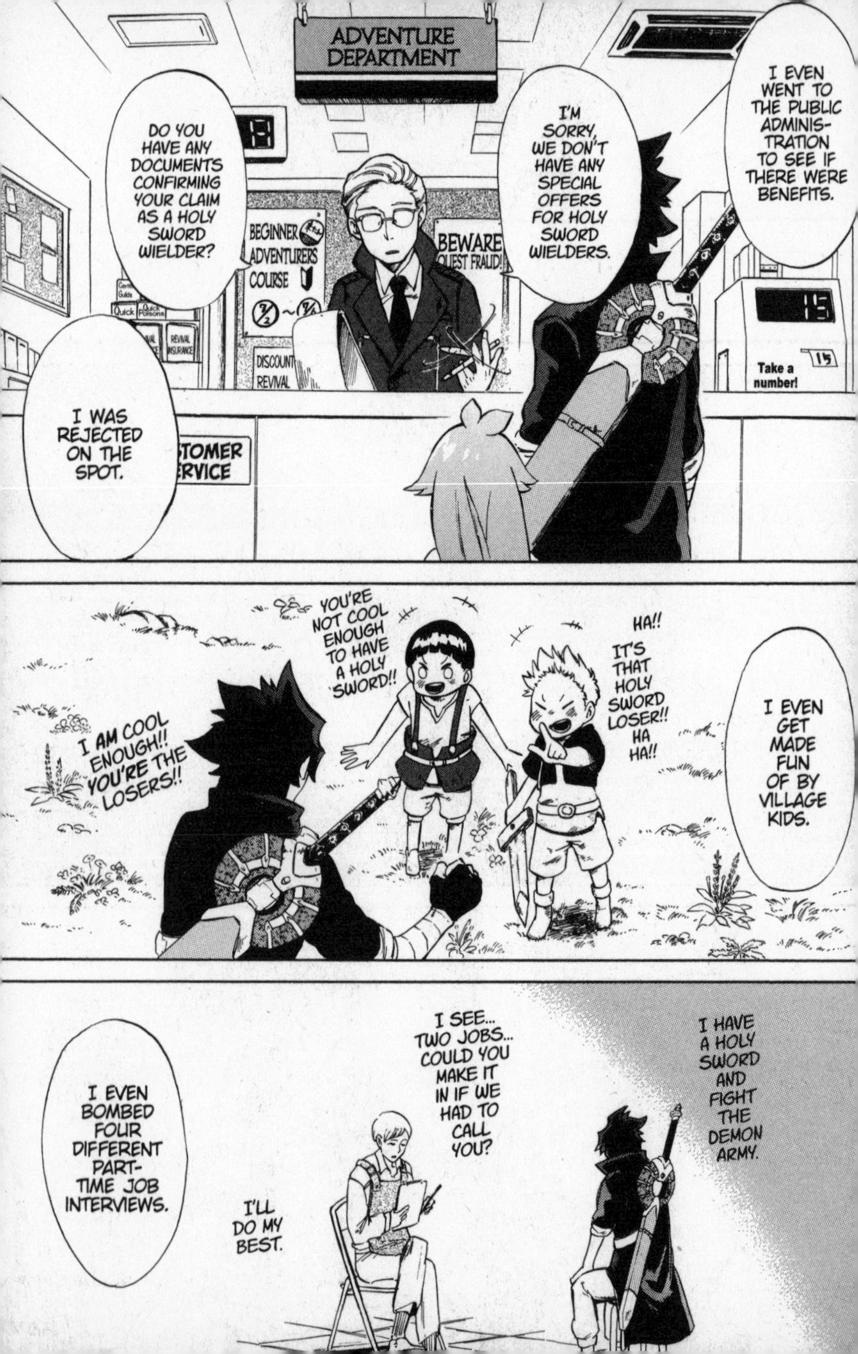
ADVENTURE DEPARTMENT
I EVEN WENT TO THE PUBLIC ADMINISTRATION TO SEE IF THERE WERE BENEFITS.
I'M SORRY, WE DON'T HAVE ANY SPECIAL OFFERS FOR HOLY SWORD WIELDERS.
DO YOU HAVE ANY DOCUMENTS CONFIRMING YOUR CLAIM AS A HOLY SWORD WIELDER?
I WAS REJECTED ON THE SPOT.
BEWARE QUEST FRAUD!
BEGINNER ADVENTURERS COURSE
DISCOUNT REVIVAL
REVIVAL INSURANCE
Quick Poisons
15
Take a number!
I EVEN GET MADE FUN OF BY VILLAGE KIDS.
HA!! IT'S THAT HOLY SWORD LOSER!! HA HA!!
YOU'RE NOT COOL ENOUGH TO HAVE A HOLY SWORD!!
I AM COOL ENOUGH!! YOU'RE THE LOSERS!!
I HAVE A HOLY SWORD AND FIGHT THE DEMON ARMY.
I SEE... TWO JOBS... COULD YOU MAKE IT IN IF WE HAD TO CALL YOU?
I'LL DO MY BEST.
I EVEN BOMBED FOUR DIFFERENT PART-TIME JOB INTERVIEWS.

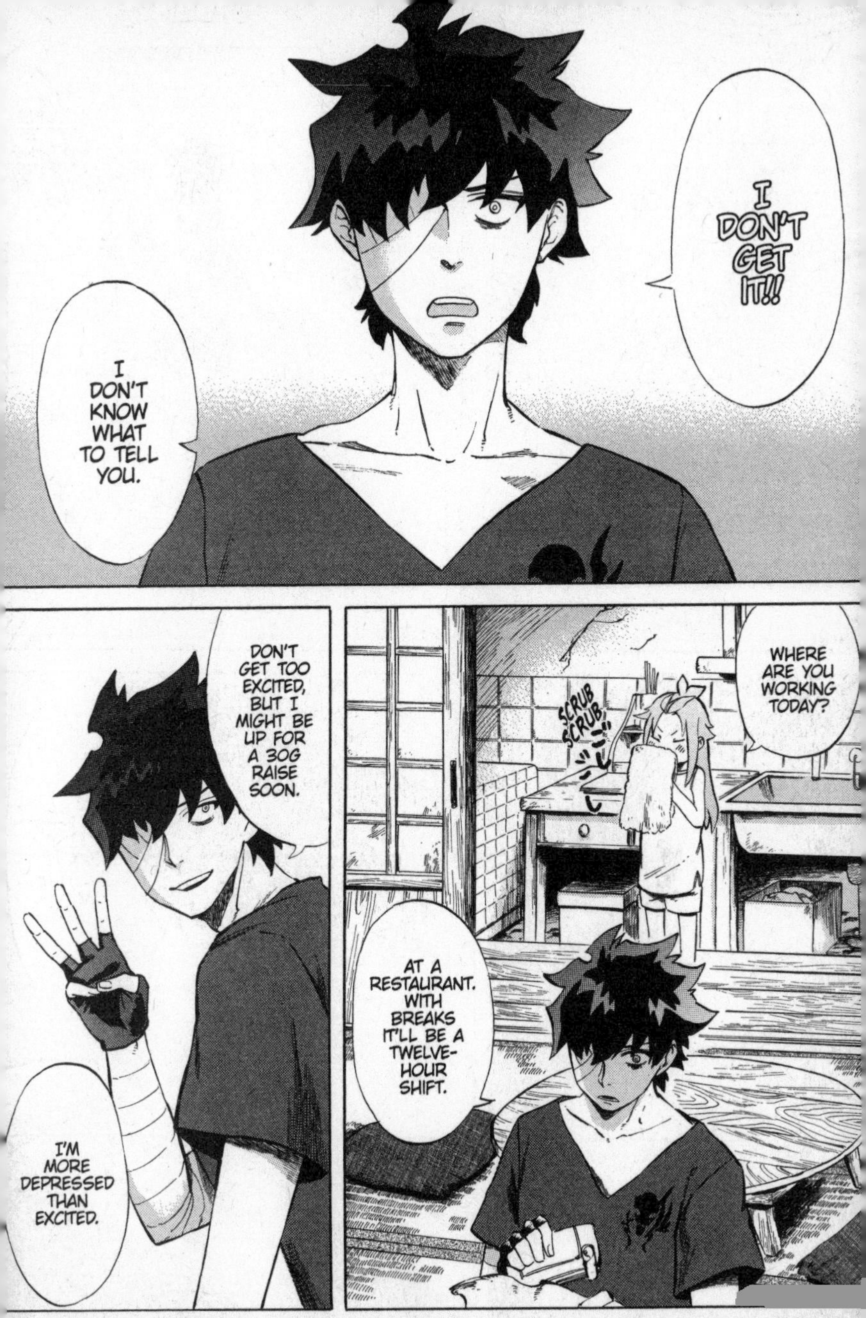
I DON'T GET IT!!
I DON'T KNOW WHAT TO TELL YOU.
WHERE ARE YOU WORKING TODAY?
SCRUB SCRUB
AT A RESTAURANT. WITH BREAKS IT'LL BE A TWELVE-HOUR SHIFT.
DON'T GET TOO EXCITED, BUT I MIGHT BE UP FOR A 30G RAISE SOON.
I'M MORE DEPRESSED THAN EXCITED.

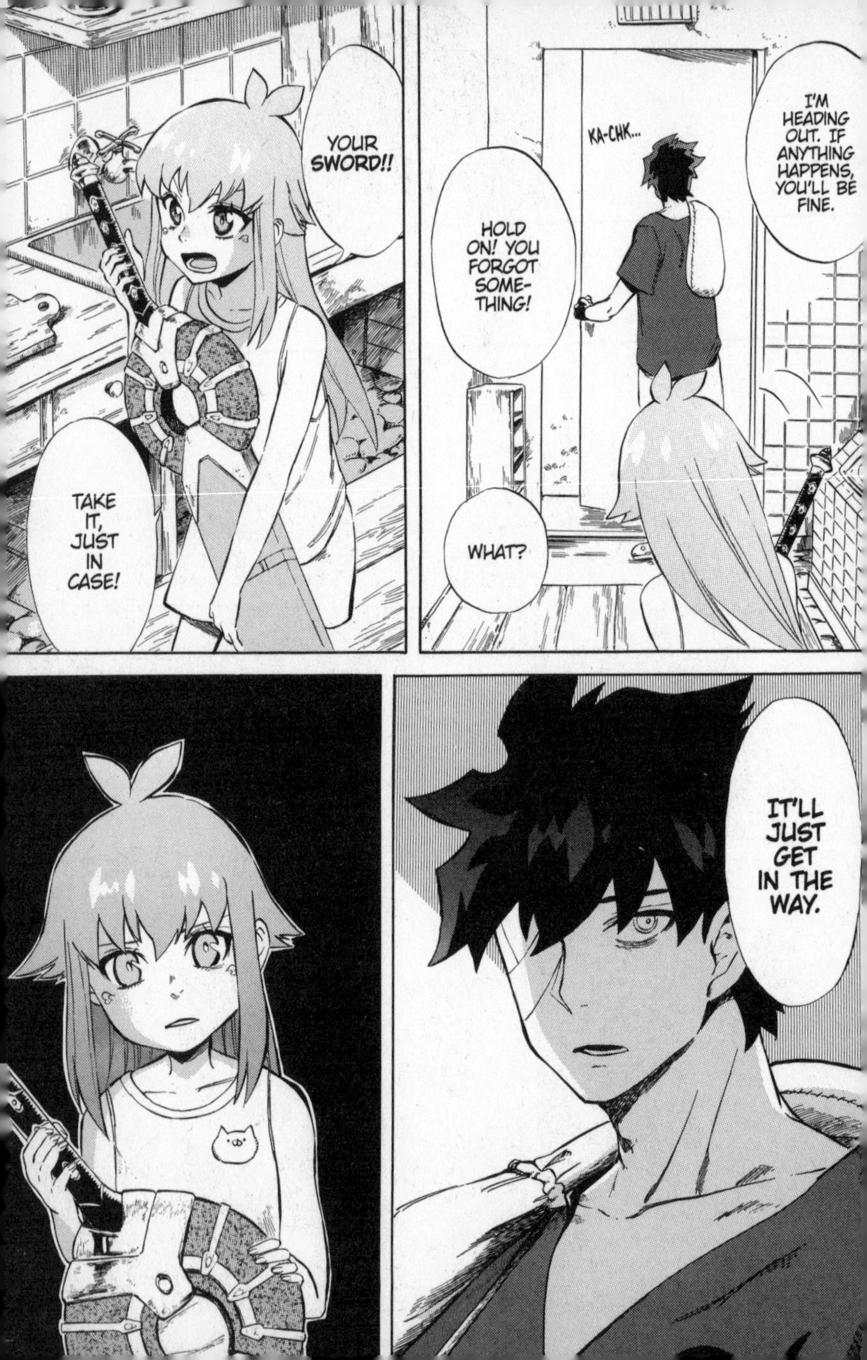
I'M HEADING OUT. IF ANYTHING HAPPENS, YOU'LL BE FINE.
KA-CHK...
HOLD ON! YOU FORGOT SOME-THING!
WHAT?
YOUR SWORD!!
TAKE IT, JUST IN CASE!
IT'LL JUST GET IN THE WAY.

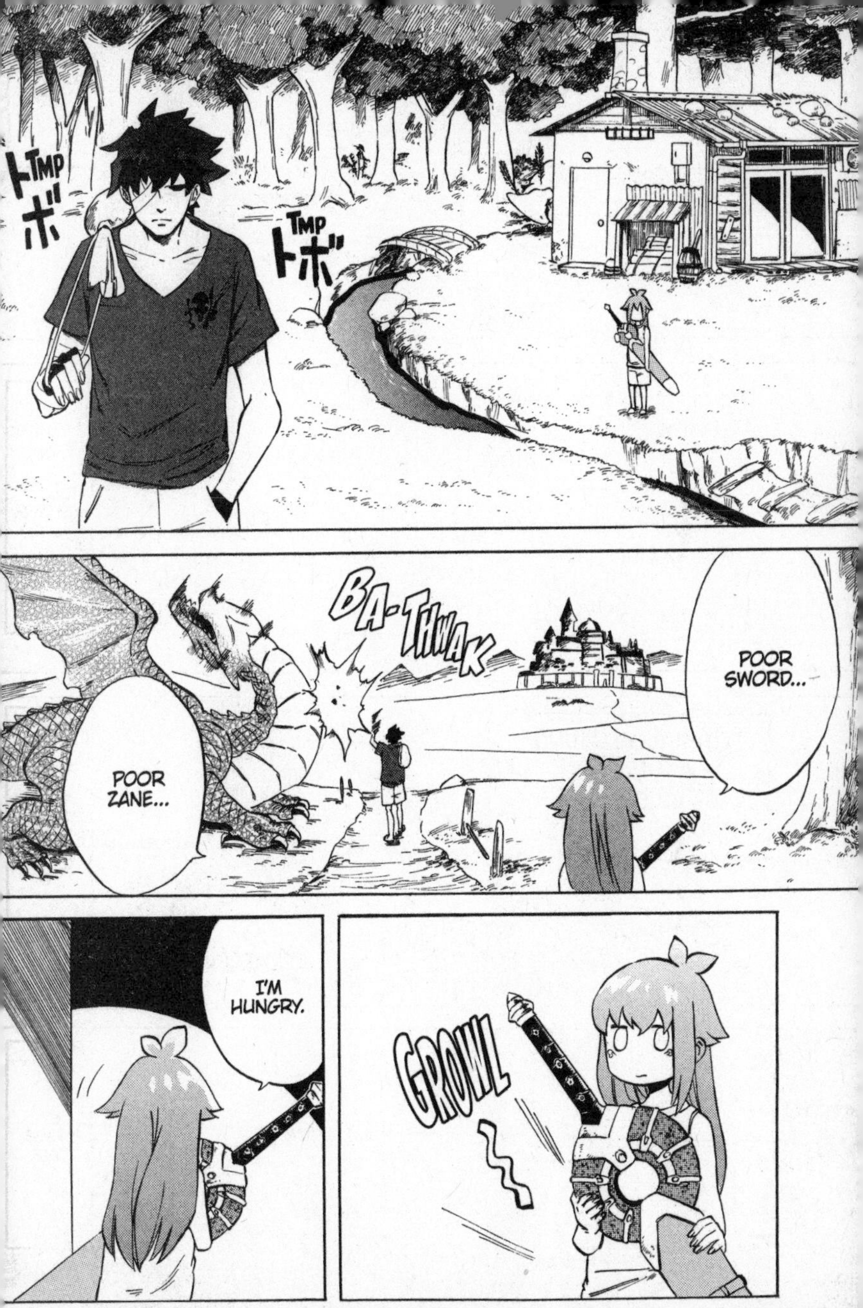
TMP
トボ
TMP
トボ
POOR SWORD...
BA-THWAK
POOR ZANE...
GROWL
I'M HUNGRY.

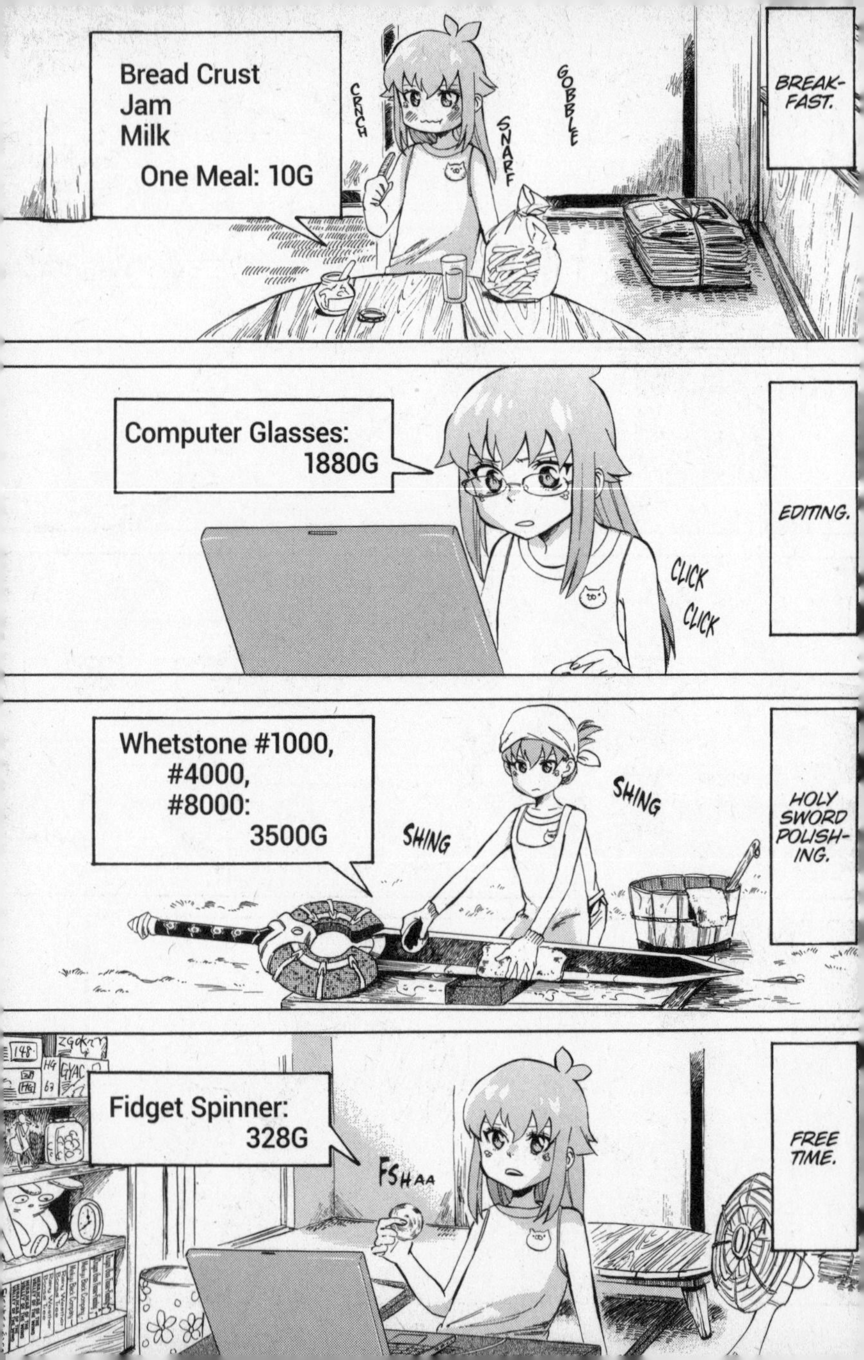
BREAK-
FAST.
GOBBLE
SNARF
CRNCH
Bread Crust
Jam
Milk
One Meal: 10G
EDITING.
CLICK
CLICK
Computer Glasses:
1880G
HOLY
SWORD
POLISH-
ING.
SHING
SHING
Whetstone #1000,
#4000,
#8000:
3500G
FREE
TIME.
FSHAA
Fidget Spinner:
328G

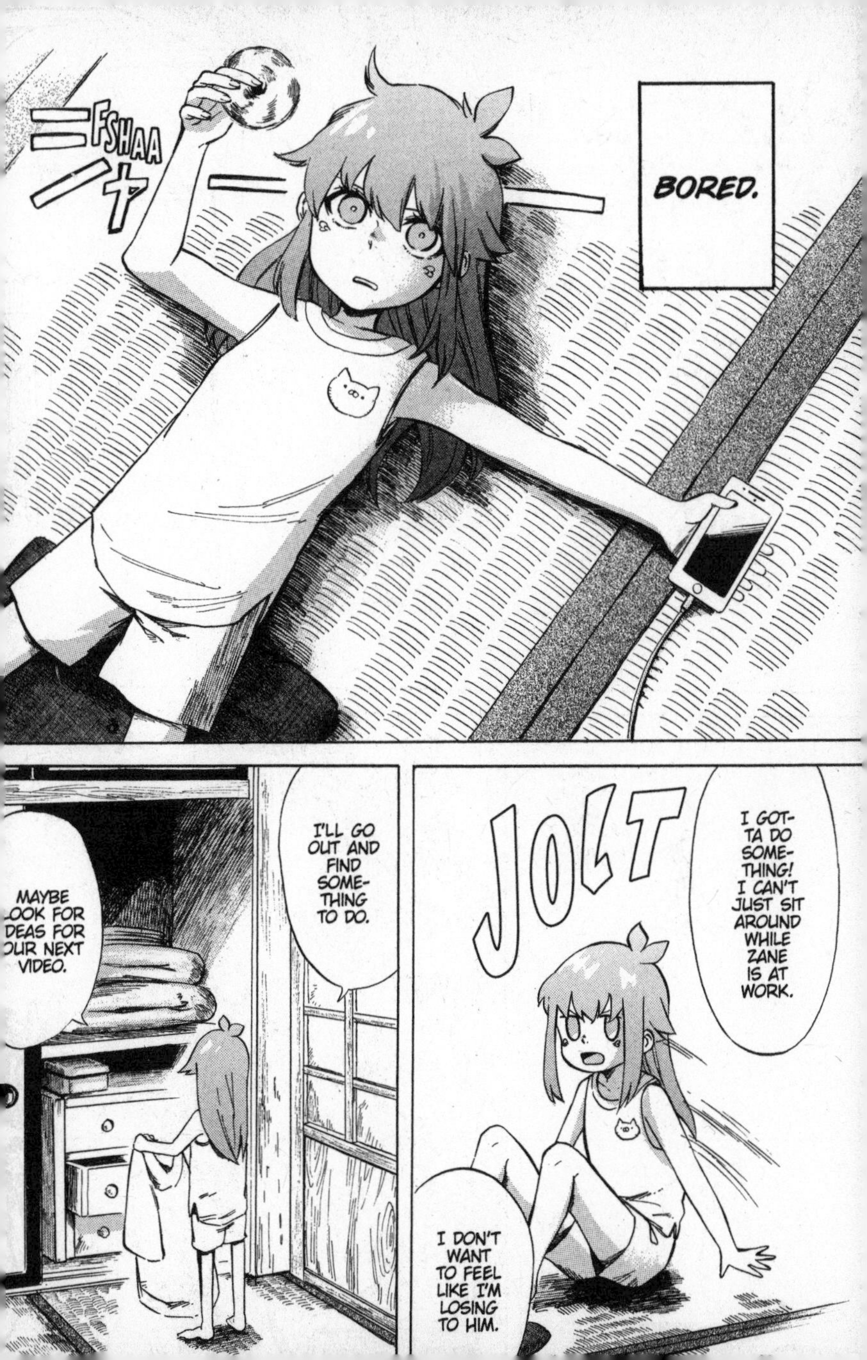
BORED.
FSHAA
JOLT
I GOTTA DO SOMETHING! I CAN'T JUST SIT AROUND WHILE ZANE IS AT WORK.
I DON'T WANT TO FEEL LIKE I'M LOSING TO HIM.
I'LL GO OUT AND FIND SOMETHING TO DO.
MAYBE LOOK FOR DEAS FOR OUR NEXT VIDEO.

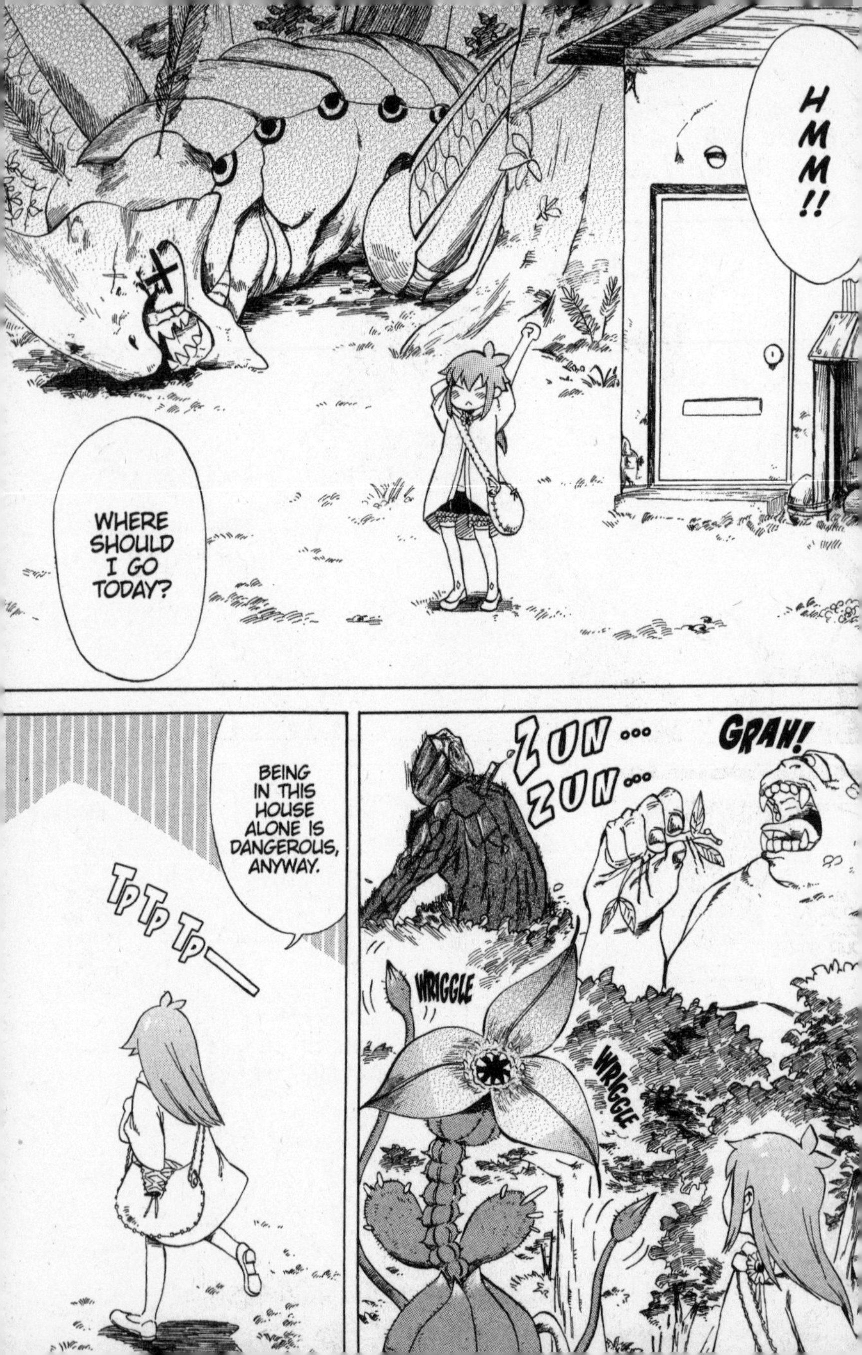
HMM!!
WHERE SHOULD I GO TODAY?
ZUN... ZUN...
GRAH!
WRIGGLE
WRIGGLE
BEING IN THIS HOUSE ALONE IS DANGEROUS, ANYWAY.
TpTp Tp—

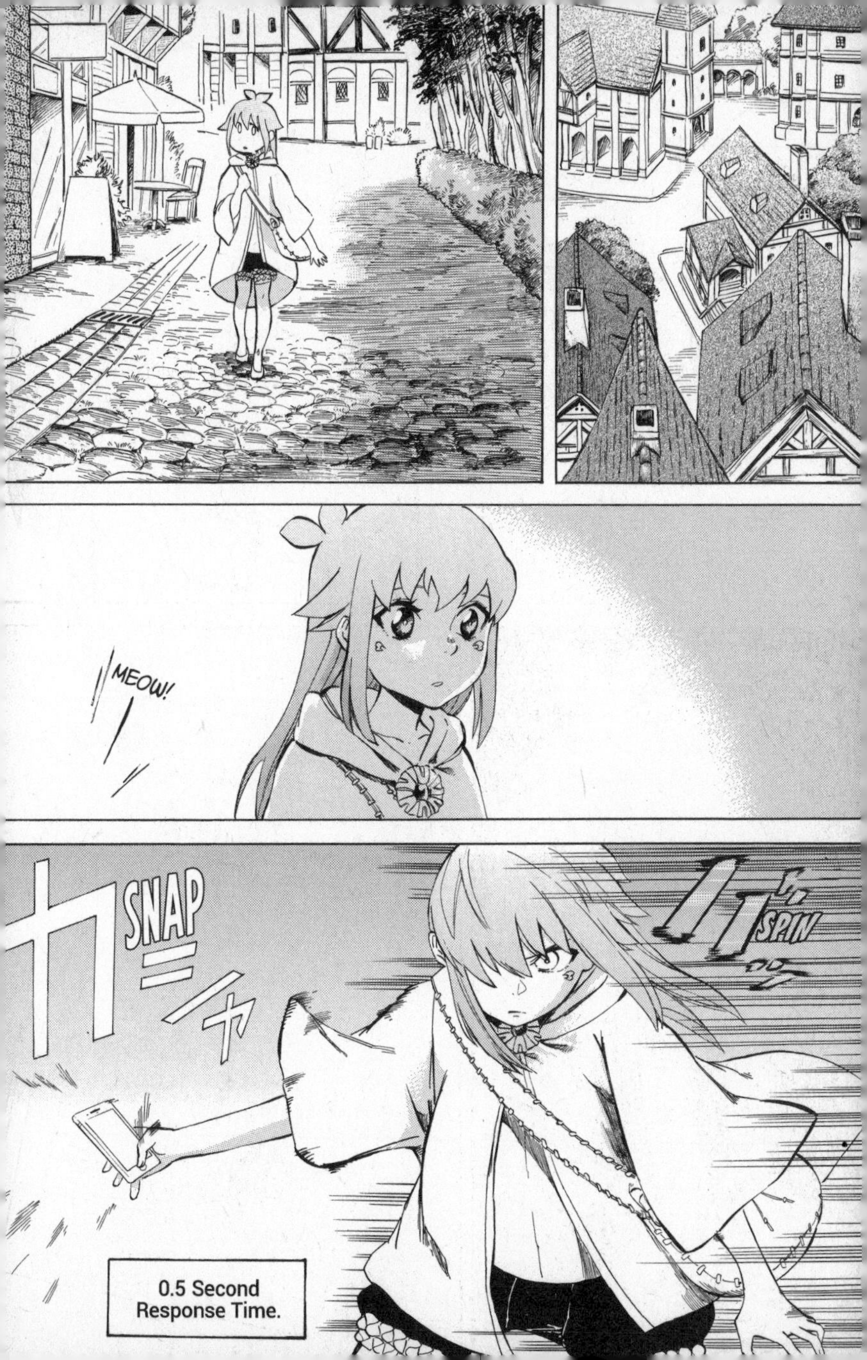
MEOW!
SPIN
SNAP
0.5 Second Response Time.

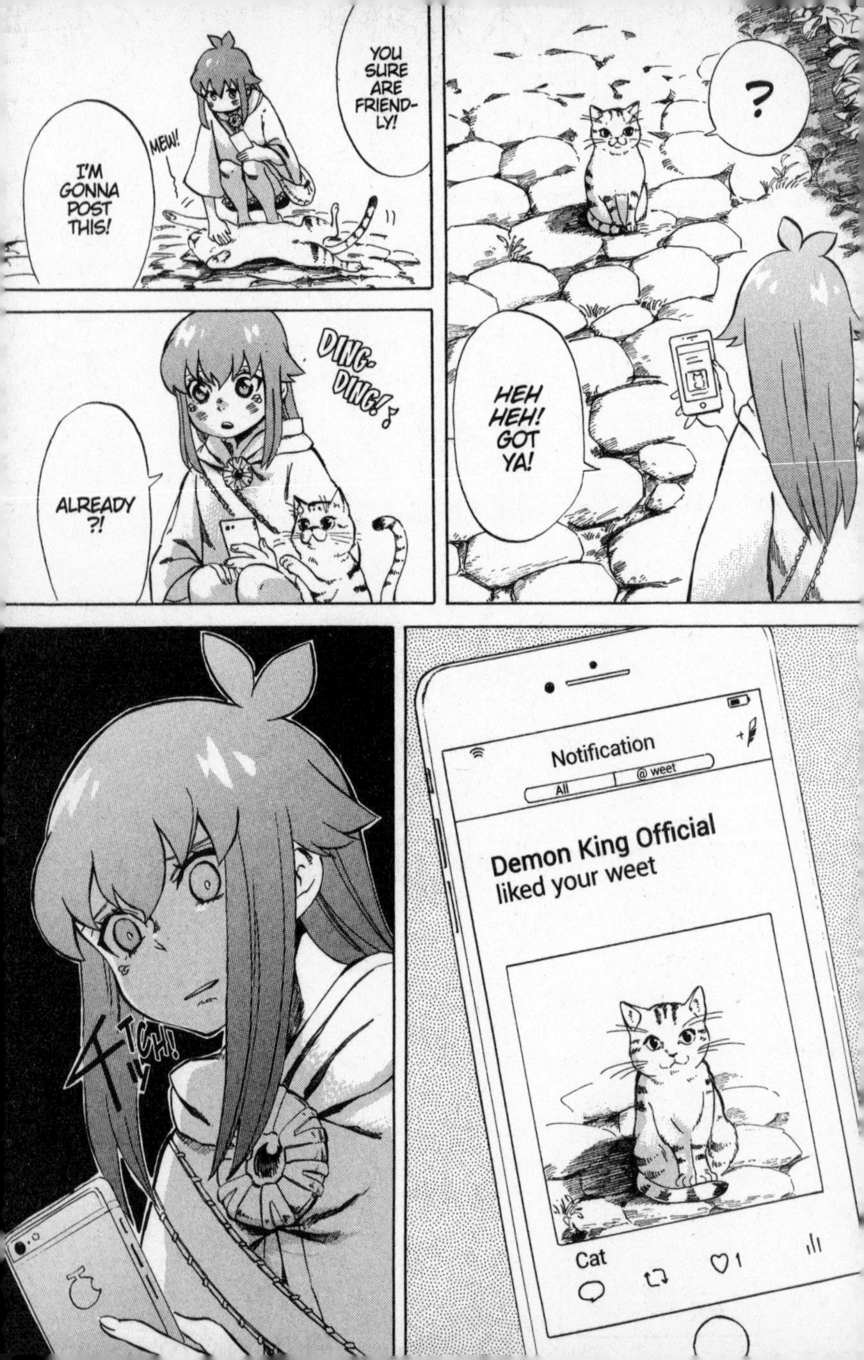
?
HEH HEH! GOT YA!
YOU SURE ARE FRIEND-LY!
MEW!
I'M GONNA POST THIS!
DING-DING! ♪
ALREADY ?!
Notification
All
@ weet
Demon King Official liked your weet
Cat
1
TCH!

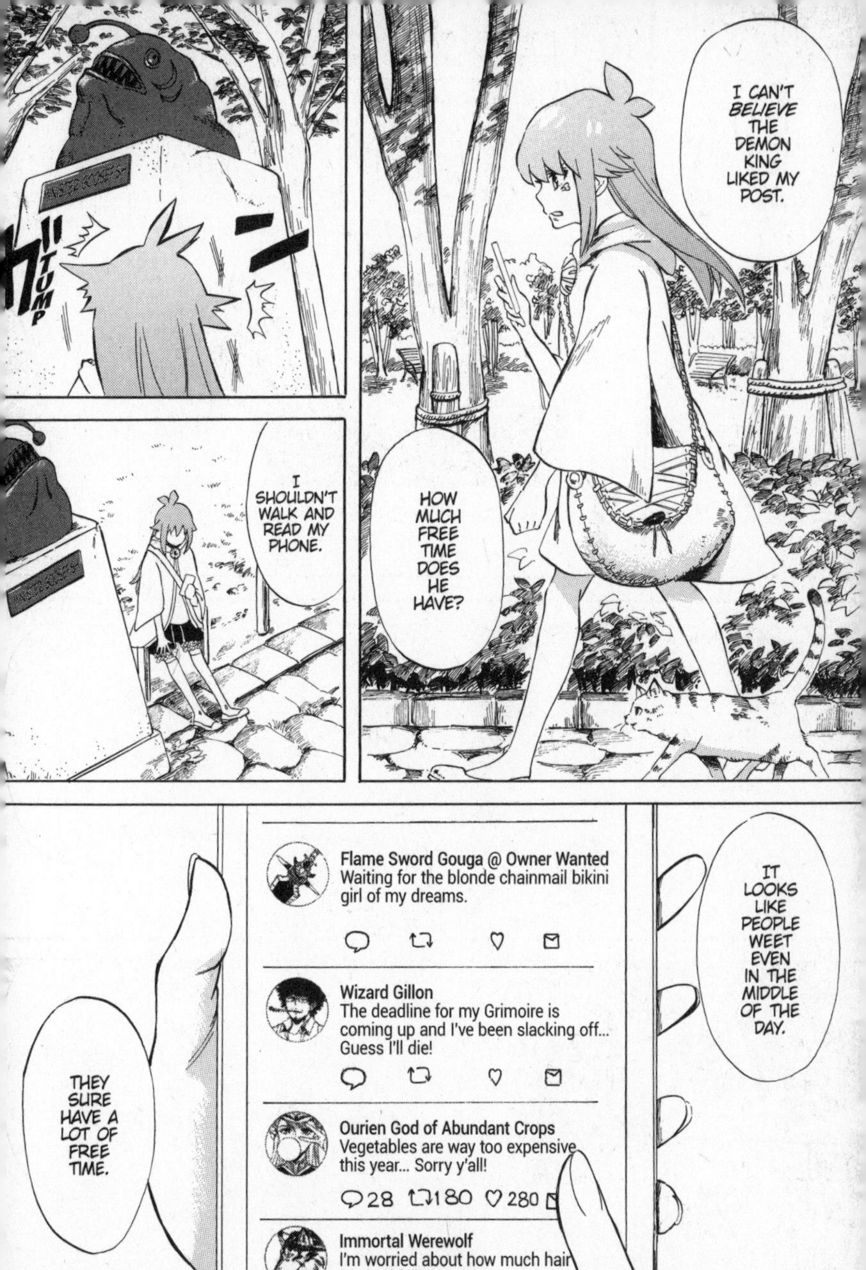
I CAN'T BELIEVE THE DEMON KING LIKED MY POST.
HOW MUCH FREE TIME DOES HE HAVE?
TUMP
I SHOULDN'T WALK AND READ MY PHONE.
IT LOOKS LIKE PEOPLE WEET EVEN IN THE MIDDLE OF THE DAY.
Flame Sword Gouga @ Owner Wanted
Waiting for the blonde chainmail bikini girl of my dreams.
Wizard Gillon
The deadline for my Grimoire is coming up and I've been slacking off... Guess I'll die!
Ourien God of Abundant Crops
Vegetables are way too expensive this year... Sorry y'all!
28 180 280
Immortal Werewolf
I'm worried about how much hair I've had falling out...!
THEY SURE HAVE A LOT OF FREE TIME.

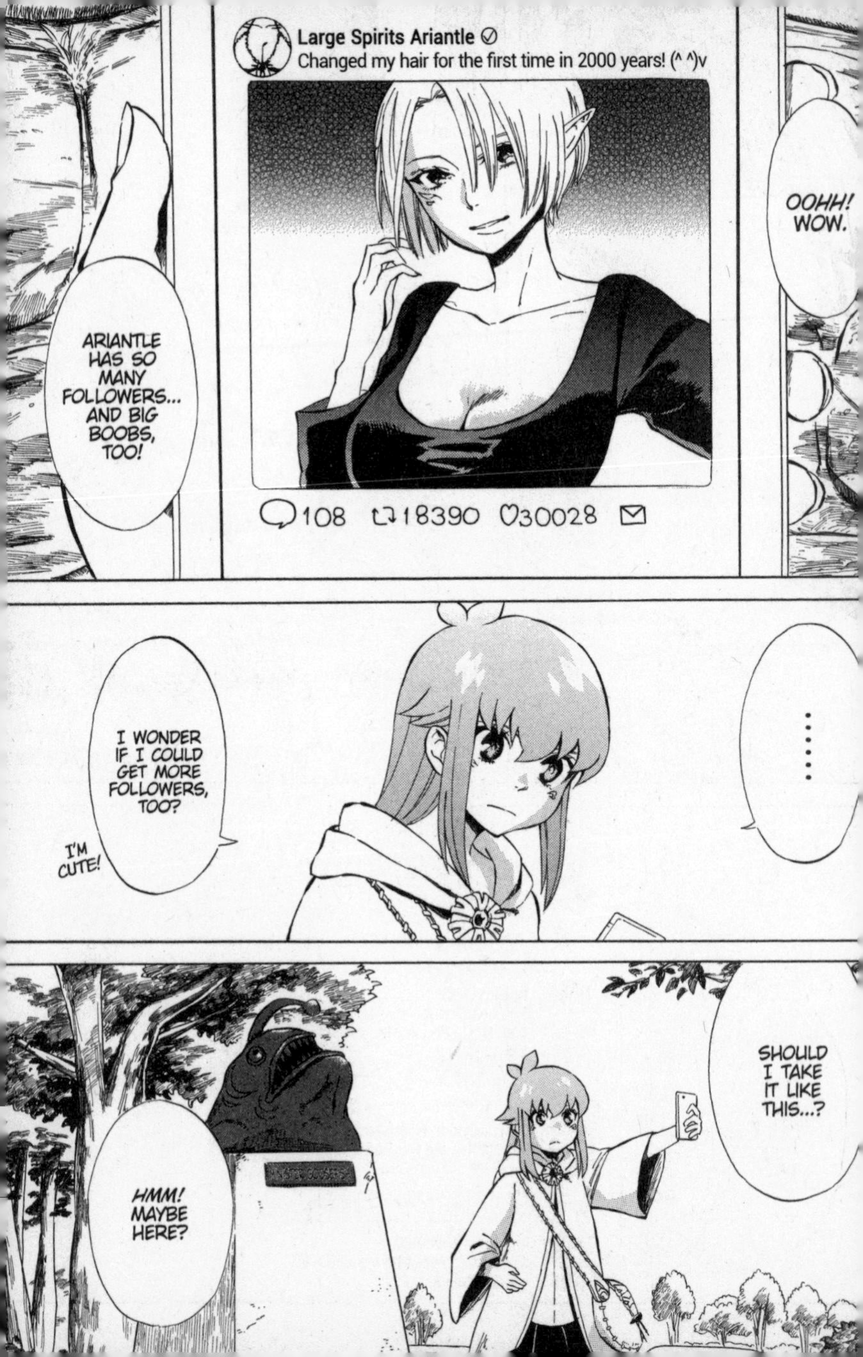
Large Spirits Ariantle
Changed my hair for the first time in 2000 years! (^ ^)v
108 18390 30028
OOHH! WOW.
ARIANTLE HAS SO MANY FOLLOWERS... AND BIG BOOBS, TOO!
......
I WONDER IF I COULD GET MORE FOLLOWERS, TOO?
I'M CUTE!
SHOULD I TAKE IT LIKE THIS...?
HMM! MAYBE HERE?

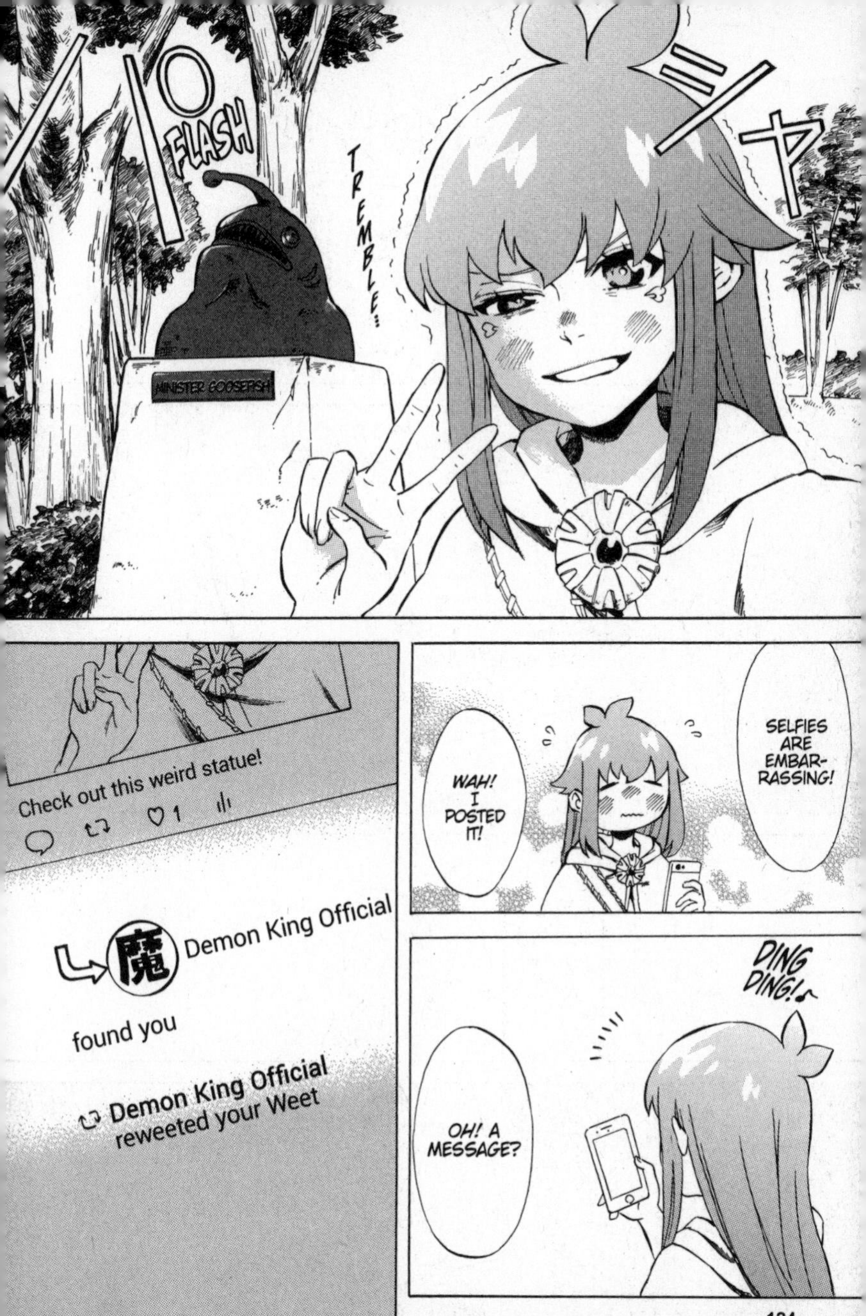
FLASH
TREMBLE...
MINISTER GOOSEFISH
SELFIES ARE EMBARRASSING!
WAH! I POSTED IT!
DING DING!♪
OH! A MESSAGE?
Check out this weird statue!
1
Demon King Official
魔
found you
Demon King Official reweeted your Weet

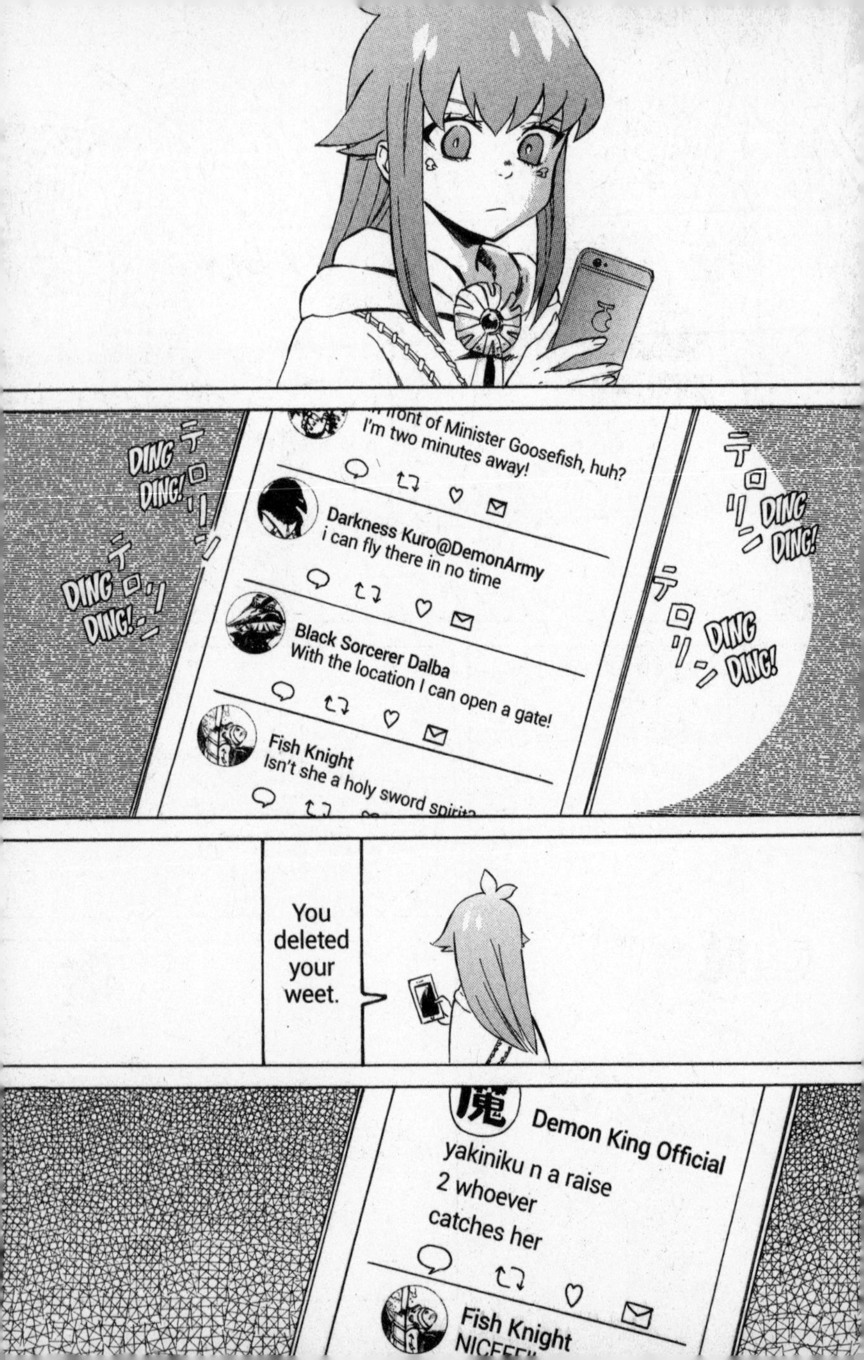
テロリン
DING DING!
テロリン
DING DING!
front of Minister Goosefish, huh?
I'm two minutes away!
Darkness Kuro@DemonArmy
i can fly there in no time
Black Sorcerer Dalba
With the location I can open a gate!
Fish Knight
Isn't she a holy sword spirit
テロリン
DING DING!
テロリン
DING DING!
You deleted your weet.
魔
Demon King Official
yakiniku n a raise
2 whoever
catches her
Fish Knight

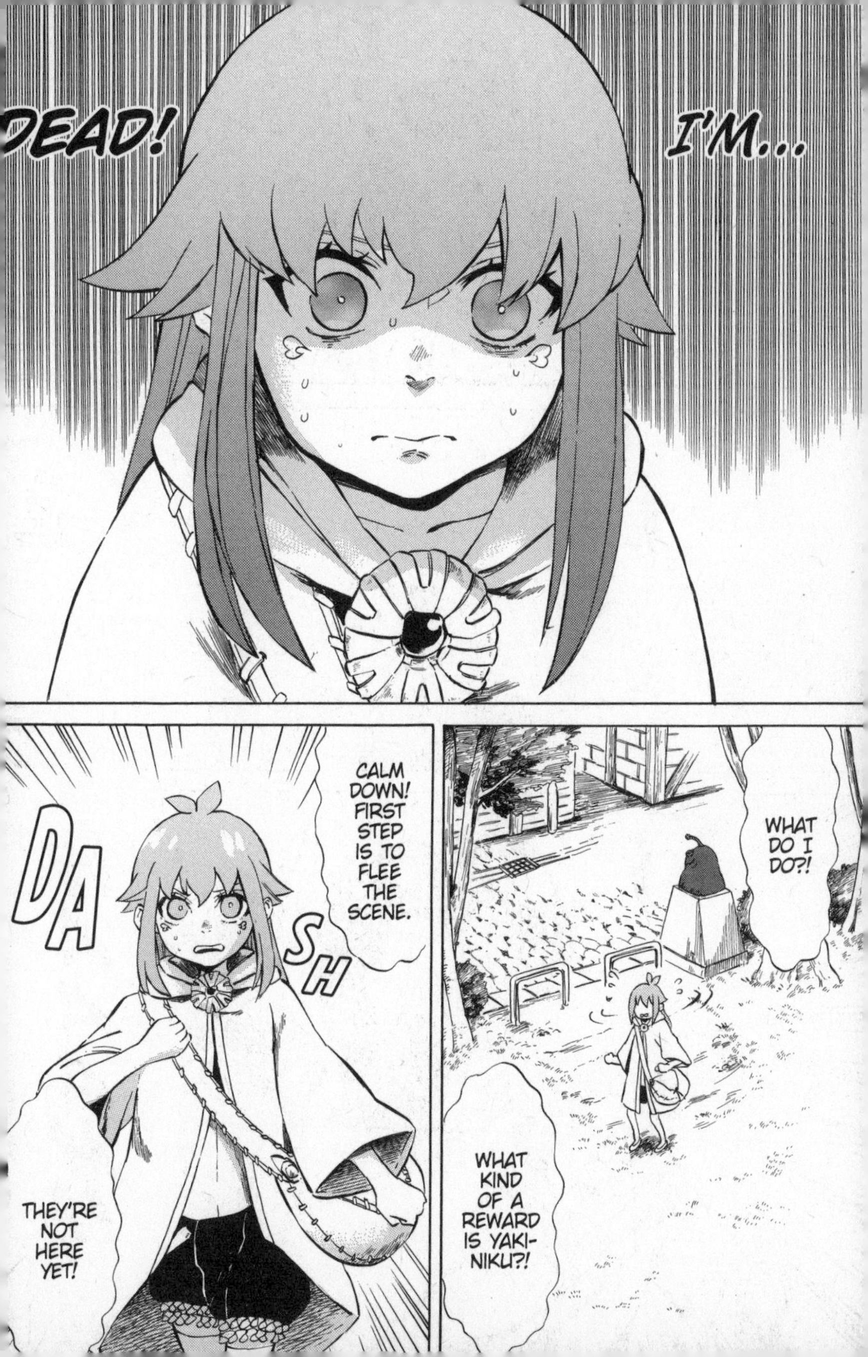
I'M...
DEAD!
WHAT DO I DO?!
WHAT KIND OF A REWARD IS YAKI-NIKU?!
CALM DOWN! FIRST STEP IS TO FLEE THE SCENE.
DASH
THEY'RE NOT HERE YET!

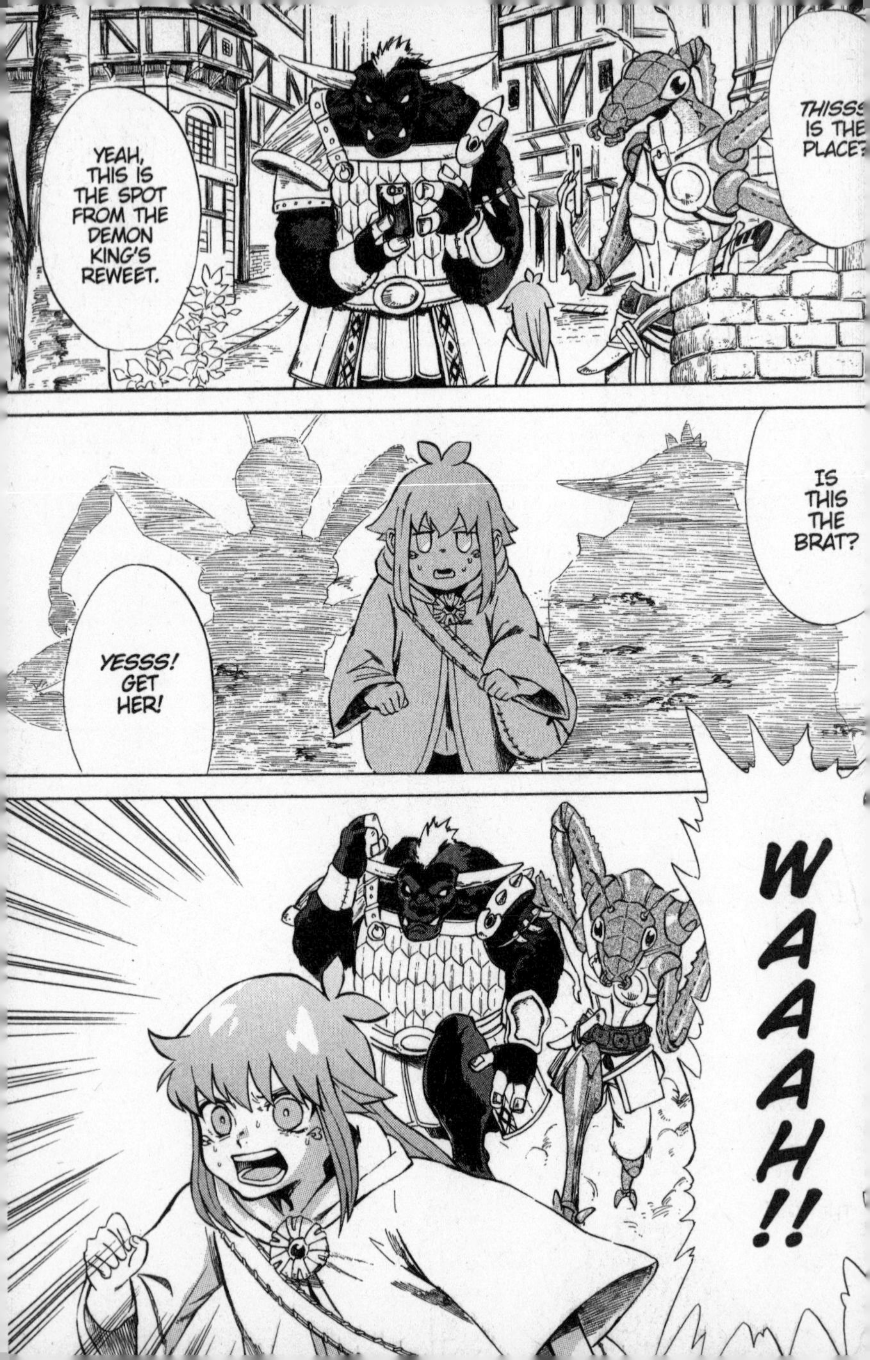
THISSS IS THE PLACE?
YEAH, THIS IS THE SPOT FROM THE DEMON KING'S REWEET.
IS THIS THE BRAT?
YESSS! GET HER!
WAAAAH!!

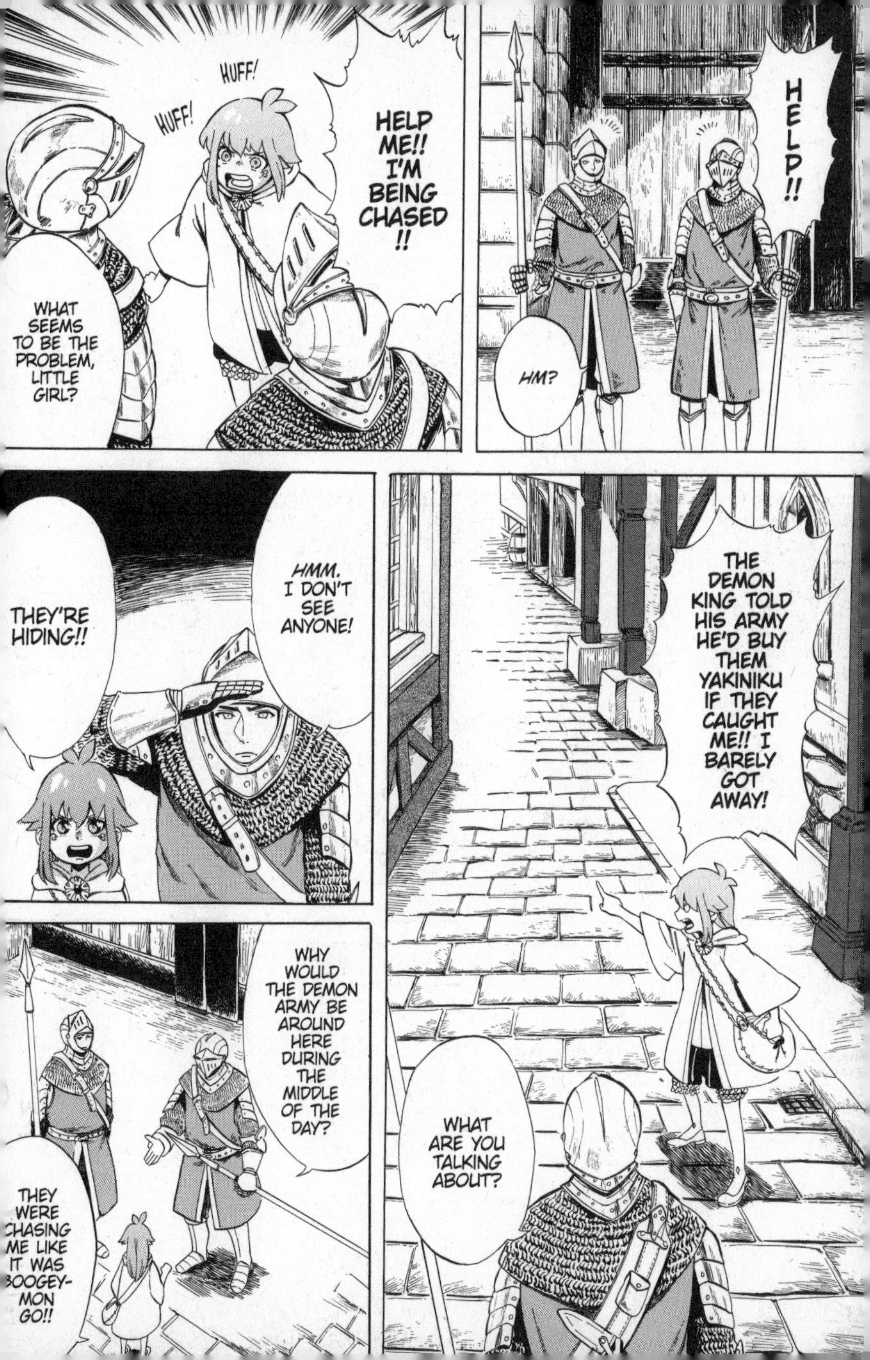
HELP!!
HM?
HELP ME!! I'M BEING CHASED!!
HUFF!
HUFF!
WHAT SEEMS TO BE THE PROBLEM, LITTLE GIRL?
THE DEMON KING TOLD HIS ARMY HE'D BUY THEM YAKINIKU IF THEY CAUGHT ME!! I BARELY GOT AWAY!
WHAT ARE YOU TALKING ABOUT?
HMM. I DON'T SEE ANYONE!
THEY'RE HIDING!!
WHY WOULD THE DEMON ARMY BE AROUND HERE DURING THE MIDDLE OF THE DAY?
THEY WERE CHASING ME LIKE IT WAS BOOGEY-MON GO!!

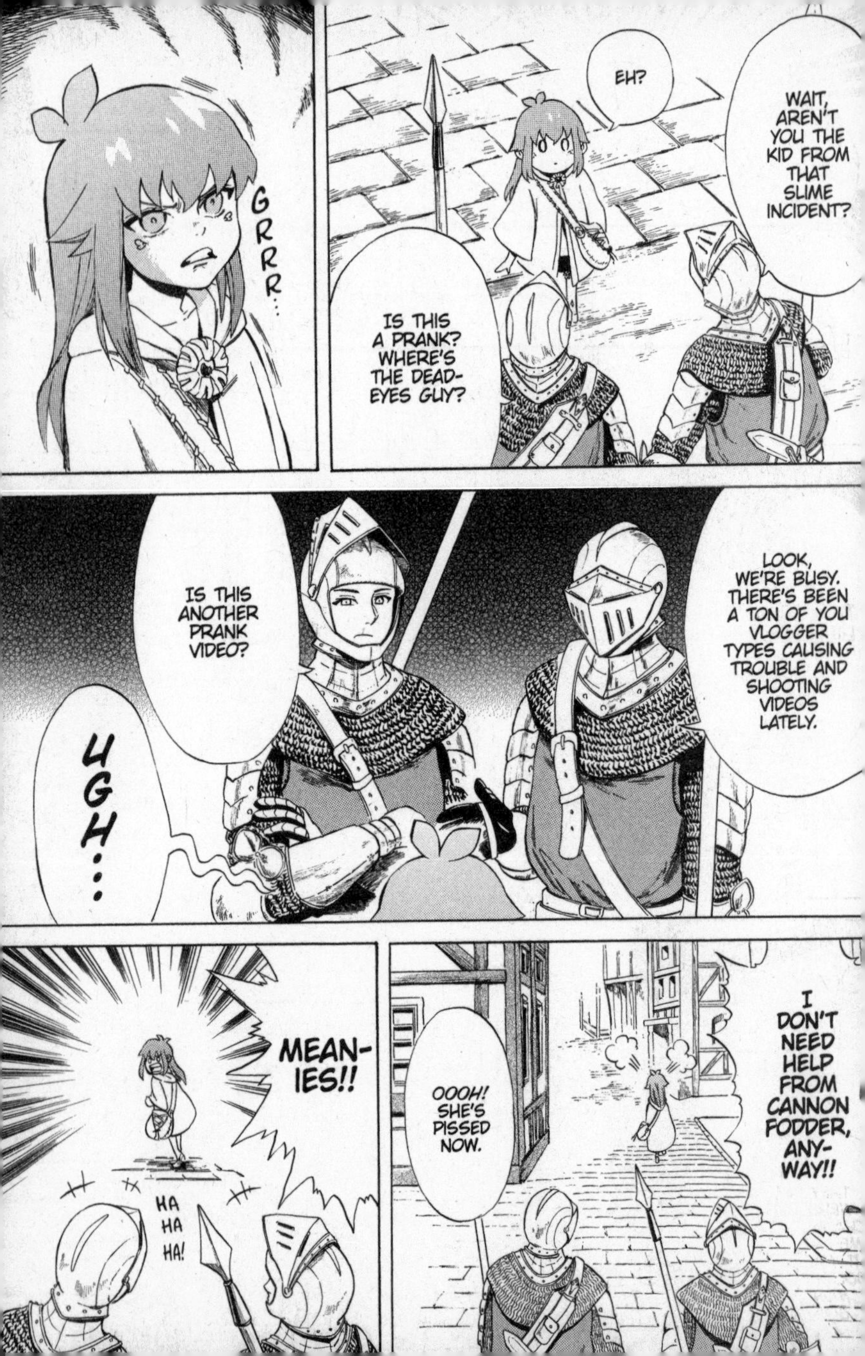
WAIT, AREN'T YOU THE KID FROM THAT SLIME INCIDENT?
EH?
IS THIS A PRANK? WHERE'S THE DEAD-EYES GUY?
GRRR...
LOOK, WE'RE BUSY. THERE'S BEEN A TON OF YOU VLOGGER TYPES CAUSING TROUBLE AND SHOOTING VIDEOS LATELY.
IS THIS ANOTHER PRANK VIDEO?
UGH...
I DON'T NEED HELP FROM CANNON FODDER, ANY-WAY!!
OOOH! SHE'S PISSED NOW.
MEAN-IES!!
HA HA HA!

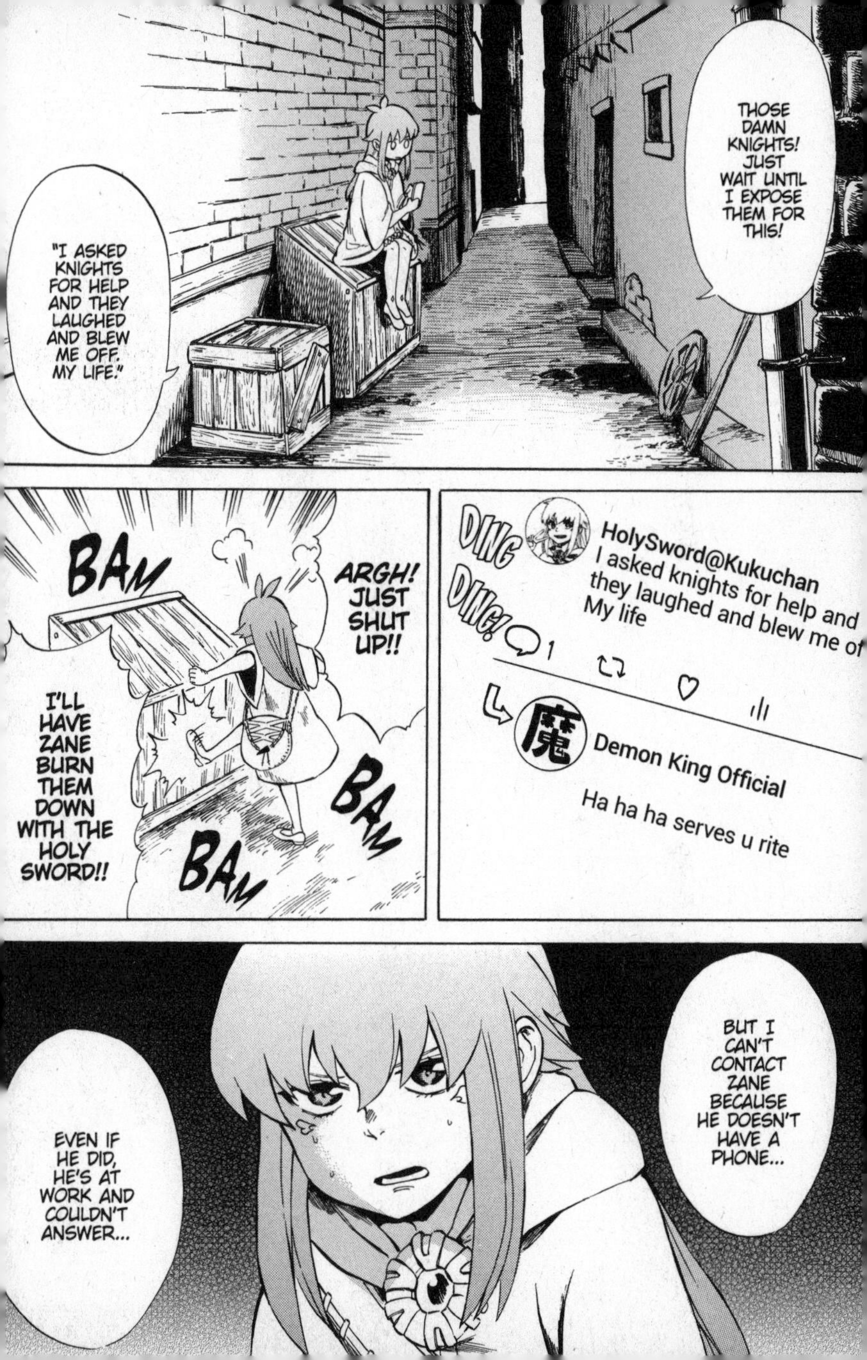
THOSE DAMN KNIGHTS! JUST WAIT UNTIL I EXPOSE THEM FOR THIS!
"I ASKED KNIGHTS FOR HELP AND THEY LAUGHED AND BLEW ME OFF. MY LIFE."
DING
DING!
HolySword@Kukuchan
I asked knights for help and they laughed and blew me of
My life
1
魔
Demon King Official
Ha ha ha serves u rite
ARGH! JUST SHUT UP!!
BAM
I'LL HAVE ZANE BURN THEM DOWN WITH THE HOLY SWORD!!
BAM
BAM
BUT I CAN'T CONTACT ZANE BECAUSE HE DOESN'T HAVE A PHONE...
EVEN IF HE DID, HE'S AT WORK AND COULDN'T ANSWER...

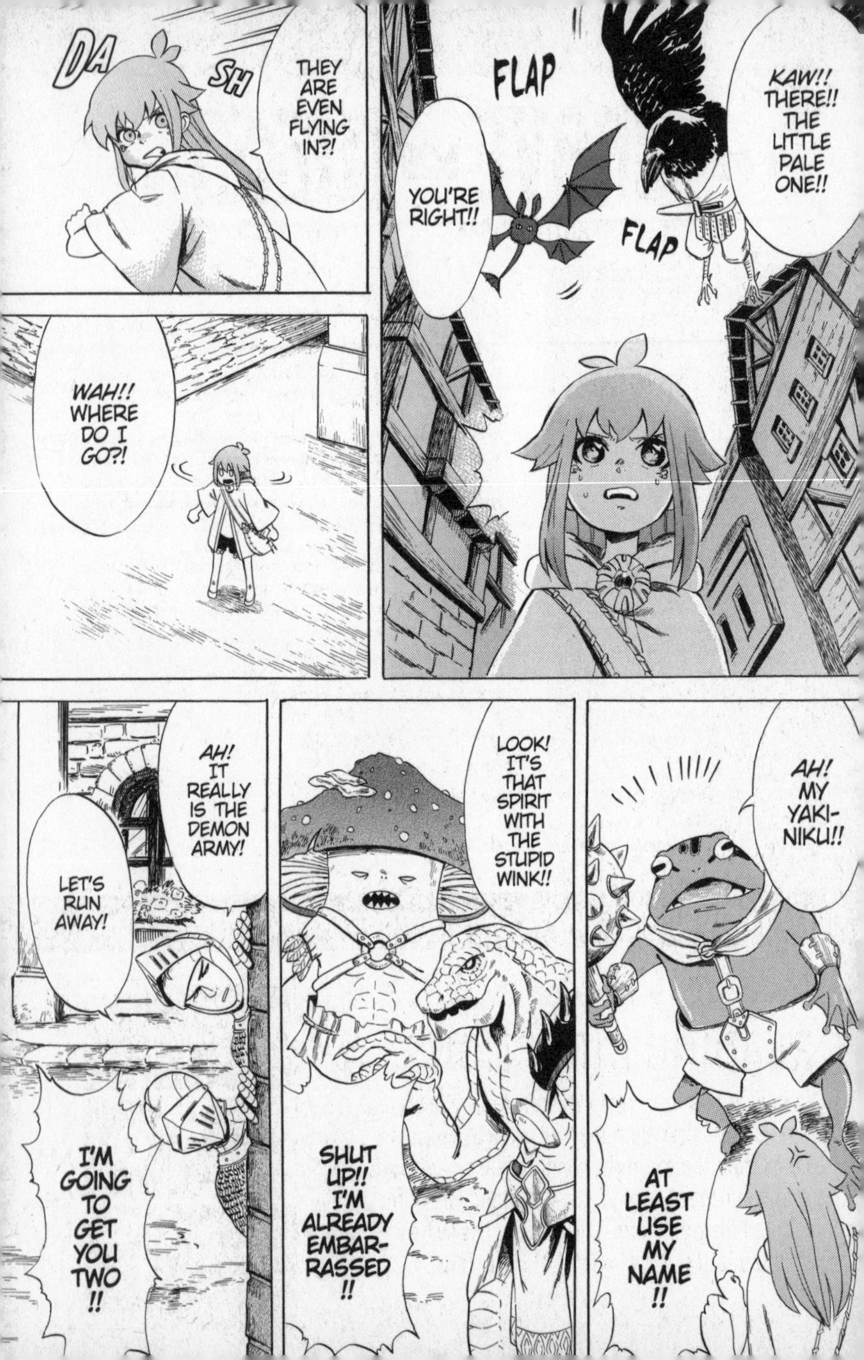
KAW!! THERE!! THE LITTLE PALE ONE!!
FLAP
FLAP
YOU'RE RIGHT!!
DASH
THEY ARE EVEN FLYING IN?!
WAH!! WHERE DO I GO?!
AH! MY YAKI-NIKU!!
AT LEAST USE MY NAME!!
LOOK! IT'S THAT SPIRIT WITH THE STUPID WINK!!
SHUT UP!! I'M ALREADY EMBARRASSED!!
AH! IT REALLY IS THE DEMON ARMY!
LET'S RUN AWAY!
I'M GOING TO GET YOU TWO!!

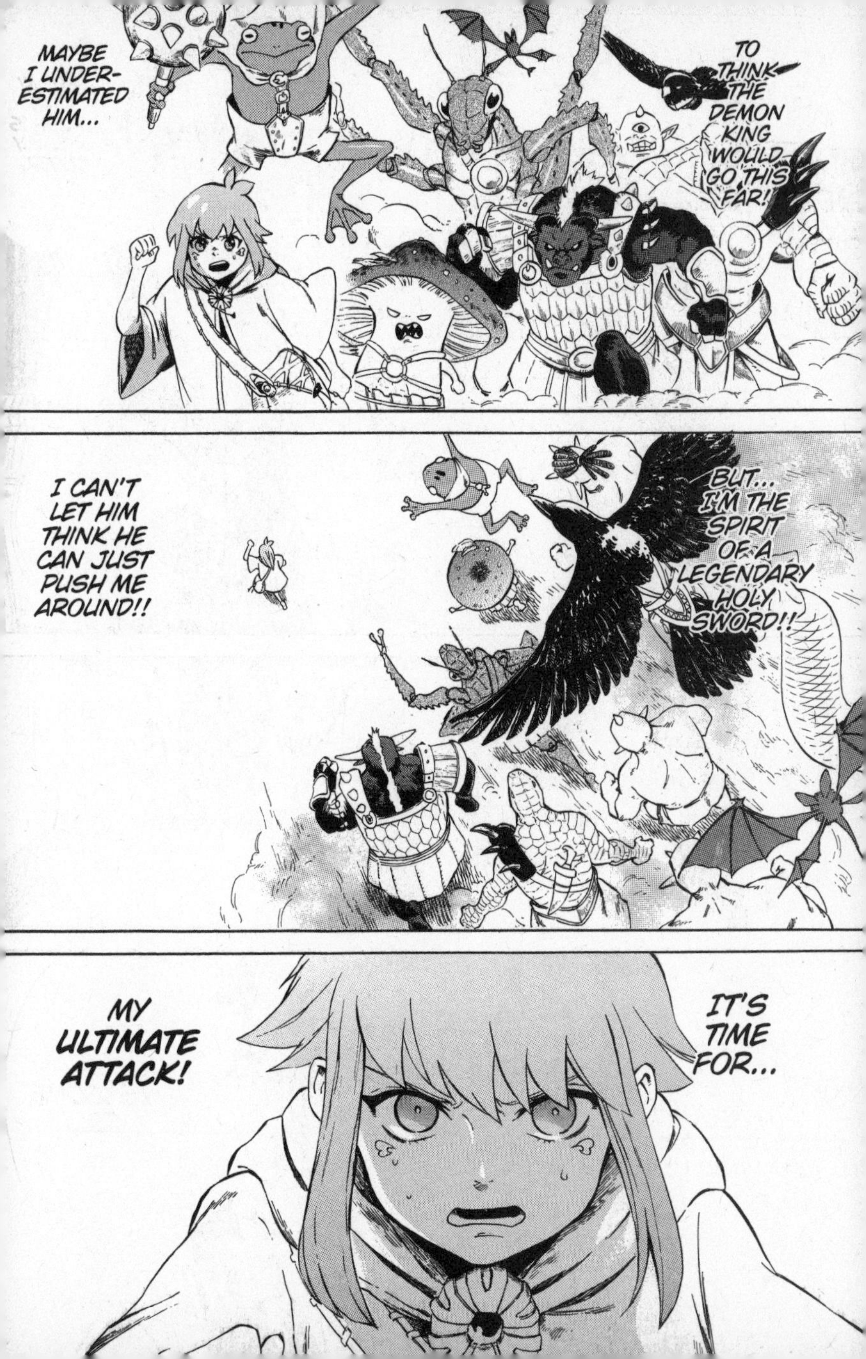
TO THINK THE DEMON KING WOULD GO THIS FAR!
MAYBE I UNDER-ESTIMATED HIM...
BUT... I'M THE SPIRIT OF A LEGENDARY HOLY SWORD!!
I CAN'T LET HIM THINK HE CAN JUST PUSH ME AROUND!!
IT'S TIME FOR...
MY ULTIMATE ATTACK!

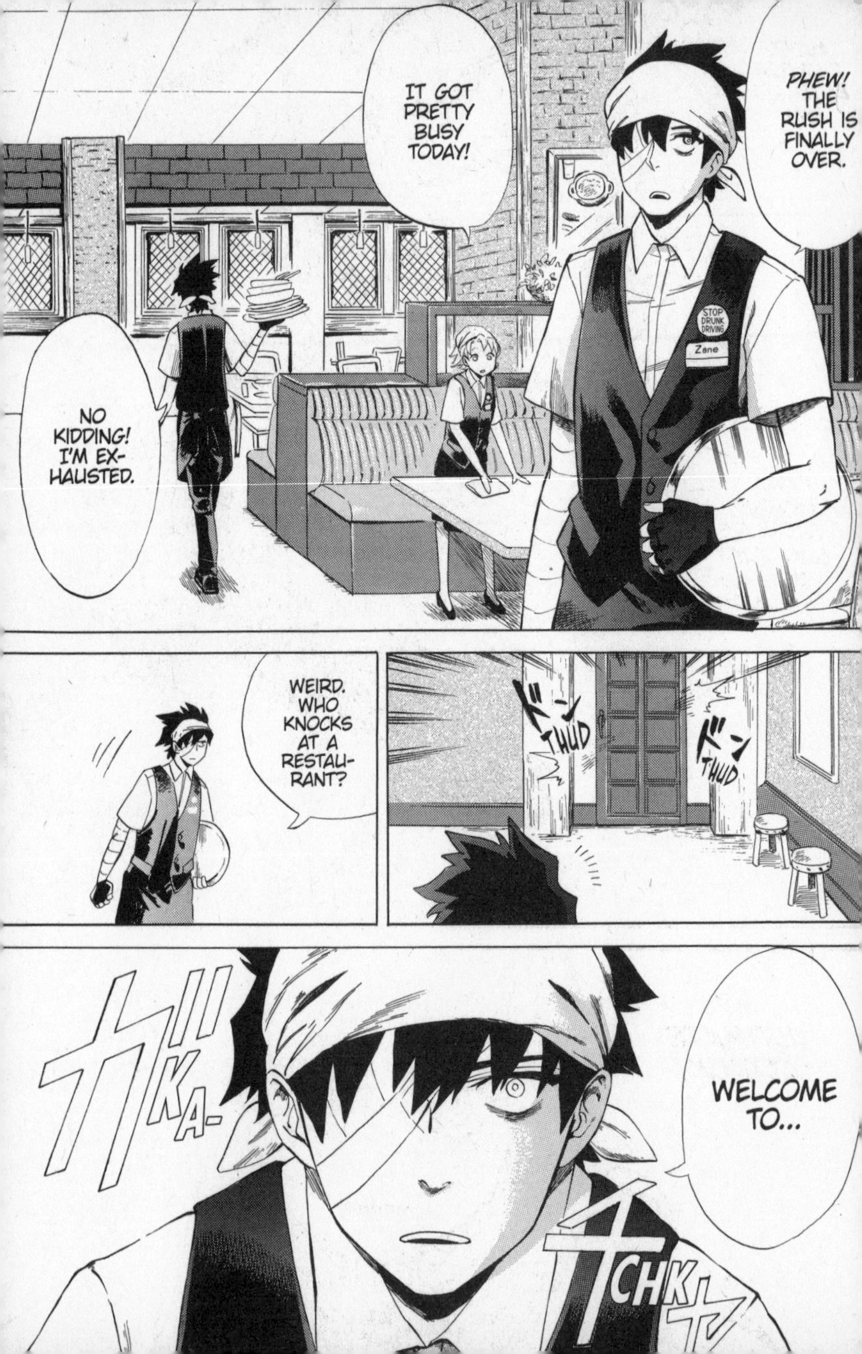
PHEW! THE RUSH IS FINALLY OVER.
STOP DRUNK DRIVING
Zane
IT GOT PRETTY BUSY TODAY!
NO KIDDING! I'M EXHAUSTED.
ドン THUD
ドン THUD
WEIRD. WHO KNOCKS AT A RESTAURANT?
WELCOME TO...
CHK
KA-

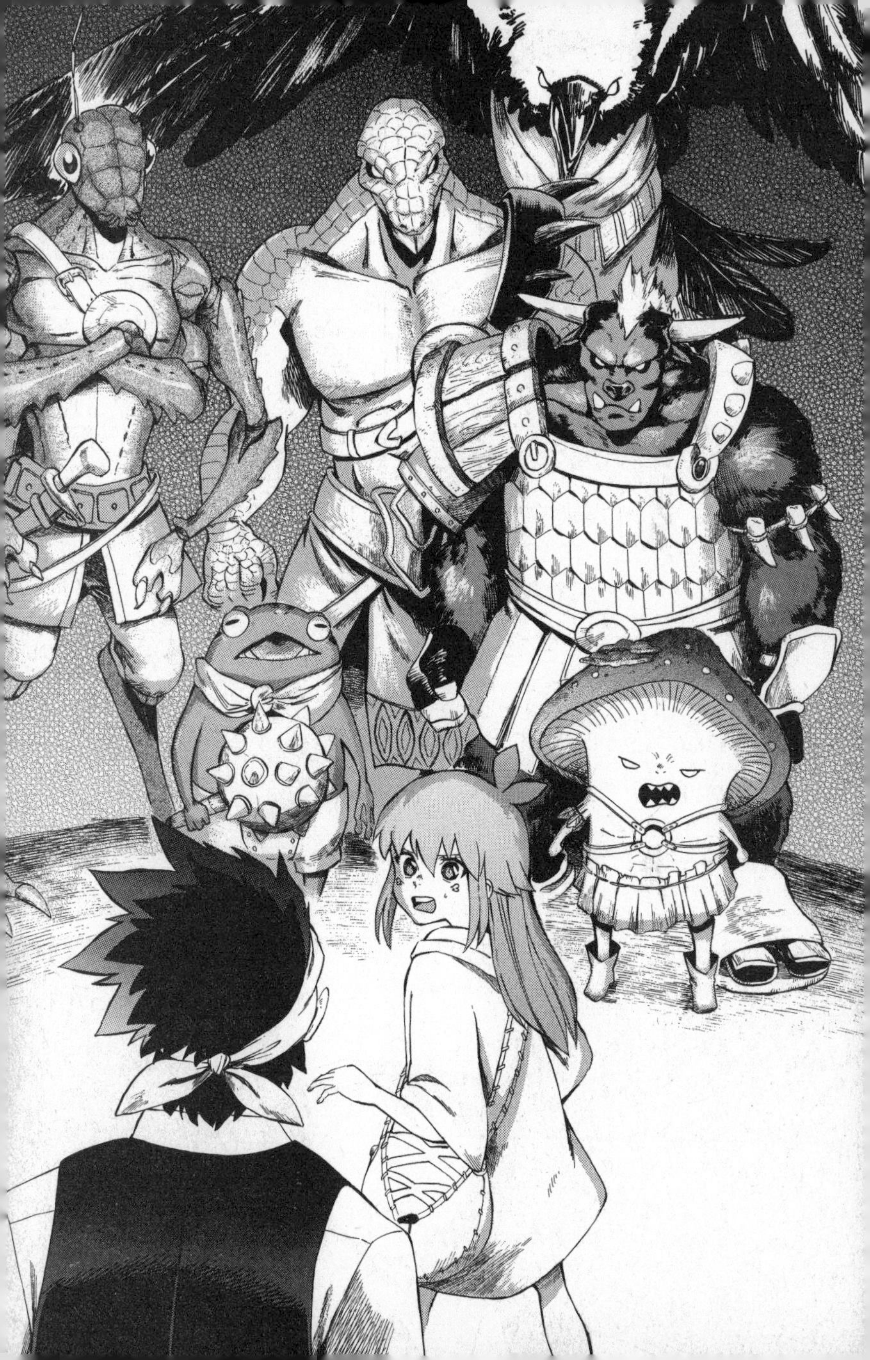

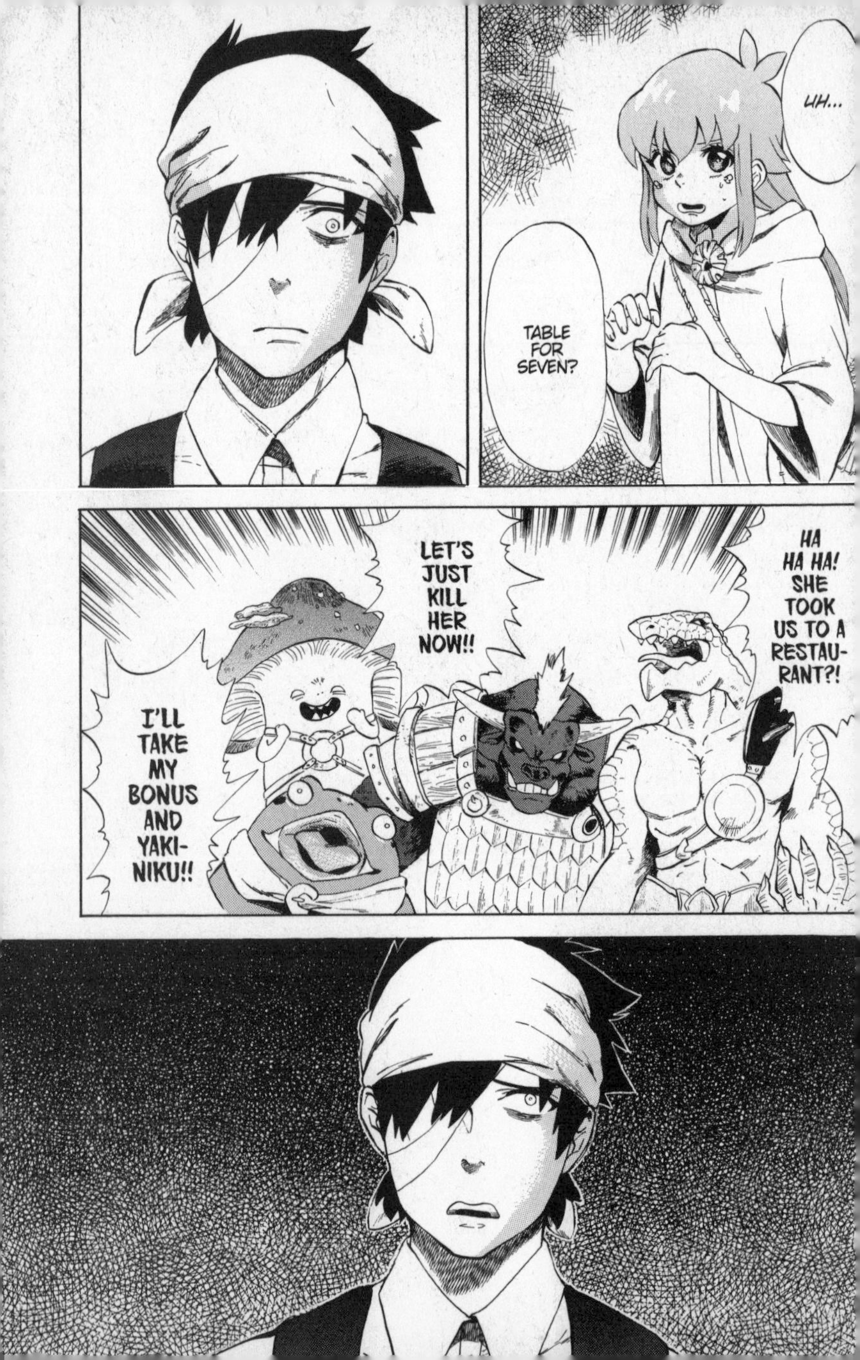
UH...
TABLE FOR SEVEN?
HA HA HA! SHE TOOK US TO A RESTAU-RANT?!
LET'S JUST KILL HER NOW!!
I'LL TAKE MY BONUS AND YAKI-NIKU!!

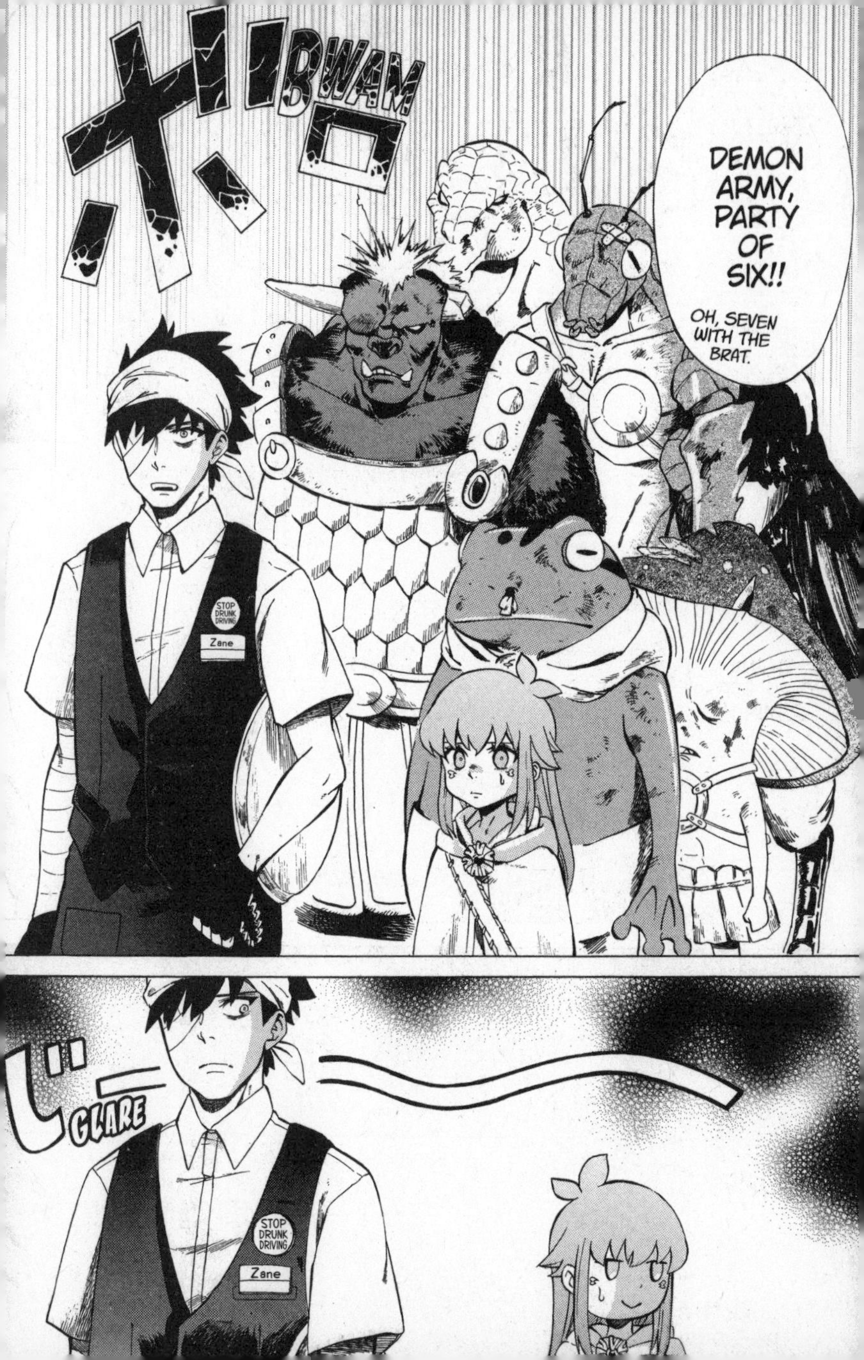
BWAM
DEMON ARMY, PARTY OF SIX!!
OH, SEVEN WITH THE BRAT.
STOP DRUNK DRIVING
Zane
GLARE
STOP DRUNK DRIVING
Zane

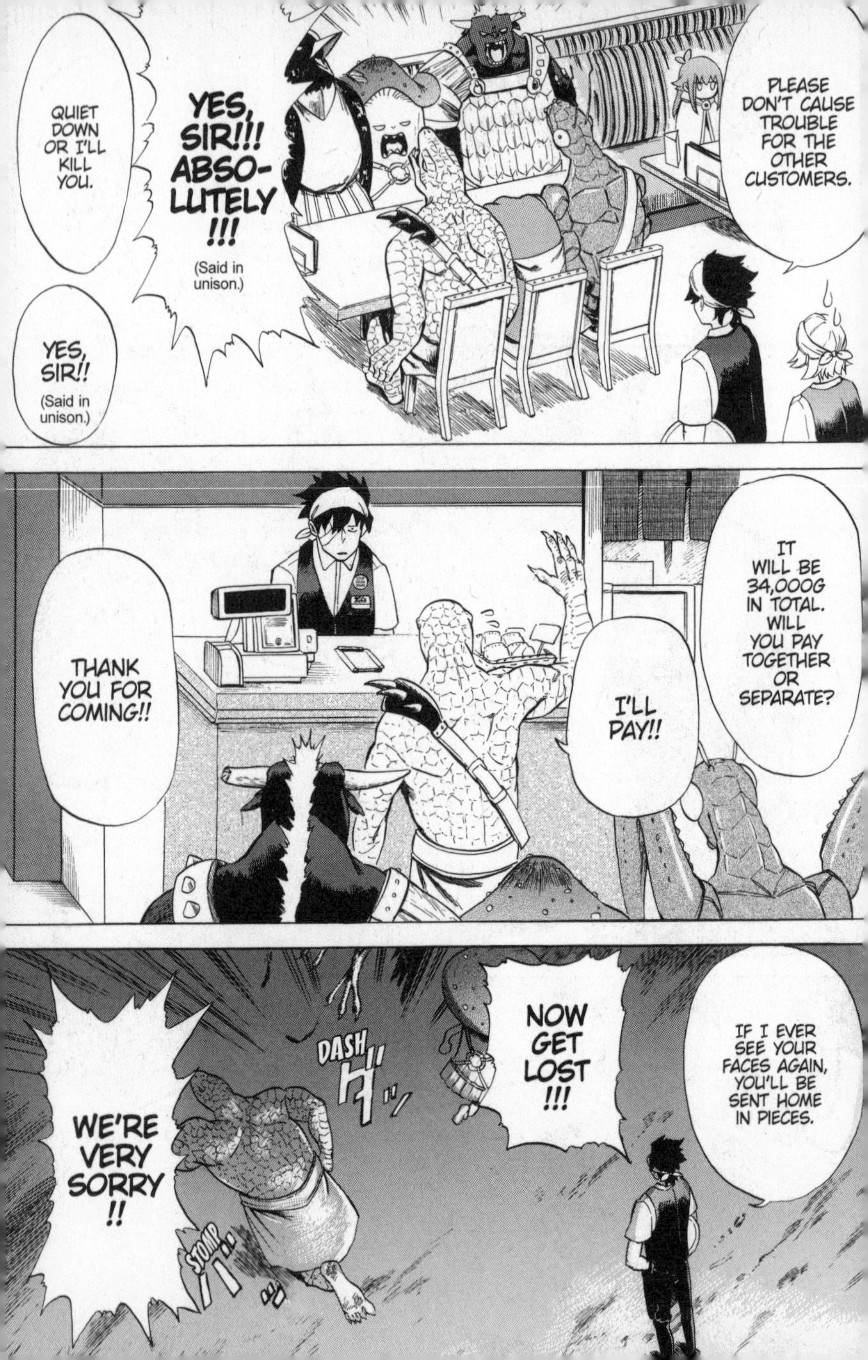
PLEASE DON'T CAUSE TROUBLE FOR THE OTHER CUSTOMERS.
YES, SIR!!! ABSOLUTELY!!!
(Said in unison.)
QUIET DOWN OR I'LL KILL YOU.
YES, SIR!!
(Said in unison.)
IT WILL BE 34,000G IN TOTAL. WILL YOU PAY TOGETHER OR SEPARATE?
I'LL PAY!!
THANK YOU FOR COMING!!
IF I EVER SEE YOUR FACES AGAIN, YOU'LL BE SENT HOME IN PIECES.
NOW GET LOST!!!
DASH
WE'RE VERY SORRY!!
STOMP

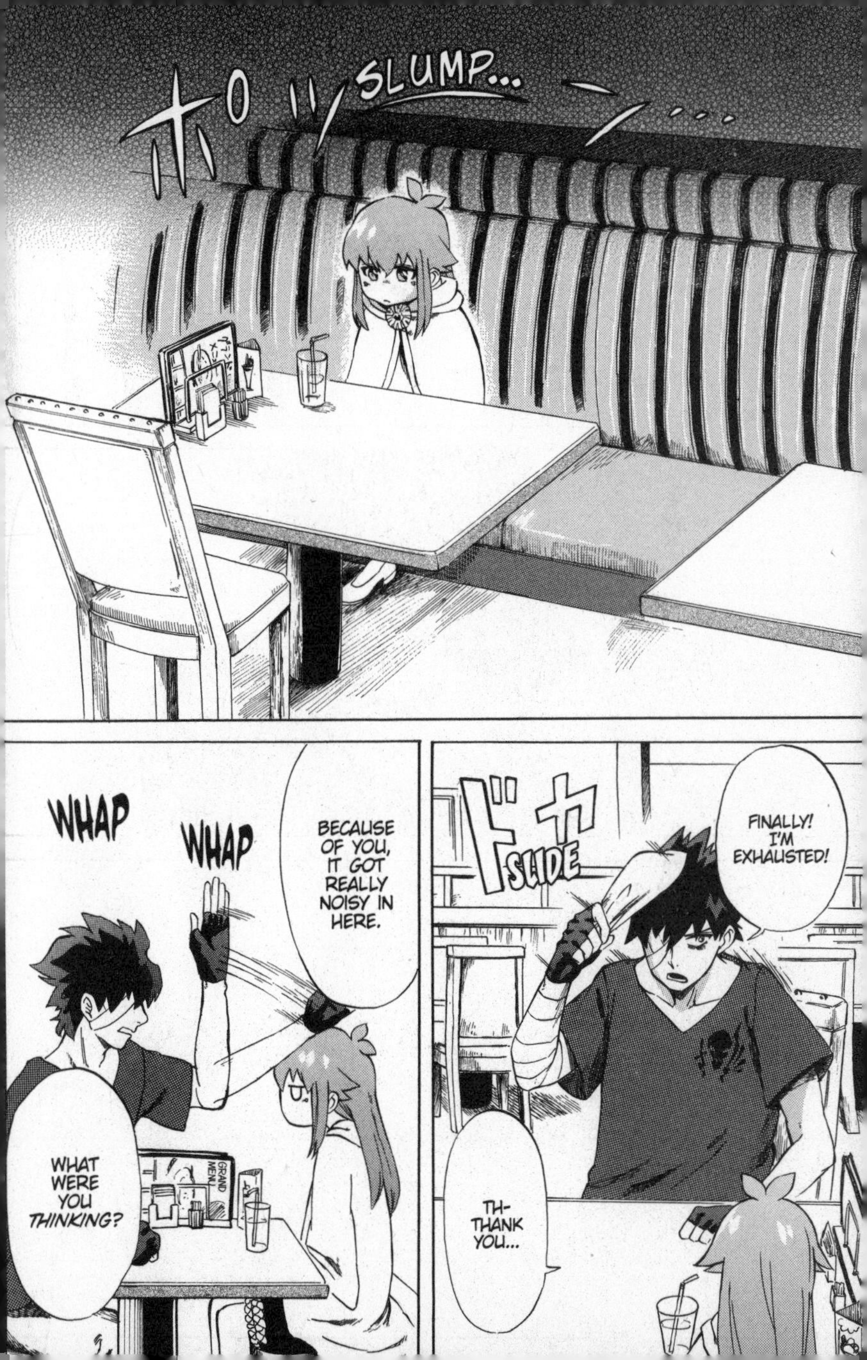
ホッ
SLUMP...
FINALLY! I'M EXHAUSTED!
ドサ
SLIDE
TH-THANK YOU...
BECAUSE OF YOU, IT GOT REALLY NOISY IN HERE.
WHAP
WHAP
GRAND MENU
WHAT WERE YOU *THINKING?*

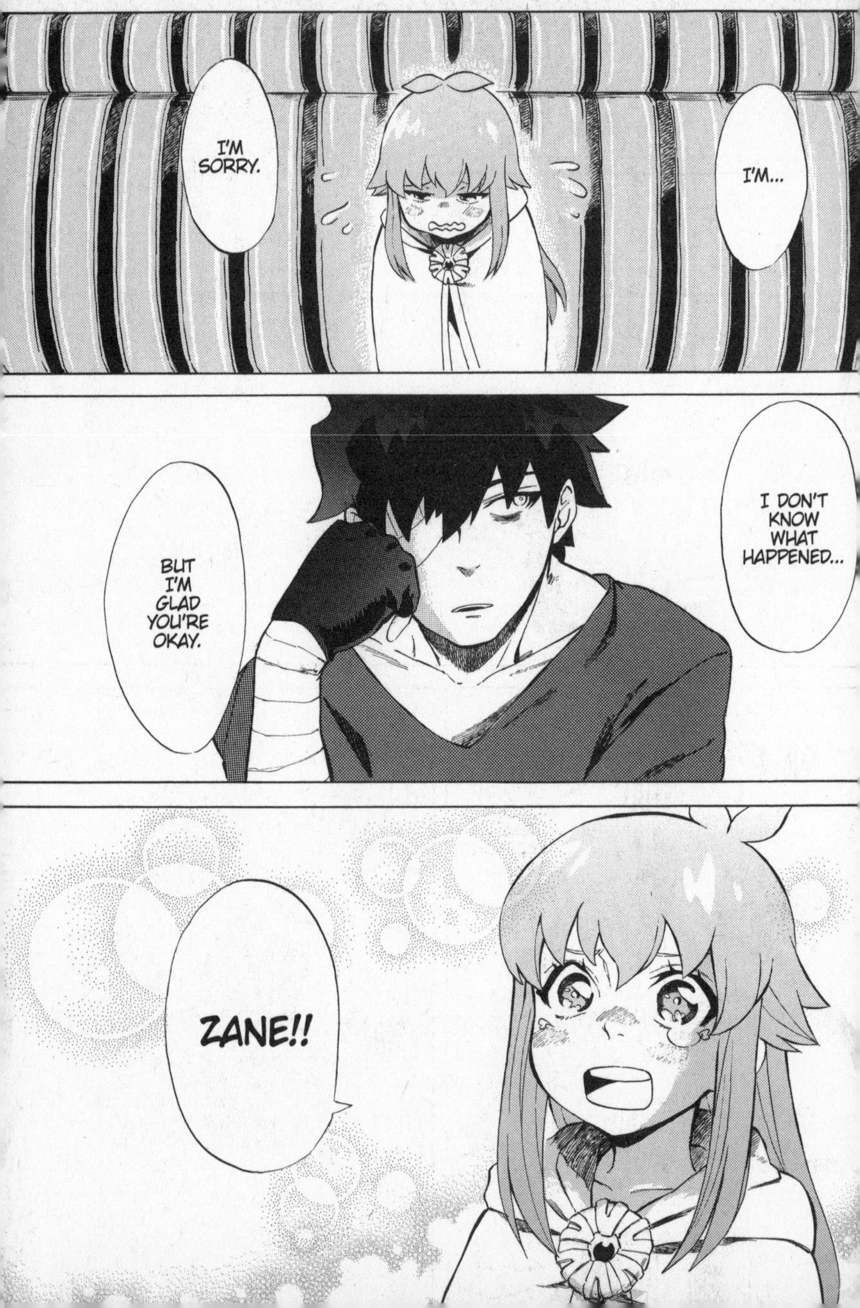
I'M...
I'M SORRY.
I DON'T KNOW WHAT HAPPENED...
BUT I'M GLAD YOU'RE OKAY.
ZANE!!

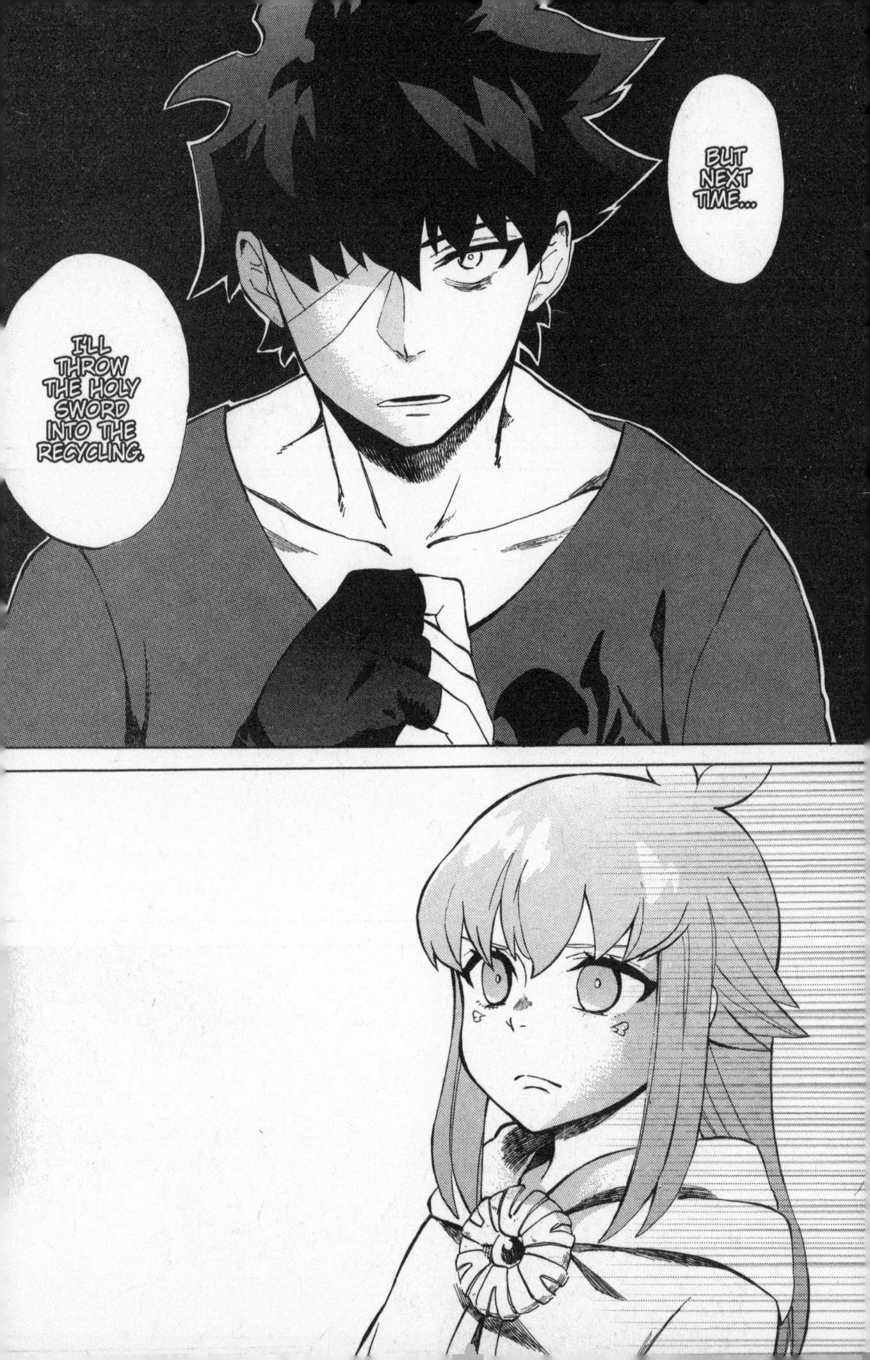
BUT NEXT TIME...
I'LL THROW THE HOLY SWORD INTO THE RECYCLING.

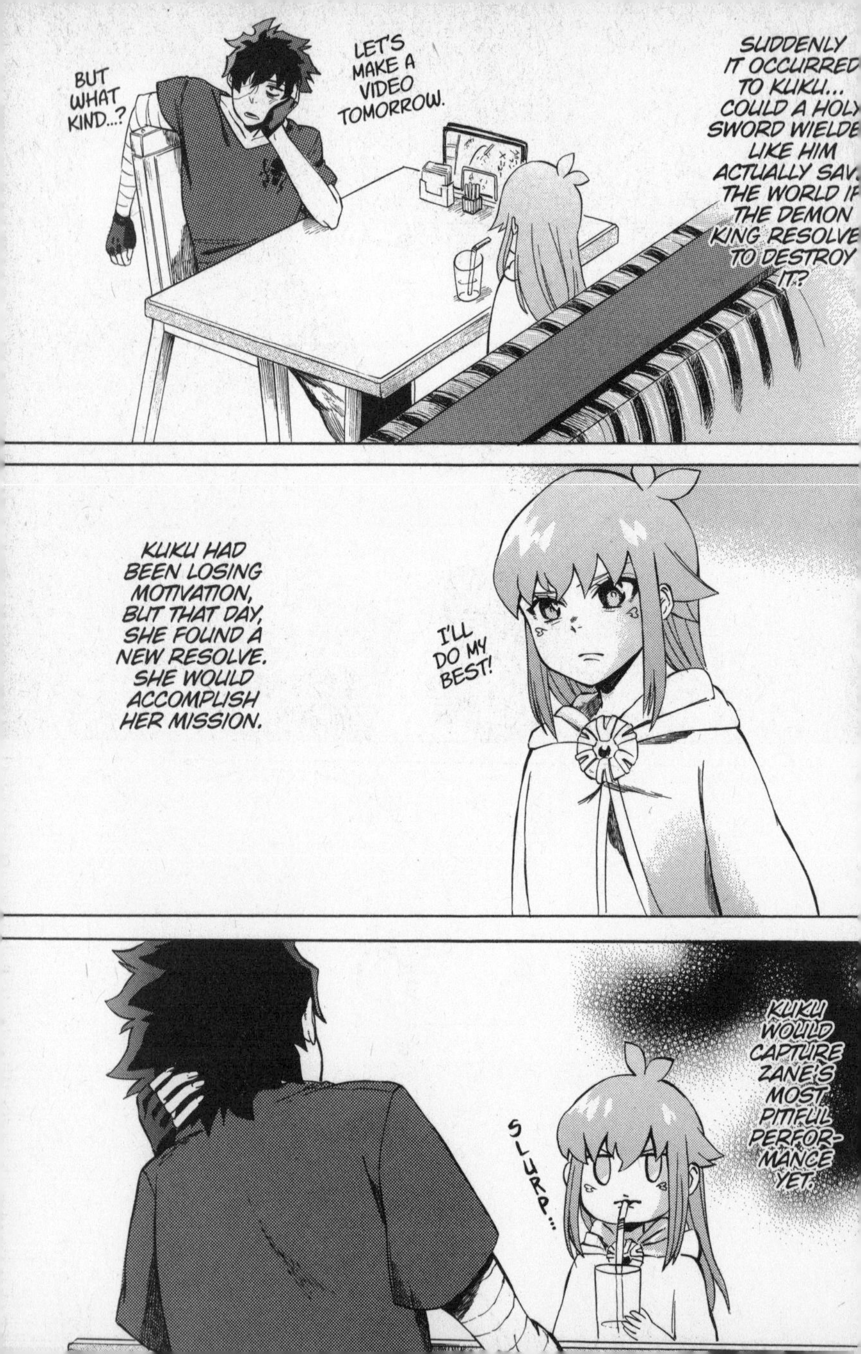
SUDDENLY IT OCCURRED TO KUKU... COULD A HOLY SWORD WIELDE LIKE HIM ACTUALLY SAV THE WORLD IF THE DEMON KING RESOLVE TO DESTROY IT?
LET'S MAKE A VIDEO TOMORROW.
BUT WHAT KIND...?
I'LL DO MY BEST!
KUKU HAD BEEN LOSING MOTIVATION, BUT THAT DAY, SHE FOUND A NEW RESOLVE. SHE WOULD ACCOMPLISH HER MISSION.
KUKU WOULD CAPTURE ZANE'S MOST PITIFUL PERFOR-MANCE YET.
SLURP...

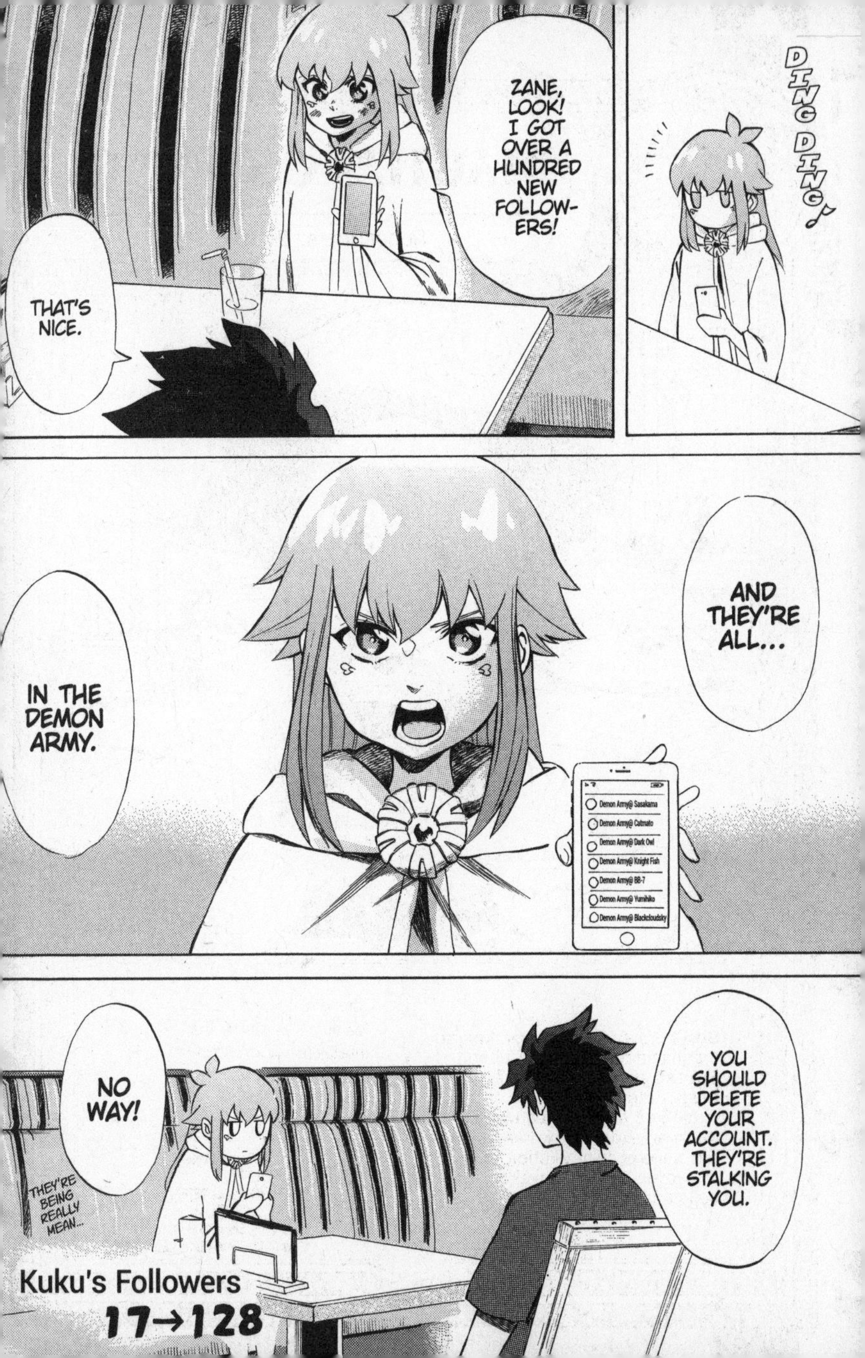
DING DING♪
ZANE, LOOK! I GOT OVER A HUNDRED NEW FOLLOW-ERS!
THAT'S NICE.
AND THEY'RE ALL...
IN THE DEMON ARMY.
Demon Army@ Sasakama
Demon Army@ Catmato
Demon Army@ Dark Owl
Demon Army@ Knight Fish
Demon Army@ BB-7
Demon Army@ Yumihiko
Demon Army@ Blackcloudsky
YOU SHOULD DELETE YOUR ACCOUNT. THEY'RE STALKING YOU.
NO WAY!
THEY'RE BEING REALLY MEAN...
Kuku's Followers
17→128

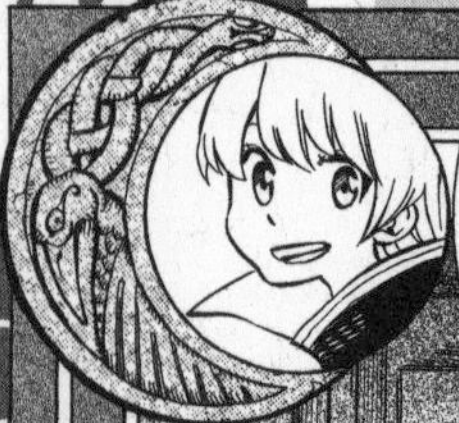

MAGIL'S CHANNEL

Subscribers: 21,384,254

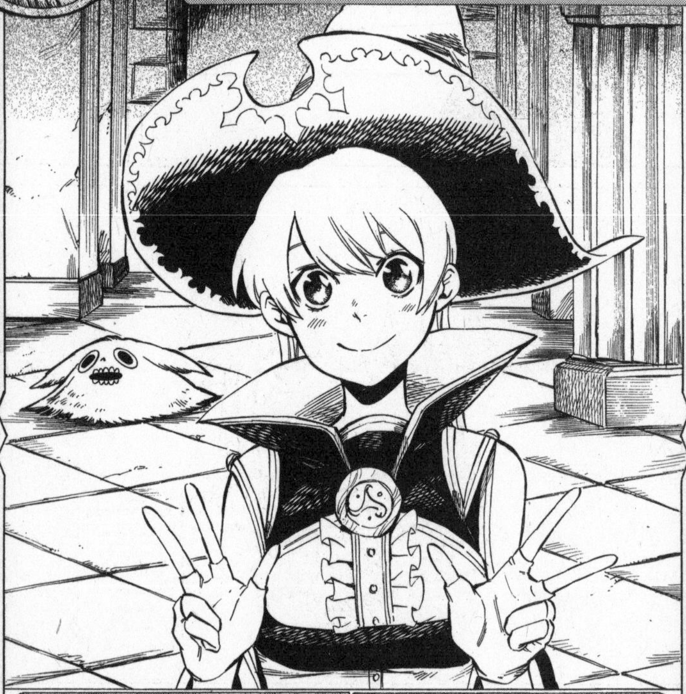

Second only to the Ashen Knight, Magil is a top class WizTuber. Praised as a genius, Magil posts magic tutorial videos for beginners to advanced users. She's an expert networker and has several collaboration videos. She loves trying out weird capsule toy machines.

Strength	☆☆
Magic	☆☆☆☆☆
Intelligence	☆☆☆☆☆
Editing	☆☆☆☆☆
Speech	☆☆☆
Networking	☆☆☆☆☆☆☆☆☆☆

RECOMMENDED VIDEOS

- Magil's Magic Course [COMPLETE]
- NO BOYS ALLOWED!!! <*。ヽ(。>v<。)/。*> Girls Only Secret Meeting
- How to Let Them Down Easy[#127]

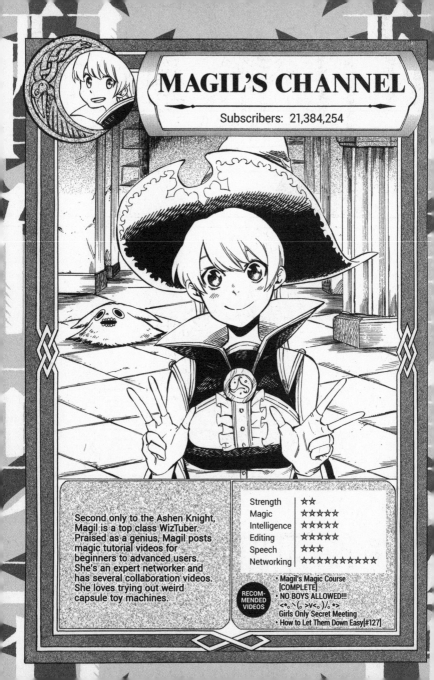

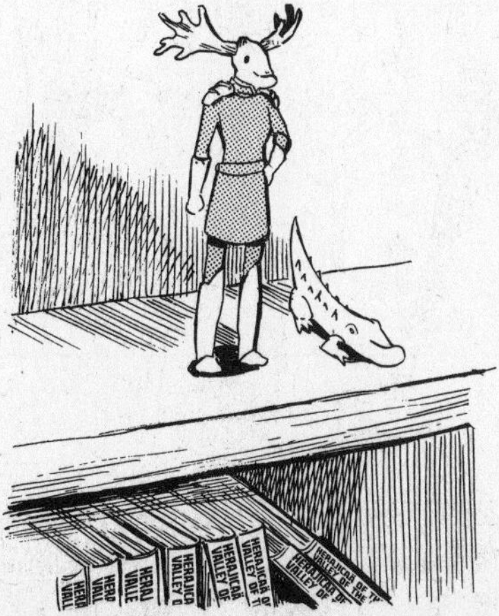

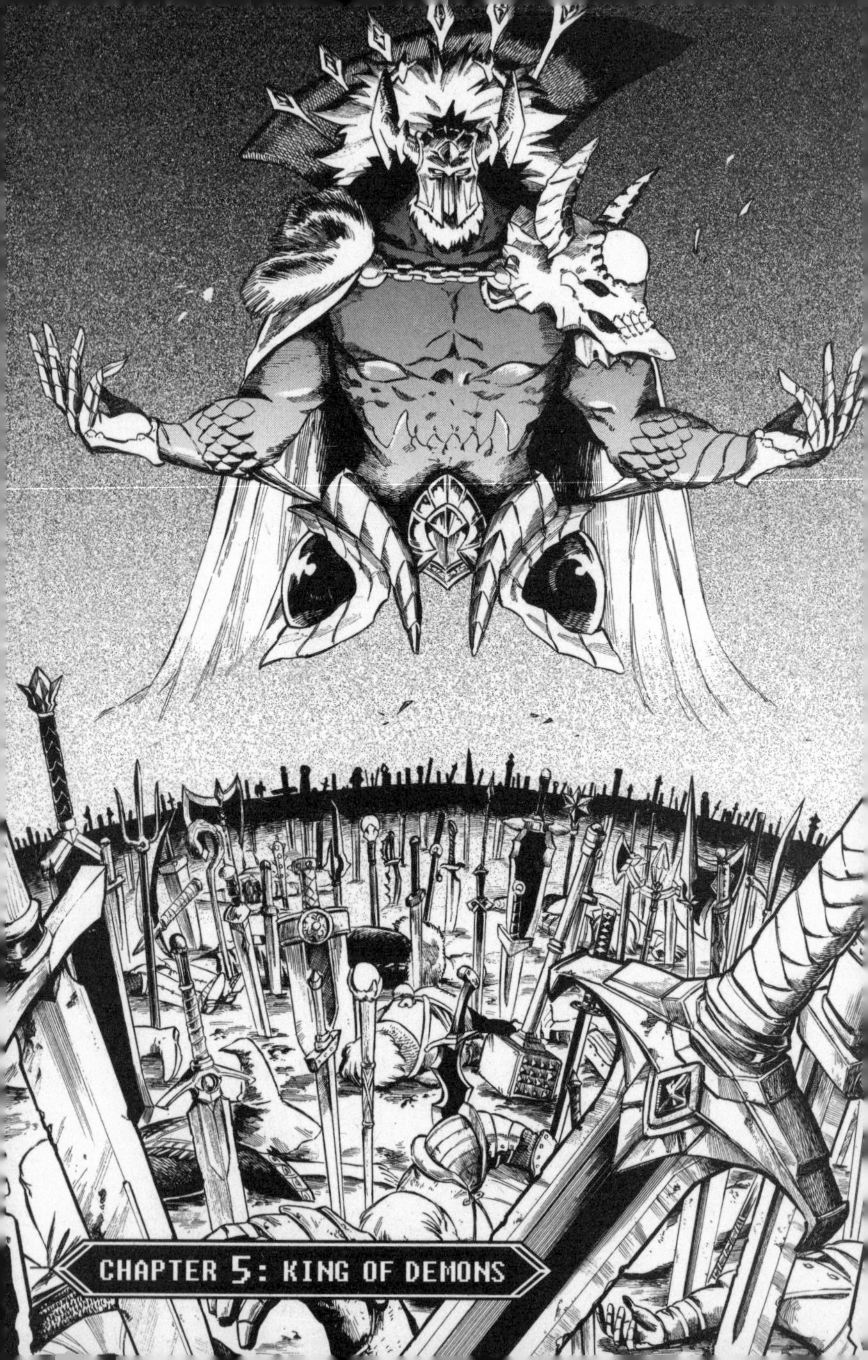
CHAPTER 5: KING OF DEMONS

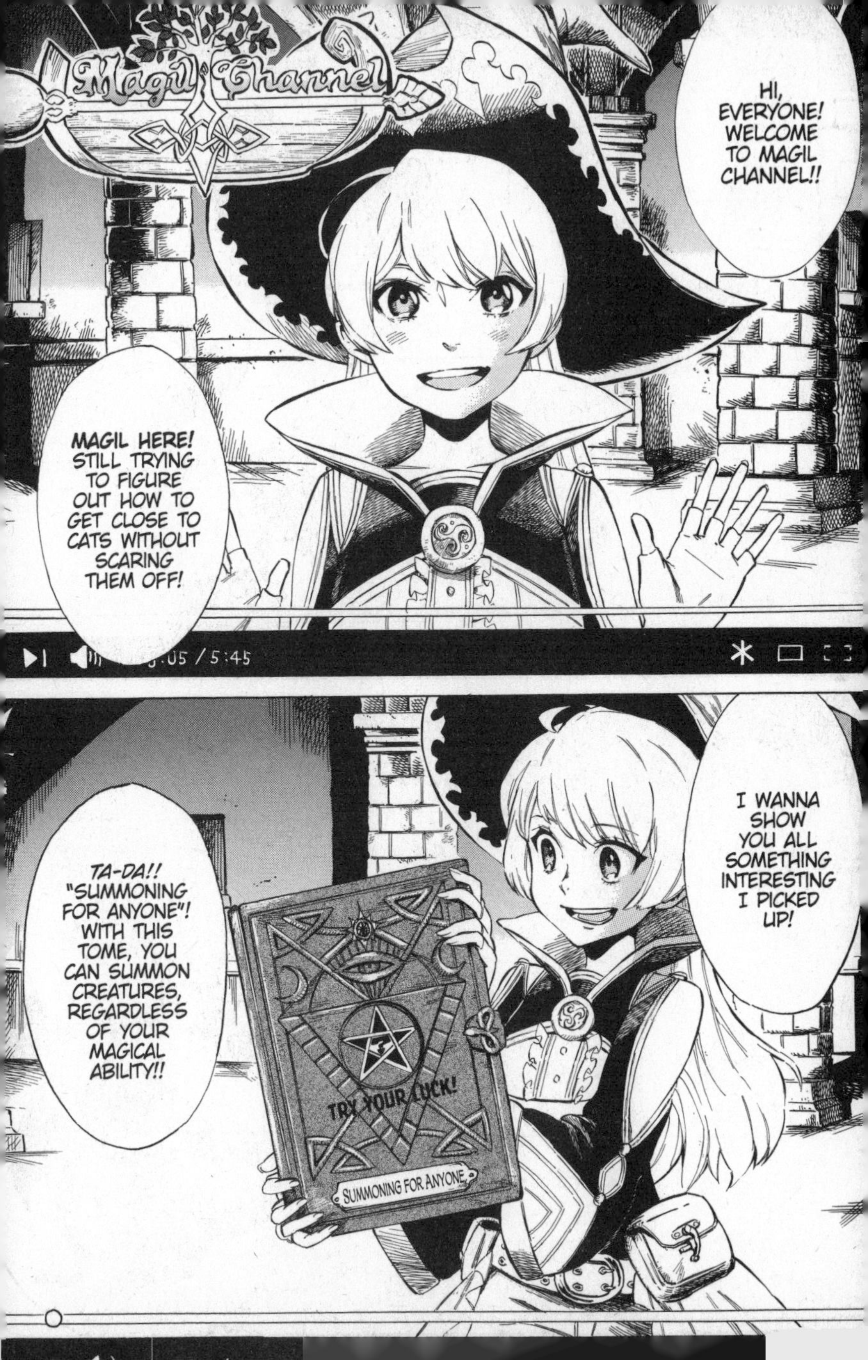
Magil Channel
HI, EVERYONE! WELCOME TO MAGIL CHANNEL!!
MAGIL HERE! STILL TRYING TO FIGURE OUT HOW TO GET CLOSE TO CATS WITHOUT SCARING THEM OFF!
5:45
I WANNA SHOW YOU ALL SOMETHING INTERESTING I PICKED UP!
TA-DA!! "SUMMONING FOR ANYONE"! WITH THIS TOME, YOU CAN SUMMON CREATURES, REGARDLESS OF YOUR MAGICAL ABILITY!!
TRY YOUR LUCK!
SUMMONING FOR ANYONE

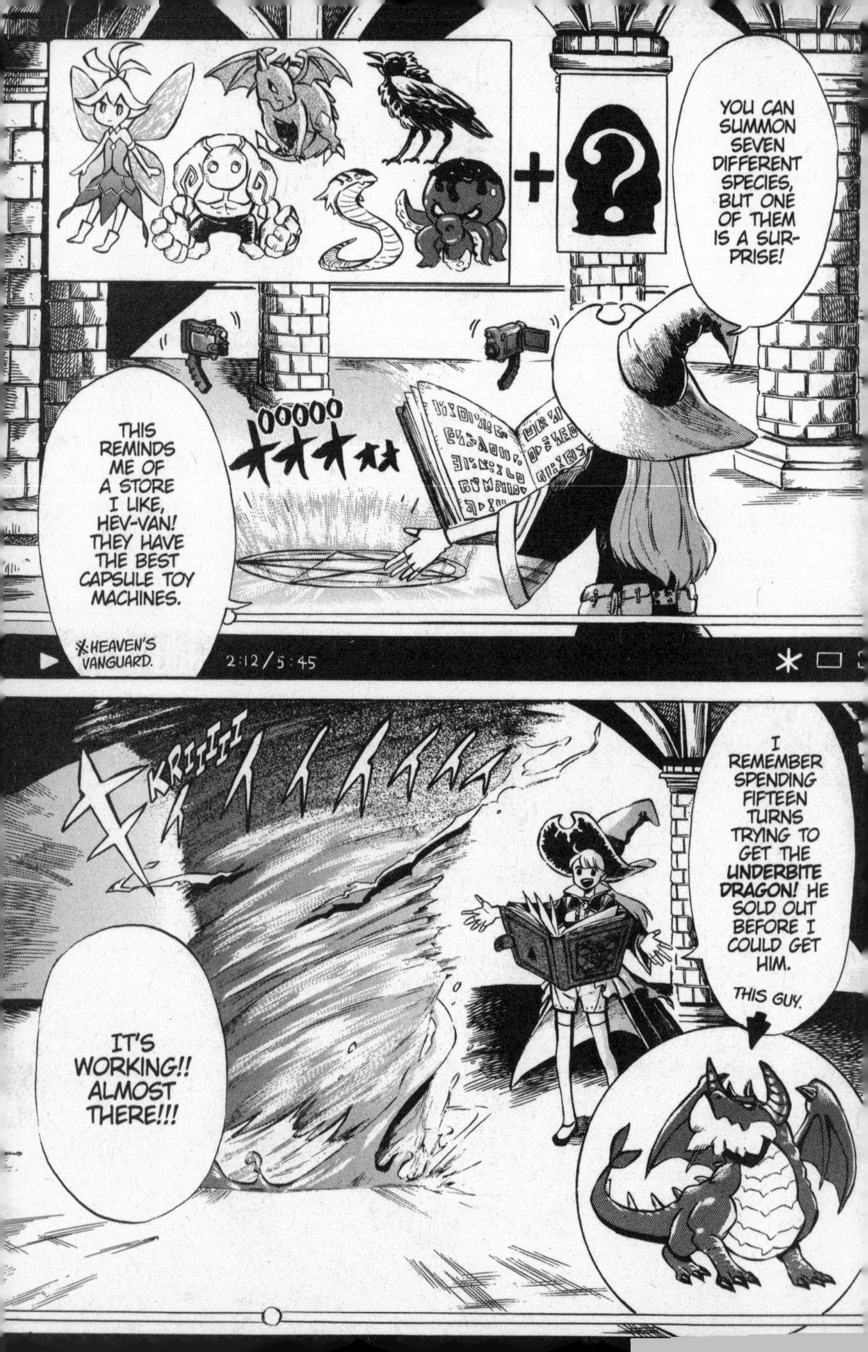
YOU CAN SUMMON SEVEN DIFFERENT SPECIES, BUT ONE OF THEM IS A SUR-PRISE!
OOOOO
THIS REMINDS ME OF A STORE I LIKE, HEV-VAN! THEY HAVE THE BEST CAPSULE TOY MACHINES.
※HEAVEN'S VANGUARD.
2:12/5:45
I REMEMBER SPENDING FIFTEEN TURNS TRYING TO GET THE UNDERBITE DRAGON! HE SOLD OUT BEFORE I COULD GET HIM.
THIS GUY.
KRIIIII
IT'S WORKING!! ALMOST THERE!!!

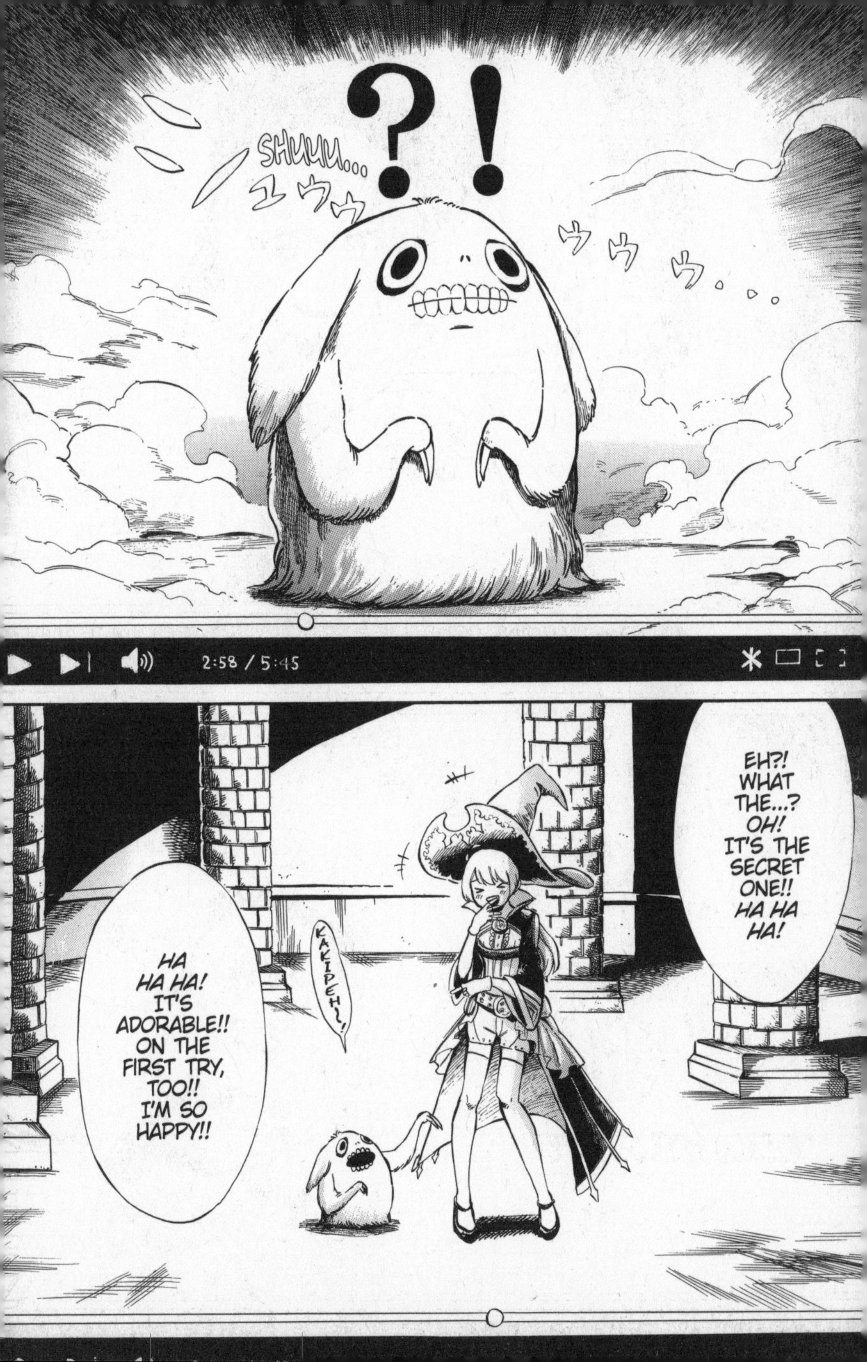
?!
SHUUU...
ユウウ
ウウウ。。。
2:58 / 5:45
EH?! WHAT THE...? OH! IT'S THE SECRET ONE!! HA HA HA!
KAKIPEH~!
HA HA HA! IT'S ADORABLE!! ON THE FIRST TRY, TOO!! I'M SO HAPPY!!

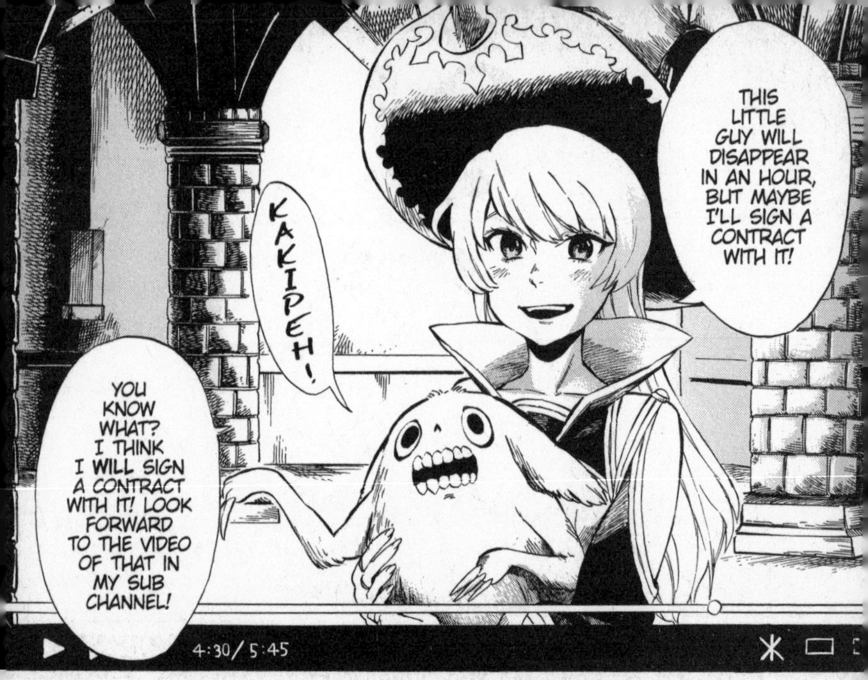
THIS LITTLE GUY WILL DISAPPEAR IN AN HOUR, BUT MAYBE I'LL SIGN A CONTRACT WITH IT!
KAKIPEH!
YOU KNOW WHAT? I THINK I WILL SIGN A CONTRACT WITH IT! LOOK FORWARD TO THE VIDEO OF THAT IN MY SUB CHANNEL!
4:30 / 5:45

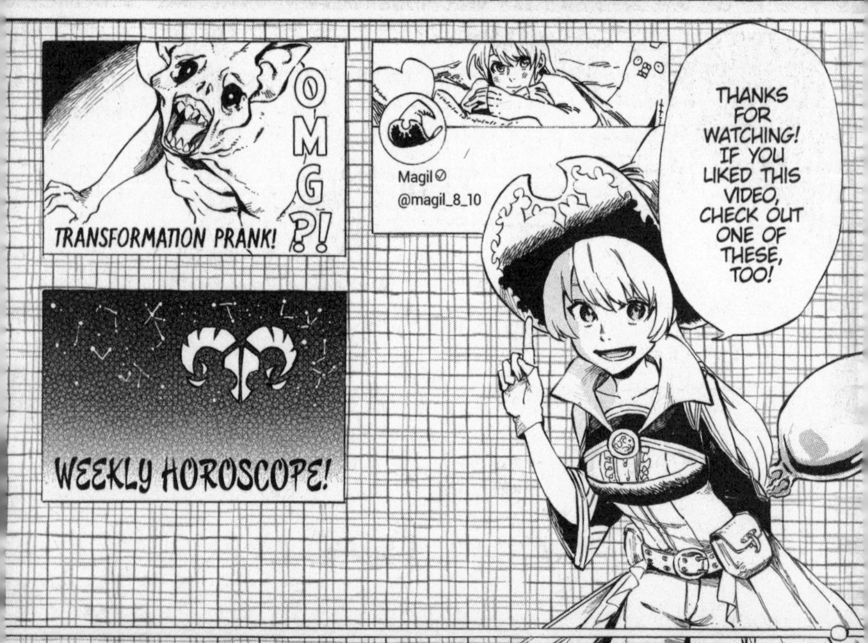
THANKS FOR WATCHING! IF YOU LIKED THIS VIDEO, CHECK OUT ONE OF THESE, TOO!
Magil
@magil_8_10
OMG?!
TRANSFORMATION PRANK!
WEEKLY HOROSCOPE!

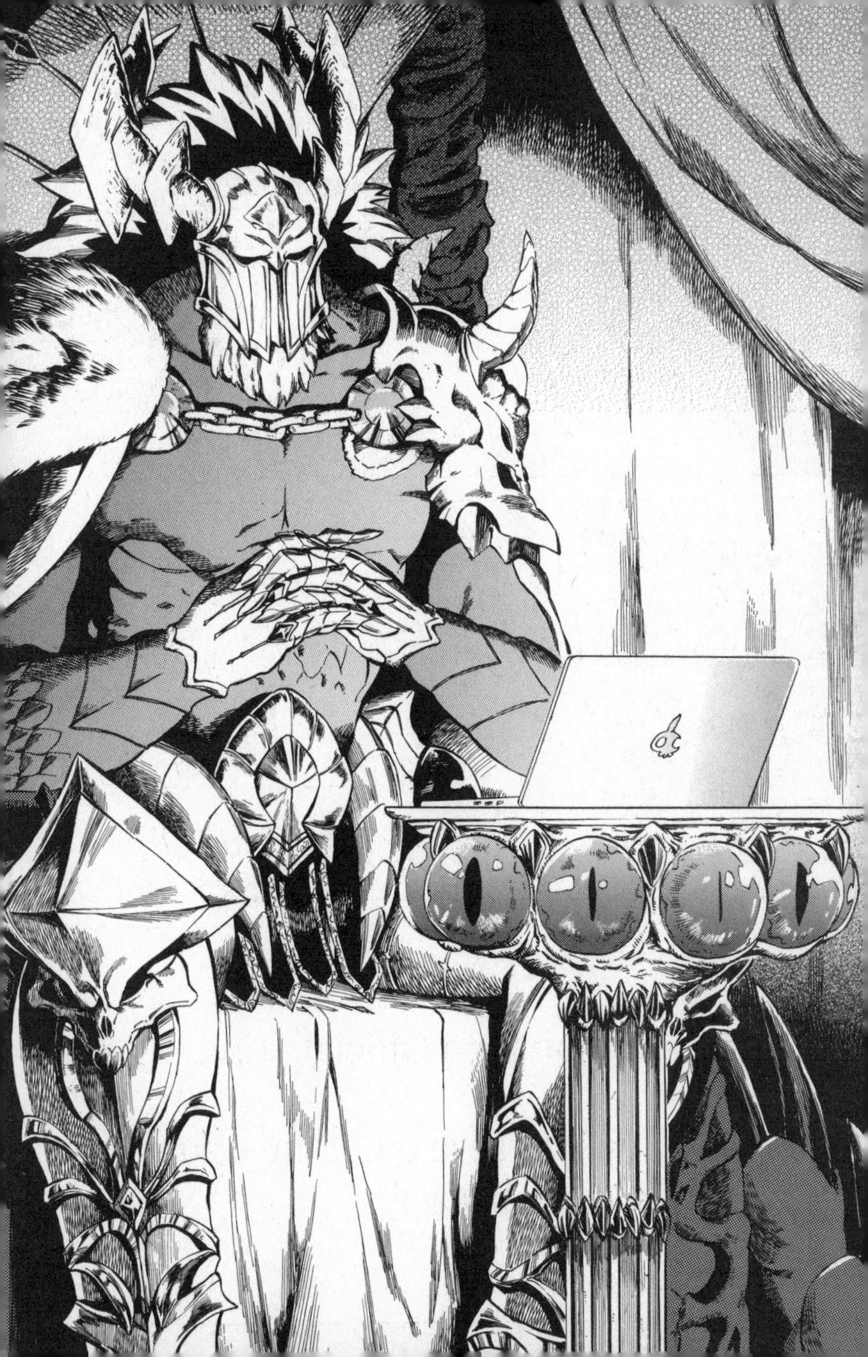

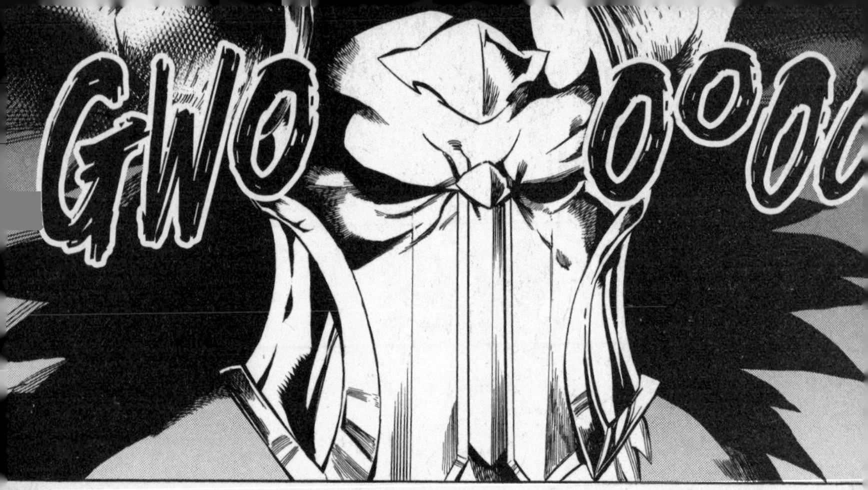
GWOOOO

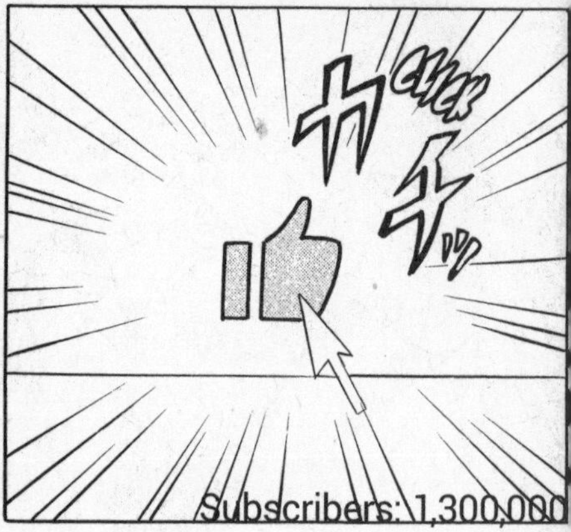
カチッ
CLICK
Subscribers: 1,300,000

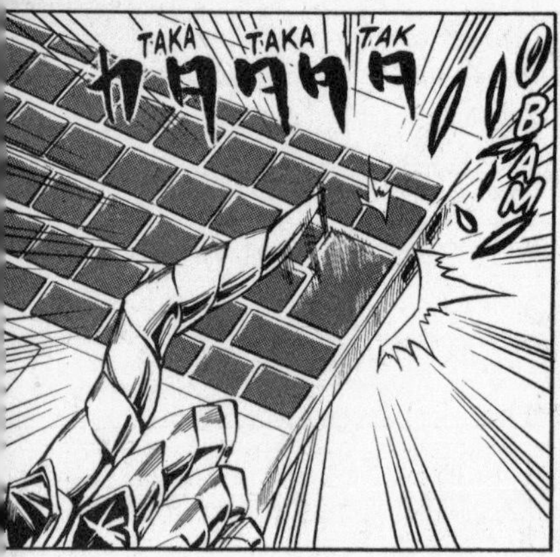
カタタタタ
TAKA TAKA TAK
BAM

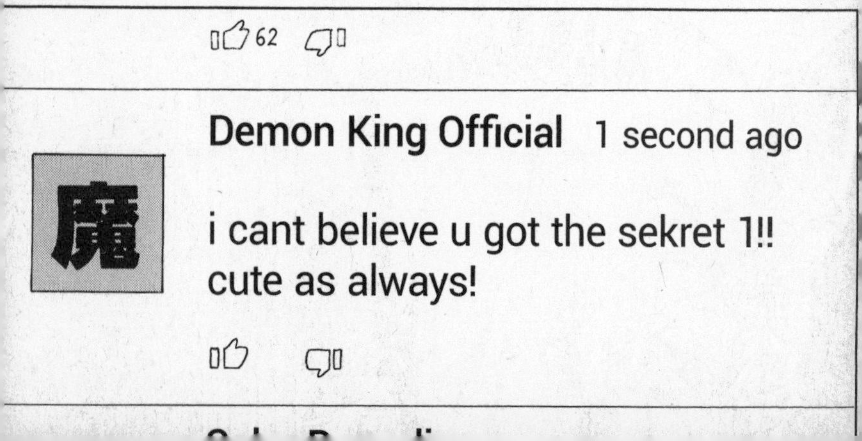
62
Demon King Official 1 second ago
魔
i cant believe u got the sekret 1!!
cute as always!

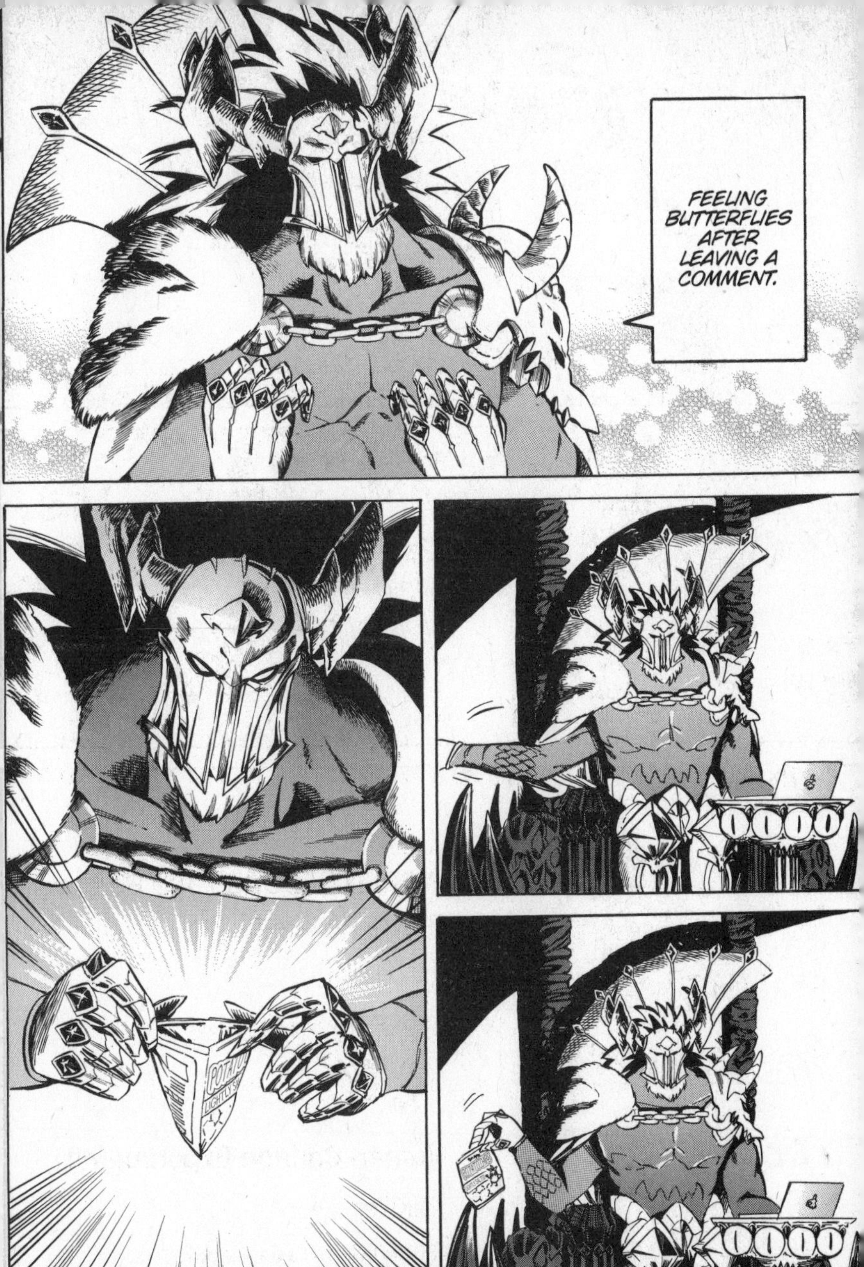
FEELING BUTTERFLIES AFTER LEAVING A COMMENT.

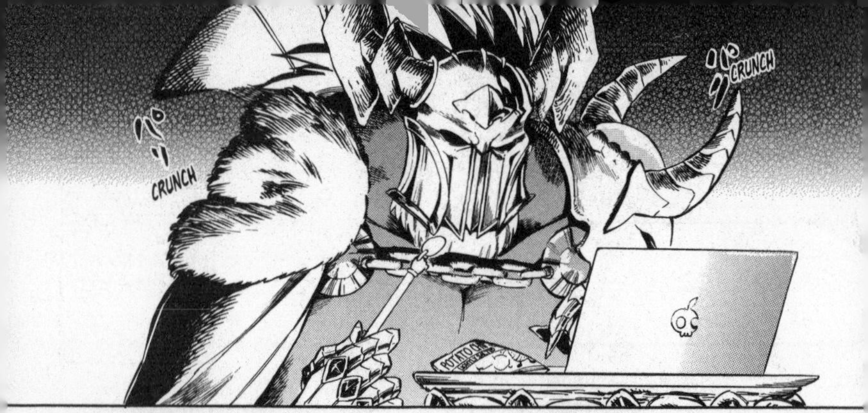
CRUNCH
CRUNCH

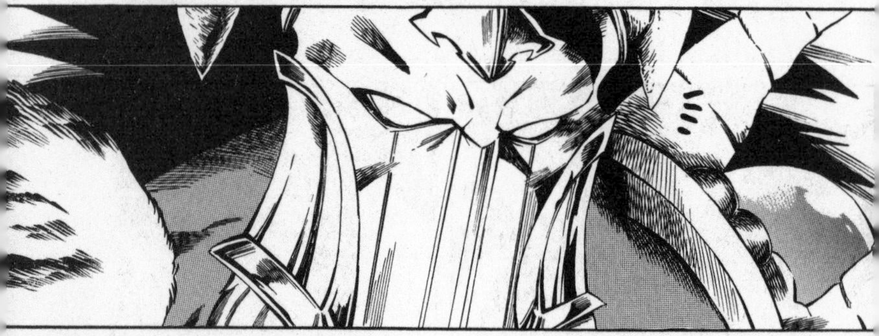

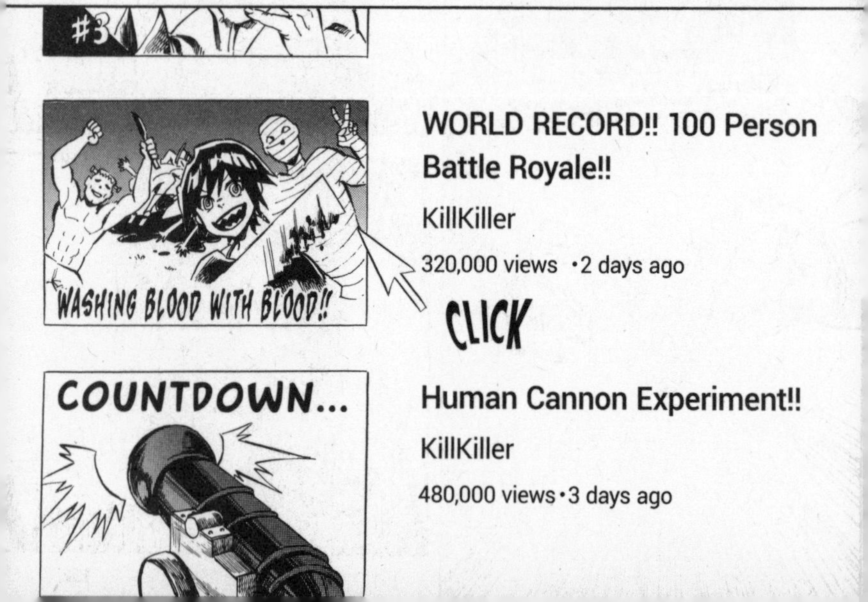
#3
WORLD RECORD!! 100 Person Battle Royale!!
KillKiller
320,000 views •2 days ago
WASHING BLOOD WITH BLOOD!!
CLICK
Human Cannon Experiment!!
KillKiller
480,000 views•3 days ago
COUNTDOWN...

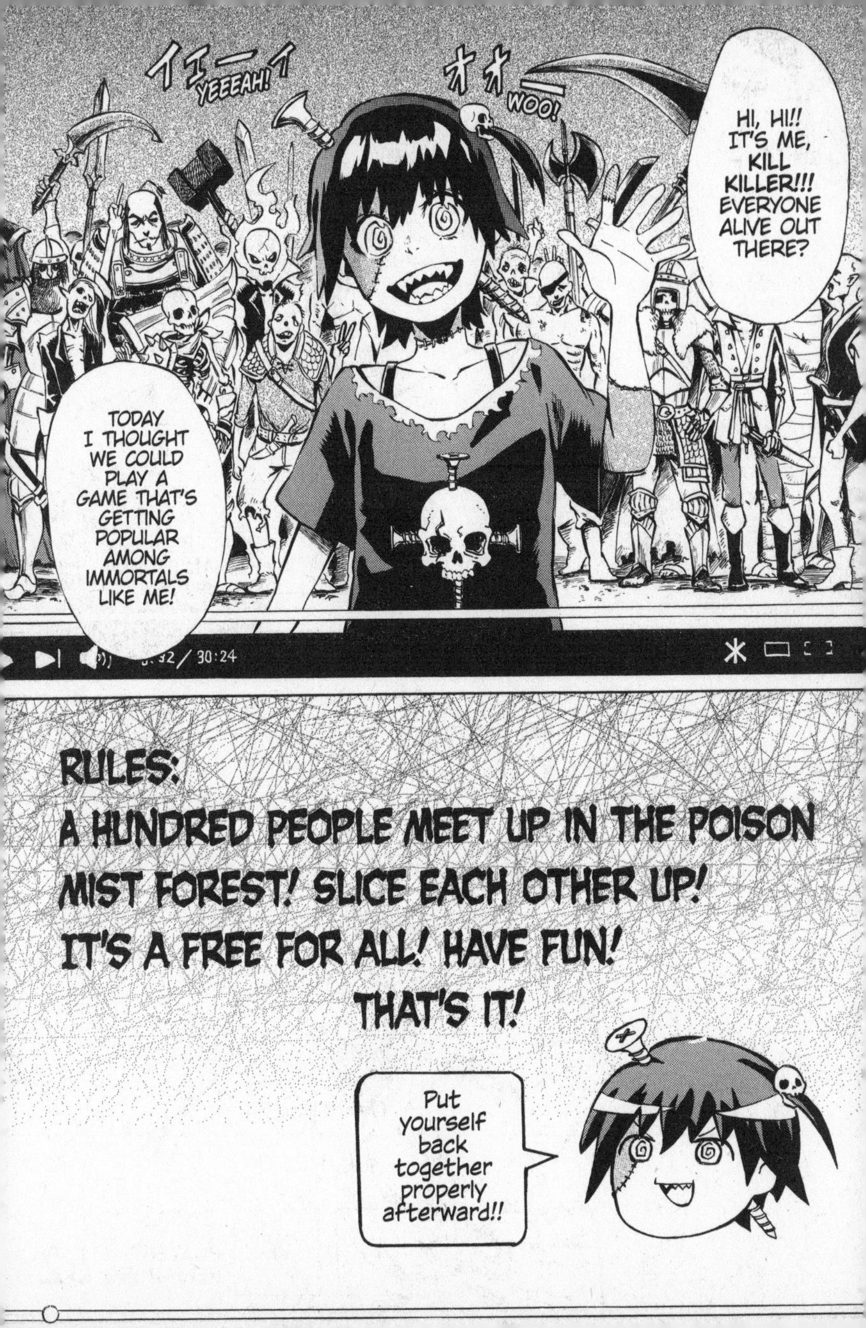
HI, HI!! IT'S ME, KILL KILLER!!! EVERYONE ALIVE OUT THERE?
オオー
WOO!
イエーイ
YEEEAH!
TODAY I THOUGHT WE COULD PLAY A GAME THAT'S GETTING POPULAR AMONG IMMORTALS LIKE ME!
30:24
RULES:
A HUNDRED PEOPLE MEET UP IN THE POISON MIST FOREST! SLICE EACH OTHER UP! IT'S A FREE FOR ALL! HAVE FUN!
THAT'S IT!
Put yourself back together properly afterward!!

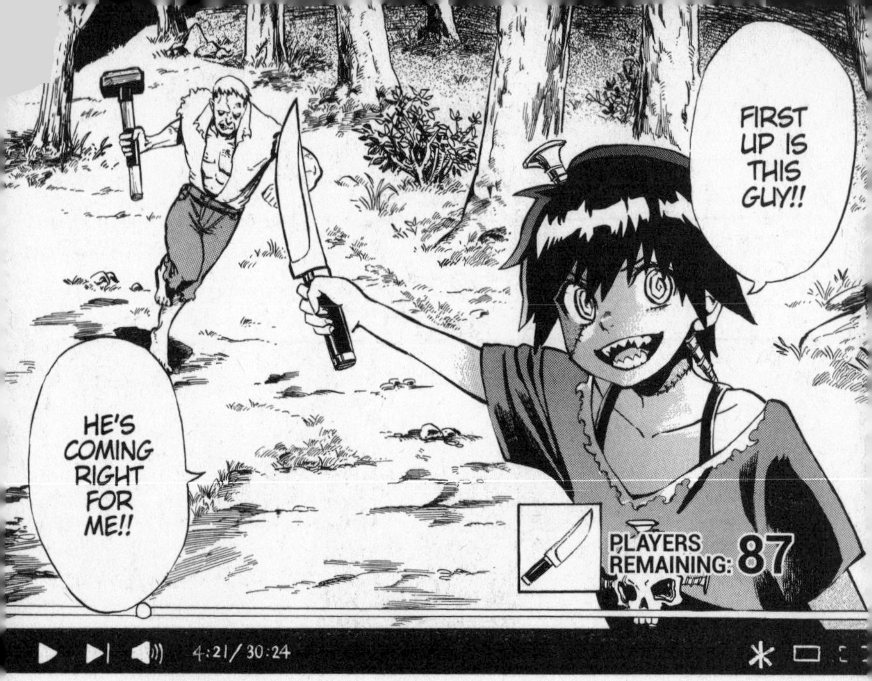
FIRST UP IS THIS GUY!!
HE'S COMING RIGHT FOR ME!!
PLAYERS REMAINING: 87
4:21/30:24

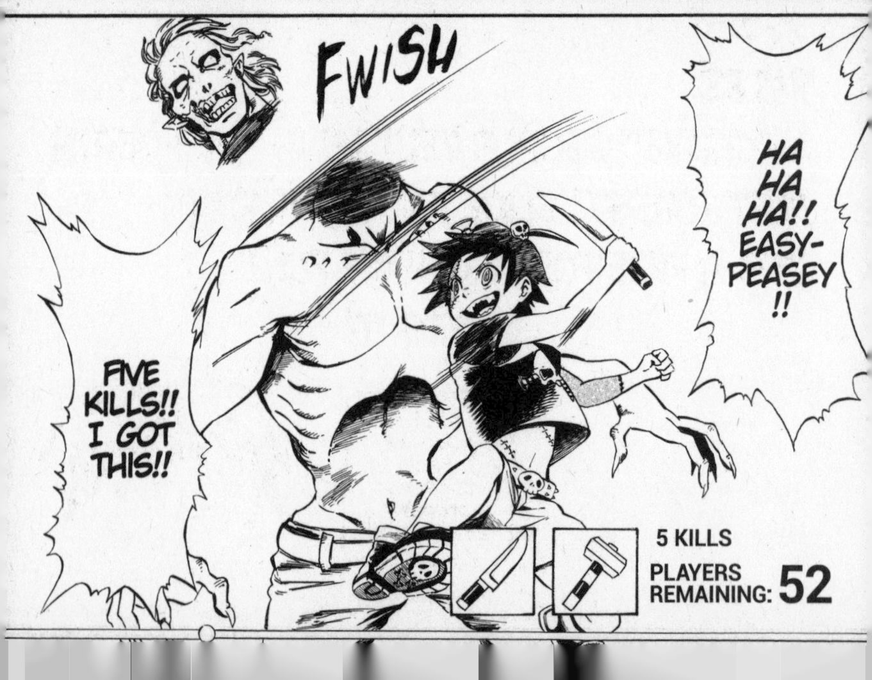
HA HA HA!! EASY-PEASEY!!
FWISH
FIVE KILLS!! I GOT THIS!!
5 KILLS
PLAYERS REMAINING: 52

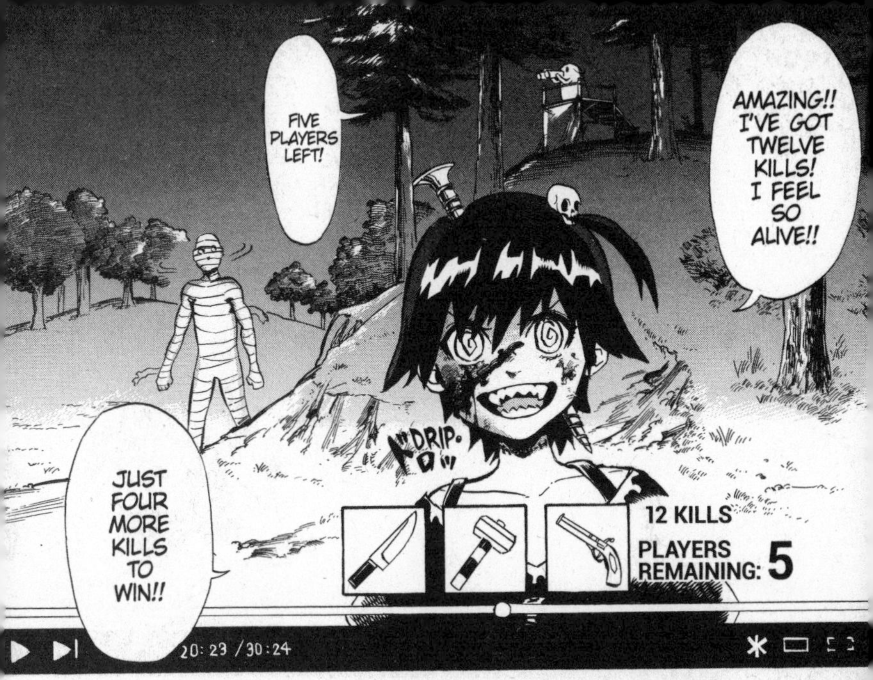
AMAZING!! I'VE GOT TWELVE KILLS! I FEEL SO ALIVE!!
FIVE PLAYERS LEFT!
DRIP
JUST FOUR MORE KILLS TO WIN!!
12 KILLS
PLAYERS REMAINING: 5
20:23 / 30:24

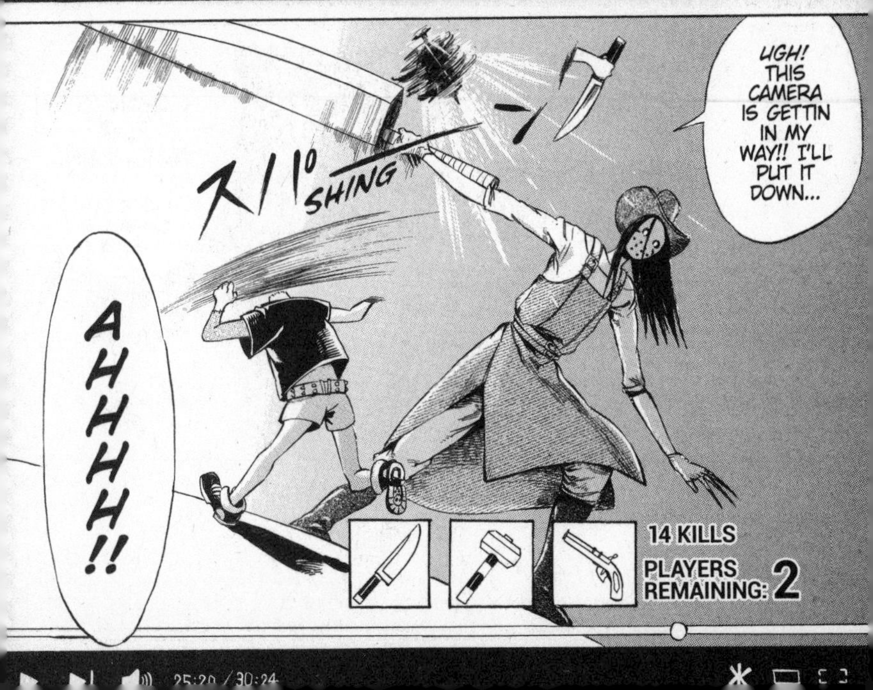
UGH! THIS CAMERA IS GETTIN IN MY WAY!! I'LL PUT IT DOWN...
SHING
AHHHHH!!
14 KILLS
PLAYERS REMAINING: 2
25:20 / 30:24

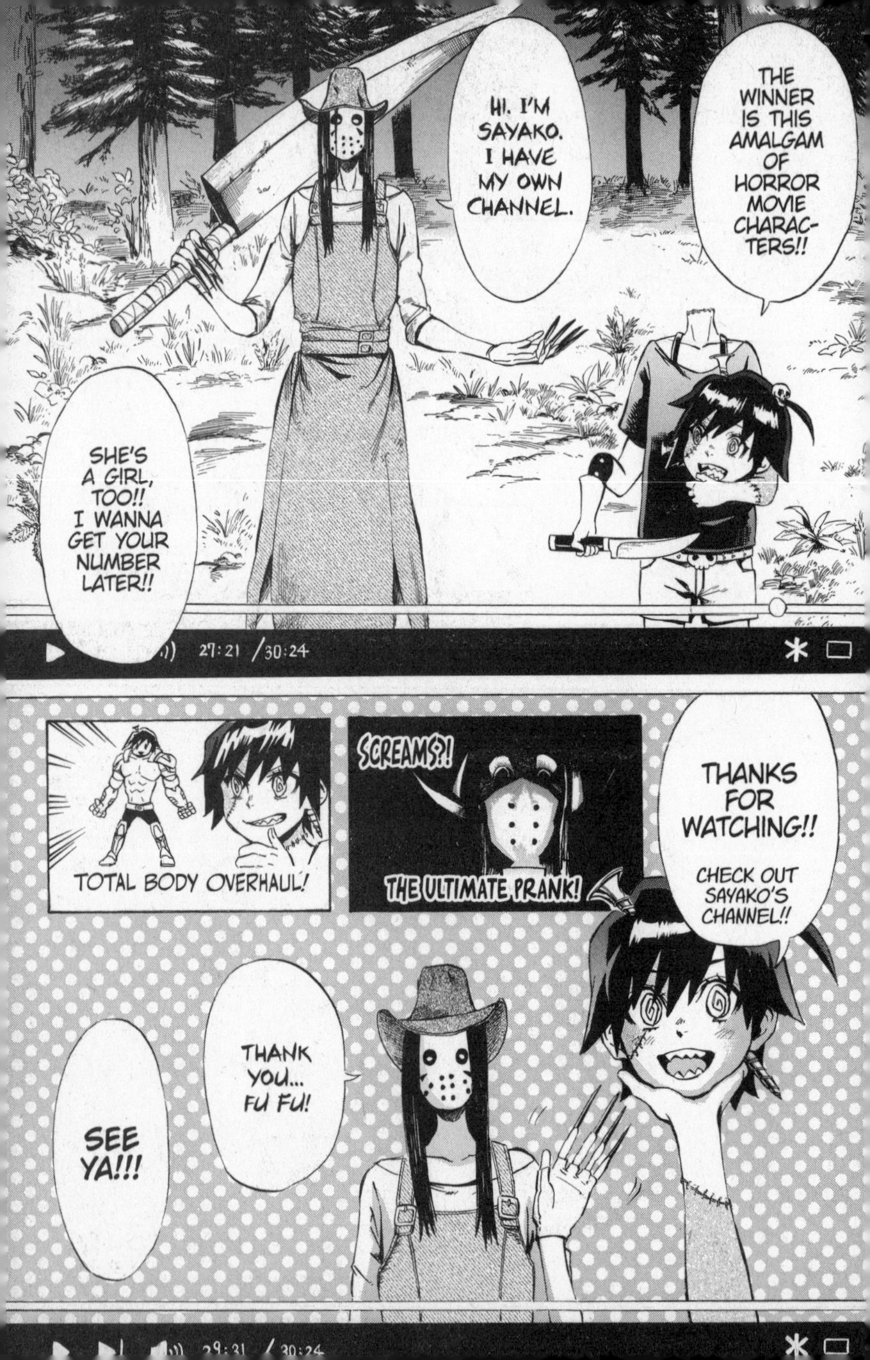
THE WINNER IS THIS AMALGAM OF HORROR MOVIE CHARAC-TERS!!
HI. I'M SAYAKO. I HAVE MY OWN CHANNEL.
SHE'S A GIRL, TOO!! I WANNA GET YOUR NUMBER LATER!!
27:21 /30:24
THANKS FOR WATCHING!!
CHECK OUT SAYAKO'S CHANNEL!!
SCREAMS?!
THE ULTIMATE PRANK!
TOTAL BODY OVERHAUL!
THANK YOU... FU FU!
SEE YA!!!
29:31 / 30:24

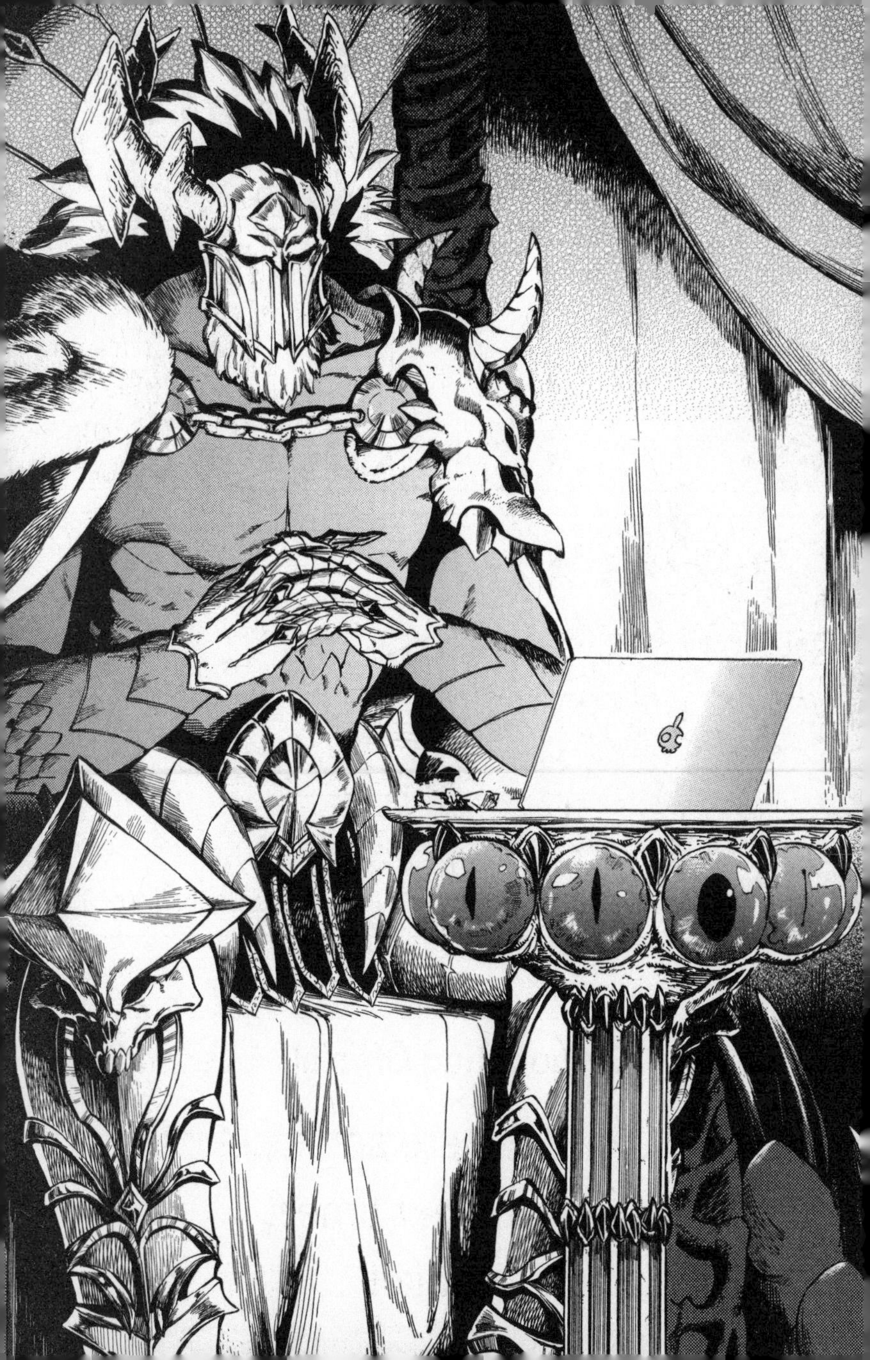

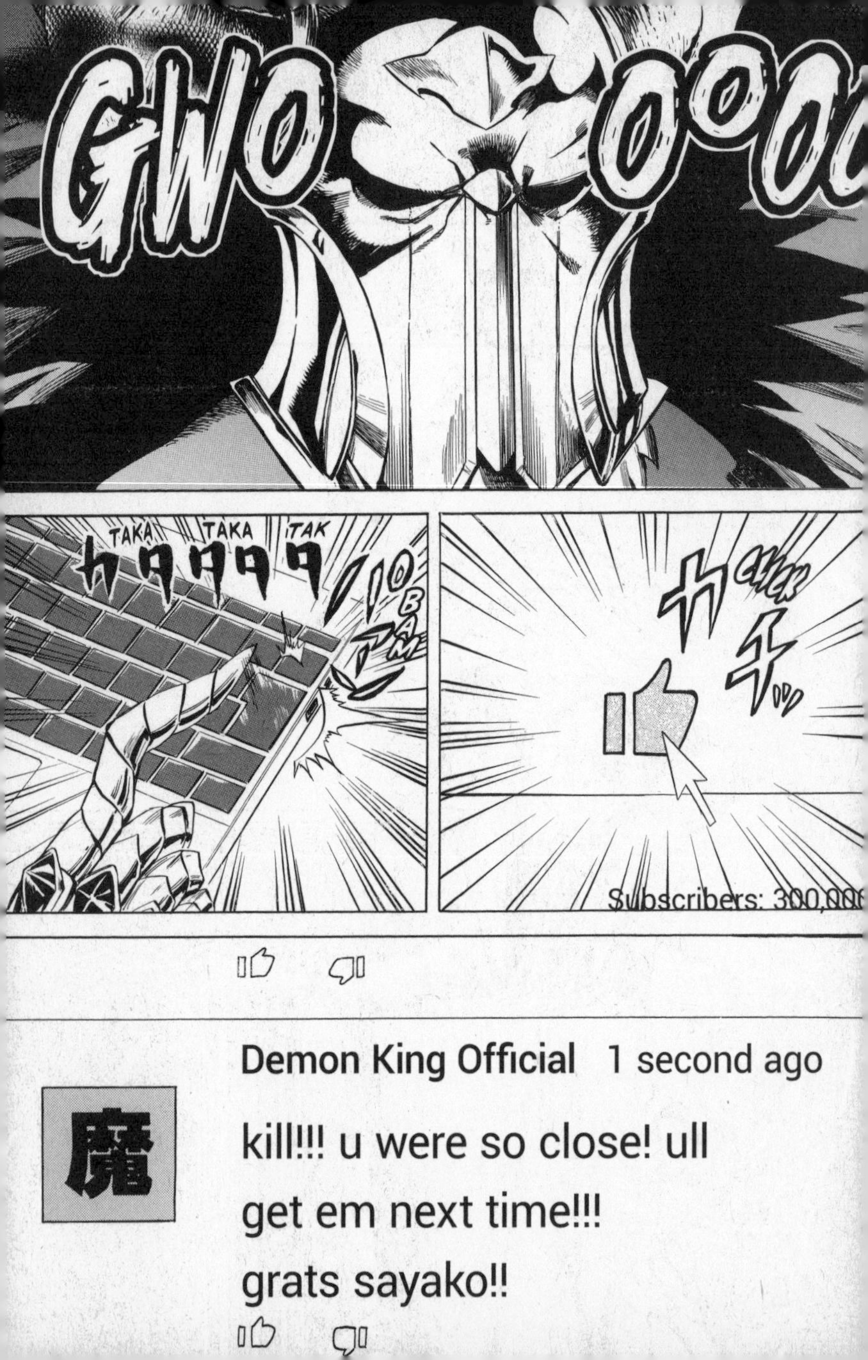
GWOOOO
カチッ
CLICK
Subscribers: 300,00
カタタタタ
TAKA TAKA TAK
BAM
Demon King Official 1 second ago
魔
kill!!! u were so close! ull get em next time!!!
grats sayako!!

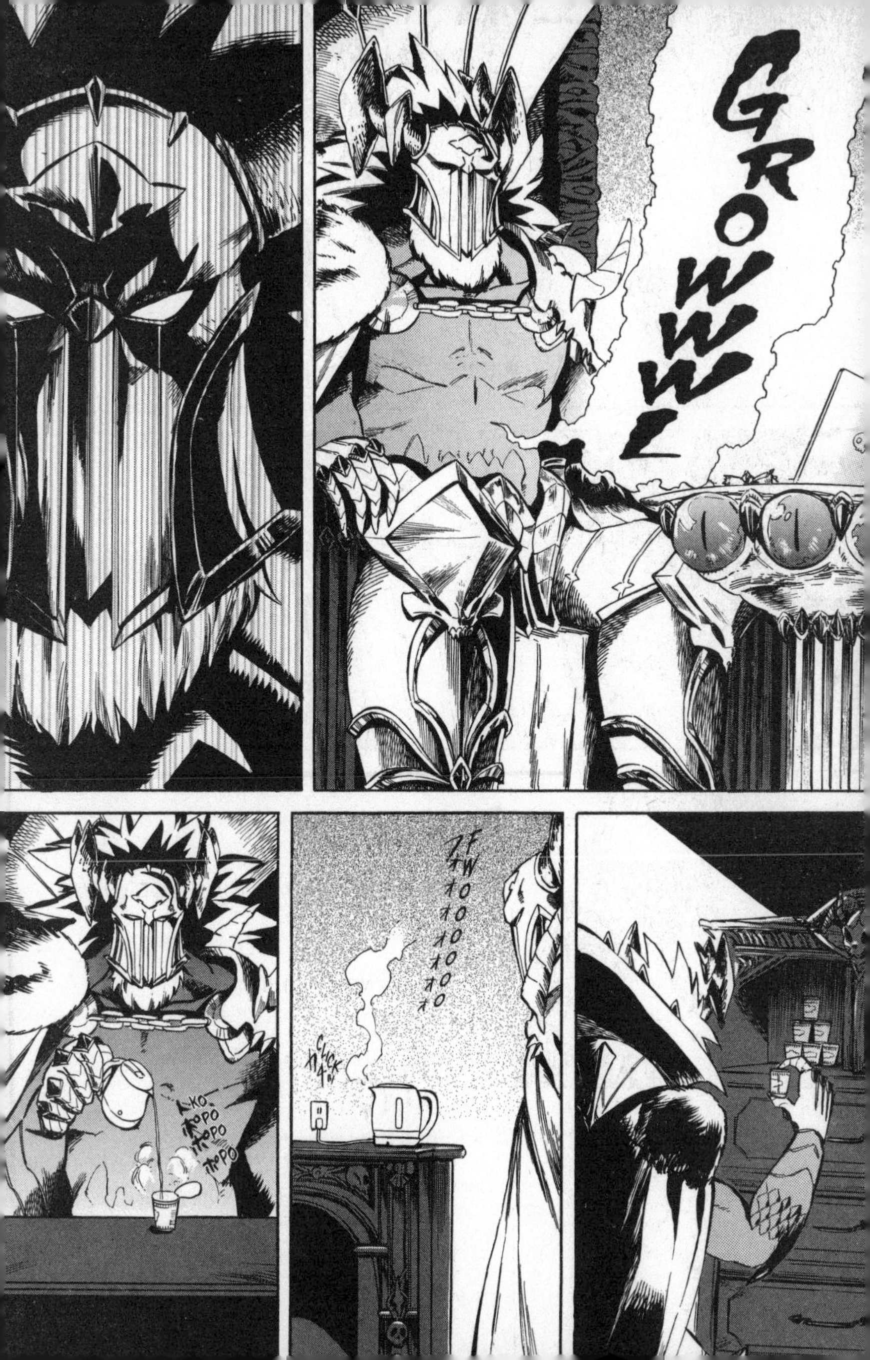
GROWWWL
FWOOOOOO
CLICK
KO
PO
PO
PO

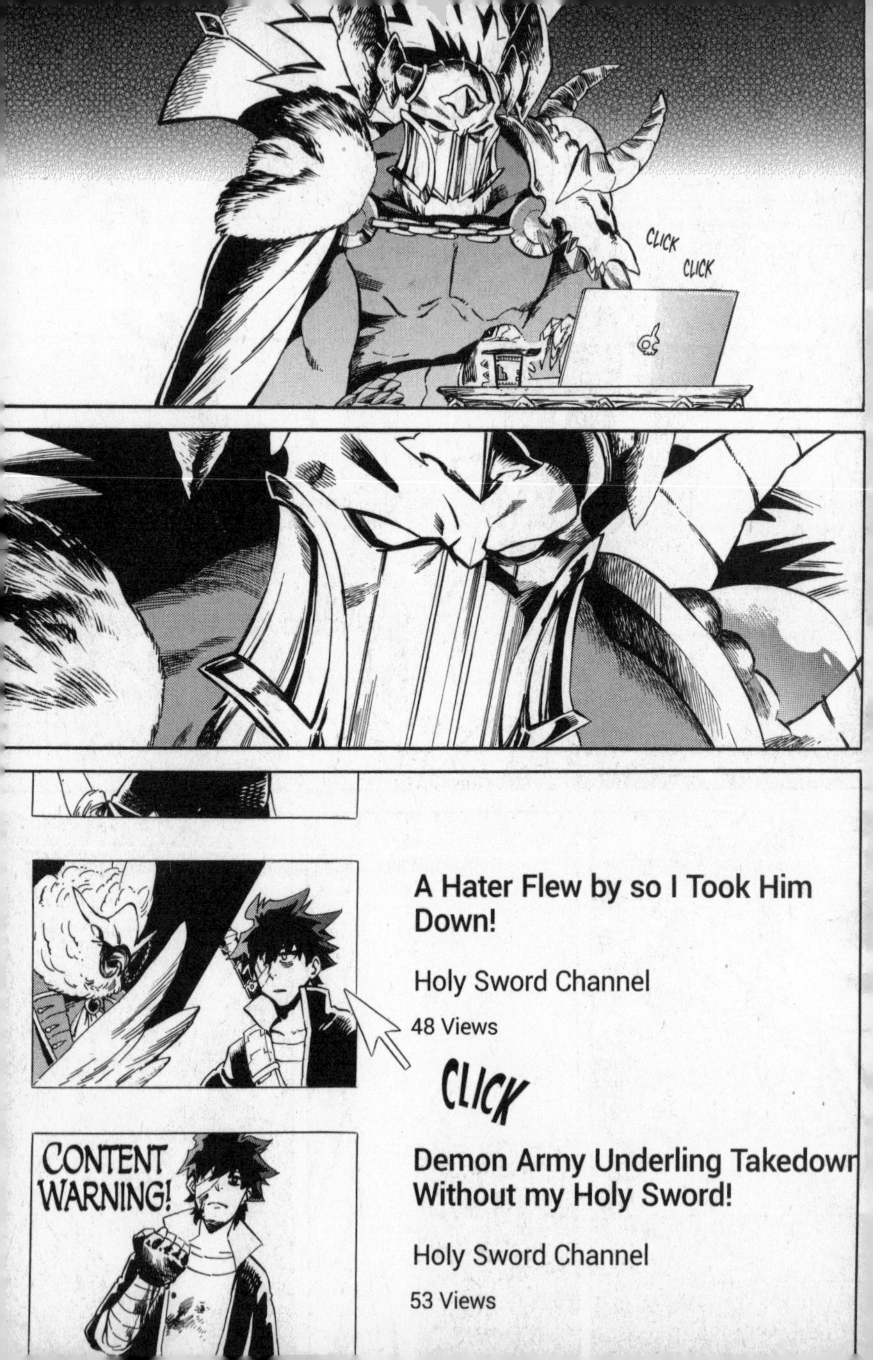
CLICK
CLICK
A Hater Flew by so I Took Him Down!
Holy Sword Channel
48 Views
CLICK
Demon Army Underling Takedown Without my Holy Sword!
CONTENT WARNING!
Holy Sword Channel
53 Views

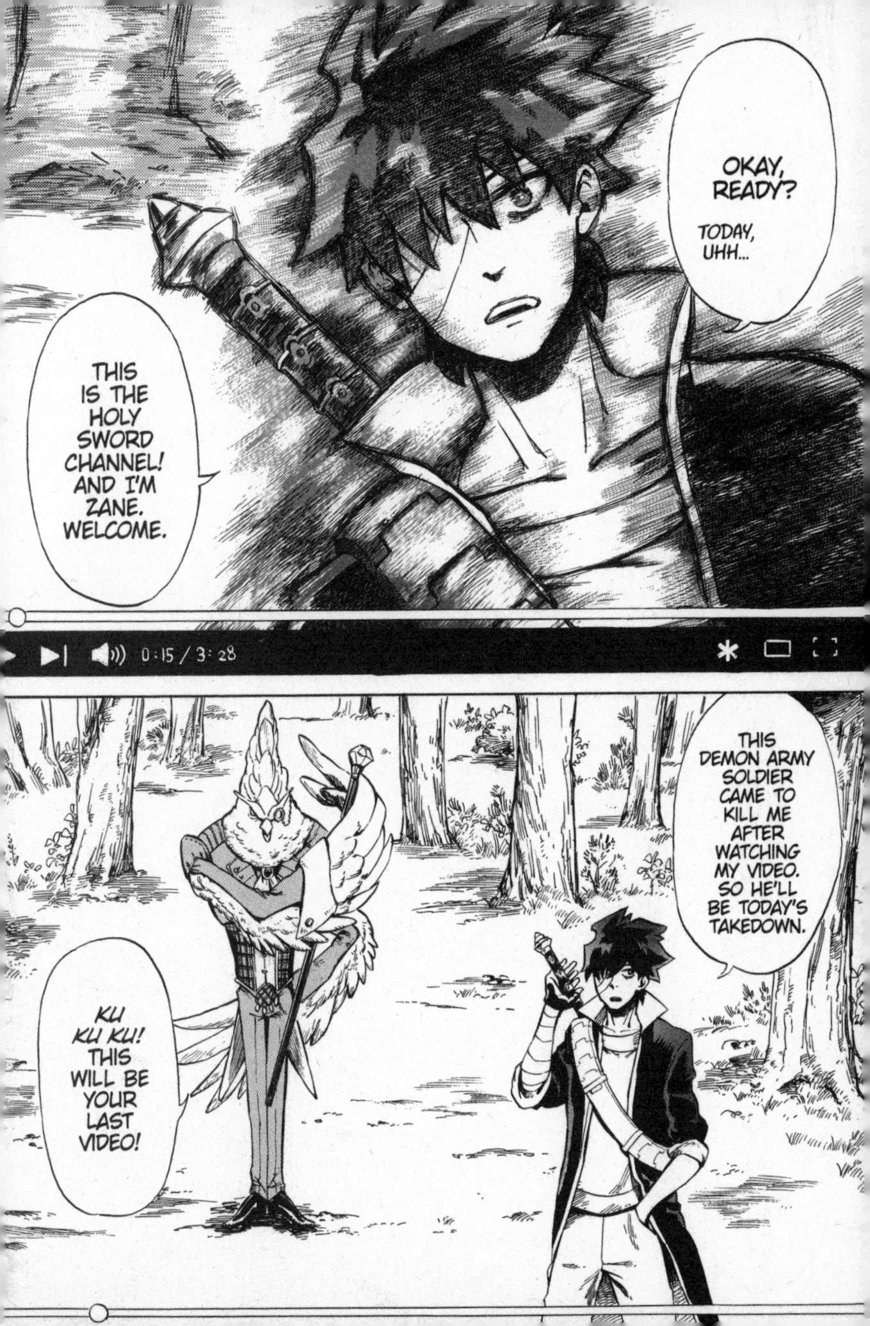
OKAY, READY?
TODAY, UHH...
THIS IS THE HOLY SWORD CHANNEL! AND I'M ZANE. WELCOME.
0:15 / 3:28
THIS DEMON ARMY SOLDIER CAME TO KILL ME AFTER WATCHING MY VIDEO. SO HE'LL BE TODAY'S TAKEDOWN.
KU KU KU! THIS WILL BE YOUR LAST VIDEO!

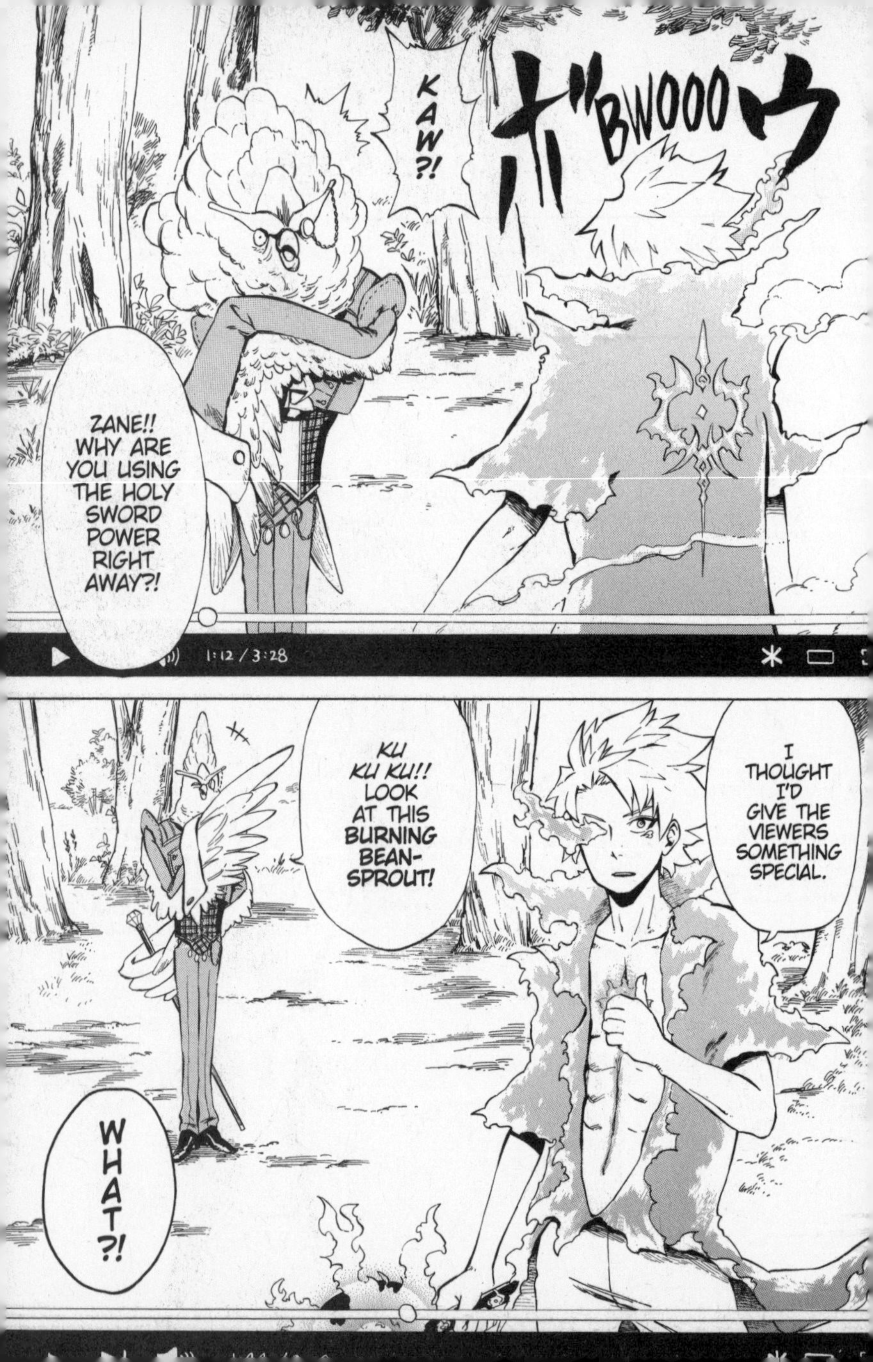
ボ BWOOO ウ
KAW?!
ZANE!! WHY ARE YOU USING THE HOLY SWORD POWER RIGHT AWAY?!
1:12 / 3:28
I THOUGHT I'D GIVE THE VIEWERS SOMETHING SPECIAL.
KU KU KU!! LOOK AT THIS BURNING BEAN-SPROUT!
WHAT?!

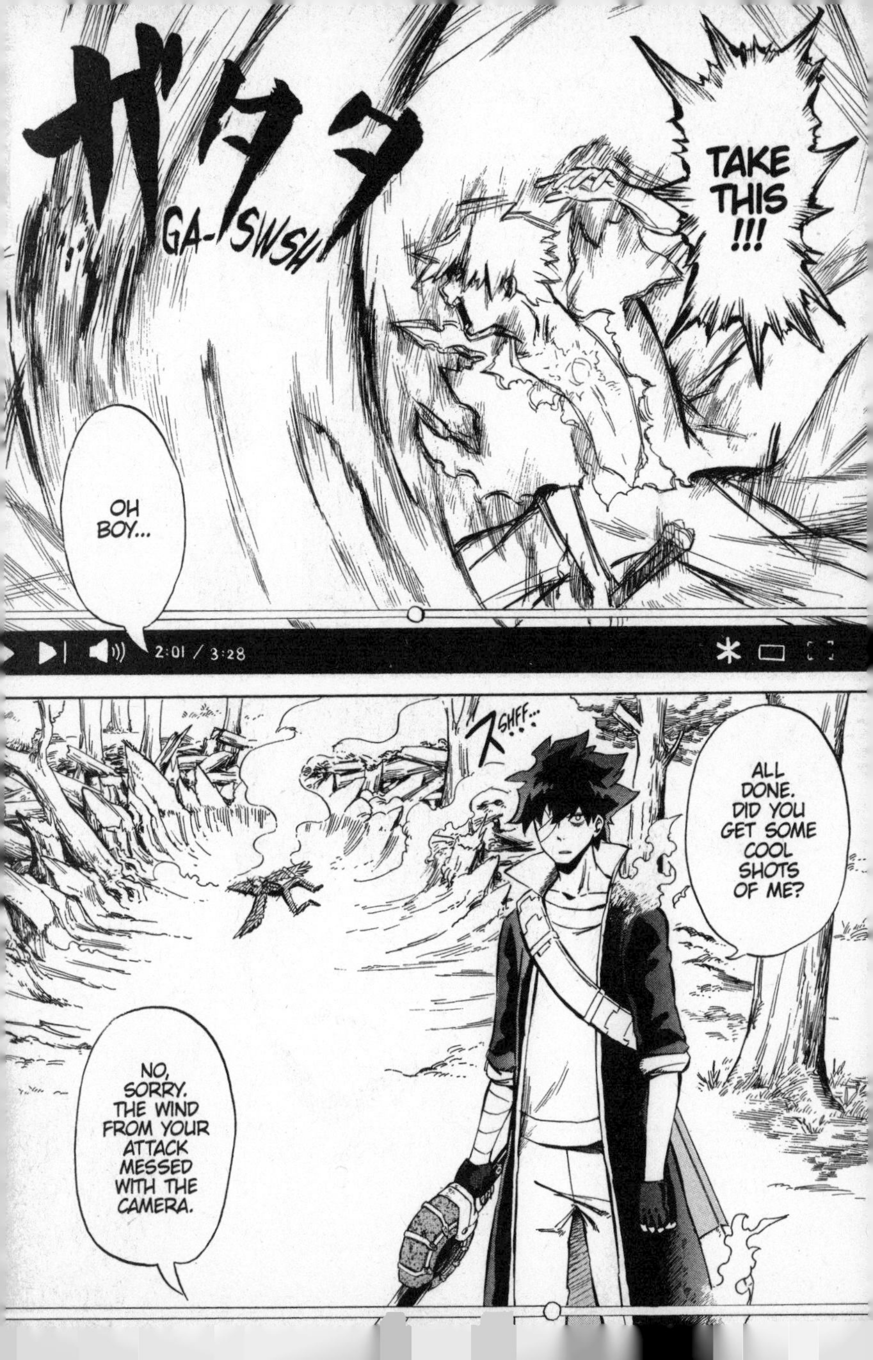
TAKE THIS!!!
GA-SWSH
OH BOY...
2:01 / 3:28
ALL DONE. DID YOU GET SOME COOL SHOTS OF ME?
ス SHFF...
NO, SORRY. THE WIND FROM YOUR ATTACK MESSED WITH THE CAMERA.

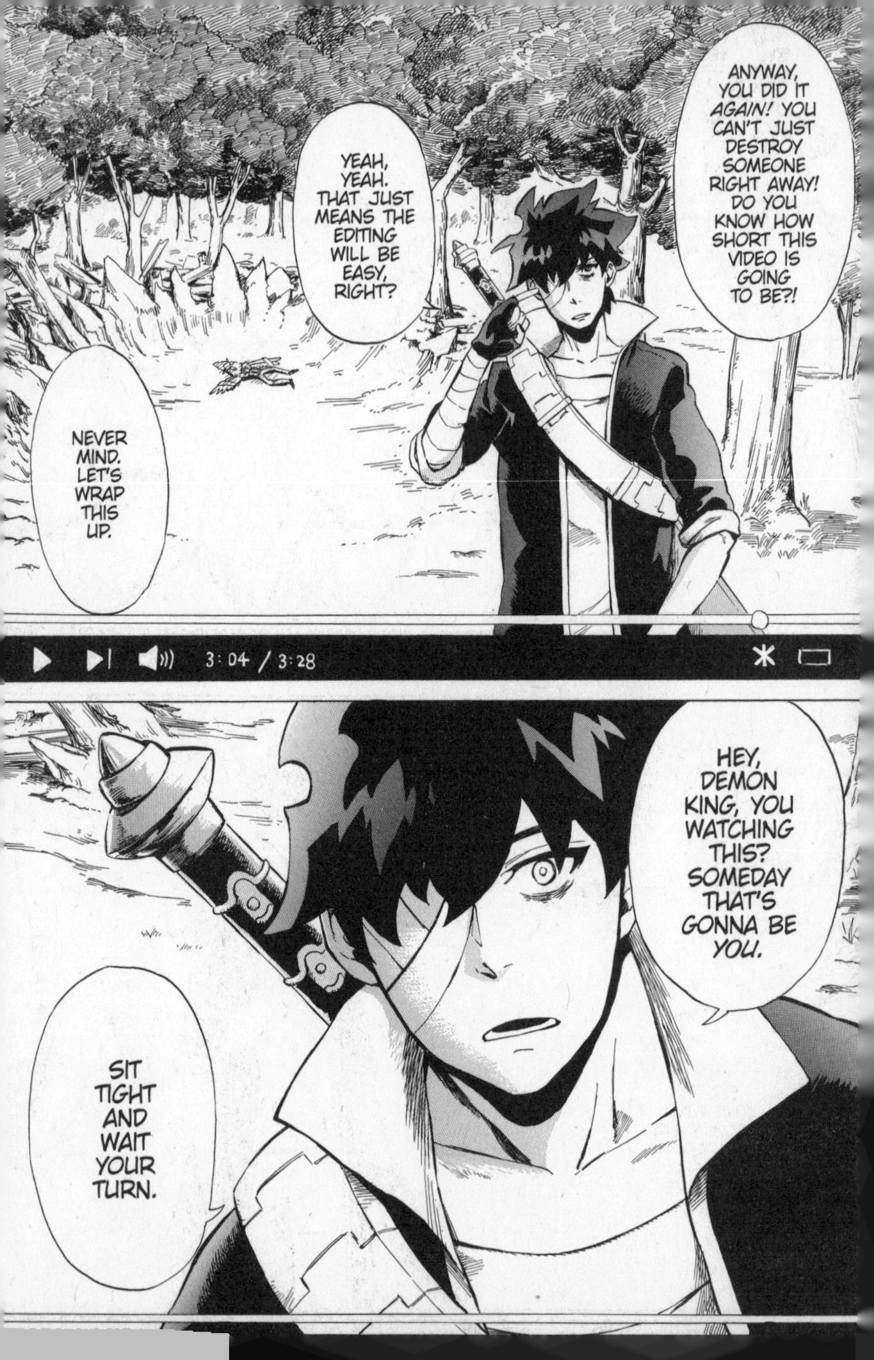
ANYWAY, YOU DID IT *AGAIN!* YOU CAN'T JUST DESTROY SOMEONE RIGHT AWAY! DO YOU KNOW HOW SHORT THIS VIDEO IS GOING TO BE?!
YEAH, YEAH. THAT JUST MEANS THE EDITING WILL BE EASY, RIGHT?
NEVER MIND. LET'S WRAP THIS UP.
3:04 / 3:28
HEY, DEMON KING, YOU WATCHING THIS? SOMEDAY THAT'S GONNA BE *YOU.*
SIT TIGHT AND WAIT YOUR TURN.

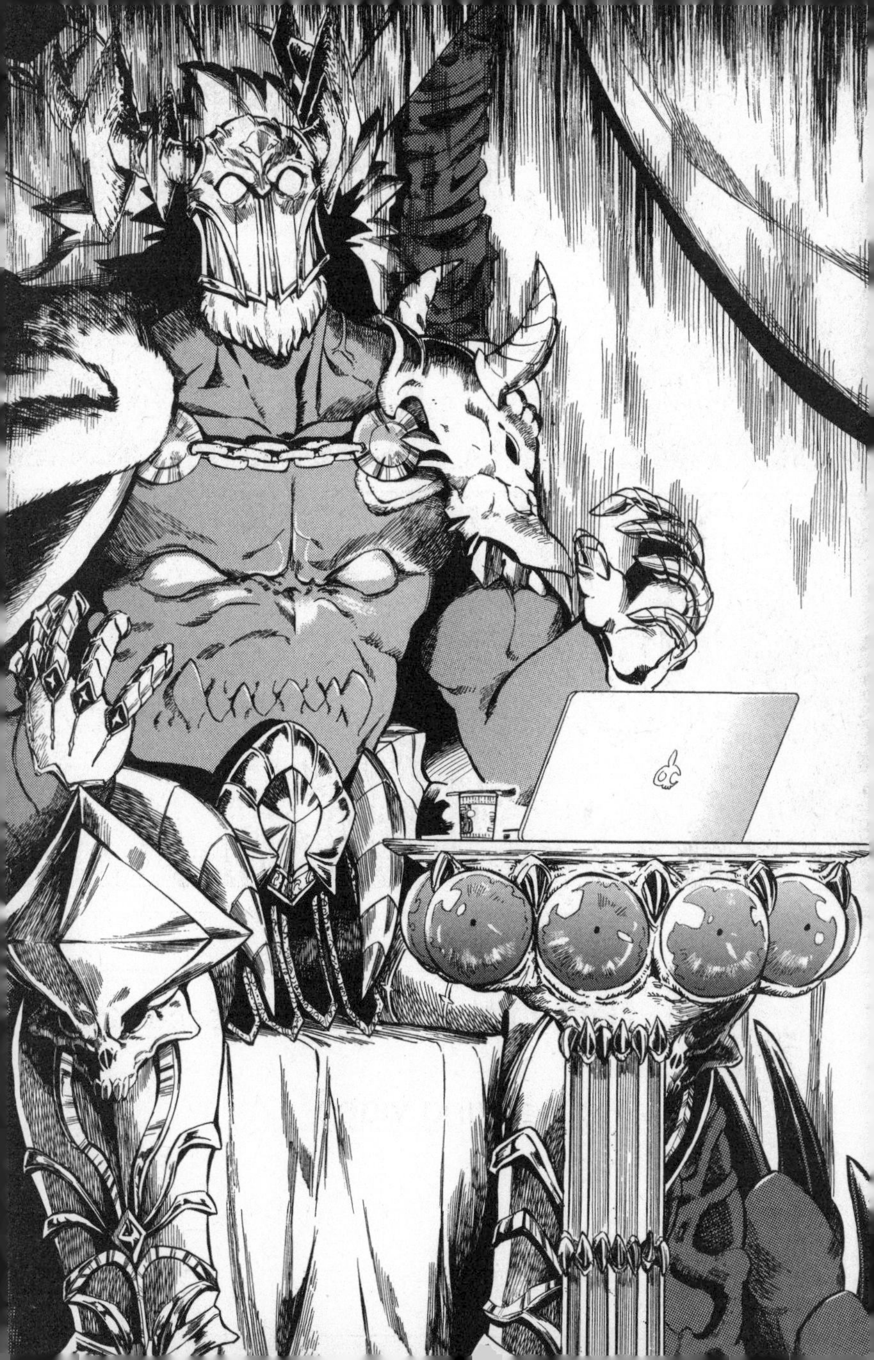

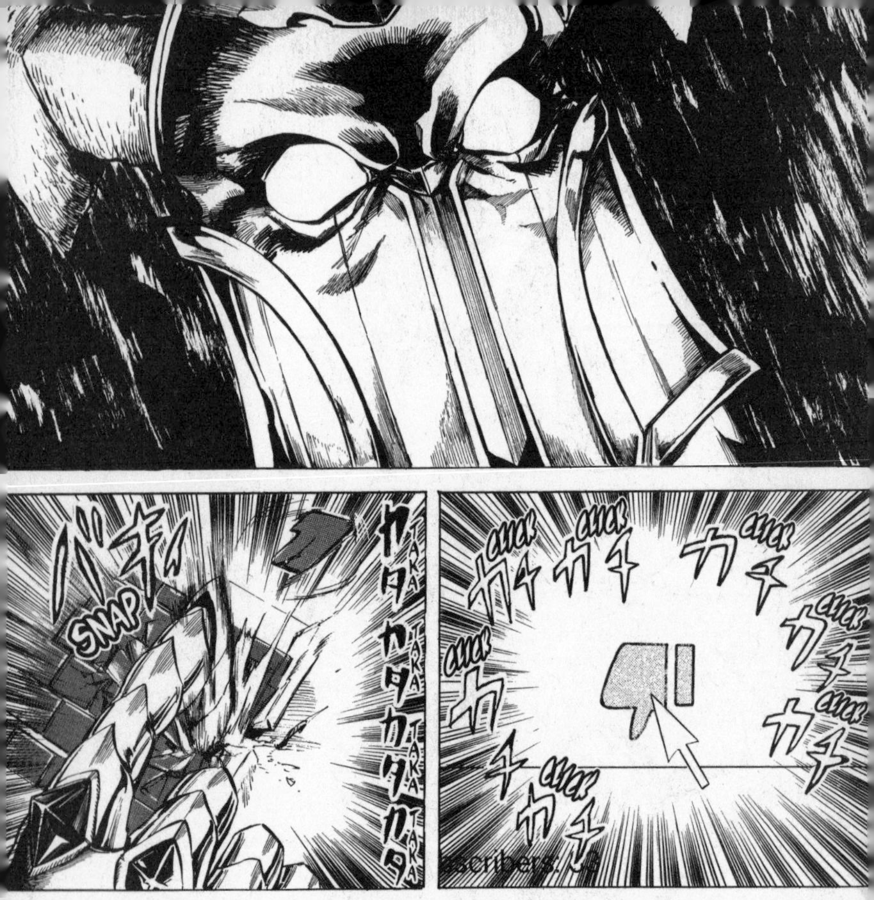
カチ CLICK
カチ CLICK
カチ CLICK
カチ CLICK
カチ CLICK
カチ CLICK
カチ CLICK
バキッ SNAP
カタカタカタカタ TAKA TAKA TAKA TAKA

魔

Demon King Official 1 second ago

most boring video
ever...
die.

0 0

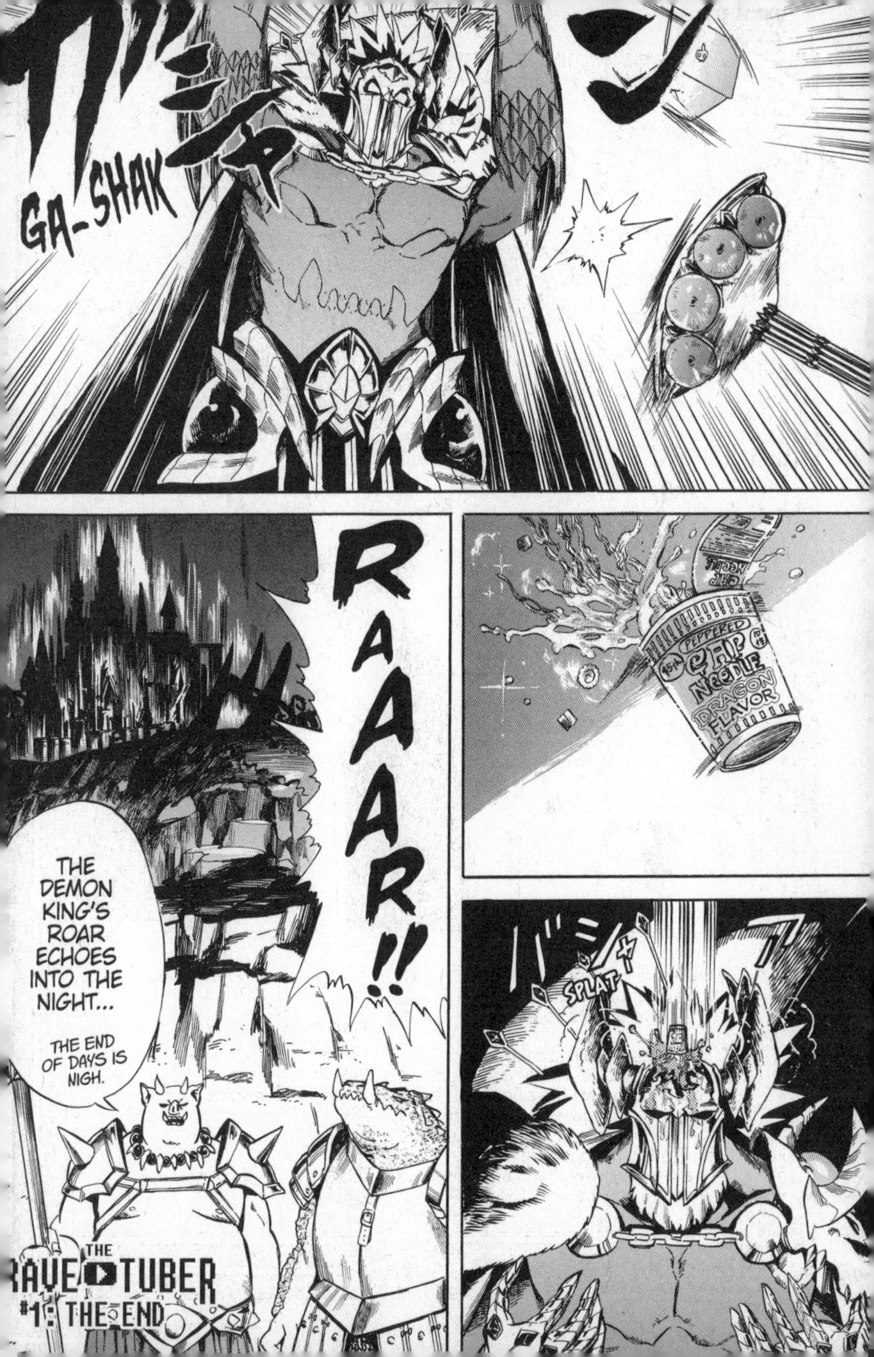
GA-SHAK
PEPPERED CHIP NOODLE DRAGON FLAVOR
SPLAT
RAAAR!!
THE DEMON KING'S ROAR ECHOES INTO THE NIGHT...
THE END OF DAYS IS NIGH.
THE
RAVE TUBER
#1: THE END

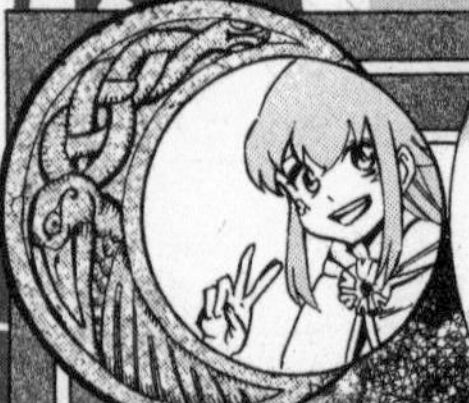

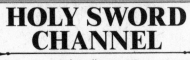

HOLY SWORD CHANNEL

Subscribers: 83

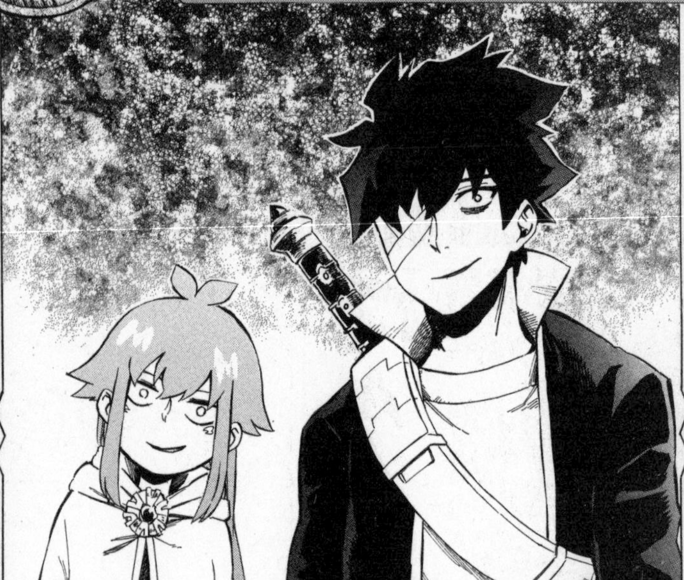

These two content creators are the self-proclaimed wielder of a holy sword and its spirit.

Their videos make little sense, and most involve a violent assault. They're known for hijacking the Demon Army Beldeenos's streams and creating nuisance homunculi, earning them a poor reputation. It's a mystery why they have been chosen to wield a Holy Sword.

Strength	☆☆☆☆☆☆☆☆☆☆
Magic	☆
Intelligence	☆
Editing	☆
Speech	☆
Suspicious-ness	☆☆☆☆☆☆☆☆☆☆

RECOMMENDED VIDEOS

None

Galbee
POTATO CHIPS
Lightly Salted
CRISPY AND DELICIOUS!
60g

BRAVE-TUBER FOUR PANEL MANGA

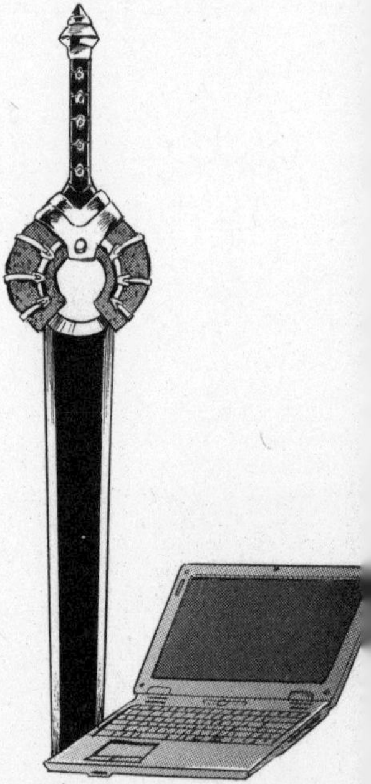

KILLING MOVE

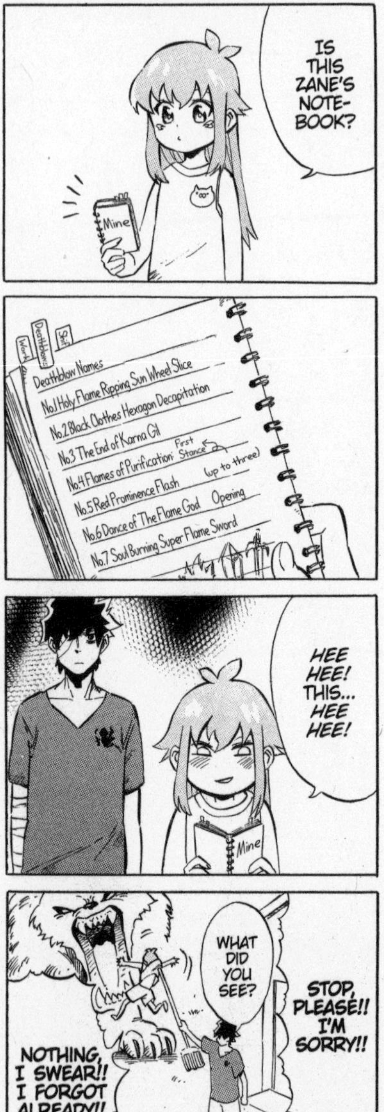

IS THIS ZANE'S NOTE-BOOK?
Mine
Work
Deathblows
Skill
Deathblow Names
No.1 Holy Flame Ripping Sun Wheel Slice
No.2 Black Clothes Hexagon Decapitation
No.3 The End of Karna Gil
No.4 Flames of Purification: First Stance
(up to three)
No.5 Red Prominence Flash
No.6 Dance of The Flame God Opening
No.7 Soul Burning Super Flame Sword
HEE HEE! THIS... HEE HEE!
Mine
STOP, PLEASE!! I'M SORRY!!
WHAT DID YOU SEE?
NOTHING, I SWEAR!! I FORGOT ALREADY!!

WALK DOWN THE STREET (KUKU)

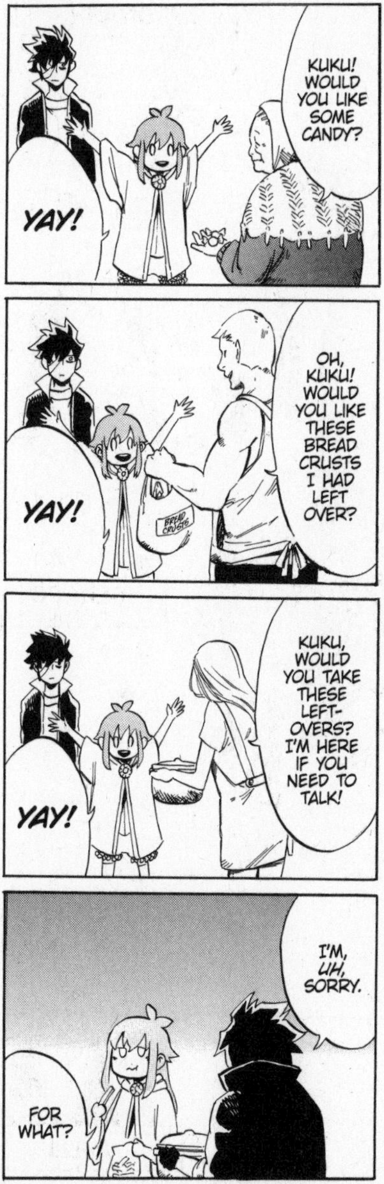
KUKU! WOULD YOU LIKE SOME CANDY?
YAY!
OH, KUKU! WOULD YOU LIKE THESE BREAD CRUSTS I HAD LEFT OVER?
BREAD CRUSTS
YAY!
KUKU, WOULD YOU TAKE THESE LEFT-OVERS? I'M HERE IF YOU NEED TO TALK!
YAY!
I'M, UH, SORRY.
FOR WHAT?

STROLLING DOWN THE STREET (ZANE)

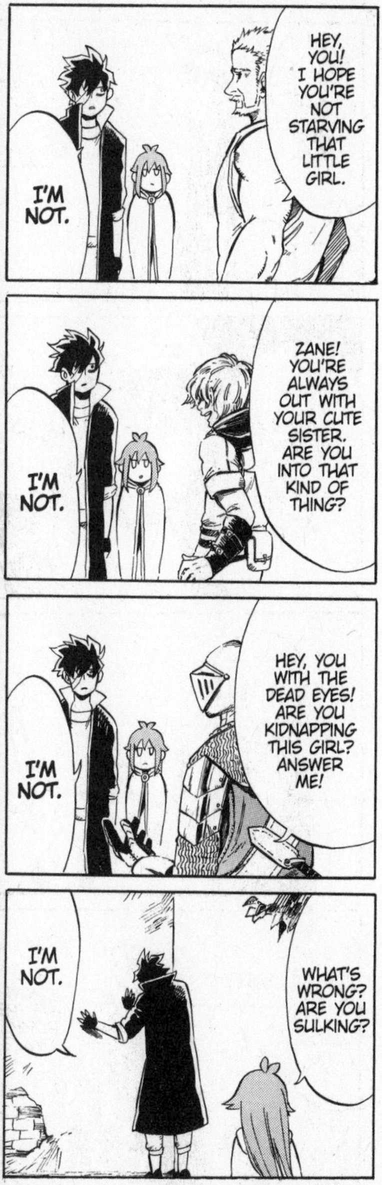
HEY, YOU! I HOPE YOU'RE NOT STARVING THAT LITTLE GIRL.
I'M NOT.
ZANE! YOU'RE ALWAYS OUT WITH YOUR CUTE SISTER. ARE YOU INTO THAT KIND OF THING?
I'M NOT.
HEY, YOU WITH THE DEAD EYES! ARE YOU KIDNAPPING THIS GIRL? ANSWER ME!
I'M NOT.
WHAT'S WRONG? ARE YOU SULKING?
I'M NOT.

SKETCHY NEWBIE

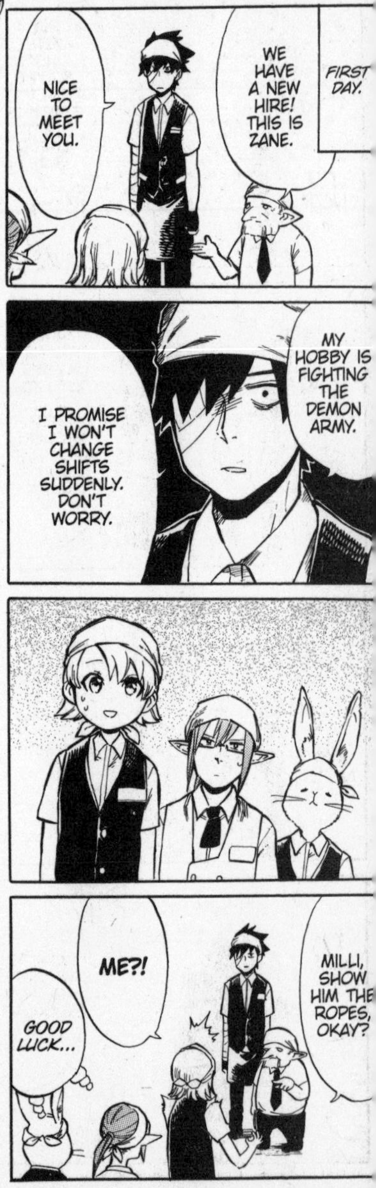
FIRST DAY.
WE HAVE A NEW HIRE! THIS IS ZANE.
NICE TO MEET YOU.
MY HOBBY IS FIGHTING THE DEMON ARMY.
I PROMISE I WON'T CHANGE SHIFTS SUDDENLY. DON'T WORRY.
MILLI, SHOW HIM THE ROPES, OKAY?
ME?!
GOOD LUCK...

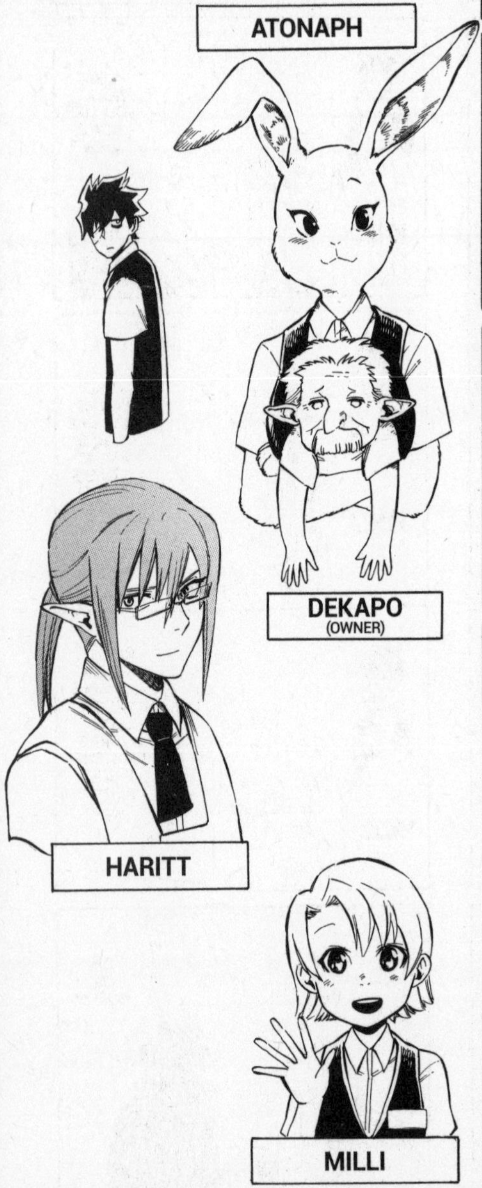
ATONAPH
DEKAPO
(OWNER)
HARITT
MILLI

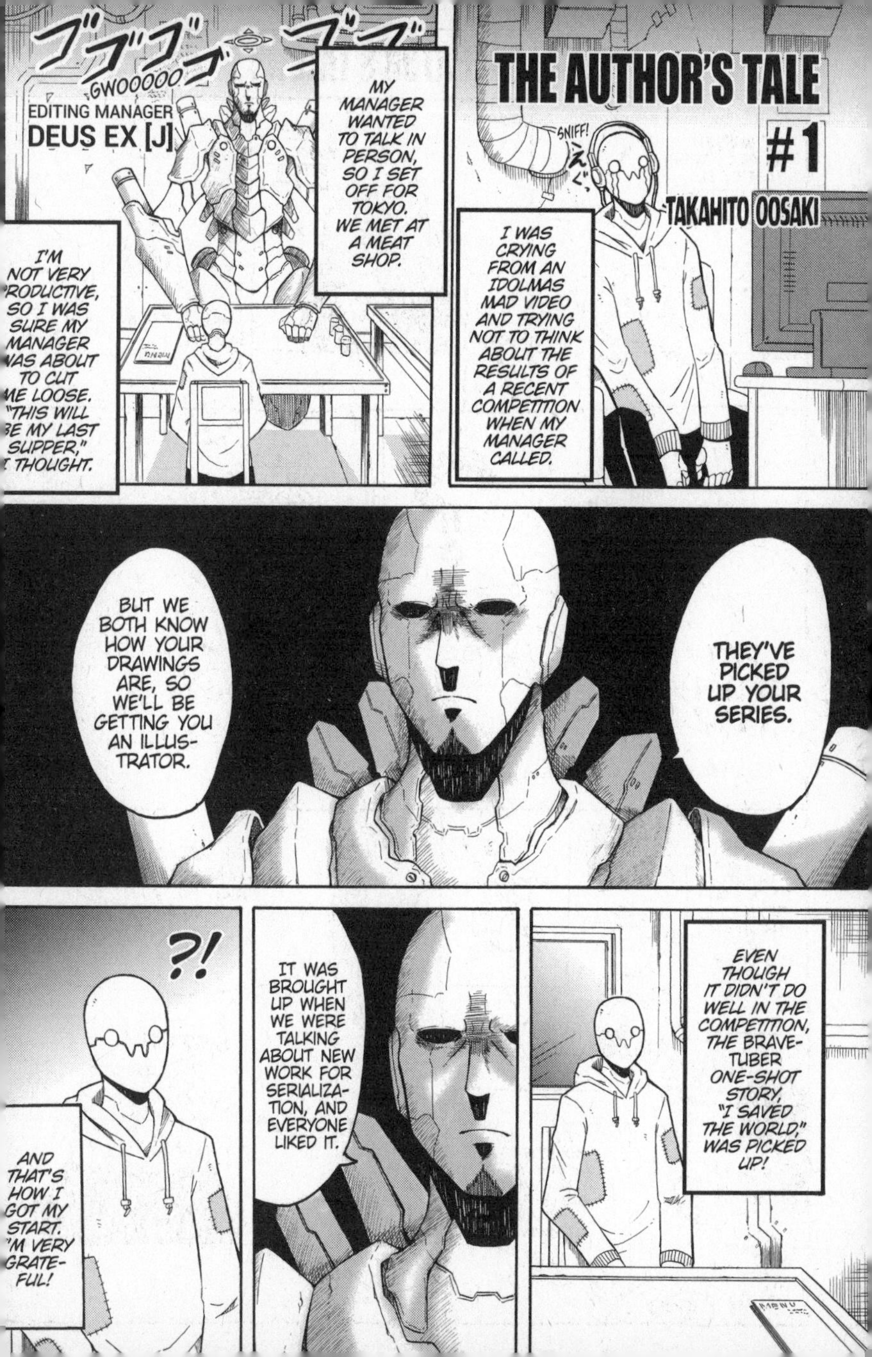
THE AUTHOR'S TALE
#1
TAKAHITO OOSAKI
SNIFF!
えぐっ
I WAS CRYING FROM AN IDOLMAS MAD VIDEO AND TRYING NOT TO THINK ABOUT THE RESULTS OF A RECENT COMPETITION WHEN MY MANAGER CALLED.
ゴゴゴゴゴゴ
GWOOOOO
MY MANAGER WANTED TO TALK IN PERSON, SO I SET OFF FOR TOKYO. WE MET AT A MEAT SHOP.
EDITING MANAGER
DEUS EX [J]
I'M NOT VERY PRODUCTIVE, SO I WAS SURE MY MANAGER WAS ABOUT TO CUT ME LOOSE. "THIS WILL BE MY LAST SUPPER," I THOUGHT.
THEY'VE PICKED UP YOUR SERIES.
BUT WE BOTH KNOW HOW YOUR DRAWINGS ARE, SO WE'LL BE GETTING YOU AN ILLUSTRATOR.
EVEN THOUGH IT DIDN'T DO WELL IN THE COMPETITION, THE BRAVE-TUBER ONE-SHOT STORY, "I SAVED THE WORLD," WAS PICKED UP!
IT WAS BROUGHT UP WHEN WE WERE TALKING ABOUT NEW WORK FOR SERIALIZATION, AND EVERYONE LIKED IT.
?!
AND THAT'S HOW I GOT MY START. I'M VERY GRATEFUL!

THE ILLUSTRATOR'S TALE #1 BY IKURO

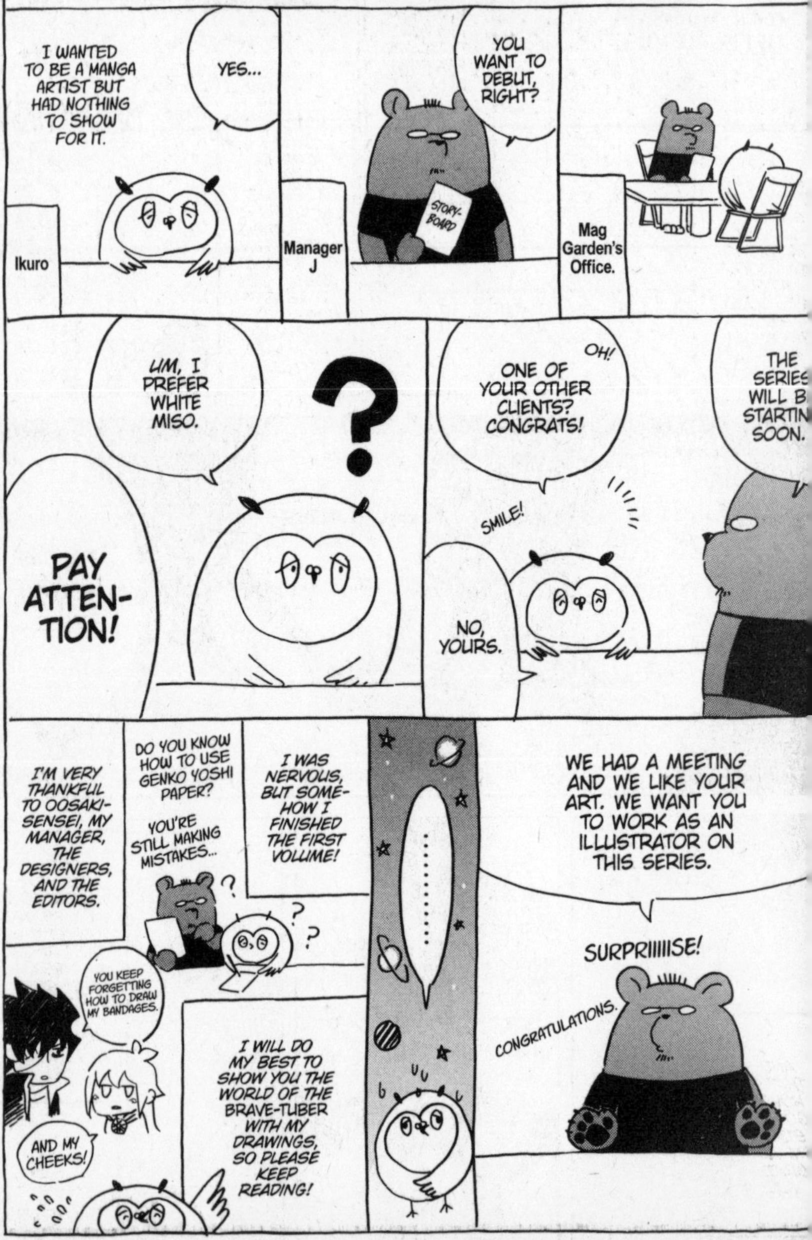
Mag Garden's Office.
YOU WANT TO DEBUT, RIGHT?
STORY-BOARD
Manager J
I WANTED TO BE A MANGA ARTIST BUT HAD NOTHING TO SHOW FOR IT.
YES...
Ikuro
THE SERIES WILL B STARTIN SOON.
OH!
ONE OF YOUR OTHER CLIENTS? CONGRATS!
SMILE!
NO, YOURS.
UM, I PREFER WHITE MISO.
?
PAY ATTENTION!
WE HAD A MEETING AND WE LIKE YOUR ART. WE WANT YOU TO WORK AS AN ILLUSTRATOR ON THIS SERIES.
SURPRIIIIISE!
CONGRATULATIONS.
......
I WAS NERVOUS, BUT SOMEHOW I FINISHED THE FIRST VOLUME!
DO YOU KNOW HOW TO USE GENKO YOSHI PAPER?
YOU'RE STILL MAKING MISTAKES...
I'M VERY THANKFUL TO OOSAKI-SENSEI, MY MANAGER, THE DESIGNERS, AND THE EDITORS.
I WILL DO MY BEST TO SHOW YOU THE WORLD OF THE BRAVE-TUBER WITH MY DRAWINGS, SO PLEASE KEEP READING!
YOU KEEP FORGETTING HOW TO DRAW MY BANDAGES.
AND MY CHEEKS!

EXTRAS

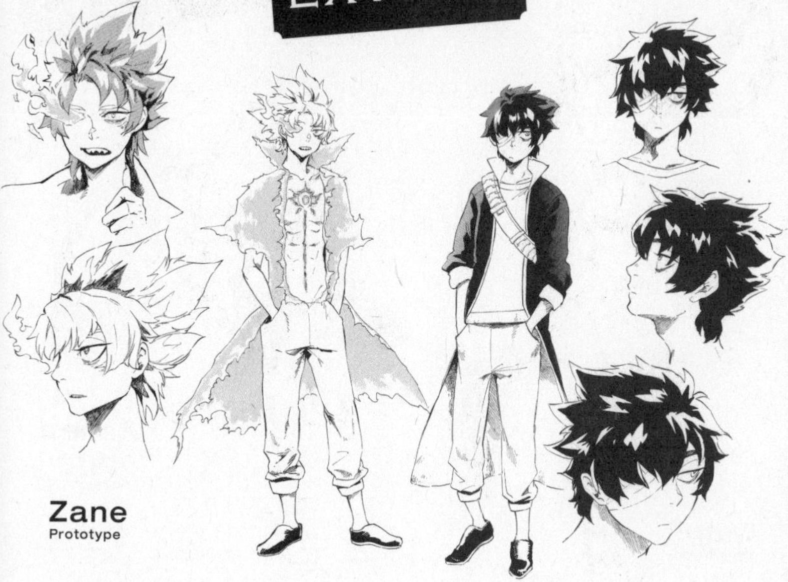

Zane
Prototype

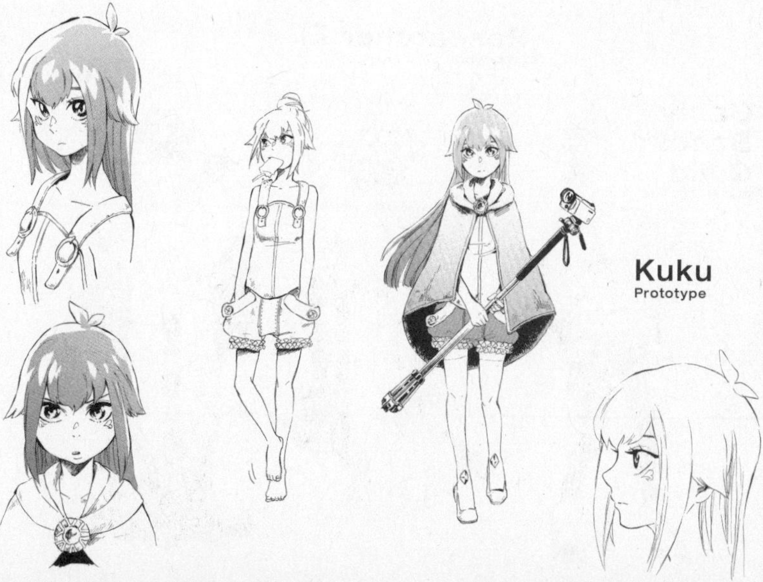

Kuku
Prototype

EXTRAS

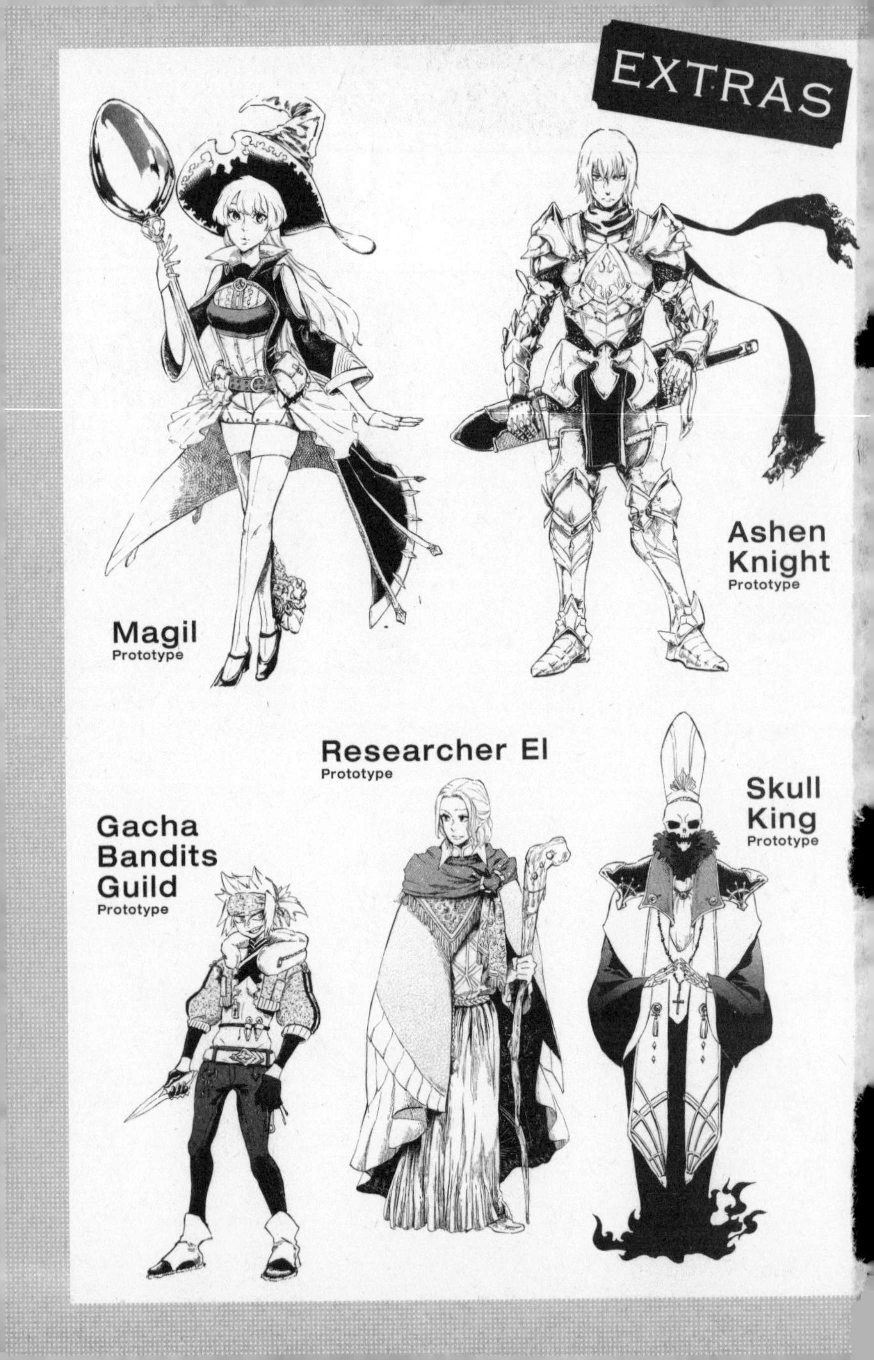
Ashen Knight
Prototype
Magil
Prototype
Skull King
Prototype
Researcher El
Prototype
Gacha Bandits Guild
Prototype

SEVEN SEAS ENTERTAINMENT PRESENTS

THE BRAVE-

story by **TAKAHITO OOSAKI**

TRANSLATION
Thomas Zimmerman

ADAPTATION
Dawn Davis

LETTERING
James Gaubatz

COVER DESIGN
KC Fabellon

PROOFREADER
Kurestin Armada
Nicole Riebe

EDITOR
Shannon Fay

PRODUCTION MANAGER
Lissa Pattillo

MANAGING EDITOR
Julie Davis

EDITOR-IN-CHIEF
Adam Arnold

PUBLISHER
Jason DeAngelis

HAISHIN YUUSHA VOLUME 1
© Takahito Oosaki 2018
© Ikuro 2018
Originally published in Japan in 2018 by MAG Garden Corporation, Tokyo.
English translation rights arranged through TOHAN CORPORATION, Tokyo.

Seven Seas press and purchase enquiries can be sent to Marketing Manager Lianne Sentar at press@gomanga.com. Information regarding the distribution and purchase of digital editions is available from Digital Manager CK Russell at digital@gomanga.com.

Seven Seas and the Seven Seas logo are trademarks of Seven Seas Entertainment. All rights reserved.

ISBN: 978-1-64275-486-5

Printed in Canada

First Printing: September 2019

10 9 8 7 6 5 4 3 2 1

FOLLOW US ONLINE: *www.sevenseasentertainment.com*

READING DIRECTIONS

This book reads from *right to left*, Japanese style. If this is your first time reading manga, you start reading from the top right panel on each page and take it from there. If you get lost, just follow the numbered diagram here. It may seem backwards at first, but you'll get the hang of it! Have fun!!

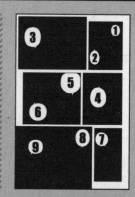